living in...
THE ACTIVE WORD
WITH PASTOR BOB COY

A year long devotional
for setting your heart and mind
heavenward

365 -- A year-long devotional for setting your heart and mind heavenward

Published in Fort Lauderdale, Florida, by Calvary Chapel Church, Inc.

Requests for information should be addressed to:
Calvary Chapel Church, Inc.
The Active Word – Media Ministry
2401 West Cypress Creek Road, Fort Lauderdale, Florida 33309
Calvary Chapel Church Web site: www.calvaryftl.org

ISBN: 1-932283-28-5

Content from *Living in the Active Word* Devotional Magazine
Printed in the United States of America

introduction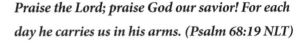

Praise the Lord; praise God our savior! For each day he carries us in his arms. (Psalm 68:19 NLT)

No matter how long I am a Christian, I still find myself startled and astounded by the pictures painted in Scripture. It is as difficult as it is comforting to imagine being carried by God Almighty day after day.

I think the trouble we have in getting our minds around this amazing truth stems not from our imagination but rather from our preoccupation with the world around us. I have found that if I take time first thing in the morning—before my day gets too busy—to set my heart and mind heavenward, my imagination has no problem whatsoever seeing God in this light.

That's what I want for you. And that's why our team here at The Active Word has put together this 365-day devotional. Whether it is from an illustration in my own life or the insights of Scripture, we are praying that this book you hold in your hands will be a catalyst that brings you to a quiet time each day with God. We've prepared the means, but only you can make it happen. I urge you to shut out the noise of everyday life long enough to recognize the open arms of our Savior. He's waiting to carry you through the ups and downs of this thing we call life on planet earth. I promise you'll find it contagious and you won't believe what a difference it will make in your day: . . . *I will praise you more and more. I will tell everyone about your righteousness. All day long I will proclaim your saving power, for I am overwhelmed by how much you have done for me (Psalm 71:14–15 NLT).*

Until the whole world hears,

Pastor Bob Coy

PASTOR BOB COY
Senior Pastor

"Can I not do with you as this potter?" says the LORD. "Look, as the clay is in the potter's hand, so are you in My hand . . . ." (Jeremiah 18:6 NKJV)

God is in the business of changing lives; it's an essential part of who He is. He even compares Himself to a potter who takes a useless lump of clay and changes it into a useful and beautiful vessel. Those who have experienced the Potter's touch firsthand can attest to the truthfulness of this comparison. But there are three things that we, as pieces of clay, must acknowledge about the Potter before we can truly be transformed by His hand.

His prerogative. It is God's divine right to change us because He also created us. None of us called ourselves into existence; therefore, none of us can claim ownership of ourselves. We are the Potter's property, and the sooner we submit to this truth, the sooner we will see His wonderful work revealed in us.

His power. People are incapable of changing who they are at heart, and this is bad news because everyone has a wicked and sinful heart (Jeremiah 17:9). Despite our promises and commitments to change who we are deep down inside, we simply lack the power to do so. Real and lasting change is only possible with the Potter because He is capable of doing what we cannot.

His passion. Sometimes we forget that the Lord has intense feelings toward us. Only an intense desire to see us transformed could justify the precious sacrifice that God willingly laid down upon Calvary's cross. Change is not just something we long for; it is also something the Potter is intensely passionate about, and He will not be satisfied until He sees it accomplished.

Let's be open to being transformed and shaped by the Potter. When we want to stubbornly resist Him, let's remember His prerogative; when we grow discouraged by our inability to change ourselves, let's remember His power; and when we're feeling lonely and unloved, let's remember His passion.

What areas of your life would you like to see the Lord change? Write them down.

What are you willing to give up in exchange for these changes?

FIXED BY BROKENNESS
DAY 2

So He said to him, "What is your name?" He said, "Jacob." And He said, "Your name shall no longer be called Jacob, but Israel; for you have struggled with God and with men, and have prevailed." (Genesis 32:27–28 NKJV)

In biblical times, people's names were a snapshot of their nature as there was often a direct correlation between people's character and the definition of their name. The name *Jacob* means "heel catcher, conniver, and deceiver," and fewer names have ever fit a person so perfectly. From the womb, Jacob was determined to do all that he could to "get his" (Genesis 25:26). His existence was dominated by his sense of self, which enabled him to survive in the "real world." But it also prevented him from becoming the spiritual man that God had called him to be. A drastic dose of change was needed, and the Lord had the perfect prescription—brokenness.

The Lord appeared to Jacob and deliberately put his hip out of joint. This wasn't a minor injury, but apparently it remained with him for the rest of his natural life (Hebrews 11:21). It was a life-changing moment, designed not just to cripple him physically, but also to break him spiritually. Without the ability to fend for himself, Jacob would now be forced to rely on the Lord for his strength and sufficiency.

To illustrate this pivotal moment, the Lord renamed Jacob. No longer would Jacob live as the self-centered deceiver, but now he would be known as *Israel*, which means "governed by God," thus indicating his new nature as a God-dominated man. From this point forward, Jacob began to manifest the spiritual characteristics that would immortalize him as one of the great patriarchs.

Missionary Alan Redpath once said, "God has one great purpose for His people above everything else: it is to destroy in us forever any possible confidence in the flesh; it is to bring us to the place where self-confidence has passed into history and has been exchanged for a confidence in God, who raises the dead." Before God can fully **bless** us, He needs to fully **break** us of our "Jacob-like" ways. Such breaking is all part of the process of being rebuilt by our Master Maker.

Where are you at in God's breaking process in your life?

How is brokenness a blessing?

Beloved, let us love one another, for love is of God; and everyone who loves is born of God and knows God. (1 John 4:7 NKJV)

This familiar exhortation to love others comes to us from the pen of the apostle John. We frequently refer to John as "the apostle of love" and with very good reason. His first epistle alone contains the word *love* or its equivalent fifty-six times in just five short chapters. The theme of love also has a prominent place in John's gospel, including its best-known passage, *"For God so **loved** the world that He gave . . ." (John 3:16 NKJV).*

But it's important for us to understand that the apostle John wasn't always a loving individual. Luke's gospel gives us an interesting snapshot of John when he began to follow Christ. Notice how he reacted to a village of people that had rejected the Gospel message:

And when His disciples James and John saw this, they said, "Lord, do You want us to command fire to come down from heaven and consume them, just as Elijah did?" But He turned and rebuked them, and said, "You do not know what manner of spirit you are of." (Luke 9:54–55 NKJV)

We also discover in Mark's gospel that Jesus had given John and his brother, James, the nickname "the sons of thunder," presumably because of their fiery disposition to judge others (Mark 3:17). This shows us that John had started out with a somewhat judgmental and volatile heart, but over the years, it had been tenderly transformed through continual exposure to the Lord of Love.

Lives that are yielded to Christ become more and more loving. Initially, a believer might be quick to call down judgment on others, but over time, the transforming influence of Jesus softens a heart and fills it with gentleness and kindness. This ought to cause us to pause and ponder where we are at in this process. Do we resemble a son of thunder, or are we known and identified by our love toward others?

What personal experiences prove that God has made you into a more loving person?

How can you better express love for others?

TAKE COURAGE
DAY 4

After this, Joseph of Arimathea, being a disciple of Jesus, but secretly, for fear of the Jews, asked Pilate that he might take away the body of Jesus; and Pilate gave him permission. So he came and took the body of Jesus. And Nicodemus, who at first came to Jesus by night, also came, bringing a mixture of myrrh and aloes, about a hundred pounds. (John 19:38–39 NKJV)

Cowardice and courage are exact opposites. They cannot coexist, and one will always be chosen and exercised at the expense of the other. This is a principle that Joseph and Nicodemus understood all too well. As members of Israel's religious ruling class, they had become familiar with the teachings of Jesus. Over the course of time, they came to believe His claims and their hearts were changed through their exposure to this man who spoke with heavenly authority and embodied divine love.

Another change was simultaneously occurring in the hearts of their peers. The Jews' official opinion toward Jesus grew increasingly hostile. Joseph and Nicodemus found themselves in the minority whenever Jesus' name was brought up. At one point, Nicodemus tried to defend Christ against the criticism of the religious leaders, but he was quickly shot down (John 7:53). The pressure must have been intense for these men to lie low, which is what they did up until the point of Jesus' crucifixion.

Something significant happened in their hearts as they saw the love of Jesus demonstrated through His suffering on the cross. Joseph and Nicodemus crossed the line of anonymity, came out into the open, and exchanged their cowardice for courage by taking and burying Christ's body.

A heart that has been truly changed by Christ cannot rest contentedly in lying low. Eventually, believers move from a place of cowardice to a place of courage because they come to understand that the reality of Jesus' love for them is greater than their fears.

For God has not given us a spirit of fear, but of power and of love and of a sound mind. (2 Timothy 1:7 NKJV)

How can you relate to the examples of Joseph and Nicodemus?

How has Christ produced courage in your life?

DAY 5

And certain women who had been healed of evil spirits and infirmities; Mary called Magdalene, out of whom had come seven demons . . and many others who provided for Him from their substance. (Luke 8:2–3 NKJV)

Surprisingly little is known about Mary Magdalene. We don't know the facts behind her demonic possession, we don't know the details surrounding her life-changing encounter with Jesus, and we don't even have any evidence that she was the immoral character that she is often portrayed as being. The Scriptures simply introduce her to us at the point of her radical transformation from a demoniac to a devoted follower and supporter of Jesus Christ.

The next time we see Mary Magdalene in the gospels, it is at Calvary's cross (Matthew 27:56). With the sole exception of John, Jesus' disciples had all scattered and deserted Him at this point. In the hour of His greatest pain and suffering, the Lord found Himself conspicuously abandoned by those who had been by His side. Yet in their absence, there is the precious presence of Mary. This woman whom Christ had set free stood loyally by her Deliverer as the rest of the world tortured and mocked Him.

Mary's devotion embodies the truth that those who have been delivered from much will also love much (Luke 7:47). Devotion is the natural fruit of the change that Jesus produces in people's lives. If people do not return Christ's deliverance with their devotion, then they simply don't understand the depth of depravity from which they have been delivered.

It is fitting that of all the people who had come into contact with Jesus during His life, Mary Magdalene was the one who was honored to first witness Him as the risen Lord (John 20:14). In a similar sense, those who abide by Jesus because they understand what He's done for them will also be those who enjoy the Lord's presence. Let us never forget what Jesus has saved us from, and may our lives be an expression of profound gratitude for the change He has produced in us.

Where would you be today apart from the Lord's work in your life?

How can you be more mindful of what God has delivered you from?

TERMS OF TRANSFORMATION
DAY 6

Now Naaman, commander of the army of the king of Syria, was a great and honorable man in the eyes of his master, because by him the LORD had given victory to Syria. He was also a mighty man of valor, but a leper. (2 Kings 5:1 NKJV)

Naaman was a leper and, therefore, in need of change. He had tried everything, but in the end, nothing was capable of changing his condition. The prospect of being well seemed hopelessly lost until his wife's handmaiden suggested that he make his way to the prophet Elijah through whom the Lord had performed many mighty miracles. Naaman's options were limited, so he decided to seek Elijah's help.

Despite his critical condition, Naaman was also a man who was used to calling the shots, and he had some definite ideas on how the Lord should heal him. Elijah upset these expectations by commanding Naaman to go and wash himself in the Jordan River seven times. He was furious when he heard this and almost walked away from the incredible transformation that God had in store for him. Fortunately, his servants were able to convince Naaman to set aside his expectations and do what Elijah had said. What followed is a testimony to God's transforming power:

So he went down and dipped seven times in the Jordan, according to the saying of the man of God; and his flesh was restored like the flesh of a little child, and he was clean. (2 Kings 5:14 NKJV)

We see that Naaman did indeed experience God's transforming touch upon his life, but notice that it came on God's terms, not his own. It's crucial to comprehend this because so many of us long for God to change us, yet it never happens because we aren't willing to submit to His terms. We often want God to do *His* work *our* way, and this simply will never happen. Let us learn from Naaman's example by abandoning our own expectations and accepting God's terms for transformation.

When have you stubbornly resisted God's terms for transforming your life?

What was the outcome and why?

SPIRITUAL IN-SIGHT
DAY 7

Now as Jesus passed by, He saw a man who was blind from birth. (John 9:1 NKJV)

Try to imagine what life must have been like for this man. Born blind, he grew up without ever seeing the approving smile of his parents. He never had the opportunity to take in the glorious rising of the Middle-Eastern sun or stare in awe at a star-studded evening sky. He probably felt that God had singled him out for some special form of punishment, an impression that even the disciples were under as they asked Jesus, *"Who sinned, this man or his parents, that he was born blind?" (John 9:2 NKJV)* Jesus dispelled this false notion and with a single touch forever changed the way this man would look at life:

. . . He spat on the ground and made clay with the saliva; and He anointed the eyes of the blind man with the clay. And He said to him, "Go, wash in the pool of Siloam" . . . . So he went and washed, and came back seeing. (John 9:6–7 NKJV)

The impossible had occurred: a man who had been born without sight now could see. Rather than rejoice over this miraculous manifestation, the religious authorities were bugged by the fact that this had happened on the Sabbath. In the middle of the most incredible moment of this man's life, they interrogated him about the identity of the "troublemaker" who was responsible for this. His answers to their questions reveal an important progression.

When first asked about Jesus, he refers to Him as "a man" (John 9:11). Then he identifies Jesus as "a prophet" (John 9:17). When he eventually reencounters Jesus, he calls Him by His rightful title of "Lord" and worships Him (John 9:38). We can't miss his progressive journey as he draws closer and closer to the heart of who Jesus truly is. He is a man but much more than a man; He is a prophet but much more than a prophet; He is the Lord who alone is worthy of praise.

When Jesus opens our spiritual eyes, we embark on the same journey. The depth of His glory grows deeper and deeper as we grow in our relationship with Him.

How has your understanding of Jesus changed in the past year?

Ask the Lord to reveal His glory to you throughout this week.

BLESSED BLINDNESS
DAY 8

As he journeyed he came near Damascus, and suddenly a light shone around him from heaven. Then he fell to the ground, and heard a voice saying to him, "Saul, Saul, why are you persecuting Me?" (Acts 9:3–4 NKJV)

This is perhaps the most well-known conversion in the Bible. Saul was the arch-adversary of the church. His heart was filled with such hatred for those who followed Jesus of Nazareth that he made it his mission in life to eradicate them from every corner of the world. After having set out on one of these unholy "mission trips," Saul came face to face with Jesus in His blinding glory and was confronted with the fact that when he persecuted the church, he actually persecuted Jesus. Saul came to his senses, surrendering himself to Christ right there on the spot:

So he, trembling and astonished, said, "Lord, what do You want me to do?" (Acts 9:6 NKJV)

God answered Saul's question by giving him a new name, Paul, and by calling him to take the Gospel message to every corner of the world. Without a doubt, this is one of the most dramatic transformations to have ever taken place in a person's life. But many of us miss a small detail that followed in the wake of this work: *And he was three days without sight . . . (Acts 9:9 NKJV).*

The first lesson Paul had to learn as a Christian was dependency. For three whole days, Paul was forced to rely on the gracious help of others; the leader needed to be led. This was a fundamental principle that would support and secure him over a lifetime of missions work. Paul always sought the leading of God before stepping out, and as a result, he was always headed in the right direction.

When we surrender ourselves to Jesus, He often blinds us in order to give us greater spiritual sight. He knows that before we can make true and lasting progress in the Christian life, our self-sufficiency must be broken. Initially, we can't see the purpose for this breaking process, but hindsight reveals that God deserves praise for teaching us how to depend on Him instead of ourselves.

How did the Lord blind/break you when you first came to Him?

Why is brokenness an important part of God's process of changing us?

But Peter, standing up with the eleven, raised his voice and said to them, "Men of Judea and all who dwell in Jerusalem, let this be known to you, and heed my words." (Acts 2:14 NKJV)

This is one of those "Hollywood moments" when the lovable underdog rises up against all odds and accomplishes the unthinkable—only this isn't a movie. It's perhaps the most significant moment in church history, the turning point for sincere yet incapable disciples.

As the verse indicates, Peter is the one who stands and shouts these words. Just fifty days earlier, Peter was humbled and exposed as a coward. As his Master was interrogated and tortured, Peter denied that he ever knew Him, fearing for his own safety. He didn't even gather the courage to show up during Christ's dying moments on the cross. In the following days, Peter was so paranoid of being arrested by the same authorities who had killed Jesus that he hid (along with the other disciples) behind a locked door. This is not a heroic portrait, so it's all the more amazing when just fifty days after the resurrection, he stands up and boldly preaches to those same authorities that he had feared. How was such a transformation possible?

Prior to ascending to heaven, Jesus commanded Peter and the rest of His followers to wait in Jerusalem for the Holy Spirit to come upon them in a way that would enable them to exchange their fearfulness for boldness (Acts 1:4–8). In essence, Christ was telling them that they would no longer be limited by themselves but would be given spiritual access to the vaults of heaven. Through the Spirit's work in his life, Peter accessed those resources and neither he nor the world has been the same since.

The same transformation can also occur in our lives. We too have access to the Spirit's empowering presence, which will provide us with the resources we don't have in ourselves. All we need to do is ask:

"How much more will your heavenly Father give the Holy Spirit to those who ask Him!" (Luke 11:13 NKJV)

Why do you need the Holy Spirit?

How will you ensure that His empowering presence is upon your life?

Then they compelled a certain man, Simon a Cyrenian, the father of Alexander and Rufus, as he was coming out of the country and passing by, to bear His cross. (Mark 15:21 NKJV)

Simon had journeyed all the way from Cyrene in northern Africa in order to celebrate the Passover feast in Jerusalem. His heart must have been flush with reverence as he approached the holy temple. Perhaps he was even carrying a sacrificial lamb. But something caught his attention. There was a noisy crowd congregating along the pathway that led out of the city.

As he drew near, he could see that a man was causing the commotion—but not just any man. This was a condemned man who was being forced to carry His own cross. He had already been horribly beaten, but rather than being reviled by the sight, something drew Simon's heart and caused him to follow along at a distance. Suddenly, the man's frame crumbled under the weight of His cross; He was physically incapable of going on.

Perhaps that would have been the end of Simon's interaction with Jesus, but one of the attending soldiers invoked Roman law and ordered Simon to carry the cross to its destination. The Bible doesn't elaborate on what happened inside Simon at this point, but we can reasonably see that his life was changed during the moments between picking up the cross and setting it down at Calvary.

Notice that Mark identifies Simon as the father of Alexander and Rufus. This means that Alexander and Rufus were well-known in the early church, and perhaps this is even the same Rufus mentioned in Romans 16:13. This would make sense since it's generally accepted that Mark wrote his gospel from Rome. All of these factors point to Simon becoming a believer and passing his spiritual heritage on to his sons.

Whenever we have a life-changing encounter with Christ, there should be a natural desire to pass it on to the next generation. By doing so, we help ensure that He continues to receive glory as He continues to change lives.

Whom can you pass your spiritual legacy on to?

What are some practical steps that you can take in order to make sure this happens?

LIVE TO GIVE
DAY 11

Then Jesus entered and passed through Jericho. Now behold, there was a man named Zacchaeus who was a chief tax collector, and he was rich. (Luke 19:1–2 NKJV)

Some people just seem beyond God's reach. The world's claws appear too deeply embedded in their hearts to hope for any change. If we were alive during Jesus' day, we would have probably looked at Zacchaeus and placed him into this category. In those days, tax collectors were typically very wealthy and very dishonest because they were at liberty to pocket any residuals after Rome had received its fair share. And the Scriptures tell us that Zacchaeus was a *chief* tax collector, placing him at the top of the taxation food chain. Just in case we may have missed the significance here, the Spirit spells it out for us: *he was rich.*

Zacchaeus had dedicated his life to accumulating money for himself, but deep down there lingered the unfulfilled desire to give. Jesus opened the door for him to give by inviting Himself over for dinner. The Scriptures tell us that when Zacchaeus heard this, *he made haste and came down, and received Him joyfully (Luke 19:6 NKJV).* As the Lord continued to perform His work in Zacchaeus' life, he was moved to give to a much greater degree:

Zacchaeus stood and said to the Lord, "Look, Lord, I give half of my goods to the poor; and if I have taken anything from anyone by false accusation, I restore fourfold." (Luke 19:8 NKJV)

Part of the transformation that Jesus accomplishes in us is a desire to give rather than get. This world encourages us to look out for ourselves first, last, and always, but we should be headed in the opposite direction. Rather than living self-centered lives that are consumed with our own wealth and possessions, we experience a desire within us to meet the needs of others. This is because it is the Lord's desire within us; for just as He devoted Himself to giving while on this earth, He continues to give now through those He inhabits.

Where is your heart in relation to your desire to give to others?

What are the spiritual and practical advantages to giving versus getting? (Hint: read Mark 4:18–19.)

EXCEEDED EXPECTATIONS
DAY 12

Then Abram fell on his face, and God talked with him, saying: "As for Me, behold, My covenant is with you, and you shall be a father of many nations. No longer shall your name be called Abram, but your name shall be Abraham; for I have made you a father of many nations." (Genesis 17:3–5 NKJV)

There are only a few examples in Scripture where God personally renames a person, and this is one of them. In that day and culture, people's names were indicative of who they were, and so when God changes people's names, it always represents a deeper change that encompasses their character and nature.

The name *Abram* literally means "high father," which speaks of the honor of a father. At this point in his life, Abram had one son, Ishmael, through his servant Hagar. At ninety-nine years of age, he was probably settled and content with just the honor of being a father to Ishmael—but God had much bigger plans.

Abram was a noble moniker, but God changed his name to *Abraham*, which means "father of many." As wonderful as it was to be a "high father," the Lord went above and beyond this and gave him a new nature in which the joys of his prior nature would be marvelously multiplied.

This reveals a precious aspect of the way God operates in the lives of those who surrender to Him. When the Lord takes over a life, He always exceeds the expectation and imagination of that person. We all come to the Lord with a limited view of who He is and of what He is capable of accomplishing in us. How many of us can honestly say that we anticipated and expected Him to do all that He has done? The truth is that we are being constantly amazed by the One who is constantly replacing who we were with something infinitely better.

Now to Him who is able to do exceedingly abundantly above all that we ask or think, according to the power that works in us . . . . (Ephesians 3:20 NKJV)

How has the Lord exceeded your expectations?

How would you answer someone who asked, "What can God do with my life?"

NEW NEWS
DAY 13

"Behold, I will do a new thing . . . " (Isaiah 43:19 NKJV)

There is some great news given to us in the Bible: God is doing new things. He isn't satisfied with the status quo when there is a need for improvement. We see this aspect of His heart expressed in three distinct ways.

First, God desires to do something new in **creation**. When the world was created, God declared that it was good because at that time, it was perfect in every way. But when Adam and Eve fell, their sin had a devastating ripple effect on the world, and it too became corrupted. The natural disasters that are so common today were never a part of the original plan. The Lord is not pleased with the present situation and has promised to create something new at the end of this age:

Nevertheless we, according to His promise, look for new heavens and a new earth in which righteousness dwells. (2 Peter 3:13 NKJV)

Second, God established a new **covenant**. The word *covenant* means "a contract or agreement." Before Jesus, God had established an agreement with His people that was predicated on the law of Moses. Man was required to strictly observe the law's 613 commands in order to be right before God. The law was perfect, but man's imperfection prevented him from being able to keep it. So, God established a new covenant in which the law was set aside and belief in Jesus' sacrificial death on the cross became the basis for being right with God:

Christ is the end of the law for righteousness to everyone who believes. (Romans 10:4 NKJV)

Finally, God's desire to do something new is demonstrated in our **conversion**. God loves us too much to allow us to stay stuck in our sins. He is constantly calling people to surrender so that He can take over their lives and replace their painful emptiness with a sense of fulfillment that they could never know otherwise:

"I have come that they may have life, and that they may have it more abundantly."
(John 10:10 NKJV)

Has God done something new in you? If so, how, and if not, why?

Whom can you share this new news with?

DAY 14

So Judah said to his brothers, "What profit is there if we kill our brother and conceal his blood? Come and let us sell him . . . ." (Genesis 37:26–27 NKJV)

Joseph's brothers were sick of him. Not only was he their father's undisputed favorite, but lately Joseph had begun to have dreams of them bowing down to him. The mere presence of Joseph became an increasingly difficult burden for them to bear, and so, at the first opportunity to get rid of him, they threw him into a pit and left him for dead. But off on the horizon, they spotted a caravan of traders headed for Egypt, so Judah got the idea to make some money by selling Joseph as a slave. This reveals important insight into Judah's self-centered nature.

Fast-forward twenty years, and now the roles are reversed. Joseph had become the second most powerful man in Egypt, and through a set of divinely ordained events, his brothers are forced to approach him and beg for food. They don't recognize Joseph, but he recognizes them. Amazingly, he does not seek revenge but wants to be reconciled to them. But before there could be **reconciliation,** he needs to see **transformation**, so Joseph sets up a test to see if their hearts have changed over the years.

He gives them the same opportunity to selfishly sell out one of their other brothers for their own benefit, and it is Judah (the one with the greatest guilt) who rises up and offers to suffer in another's place (Genesis 44:33). By doing so, Judah demonstrates that his heart has made the journey from a place of self-centeredness to a place of selflessness. Joseph wept at this point because he now knew the transformation was complete and the door to reconciliation was finally open.

The change we witness in Judah is a hint of what ought to happen in us as we become new creations in Christ. Our old motives for personal profit are exchanged for a desire to profit and benefit others. Interestingly enough, Judah's name means "praise," which is also our natural reaction toward God as He works this transformation in us.

Do other people see you as self-centered or selfless?

When was the last time you made a personal sacrifice for someone else?

Then Moses said to the LORD, "O my Lord, I am not eloquent, neither before nor since You have spoken to Your servant; but I am slow of speech and slow of tongue." (Exodus 4:10 NKJV)

We are prone to drift toward two erroneous extremes. On one side of the scale, there is the error of focusing on our abilities. When this happens, the paralysis of pride is sure to follow. On the other side, there is the error of focusing on our inabilities. This is where Moses found himself as God placed the sacred call of delivering and leading Israel upon him.

In Moses' mind, he was the wrong man for the job. He lacked the eloquence that would be needed for such an undertaking, and he was right . . . partially. He wasn't capable of fulfilling the calling on his own, but it was never God's intention for him to go it alone:

So the LORD said to him, "Who has made man's mouth? Or who makes the mute, the deaf, the seeing, or the blind? Have not I, the LORD? Now therefore, go, and I will be with your mouth and teach you what you shall say." (Exodus 4:11–12 NKJV)

Moses continued to put up a fight because he remained focused on his own deficiencies, but in the end, he learned that man's inabilities are easily overcome when God fulfills His purposes. He will be faithful to fill the vessel that simply submits to the will of the great I AM. As God changed Moses from a simple shepherd into the deliverer of a nation, He also needed to change the way that Moses looked at his inabilities.

Perhaps we know better than to focus on our achievements and accomplishments, but how well do we detect the danger in focusing on our ineptitude? One is just as dishonoring to the Lord as the other, and both will bring God's transforming work in our lives to a halt. Let's ask the Lord to take away our tendency to focus on our lack rather than on His sufficiency as He continues to change us!

When are you tempted to focus on your inabilities, and does this affect your obedience toward God?

How can you prevent this from happening?

ANY QUESTIONS?
DAY 16

O LORD, how long shall I cry, And You will not hear? Even cry out to You, "Violence!" And You will not save. (Habakkuk 1:2 NKJV)

Notice how the book of Habakkuk begins. It starts with a question, *"How long shall I cry, And You will not hear?"* This sets the tone for the first chapter of this book as Habakkuk goes on to ask God a series of "why" questions (vv. 3, 13, 14). One Bible commentator has made the observation that this prophet had a question mark for a brain.

Habakkuk had so many questions because his homeland was being invaded and overrun by the Babylonians. In reality, these questions were actually statements that were calling God's goodness and faithfulness into question, essentially saying, *If you were a good and faithful God, things would not be as they are!* Habakkuk had fallen into the snare of measuring God's character by the circumstances presently affecting him. This is a huge mistake because the Lord is eternal, and His good and faithful nature cannot be gauged according to a momentary situation. He is who He is, whether our circumstances seem to reflect it or not. Habakkuk's problem was that he was looking at God through the lens of what was temporary rather than looking at what was temporary through the lens of who God was, is, and always will be. So, God reminds him:

"But the LORD is in His holy temple. Let all the earth keep silence before Him." (Habakkuk 2:20 NKJV)

In the process of our spiritual transformation, we need to learn this same lesson. The transient trials of life will tempt us to question God's nature, but blessed are the believers who embrace the Lord's eternal and unchanging heart toward them. In Hebrew, the name *Habakkuk* literally means "to embrace." This is fitting due to the fact that by the end of his book, he is no longer questioning God but confidently embracing His character:

The LORD God is my strength; He will make my feet like deer's feet, And He will make me walk on my high hills. (Habakkuk 3:19 NKJV)

When have you questioned God because of your circumstances?

What should you do the next time you're tempted to question God's goodness and faithfulness?

TRAGEDY TRANSFORMED
DAY 17

And there was a certain nobleman whose son was sick at Capernaum. When he heard that Jesus had come out of Judea into Galilee, he went to Him and implored Him to come down and heal his son, for he was at the point of death. (John 4:46–47 NKJV)

Tragedy brings people from different walks of life together like nothing else can. We get a glimpse of this in the passage above. We're introduced to a nobleman, who in our day would be comparable to a politician. As a wealthy and prestigious person, he ordinarily would have had nothing to do with an itinerant preacher like Jesus. But that changed when his son was brought to the brink of death.

The Bible tells us he traveled twenty-five miles from Capernaum in order to see Jesus and he was willing to implore (or beg) Him to come and heal his son. Tragedy brought this nobleman to the Lord, and the Lord used it to transform him into a man of faith. Keep in mind that the nobleman wanted Jesus to make the trip to see and heal his son, showing that his faith in Christ was limited to His visible presence. Jesus challenged this shallow sense of trust by calling him to believe in what he couldn't see:

Jesus said to him, "Go your way; your son lives." (John 4:50 NKJV)

At this point, the nobleman's faith was being tested. Would he still insist that Jesus accompany him so he could make sure his son was healed? Or would he make the long journey home equipped with nothing more than Christ's promise? He passed the test, went his way, and discovered that his son had been healed just as Jesus had said. As a result, he and his entire household became believers (John 4:53). As He so gloriously does, the Lord used this tragedy as a means of spiritual transformation.

The Lord does the same thing in our lives. Every tragic moment is an opportunity for us to trust in the promises we find in God's Word. The nobleman's example shows us that those who simply take God at His Word are those who experience the greatest degree of spiritual transformation in their lives.

What would you have done in the nobleman's position?

When has God used a tragedy to transform you?

CHOOSE CHANGE
DAY 18

Now a certain man was there who had an infirmity thirty-eight years. When Jesus saw him lying there, and knew that he already had been in that condition a long time, He said to him, "Do you want to be made well?" (John 5:5–6 NKJV)

In Jesus' day, there was a public pool in Jerusalem that was noted for having miraculous healing properties. The Scriptures tell us that the people believed that an angel would stir up the waters and the first person in would be supernaturally healed. At the edge of this pool, there was a man who had been suffering for an excruciating thirty-eight years! Few of us can imagine dealing with *anything* for such a long time, much less a physical infirmity. Therefore, it seems a bit strange, if not comical, that Jesus asked him, *"Do you want to be made well?"* Let's be sensible for a second; after being in such a condition for so long, it was a given that this man *wanted* to be made well . . or was it?

It's a sad commentary on our human nature, but true nonetheless, that it's possible for people to become comfortable in a condition of sickness. Rather than receive the healing and transforming touch of God upon their lives, they would rather stay sick because it provides security and comfort for them. Perhaps this man had been sick for so long because deep down he didn't want to accept the requirements and responsibilities that would come along with change.

C. S. Lewis remarked in a sermon that

> . . . it would seem that our Lord finds our desires not too strong, but too weak. We are half-hearted creatures, fooling about with drink and sex and ambition when infinite joy is offered us, like an ignorant child who wants to go on making mud pies in a slum because she cannot imagine what is meant by the offer of a holiday at the sea. We are far too easily pleased.

Even though the Lord wants to make us spiritually well, we must decide if we want His touch upon our lives. He requires that we leave our old ways and adopt a new way of living godly in Christ Jesus. Though it breaks His heart, the Lord will not change a life that is unwilling to accept change or to be made well.

When have you gotten comfortable with an unhealthy condition?

What requirements accompany the Lord's touch upon a life?

DAY 19

At that time the disciples came to Jesus, saying, "Who then is greatest in the kingdom of heaven?" (Matthew 18:1 NKJV)

The disciples had been following Jesus for the past two to three years. Consider how awesome this was—God was literally eating, walking, and sleeping right alongside of these simple men! Perfection was being expressed in their midst in every conceivable scenario of life. With this incredible privilege came an incredible responsibility; for since these men had the advantage of being in the presence of God, they were also expected to live in godliness.

They failed miserably . . . several times. They even went so far as to ask Jesus which of them would be the *"greatest in the kingdom of heaven."* They were not asking so they could congratulate someone else; they were asking in hopes of pushing their way past their peers to the top of the ladder of spiritual status. This spirit of self-promotion was the polar opposite of God, whom they were supposedly representing! After investing so much time, teaching, and training into these men, we might have been tempted to throw in the proverbial towel on them.

Not Jesus. He knew change was possible in them because all things are possible with Him. Therefore, He persistently and patiently invested more time, teaching, and training into these twelve men. Eventually, the evidence of their altered hearts became more and more apparent until they began to bear the likeness of their Master.

What an encouragement to us. If we were completely honest, we would have to confess that we aren't much different from the disciples. The real difference is that instead of dwelling alongside Jesus as they did, we have Jesus dwelling within us by the power of the Holy Spirit (Colossians 1:27). You can't get any closer than that! This makes us all the more accountable to live in godliness. But even when we fail (and we will certainly fail), the Lord shows the same persistent patience in changing us into people who resemble Him.

How does Christ respond to your failures, and how can you keep this in mind the next time you fail?

What advantage do you have over the twelve disciples?

Now they came to Jericho. As He went out of Jericho with His disciples and a great multitude, blind Bartimaeus, the son of Timaeus, sat by the road begging. And when he heard that it was Jesus of Nazareth, he began to cry out and say, "Jesus, Son of David, have mercy on me!" (Mark 10:46-47 NKJV)

This is one of the most memorable moments in the gospels. It begins with a blind man named Bartimaeus desperately crying out to Jesus for healing. He was told to keep quiet by the crowd surrounding Christ, but he didn't let man's rejection prevent him from seeking the Lord's restoration and cried out all the more. Jesus stood still for him and asked, *"What do you want Me to do for you?"* Bartimaeus responded, *"That I may receive my sight"* (Mark 10:51 NKJV). These details are familiar to most of us, but what might not be so familiar is the subtlety seen in the following verse:

Then Jesus said to him, "Go your way; your faith has made you well." (Mark 10:52 NKJV)

Christ didn't promise to help Bartimaeus in exchange for anything. He simply said, *"Go your way."* Jesus wasn't telling him to go away but rather was telling him that he was now free to do what he wanted. Christ wasn't interested in forcing or guilt-tripping people into following Him but wanted them to follow because that's what they wanted to do. Notice the reaction of Bartimaeus after he experienced the transforming touch of the Lord:

And immediately he received his sight and followed Jesus on the road. (Mark 10:52 NKJV)

Jesus had released Bartimaeus to go his own way, but by choosing to follow Jesus, he was declaring that the Lord's way was now his way. Life itself was now redefined as Christ became the axis around which his world revolved. Who could blame him? Why wouldn't he want to follow the One who had produced such incredible change in him?

We're no different. At one point, we were spiritually blind and graciously given sight by the Healer; and the change that Jesus has brought to us compels us to follow Him because we *want* to, not because we *have* to. Let's not lose sight of this.

Why do you follow Jesus?

What are some bad reasons for following Jesus?

MADE WHOLE
DAY 21

And behold, a leper came and worshiped Him, saying, "Lord, if You are willing, You can make me clean." (Matthew 8:2 NKJV)

Life couldn't get much worse for lepers in biblical times. They were forced to face the physical suffering of their disease, which would begin to show itself in large reddish blisters that would eventually burst. These sores would then putrefy and deteriorate until extremities, such as fingers and toes, were eventually lost. And their suffering wasn't just skin deep; there was a social stigma attached to lepers. In Jesus' day, they were forced to stay a hundred feet away from everyone else and it was illegal to greet or touch a leper. Imagine the pain of being quarantined from your loved ones. But the worst effect was on the spiritual level. Not only were lepers forbidden from entering the temple (which signified God's presence), but the Pharisees taught that lepers were being afflicted by the hand of God for their sins.

As this leper approached Jesus, he was suffering on three different levels. **Physically**, his body was rotting away; **emotionally**, he was a social outcast incapable of enjoying companionship; and **spiritually**, he was under the impression that God Himself had rejected him. Even though religion taught that the hand of God was against this leper, Jesus lovingly extending the healing hand of God toward him:

Then Jesus put out His hand and touched him, saying, "I am willing; be cleansed." Immediately his leprosy was cleansed. (Matthew 8:3 NKJV)

This leper's healing was instantaneous and thorough. Not only was his flesh made fresh and new, but he was able to reenter society and embrace those whom he loved. Most significantly, he was now able to enter the temple where he would now be looked upon as a recipient of God's miraculous favor. Through the transforming touch of Jesus, this man was made completely whole. So it is with all who experience the Lord's touch upon their lives. Physical healing may be withheld in order to draw us closer to Christ, but the end result is the same sense of wholeness that flooded this former leper's body, soul, and spirit.

How can you relate to this leper?

What does his story teach you about the Lord?

. . . there met Him out of the tombs a man with an unclean spirit . . . . (Mark 5:2 NKJV)

As Jesus came to the coastal region of the Gadarenes, He immediately stepped into one of the most spectacular scenes in Scripture. A demon-possessed man suddenly rushed forward to confront Christ, and our imagination can go on overload when we consider what he must have looked like.

The Bible tells us he had been possessed for a long time (Luke 8:27), he had supernatural strength and was absolutely untamable (Mark 5:4), the demons that tortured him drove him into the wilderness (Luke 8:29), he would cut and gouge himself with sharp stones and howl day and night (Mark 5:5), and in all of this, he ran naked and lived among the graves of the dead (Luke 8:27). He was a pathetic portrait of what the devil does to those under his dominion, but at the same time, he was also a perfect candidate for God's kingdom! Jesus cast the demons out of this poor creature and instantly began to produce change in his life.

They came to Jesus, and saw the one who had been demon-possessed and had the legion, sitting and clothed and in his right mind. (Mark 5:15 NKJV)

There are three changes we see in this man, and the first is that he was **sitting**. Throughout Scripture, sitting represents a sense of peace and stillness. Jesus had replaced this man's rage with repose, torment with tranquility, and chaos with calm. The second change is that this man was now **clothed**. The shame and humiliation of his nakedness was now covered. Third, he was also **in his right mind**. In Greek, the words used for "right mind" convey a sense of sobriety and sound judgment. His instability had turned into surety as he was now able to think reasonably and rationally.

So it is with those of us who have been changed by Jesus. We enjoy the peace of God that surpasses all earthly understanding, our sinful shame has been clothed in the robe of Christ's righteousness, and we are given the mind of Christ so that we can make sound decisions in life.

How does Jesus' treatment of people differ from the devil's?

How many godly changes can you list in your life?

YOU'RE FINISHED!
DAY 23

And Barnabas and Saul returned from Jerusalem when they had fulfilled their ministry, and they also took with them John whose surname was Mark. (Acts 12:25 NKJV)

John-Mark is an encouragement to those who have trouble finishing what they start. His life also shows that in taking over our lives, Jesus makes us into people who are faithful finishers. This young man had made the commitment to accompany Paul and Barnabas on their first missionary journey. What an exciting adventure lay ahead for the three of them! They would face unknown dangers together and share in witnessing the miraculous moving of God. John-Mark was fired-up to go along on this trip, but his fire was fueled by enthusiasm, not faithfulness.

His zeal sustained him through their adventures on the island of Cyprus (Acts 13:4–12), but the flame flickered and went out as they came to the notoriously dangerous region of Pamphylia:

Now when Paul and his party set sail from Paphos, they came to Perga in Pamphylia; and John, departing from them, returned to Jerusalem. (Acts 13:13 NKJV)

Scholars disagree over exactly why John-Mark split at this point, but one thing is certain—Paul was displeased by his departure because he refused to take him along on his next journey (Acts 15:38). The apostle felt that this kid had proven he was unreliable and, therefore, couldn't be trusted with such an important task. Imagine the sense of guilt and dejection John-Mark must have wrestled with. As a young man, his ministry career seemed finished.

Fortunately, God was not finished with him. Barnabas was led to give John-Mark a second chance and took him on another journey without Paul. This small token of kindness brought a huge return for the kingdom because John-Mark later became a key member of the early church. He was one of only four men whom God chose to write the gospels (Mark), and as Paul closed the last epistle he would write, he referred to John-Mark as being *useful to me for ministry (2 Timothy 4:11 NKJV)*. He had a shaky start but finished well, which is what is to be expected from a life that Jesus is working in and working on.

How has Christ made you into a better finisher?

Why is finishing important? How is this demonstrated in Christ's life and death?

"Is this not the carpenter's son? Is not His mother called Mary? And His brothers <u>James</u>, Joses, Simon, and <u>Judas</u>?" (Matthew 13:55 NKJV)

For even His brothers did not believe in Him. (John 7:5 NKJV)

It's an incredible fact that Jesus' own brothers did not believe in Him during His earthly ministry. If anyone had the advantage of believing in Jesus, it would seem to have been these men. They had witnessed His many miracles and His moral perfection for years, yet they had not committed themselves to Him. They were non-believers, and at one point, they even thought their older brother had lost His mind (Mark 3:32).

This changed after Jesus' death, burial, and resurrection. James came to believe in his brother as his Lord and Savior in the wake of these momentous events (Galatians 1:19). This sibling became a foundational leader in the Jerusalem church, and he went on to author the epistle that bears his name. Another brother, Judas (or Jude), came to a saving faith in Christ and authored the book of Jude.

This shows us that the Lord even changed lives within His own natural family, but they were not changed by His morality or mighty miracles. It was not until the gospel message (which is Jesus' death, burial, and resurrection according to 1 Corinthians 15:1–4) was revealed to them that they became believers.

Lives are not radically changed by morality or miracles. Only the gospel has the power to produce the type of transformation that occurs at the core of a person. Before *we* can be changed, we need to believe the gospel, and before *others* can be changed, we need to share the gospel with them.

What is the best way to help a person change?

Whom will you commit to sharing the Gospel with this day, this week?

AFFLICTION IS . .

It is good for me that I have been afflicted, That I may learn Your statutes. (Psalm 119:71 NKJV)

There is evidence when God has renovated people's hearts. One such proof is found in their attitude toward affliction. It's a mark of deep spiritual maturity when servants of God look at their affliction in life and say with the psalmist, *"It is good."* Those who have been altered by God see affliction differently than the rest of this world.

For one thing, they see **affliction is an education**. There are certain spiritual realities that simply cannot be comprehended apart from pain and suffering. In the midst of such times, we become uniquely qualified to learn God's ways and statutes. Two friends were once discussing the insensitivity of an acquaintance. One turned to the other and explained, "He doesn't know how to be sensitive because he hasn't suffered."

They also recognize that **affliction is an incentive**. It was never God's intention for us to become fully satisfied here in this world. At best, we are just pilgrims passing through this life (1 Peter 2:11). Heaven is our destination, our goal, and our home. Nothing gives us greater incentive to live for the next life than the afflictions we experience in this one.

Finally, those whose hearts have been taken over by God know **affliction is a form of identification**. Although it isn't a popular topic these days, the Bible declares that we have been called to identify with Jesus through suffering (Philippians 1:29). When we suffer, it cements our personal relationship with Christ in a special way. People see that we are truly servants of the Master because we are treading down the same trail of trials.

Those of us who have been made anew in Christ can begin to see affliction as a positive presence in our lives. C. S. Lewis wrote, "Tribulations cannot cease until God either sees us remade or sees that our remaking is now hopeless." Let's use our present afflictions as a conduit for change by seeing them as an education, an incentive, and a form of identification.

What is afflicting you, and what should your attitude be toward it?

How has God used your suffering in the past to produce positive changes?

WHY NOT ME?
DAY 26

"I have heard of You by the hearing of the ear, But now my eye sees You. Therefore I abhor myself, And repent in dust and ashes." (Job 42:5–6 NKJV)

From an earthly perspective, it seems like Job had a lot to complain about. The Bible tells us that Job was blameless and upright (Job 1:1), feared God and shunned evil (Job 1:1), and was even singled out as one of the three most righteous men to have ever lived (Ezekiel 14:14, 20). Therefore, when calamity came crashing down on Job, it naturally raised questions in his heart, and it also raises questions in us.

We tend to think that good people like Job aren't supposed to suffer. The problem with this type of thinking is that nobody is "good" when it comes to God's definition of goodness. Every human being is part of a rebellious race that has been separated from the Creator since the garden of Eden. The whole of humanity was represented in Adam, who sinned and was correspondingly condemned; as the *New England Primer* puts it, "In Adam's fall, we sinned all." Sin is something we *do* because sin is a part of who we *are*. In God's sight, no one is essentially good except for Him (Matthew 19:17).

On his very best day, Job was still a miserable sinner in comparison to the Lord. As a sinner, he was not in a position to complain about the sufferings he had experienced. When he received a vision of God in His perfect holiness, he then understood who he truly was—a wretched sinner who had no reason to complain about anything. This was a turning point in Job's life, and now instead of asking, *Why me?* he began to ask, *Why not me?*

A tremendous transformation occurs when we see God for who He is because it is only then that we see ourselves for who we are. The more we compare ourselves to God, the more humbled we are that He would have anything to do with us and the more malleable we become to His transforming touch.

Why is the statement "Good people don't suffer" untrue?

When it comes to suffering, why not you?

BE PRAY-PARED
DAY 27

Now Joshua sent men from Jericho to Ai . . . And the men of Ai struck down about thirty-six men, for they chased them from before the gate . . and struck them down on the descent; therefore the hearts of the people melted and became like water. (Joshua 7:2, 5 NKJV)

The children of Israel seemed unstoppable as they crossed over the river Jordan to possess the land that God had promised to them. They had just witnessed a miraculous victory over the walled city of Jericho, and under the strong leadership of Joshua, their fame had spread throughout the land. Everything was going their way . . . until they came to the city of Ai.

In comparison to Jericho, Ai looked like a cakewalk. It was less populated and fortified than Jericho; surely they could quickly take care of it. Quite the opposite—the Israelites were overrun by Ai's army and wound up losing thirty-six men. They were now confronted by a sense of their vulnerability, and the landscape suddenly took on a different, more dangerous look. Imagine the questions Joshua must have been asking himself: *How did this happen? What did I do wrong?*

It was really what Joshua *didn't* do that led to Israel's defeat. Prior to Jericho, Joshua had sought the Lord in prayer before going into battle (Joshua 5:14), and he was graciously given the plans for victory. But with the victory over Jericho came a deceptive sense of self-sufficiency. We don't see Joshua taking counsel from the Lord before attempting to take Ai. The defeat there served as a painfully effective lesson on prayer's importance. This was something the people of Israel had to learn before God could fully transform them from lowly slaves into mighty warriors.

The same principle applies to us on a spiritual level. In order to change from those who are enslaved by our sins into those capable of conquering them, we must make prayer a consistent part of our lives. Past success must never numb us to the necessity of seeking the Lord first today. If we don't, we will have our share of Ai defeats.

When has a lack of prayer led to a loss in your life?

What should you stop and pray about today? Do it!

EQUAL OPPORTUNITY SAVIOR
DAY 28

One of the rulers of the synagogue came, Jairus by name. And when he saw Him, he fell at His feet and begged Him earnestly, saying, "My little daughter lies at the point of death. Come and lay Your hands on her, that she may be healed, and she will live." (Mark 5:22–23 NKJV)

As the Lord transforms us, we experience the depth of His universal love. Don't confuse this with universalism, which is the unbiblical teaching that everyone will be saved for eternity. Universal love means that everyone is valuable and loved by God (whether they love Him is another issue). We need to understand this in order to change as God desires.

Jairus learned about Jesus' love through his encounter with Him. His daughter was deathly ill, and we can understand his anxiety as he begs Jesus to come and heal her before it's too late. The Lord immediately goes with him, and it must have been a frantic footrace for Jairus to get home before his precious daughter died. Along the way, a large crowd of people impeded their progress. Under the circumstances, Jairus must have seen them as obstacles standing in the way of his objective. As they were nearing his house, Jesus stopped and asked, *"Who touched My clothes?" (Mark 5:30 NKJV)* Perhaps Jairus thought, *Can't this wait. My daughter is on the verge of death!*

Jairus didn't realize that this crowd contained an equally beloved daughter who was also suffering. A woman who had been bleeding uncontrollably reached out to Jesus in hopes of being healed. She stepped forward to identify herself, and with Jairus right there, Jesus says, *"Be of good cheer, <u>daughter</u>; your faith has made you well" (Matthew 9:22 NKJV)*. The message to Jairus was that as much as he loved his own daughter (who was twelve; Mark 5:42), God had just as much love for this woman (who had suffered for twelve years; Matthew 9:20). Both were beloved daughters, and neither should be seen as an inconvenience or obstacle. Jesus would go on to manifest the miraculous in Jairus' daughter, but equally significant was the lesson that Jairus learned about the Lord's universal love. If He loves everyone, then so should we.

Whom do you have a hard time loving?

How can you start loving them?

That very day Pilate and Herod became friends with each other, for previously they had been at enmity with each other. (Luke 23:12 NKJV)

When the Jewish leaders brought Jesus to Pilate and insisted that He be crucified, His case had become something of a political hot potato. Pilate wanted to appease his Jewish constituency, but he was also savvy enough to know that Jesus wasn't worthy of death. He seemed to find a loophole when he heard that Jesus was from the region of Galilee and, therefore, under the jurisdiction of Herod. Pilate decided to hand the dilemma off to Herod, freeing himself from the matter. But Jesus would not even speak to Herod, so He was sent back to Pilate. The Bible tells us that Pilate and Herod's relationship was changed through this shuffle. Formerly enemies, they now found that they had something in common—neither wanted to deal with Jesus—and as a result, they became friends.

Not all changes are for the better. We see this in Pilate and Herod as they changed not only in their relationship toward each other, but also in their relationship toward Jesus. Both men became calloused to Christ through their interaction with Him. The presence of Jesus is such that people cannot remain neutral or unchanged toward Him. They will either be drawn to receive Him or struggle to reject Him. Either way, they will be changed.

Jesus had the effect of drawing out the deepest devotion as well as the most extreme enmity in people. The Pharisees took hostility to a whole new level as they responded to Christ's rebuke against their hypocrisy. The Pharisees were changed by Jesus, but it was for the worse because they chose to reject rather than receive Him.

Christ promised His followers that they would suddenly find themselves hated and despised by their loved ones (Matthew 10:21–22). This change is not brought about by us but by the fact that we are now indwelt by Jesus. By inviting Him into our hearts, we also invite the hostility of those who haven't (John 15:21). No one can escape the fact that Jesus produces change in people, one way or another.

Why isn't all change good?

How are you changing? Be specific.

HAPPY-ENDING DAY

DAY 30

Then one of the criminals who were hanged blasphemed Him, saying, "If You are the Christ, save Yourself and us." But the other, answering, rebuked him, saying, "Do you not even fear God, seeing you are under the same condemnation? And we indeed justly, for we receive the due reward of our deeds; but this Man has done nothing wrong." Then he said to Jesus, "Lord, remember me when You come into Your kingdom." (Luke 23:39–42 NKJV)

There they hung, the perfect cross section of humanity. On one side, there was a man who had rejected Christ's claim to be the Savior of the world. In his mind, if Jesus was truly capable of saving anyone, He should have been saving Himself from the cross. This response represents the majority in this world who do not understand or believe in Jesus. Little did this antagonist realize that by *not* saving Himself from the cross, Jesus was actually doing all that He could to save him.

On the other side, there was a man who saw Jesus differently. He recognized his own sinfulness as well as Christ's holiness. When a heart apprehends both of these truths, it produces a plea for salvation to the only One able to save: *"Lord, remember me."* This response represents the rest of the world who see both who they are and who Jesus is and then place their faith in Him. By the world's standards, Jesus had no reason to honor the request of this dying man, but by God's standards, this man's life was still worth saving and changing:

And Jesus said to him, "Assuredly, I say to you, today you will be with Me in Paradise." (Luke 23:43 NKJV)

Change can never come too late in life. As long as there is breath, the Lord can still take over a heart. Many push away from Christ as they mature because they think that He won't take them toward the end of their lives. This man's request and Christ's response prove that it's never too late for Him to save and change a life seeking salvation.

Which man represents you and why?

Jesus will save anyone, including those nearing the end of their lives. Whom can you share this truth with?

DAY 31

Paul, <u>called</u> to be an apostle of Jesus Christ . . . . (1 Corinthians 1:1 NKJV)

What is the meaning of life? It's a question that we've all asked ourselves at some point, and it's a question that reveals an important insight into our souls. Within our human hearts, there is a natural longing to belong to some thing or cause greater than us. For those who don't know God, this internal itch goes unscratched, and they are still left asking the question, *What is the meaning of life?*

Paul connects with this truth as he begins the first letter to the Corinthian church. At the outset, he mentions the fact that he has been *called to be an apostle of Jesus Christ*. This shows that God had an important purpose and plan for Paul's life. The Lord didn't save Paul so that he could just sit around and become spiritually stagnant. Instead, He desired to involve Paul in a work that would prove to satisfy his built-in desire for purpose, direction, and meaning. We must understand that this wasn't just something special or unique between Paul and God; the Bible tells us that every Christian is called:

For we are His workmanship, created in Christ Jesus for good works, which God prepared beforehand that we should walk in them. (Ephesians 2:10 NKJV)

In this regard, we, as Christians, are completely different from the world around us. We enjoy a sense of purpose because we have been called by God to play a part in His master plan. From time to time, it's easy to lose sight of this fact. The effect is that we start to relate more to the world's sense of emptiness than the fulfillment that God wants us to experience. When this happens, we need to remember that we've been called by the Lord to play a part in His grand design and that our lives always have a sense of purpose, direction, and meaning.

How does God's calling on your life affect your outlook on life?

What is your God-given calling, and are you being faithful to it?

AUTHORITY PRIORITY

DAY 32

Paul, called to be an apostle of Jesus Christ <u>through the will of God</u> . . . . (1 Corinthians 1:1 NKJV)

Paul's relationship with the church at Corinth had grown more and more difficult over the past few months. Despite having been the founder of this fellowship and spending several months discipling them, a movement had sprung up to challenge the apostle's authority. Their attack even turned personal when they said that Paul's letters *are weighty and powerful, but his bodily presence is weak, and his speech contemptible (2 Corinthians 10:10 NKJV).* Paul's authority was being challenged to the core, and at this critical moment, he pointed out that his calling as an apostle was not by his own design but *through the will of God.*

This sets an important precedent for us when it comes to spiritual authority. True authority is not something that can be self-appointed or self-attained; it must be given by the Lord. The greatest servants of God are those who do not seek out positions of power for themselves but are appointed by the will of God to accomplish the work of God. David was taken from the sheepfold, Moses was recruited on the backside of the wilderness, and Elisha was commissioned while he was plowing with twelve teams of oxen. These men weren't looking for positions of power, but they were enabled to be powerful leaders because they understood from where their authority came. However, God will not honor or bless those who are filled with pride and think that their authority resides in themselves (2 Samuel 22:28).

In our walk with the Lord, we need to recognize that our spiritual authority cannot be personally pursued by ourselves. Instead, it is something that God grants to us only as we are humble and faithful in the little things of life. And once God gives us His authority, it cannot be successfully challenged by anyone.

Therefore humble yourselves under the mighty hand of God, that He may exalt you in due time . . . . (1 Peter 5:6 NKJV)

When have you witnessed an example of self-appointed authority?

True authority comes from God. How can you incorporate this into your daily routine?

DAY 33

Paul, called to be an apostle of Jesus Christ through the will of God, and <u>Sosthenes</u> our brother . . . (1 Corinthians 1:1 NKJV)

Sosthenes . . . who was he, and why did Paul take the time to mention him here? In order to answer these questions, we need to understand that the Corinthians were challenging Paul's spiritual authority as he was writing this. He deliberately mentions that Sosthenes was a brother in Christ. In and of itself, there's nothing unusual about this . . until we turn to Acts 18:12–17, which records an incident that took place at Corinth several months prior:

. . . the Jews with one accord rose up against Paul and brought him to the judgment seat . . . . And when Paul was about to open his mouth, Gallio said to the Jews, ". . I do not want to be a judge of such matters." And he drove them from the judgment seat. Then all the Greeks took <u>Sosthenes</u>, the ruler of the synagogue, and beat him before the judgment seat. (Acts 18:12–17 NKJV)

Here we discover that Sosthenes used to be the ruler of the Jewish synagogue and had actually been opposed to Paul when he first came to Corinth. We aren't given the details, but, at some point, Sosthenes went from being a bother to being a brother. Presumably, he was converted to Christ through Paul because he became one of his traveling companions. Undoubtedly, the Corinthians were aware of this incredible 180, and by mentioning Sosthenes, Paul was reminding them that God had done a mighty work through him. Sosthenes was a walking witness to Paul's authority.

As Christians, our lives are supposed to have a tangible impact on those around us. After a certain amount of time, there ought to be people that we can point to as proof that God is working in our lives to impact the lives of others. If we can't honestly say this, we need to start living out our faith in ways that influence others for the Lord. Whether we sow, water, or reap, there needs to be a Sosthenes in our lives that is a walking witness to God's work in us.

Whom can you point to as a Sosthenes in your life?

Who is a potential Sosthenes, and how can you practically impact him or her for the Lord?

To the church of God which is at Corinth . . . . (1 Corinthians 1:2 NKJV)

There is something very significant about the way Paul describes the church at Corinth. Despite that fact that he really started this church from scratch, he doesn't refer to it as the church of Paul. Despite the fact that Apollos had a huge impact on teaching the Corinthian believers, he doesn't call it the church of Apollos. Instead, he refers to it as the church of God. The Bible teaches that the church ultimately belongs to God, not man. This truth is introduced by Jesus in Matthew 16, where the church is mentioned for the very first time:

". . . on this rock _I will build My church_, and the gates of Hades shall not prevail against it." (Matthew 16:18 NKJV)

Notice that Jesus is the one who promises to build the church and that He claims complete ownership of it. This truth is carried a step further in the book of Acts as we're told that the Lord was the one who was actually adding the increase when the church began to flourish and grow:

_And _the Lord added to the church_ daily those who were being saved. (Acts 2:47 NKJV)_

It's important for us to keep this in mind because we have the tendency to see the church as belonging to the leaders that God has appointed to care for it. It is entrusted to man, but God ultimately owns it. This is a source of great comfort for us as we increasingly see the church coming under attack. If the church is merely man owned and operated, we have a reason to fear the attacks of this world. But because we belong to God, we can trust that He will be faithful to protect us and provide for us. God has invested His Son's life into us and will never allow such a valuable investment to be overwhelmed or overcome. The Lord will not leave us as orphans, and we can rest secure in our eventual victory because we are His.

What are some dangers in thinking that the church belongs to a particular person?

How is it that Jesus can claim complete ownership of the church?

HE CARES!
DAY 35

To the church of God which is at <u>Corinth</u> . . . . (1 Corinthians 1:2 NKJV)

This letter was written for the body of believers who lived in Corinth. From our twenty-first-century perspective, there doesn't seem to be anything extraordinary about this. But if we do a little digging, we will come to understand that the fact that there even was a church in Corinth proves beyond a shadow of a doubt that God cares for sinners.

When Paul wrote this, Corinth had become the most important city in Greece, even surpassing Athens. Geographically, Corinth had the advantage of being located on a tiny strip of land that separated two gulfs. This made it a natural destination for shipping and trade that fueled a booming economy. It was also the location for the Isthmian Games, which were second only to the Olympics in terms of size and significance. And Corinth was the home of the temple of Aphrodite, the love goddess, which was said to have had one thousand temple prostitutes. The city of Corinth was so notorious for loose living that the term *Corinthian* became synonymous with immorality. Corinth was full of profiteering and pleasure seeking, much like our modern-day metropolises.

However, Corinth was also a place full of people, which is what mattered to God. Because He has such a strong love for sinners, God sent Paul there bearing the message of the Gospel and established a church through him. God goes to the places where sin abounds so that He can reach the people who are the most desperate for the peace and love that can only be found in Him.

Too often we think of people's sin as being a limitation for God to work in their lives, when, in fact, their sin can be an unwitting instrument to drive them to the Lord. If God could make believers out of Corinthians, He can do the same with the people we know. We must never write someone off as a lost cause because God cares for the lost.

When was the last time you told a non-believer that God cares for him or her?

When is the next time that you will?

SANCTIFICATION'S SIGNIFICANCE

DAY 36

To the church of God which is at Corinth, to those who are <u>sanctified in Christ Jesus</u> . . .
(1 Corinthians 1:2 NKJV)

The church at Corinth was struggling with sin. Paul knew this, and he understood that in order for them to overcome it, they needed to be reminded that they were *sanctified in Christ Jesus*. Sanctification is one of the most important yet misunderstood words in the Bible. It means to "set apart" or "separate," and there are at least four ways that it impacts the life of the believer.

First, sanctification sets us apart **from sin's penalty**. By placing our faith in Christ Jesus, we have already been separated from the eternal punishment we rightly deserve as sinners. Second, sanctification sets us apart **from sin's power** to control us in our day-to-day lives. This is a progressive process that we experience as we submit to God's Spirit who enables us to overcome the power of sin and temptation. Sanctification also means separation **from the world** around us. The more we walk with God, the more we will desire separation from the world's values and standards. Last, we are sanctified **unto God**. The Christian walk isn't just about the world's absence; it is more about God's presence in our lives.

Paul reminded the Corinthians of sanctification's significance because he knew it would help them navigate through their sinful struggles. Once they saw that they had been set free from sin's penalty and power, it would be easier for them to ask for the spiritual strength to resist it. Once they understood that their spiritual nature required them to move further from the world and draw closer to the Lord, they would be headed in the right direction. When temptation comes our way, and it will certainly come, may the Lord help us to remember sanctification's significance.

How can you practically measure the sanctification process in your life?

What does your reaction to sin reveal about your understanding of sanctification?

To the church of God which is at Corinth, to those who are sanctified in Christ Jesus, <u>called to be saints</u> . . . (1 Corinthians 1:2 NKJV)

Paul began his letter to the Corinthians by telling them that he had been called to be an apostle. He also makes it a point to tell them that they, too, have been called, not to be apostles but to be saints. By doing this, Paul is revealing a powerful truth—every believer in Corinth and every believer in Christ is a saint.

What is a saint? A saint **is not** a pious person who has been uniquely recognized or designated by any church. If this were the case, then being a saint would be works-based. Good works have an important place in our Christian walk, but they don't determine our identity in Christ. Simply put, a saint **is** a sinner who has been saved through placing his or her faith in Jesus Christ. This describes anyone who is a Christian, which means that every Christian, including you, is a saint. Being a saint is based on who you are in Christ, not on what you do for Him.

Some of us may have a hard time accepting this because, perhaps, our lives don't fit what we've come to believe is a saint. Those who believe in Jesus are saints, whether they act like it or not. If performance determined sainthood, then Paul would not have called the sin-ridden Corinthians saints. The fact is that he did call them saints because he understood that God looks at believers as being clothed and covered in the perfect righteousness of Christ.

All other religions operate on the premise: do good, and you will be a saint. But true Christianity teaches: you are a saint; now do good. God sees us as saints; let's honor His grace toward us by living like it.

What are some common misconceptions about what a saint is?

What does it show you about God that He would call you a saint despite your performance?

WHAT ARE YOU LOOKING AT?
DAY 38

I thank my God always concerning you for the grace of God which was given to you by Christ Jesus . . . . (1 Corinthians 1:4 NKJV)

I thank my God always concerning you . . . really? Weren't these the same people who had been trashing Paul's reputation? Perhaps a more natural reaction would have been resentment, not gratitude. However, Paul wasn't looking at the Corinthians naturally, but supernaturally. He wasn't even really looking at them, he was looking at _the grace of God which was given to [them] by Christ Jesus._

Despite the Corinthian's sinful surface, God's grace was at work deep within the foundations of their hearts. Paul understood this and didn't measure them according to their outward behavior but by the grace that God had invested in them. He understood that where there is grace, there is always hope and, therefore, always a reason to be thankful.

When a building is being built, the stage that takes the most amount of time is setting and laying the foundation. Workers will spend weeks digging and pouring concrete that will never be seen by a single soul. So much time and care is taken at this stage that an observer may think that there's nothing happening. In reality, the most important work is happening under the surface where it can't be seen. This is the way God's grace works in the human heart. It might seem for a while that nothing is happening when the foundational work is going on underneath the surface.

Let's face it, we all know people in the church who we are naturally inclined to resent. It seems like they never grow in the things of God, and the last thing we feel for them is gratitude. We need to have Paul's perspective and see past these people and look at the grace of God that's doing foundation work beneath the surface. No matter how feeble the progress may seem, there's always a reason to be thankful for a person who has been vested with God's grace.

How has God's grace changed you?

How can you use God's work in your life to affect your attitude toward others?

ARE WE BETTER OFF?

. . . you were enriched in everything by Him . . . (1 Corinthians 1:5 NKJV)

During most of the 1980 presidential race, President Jimmy Carter enjoyed a sizable margin over his challenger, Ronald Reagan. That is until the two went face to face in a memorable debate that tipped the scale in Reagan's favor. In a moment that defined the presidency for the next eight years, Ronald Reagan looked squarely at the camera and asked Americans everywhere, "Are you better off now than you were four years ago?" Americans answered the question by electing Reagan over Carter. The message was clear: people expect a good leader to make a positive difference in their personal lives.

Are we better off now than we were before Jesus Christ came into our lives? Has the Lord made good on His claim to be the Good Shepherd? Can we say that He has been a Light in our darkness? Has He proven Himself to be the Way to God and the Truth of God, and has He filled our hearts with the Life of God? Are we a new creation now that we are in Him? Do we find rest for our souls when we come to Him? Do our lives confirm Paul's statement above that we *were enriched in everything by Him*?

Of course, as Christians, we're able to answer yes to all of these questions. In fact, when we honestly examine our lives in Christ, we have to admit that there isn't a single area of our lives worth keeping that He hasn't been enriching and improving. Take some time today to reflect on the goodness of God. Consider all He has done for you and in you. Remember the place He took you from and compare it to where He has brought you to today. Thank Him for the fact that He has enriched your life in everything.

Make a list of the significant areas of your life that the Lord has enriched.

How can God's track record toward you impact the future of your faith in Him?

NECESSITY OF UNITY
DAY 40

Now I plead with you, brethren, by the name of our Lord Jesus Christ, that you <u>all speak the same thing, and that there be no divisions among you, but that you be perfectly joined together</u> in the same mind and in the same judgment. (1 Corinthians 1:10 NKJV)

Division had left an ugly scar across the church at Corinth. Paul knew that in order for them to get on spiritual track, they would have to go from being divided to being united. The apostle understood that unity was necessary for three reasons.

First, unity **pleases God**. The Lord is blessed when He looks down and sees His children dwelling in unity. He even promises in His Word to command a blessing wherever believers are united: *Behold, how good and how pleasant it is For brethren to dwell together in unity! . . . For there the LORD commanded the blessing—Life forevermore (Psalm 133 NKJV).*

Second, unity **promotes strength**. The tallest building in America, the Sears Tower in Chicago, demonstrates this truth. This skyscraper was specially designed to withstand the powerful Chicago winds that would constantly bombard it at high altitudes. Instead of being built as one single building, it is actually nine separate structures bundled together. By having this design, the stress from the winds is evenly distributed and shared throughout the massive structure. Consequently, the Sears Tower is able to ascend higher than any other building in the United States. When the house of God is united, it is strong from within and able to weather the winds of the world.

Last, unity **preaches to the world**. Jesus taught in John 17:21 that the world would be drawn to believe the church's message when they saw the church's unity. There is a direct connection between how unified a church is and its effectiveness in reaching the lost for Christ.

A divided church is out of favor with God, weak from within, and without a powerful witness for the world. Let's do all we can to preserve unity in the church.

How do divisions occur within the church?

What are some sacrifices that are necessary for unity?

WISE WARNING
DAY 41

For Christ did not send me to baptize, but to preach the gospel, <u>not with wisdom of words</u>, lest the cross of Christ should be <u>made of no effect</u>. (1 Corinthians 1:17 NKJV)

In this passage, Paul shares that he was not supposed to share the Gospel *with wisdom of words*. The term here for *wisdom* is not a reference to godly wisdom, which comes from above, but to the unspiritual wisdom of this world. It's speaking of the way that the world would see a situation and judge what to do. Paul is stating an important truth that the Gospel of God cannot, in any way, be improved upon by the wisdom of this world. This truth goes much deeper than just the gospel. In fact, ***nothing*** of God can be improved or perfected through worldly contributions.

Can you point to a single example in the Bible where the world's ways effectively improved the things of God? Of course not! Just as a corpse cannot contribute to life, the world cannot contribute to God. Though He is gracious to use man in His plans, God has never needed man's help, and He never will. His truth is perfect and sufficient for all we need in life.

Our society is increasingly putting pressure on us to combine God's truth with the wisdom of this world. Relationally, they believe that you can do whatever you want just as long as you love each other. Vocationally, they support that you shouldn't work too hard or else you'll make others look bad. Morally, they've ignored absolute truth in favor of the philosophy "If it feels good, then it must be right." These are just a few examples of how worldly wisdom attempts to improve upon God's truth. In fact, just the opposite is true because when worldly wisdom is added to the things of God, the things of God are *made of no effect*.

We need to be aware of this so we can guard against the lie that we need to impose the world's wisdom into God's truth. This is a fatal error, and may the Holy Spirit keep us from falling into this trap.

When have you tried to merge the world's wisdom with God's truth? What happened?

What are some practical ways that the world lures us into buying into its wisdom?

UNPARALLELED POWER

DAY 42

For the message of the cross is foolishness to those who are perishing, but to us who are being saved it is the power of God. (1 Corinthians 1:18 NKJV)

On August 27, 1883, at 10:02 in the morning, something happened that the world will never forget. The volcano on the small Indonesian island of Krakatoa erupted. The sound of this explosion is generally considered to be the loudest noise in human history. Its shock wave traveled seven times around the world. The actual eruption was audibly heard three thousand miles away in Madagascar. Approximately five cubic miles of molten lava and rock were instantly ejected. Some particles were propelled as far as fifty miles into the earth's atmosphere. This was an unimaginable exhibition of power by the world's standards.

In contrast, the definitive display of God's power is found in the cross. This completely contradicts the wisdom of this world. How could the brutal execution of a man be a showing of His power? After all, a man who is crucified epitomizes powerlessness. He cannot save himself; he cannot even move! Yet, it was on the cross of Christ that the most powerful event of human history took place.

The cross is unparalleled in its power because it's able to accomplish what nothing else can. Only the cross is powerful enough to alter a person's eternal destiny. The shattering effects of earthquakes, volcanoes, and hurricanes are felt here on earth, but this is where they stay. The impact of the cross extends into eternity. Christ's cross is also the only thing powerful enough to remove the guilt, bitterness, and shame that penetrate into the deepest depths of the human heart. And the cross is unique in its ability to produce peace between bitter enemies. Even the centuries-long divide between Jew and Gentile can be bridged through mutual faith in the cross:

For Christ himself has made peace between us Jews and you Gentiles by making us all one people. He has broken down the wall of hostility that used to separate us. (Ephesians 2:14 NLT)

The unbelieving world sees the cross as the embodiment of foolishness and futility. We see it as something far different. To us, the cross is the unparalleled power of God unleashed on a world that's lost and perishing.

How would you explain the power of the cross to a non-Christian?

How has the power of the cross personally impacted you?

DAY 43

. . . we preach Christ crucified, to the Jews a stumbling block and to the Greeks foolishness, but to those who are called, both Jews and Greeks, Christ the power of God and the wisdom of God. (1 Corinthians 1:23–24 NKJV)

The Bible teaches that prior to the cross, the world was divided into two classes of people: Jews and Gentiles (or Greeks as they are referred to in the verses above). Both groups were vastly different from each other, yet they shared something in common—their rejection of the gospel of Jesus Christ.

Their reasons for rejection were different. Scripture says that the Jews stumbled over the concept of Jesus being their Messiah. Their contention was that there simply wasn't enough good evidence to back up His claims. The Gentiles perceived Jesus as foolishness because His message seemed too simplistic, instead believing that the meaning of life must be deeper than the concept of a man dying on a cross.

Since both classes came up with excuses to reject Christ, He decided to create a third class of citizens who would receive Him—Christians. For us, Jesus is not a stumbling block or a form of foolishness; He is the power and wisdom of God.

As believers in Christ, we need to understand that we aren't even second-class citizens in this world. We comprise a scorned third class, criticized for having a faith that is perceived as unprovable and simplistic. Isn't this to be expected? If the world would not accept Jesus, then why should we expect it to accept us? Can the servant do any better than his master, or can the student improve upon the work of his teacher? Despite all of this, it's well worth being what we are because the same faith that makes us third-class citizens in this world also makes us first-class citizens in heaven:

For our citizenship is in heaven, from which we also eagerly wait for the Savior, the Lord Jesus Christ . . . . (Philippians 3:20 NKJV)

What type of treatment should we expect from the world as third-class citizens?

What would you say to a Christian who is striving to find acceptance in this world?

How do you get saints to stop acting like sinners? In 2 Corinthians, Paul points the church to five things "of God" that will help us overcome the sin in our lives.

. . . I came to you . . . declaring to you the <u>testimony of God</u>. (1 Corinthians 2:1 NKJV)

The testimony of God is the gospel message. The simple fact that Jesus suffered and died on the cross for our sins should have the effect of making us think twice before we engage in them.

. . . your faith should not be in the wisdom of men but in the <u>power of God</u>. (1 Corinthians 2:5 NKJV)

Our faith is not according to our own ability but according to the power of Almighty God. The more we recognize this, the more we'll see our sinful struggles as something that God is able to overcome in us.

We speak the <u>wisdom of God</u> in a mystery, the hidden wisdom which God ordained before the ages for our glory . . . . (1 Corinthians 2:7 NKJV)

Someone once defined wisdom as "the intuitive ability to do the right thing at the right time." As Christians, we have access to God's wisdom, which helps us make the right decisions against sin.

. . . no one knows the things of God except the <u>Spirit of God</u>. (1 Corinthians 2:11 NKJV)

The indwelling Holy Spirit safeguards us against our natural desires for sin. As our constant companion, He draws us away from the evil influences of the world and into God's holy presence.

But we have the <u>mind of Christ</u>. (1 Corinthians 2:16 NKJV)

Sin often starts in our thought-life. God has given us His mind so we can take our sinful thoughts captive and bring them in-line with His thoughts.

How do saints stop acting like sinners? By understanding and applying the provisions "of God." If we aren't living like we're "of God," it's only because we aren't taking advantage "of God."

Which provision of God do you tend to neglect the most and why?

How can you do better at taking advantage of God's provisions?

Eye has not seen, nor ear heard, Nor have entered into the heart of man The things which God has prepared for those who love Him. (1 Corinthians 2:9 NKJV)

The preceding verse is one of the most wonderful verses in the Bible. It describes the unfathomable blessings of God in heaven for those who love Christ Jesus. However, the most wonderful part of this verse is not in the blessings themselves but in the basis for these blessings. God's Word says that His blessings are for those who love Him. This means that all the blessings we receive and enjoy in heaven are based on our love-relationship with Jesus.

How freeing to know that love is the basis for our blessings! God isn't looking to bless us in return for some amazing act or accomplishment. He is looking for us to love Him more than anything else because He always puts His love for us first. The story was told of a young girl who had just received her driver's license. As a reward, her father let her drive his car to school. Just as she was pulling into the school parking lot, a careless driver sideswiped her. She was uninjured, but her eyes filled with tears as she thought about the mess she was now in. As she opened the glove compartment and fumbled for the insurance papers, she noticed an envelope. Inside was a letter written to her in her father's distinct handwriting: "When the time comes for you to use these papers, remember that it's you that I love . . . not the car." This is a reflection of God's heart toward us. He loves us before anything else and desires for us to put our love for Him first.

We need to continually ask God's Spirit to search our hearts and reveal where we may have strayed in putting our love for Him first. When we do so, He will be faithful to restore and revive our love for Him.

How consistently do you dwell on God's love for you?

What is the danger in loving God's blessing more than Him?

I fed you with milk and not with solid food; for until now you were not able to receive it, and even now you are still not able . . . . (1 Corinthians 3:2 NKJV)

Milk is great for babies. It contains all they need in order to mature and develop. When Paul founded the church at Corinth, the believers there were the equivalent of spiritual babes. In order to grow, they needed to drink in the milk of God, which would have included the basic truths about God's love, the forgiveness of sins, loving others, and, of course, the hope of heaven. These were wonderful things to feed the infant church, just as milk is a wonderful way to feed a baby.

However, milk is never intended to be an end unto itself; it's supposed to make babies mature so they can eventually eat solid food. How would it look if a teenager went out on prom night and pulled out a baby bottle during dinner? It would be absurd because we understand that milk has its limitations and there comes a time when every baby must grow up and eat solid food.

After a few months of being separated from Paul, the Corinthians were the spiritual equivalent of an adolescent still on a baby bottle. He shames them for not growing and for being unable to eat spiritual solid food. Solid food includes the deeper truths of God, such as an understanding of sanctification, personal responsibility with one's liberties, and the proper use of spiritual gifts.

God wants us to stay in touch with the simple truths of Scripture, but He also wants to take us deeper into the things of Him. He expects us to mature past the milk and start digesting solid food. This is God's way of gauging our growth, and from time to time, we need to ask ourselves if our diet includes spiritual solid food or if we're content with the bottle.

For everyone who partakes only of milk is unskilled in the word of righteousness, for he is a babe. (Hebrews 5:13 NKJV)

What does your spiritual diet look like?

What habits or classes can help you eat more solid food?

CHOSEN CHANNELS
DAY 47

Who then is Paul, and who is Apollos, but ministers through whom you believed, as the Lord gave to each one? I planted, Apollos watered, but God gave the increase.
(1 Corinthians 3:5–6 NKJV)

As humans, we have the built-in tendency to want to worship what we can see and touch. Throughout history, cultures have fashioned their gods according to things they could physically relate to. The Corinthians had fallen into this trap by becoming more preoccupied with the ministers of God, such as Paul and Apollos, than with God Himself.

The Bible teaches that God has chosen *some to be apostles, some prophets, some evangelists, and some pastors and teachers, for the equipping of the saints for the work of ministry, for the edifying of the body of Christ . . . (Ephesians 4:11–12 NKJV).* Those who have been chosen for this honor ought to be respected and appreciated (Hebrews 13:7). At the same time, it's important that we understand that the minister of God is not indispensable to the work of God. The success of God's kingdom rests on Him, not in any minister, no matter how gifted.

We usually don't give much thought to the pipes that bring water into our homes. They don't get our attention because they're channels through which something more valuable passes. They are only there for the sake of something else that's greater. In the same way, those who have been specially chosen to serve the church aren't there for themselves. They are there to serve as channels for something much more valuable than themselves—God. The Corinthians had lost sight of this and had begun to hang all their hopes and expectations on men.

The same mistake is made today. Many believers are more preoccupied with a particular minister than with God. This is a subtle form of idolatry, and it's bound to end in disappointment and disillusionment. May the Lord help His church avoid this snare by allowing us to see such men for what they truly are . . . chosen channels.

What is idolatry, and what subtle forms can it take in the church?

How can you protect yourself against falling into this trap?

SECRET OF SUCCESS
DAY 48

According to the grace of God which was given to me, as a wise master builder I have laid the foundation, and another builds on it. (1 Corinthians 3:10 NKJV)

It's staggering to consider the accomplishments of the apostle Paul. Practically everywhere he went, he saw success in his ministry. Whether it was in establishing a new work from the ground up or in unfolding the mysteries of Scripture to the faithful, Paul's life produced spiritual results. Given the condition of the church in our day and age, it's worth asking the question, "What was the secret of Paul's success?"

We definitely know what it wasn't. It wasn't his **education** that made him so effective in what he did. In fact, Paul had to unlearn most of what he had spent his time learning prior to coming to Christ (Philippians 3:8). Nor was his success based on his Hebrew **heritage**. For the most part, the Jews that Paul encountered actually rejected the gospel, and, in general it was the Gentiles who came to receive the message Paul preached (Acts 13:47). Paul's success can't even be attributed to his **persona**. The Bible seems to indicate that Paul was short in stature and constantly sick (2 Corinthians 12:7). Church tradition tells us that he was bow-legged and hunch-backed. So, what *was* the secret of Paul's success?

I believe the secret behind Paul's success is found in the words above: *According to the grace of God*. Paul understood that all of his success was due to God's grace and was something that he simply didn't deserve. The Lord moved so mightily through Paul because he was a man who would never take credit for the results—it was all according to God's grace.

Perhaps the Lord is waiting and willing to do much through our lives, but He's withholding it because we wouldn't attribute the success to Him. Who knows what may have been or what opportunities we've lost because our spiritual immaturity prevents them from happening in the first place. God will always accomplish His purposes; whether He uses us depends on our understanding that His grace is always the secret of success.

What five things in your life demonstrate God's grace?

How can you cultivate a greater awareness of God's grace?

For no other <u>foundation</u> can anyone lay than that which is laid, <u>which is Jesus Christ</u>.
(1 Corinthians 3:11 NKJV)

Any builder will tell you that the most important part of a building is its foundation. An office building can rise to dizzying heights, but if its foundation isn't sound, it will all amount to a pile of rubble. It's interesting that the Bible deliberately describes Jesus as being the foundation of our lives, and there are three specific ways that He fulfills this function.

First, a building's foundation must be **sufficiently deep**. Once the depth for the foundation has been determined and the hole dug, there is no need to dig any deeper. In a spiritual sense, there is no need for a person to go any deeper than Christ. There is no spiritual mystery that does not have its answer in Jesus, for we are told that in Him *are hidden all the treasures of wisdom and knowledge (Colossians 2:3 NKJV).*

Another aspect of a foundation is that it's **single**. It would be disastrous for a building to have two or more foundations because any seam would be a breach in its structural integrity. In our own lives, we need to understand that we cannot combine Jesus with another foundation. He simply will not share that place with anyone or anything else. Christ Himself taught *"if therefore thine eye be single, thy whole body shall be full of light" (Matthew 6:22 KJV).* Our lives ought to be single in their focus, and we do this when we understand that our foundation is in Him and Him alone.

Finally, and most obviously, a foundation is **supportive**. Every ounce of a building—its framework, windows, elevators, and doors—is ultimately supported by its foundation. Similarly, Jesus Christ supports every aspect of our lives. Big or small, massive or minute, there is absolutely nothing about us that isn't ultimately supported by Him, for as Jesus said, *"without Me you can do nothing" (John 15:5 NKJV).*

What a firm foundation we have in Christ! He is sufficiently deep, He is our single source of stability, and He is supportive of every aspect of our lives that we yield to Him.

What are some faulty foundations in life?

How has Jesus proven Himself as a firm foundation in your life?

MATERIALS THAT MATTER
DAY 50

Now if anyone builds on this foundation with gold, silver, precious stones, wood, hay, straw, each one's work will become clear; for the Day will declare it, because it will be revealed by fire; and the fire will test each one's work, of what sort it is. (1 Corinthians 3:12–13 NKJV)

God's Word tells us that our lives are like a building. Jesus Christ is our foundation, and we're all building upon this foundation in one way or another. How we build is up to us, and there are only two possible scenarios for us to follow: we can either build with materials that are meaningless or with materials that matter.

The materials that **matter** are *gold, silver, and precious stones*. They each have a great deal of value and worth, and their spiritual counterpart could include prayer, worship, witnessing, giving, and serving. In fact, anything that is beneficial to our walk with the Lord can be classified as a material that matters.

The **meaningless** materials are *wood, hay, and straw*. Each of these is relatively void of value, and their equivalent is anything in this world that has no spiritual significance. Examples include worldly relationships, hobbies, habits, and any form of entertainment that takes time away from God. Anything that does not advance our spiritual progress in Christ is a meaningless material.

We have a priceless foundation in Jesus Christ, but what does the rest of our building look like? Are we building with materials that are worthy of our foundation, or are we settling for less? None of us have the excuse that we can't afford the materials that matter because they are free to anyone who is willing to take advantage of them. If our building isn't beautiful, it's nobody's fault but our own. We need to make an honest inspection of our lives and replace the meaningless with what matters. The day is coming when all that we have built will be tested by fire. Our meaningless materials will count for nothing, and what will be left to us will be the materials that matter.

What qualifies as wood, hay, and straw in your life?

How can you start building with more materials that matter?

TRUE TEMPLES
DAY 51

Do you not know that <u>you are the temple of God</u> and that the Spirit of God dwells in you?
(1 Corinthians 3:16 NKJV)

It's difficult for us to fully appreciate the glory of the Jewish temple. Historians tell us that the temple that stood in Jesus' day took more than seventy-five years to complete. The walls were constructed of white marble, and its eastern facade was covered with plates of gold that reflected the brilliance of the Middle-Eastern sun. It was so impressive that the disciples were in awe of it when it was only half completed (Luke 21:5). Yet with all of its beauty and brilliance, the temple lacked the one thing that was meant to set it apart from every other building ever built—the presence of God.

God had left long ago. Ezekiel 10:18 (NKJV) records the sad event for us: *Then the glory of the LORD departed from the threshold of the temple . . .* At this precise moment, the temple became just another building. It no longer fulfilled its intended purpose of being the one place where God's presence could abide with man, the sole spot where heaven intersected with earth. Yes, it was spectacular in appearance but common in spiritual significance.

God was looking for a new place to dwell, and He found it in us. We, as Christians, now fulfill the intended function of the temple because we are now the dwelling place of God. The one thing that the temple lacked is the one thing that every believer in Christ now possesses—the indwelling presence of God's Spirit.

Apart from God's Spirit, we are just ordinary people, but with the indwelling Spirit, we become decidedly different from those around us. The temple was intended to be special; it was meant to be the place where man could find God. This is what our lives ought to always provide for the watching world. Sources say that the temple could be seen for miles by travelers as it reflected the brilliance of the sun's rays. This is the spiritual effect our lives will have when we allow the Spirit to have complete control over us.

What responsibilities do you have as the temple of God?

How will you practically meet these responsibilities?

For I know nothing against myself, yet I am not justified by this; but <u>He who judges me is the Lord</u>. (1 Corinthians 4:4 NKJV)

Paul had come under a lot of scrutiny from the Corinthian congregation. They had begun to challenge his authority as an apostle and even his motives for being in ministry. These accusations were false, and Paul justifiably could have gotten bent out of shape over them. Instead, he did something remarkable: he appealed to the higher court of God's authority in his life. It simply didn't matter what the Corinthians thought about him. The only one that Paul had to worry about pleasing was the Lord because He was the one who would ultimately judge (literally means to inspect or scrutinize) him.

The great heroes of the faith all seem to have this conviction in common. They didn't compromise under the authority of man because they saw themselves as being under a higher authority. Abraham did not succumb to the suggestion of the king of Sodom to take the spoils of battle (Genesis 14:21–23). Micaiah was obedient to the Lord even though it meant telling King Ahab something that he didn't want to hear (1 Kings 22:8–18). Peter and John judged that it was better to offend the Pharisees than God (Acts 4:19–20). Daniel preferred to face the lions' den rather than the prospect of being unfaithful to his God who had been so faithful to Him (Daniel 6:10–11).

Daniel's name literally means "God is my judge," and *judge* ought to be our watchword as well. We should be constantly aware that we are accountable to the throne of heaven over any thrones here on earth. Our lives need to be lived in light of what God thinks of us, not according to popular opinion or peer pressure. The Christian life is a high calling, and we need to remember that we are always responsible to a higher court.

And there is no creature hidden from His sight, but all things are naked and open to the eyes of Him to whom we must give account. (Hebrews 4:13 NKJV)

Where does God rate on your list of those whom you try to please? If He's not first, how will you make Him first?

How is it freeing to be ultimately accountable to God?

. . that none of you may be <u>puffed up</u> on behalf of one against the other. (1 Corinthians 4:6 NKJV)

The church at Corinth was filled with different factions. This was such a significant problem that Paul devoted chapters 3 and 4 to addressing and correcting it. Over and over, he stressed their need for unity by showing them that they are all fellow harvesters (3:6–9), fellow builders (3:10–15), and fellow stewards (4:1–5). But it's in the verse above that he finally got to the root of the problem. Their divisiveness was a symptom; the core cause was that they had become *puffed up*.

This is an important truth for us to grasp. There is a direct connection between pride and division. When we are prideful, we will always put ourselves first, and when we put ourselves first, we will always cause division. Just ask the disciples. At one point, James and John put themselves before the others by asking Jesus if they could have the top spots in His kingdom. It didn't take long before the others caught wind of this, and their reaction is recorded for us:

When <u>the ten</u> heard it, they were greatly displeased with <u>the two</u> brothers. (Matthew 20:24 NKJV)

Up until this point, the disciples were always referred to as "the Twelve." But, in the presence of pride, they became "the ten" and "the two." This shows us that pride is no respecter of persons and that it divides even the most seasoned saints. But just as we see the divisive symptoms of pride, we see Christ's remedy for it:

But Jesus called them to Himself . . . . (Matthew 20:25 NKJV)

Jesus called His divided disciples to Himself, which is the key to overcoming pride. Pride cannot thrive or survive in the glorious presence of Christ, and divisions dissolve when He becomes involved. The application is apparent. When we're out of the Lord's presence, we're prone to being prideful and divided, but as we spend time with Him, we're given the grace to overcome our pride that divides.

Look at the divisions in your own life. What part does pride play?

Do you regularly spend time in Christ's presence? If so, how?

Therefore I urge you, <u>imitate me</u>. (1 Corinthians 4:16 NKJV)

What would the body of Christ look like if every member suddenly started following your example? Would the spiritual temperature go up or down? Would God's kingdom gain or lose ground? These are sobering questions, and if most of us were completely honest, we wouldn't want our lives to be set up as the standard for Christianity. So, it's all the more amazing that Paul says, *Imitate me.*

When Paul says this to the Corinthians, he isn't being prideful or arrogant. He makes this statement for two reasons. First, he knew that it was **good for them** to have him as a role model. There is an undeniable advantage in having an example to look to in life. As someone once said, "A pint of example is worth a gallon of advice." Paul also understood that this was **good for him** because as his life came under the observation of others, he became increasingly accountable to those who were watching him. There was a healthy pressure for Paul to make sure that his deeds matched his creed and that his walk harmonized with his talk. How did he do it? There's no mystery here because Paul tells us how he was able to set himself up as an example for others to follow:

Imitate me, just as I also imitate Christ. (1 Corinthians 11:1 NKJV)

By imitating Christ, Paul's life was naturally ordered in such a way that he could confidently say, *Imitate me.* This uncovers an important spiritual truth—our effectiveness as examples is in direct proportion to our commitment to follow Christ. And following Christ means that each day we need to take our cues from Him on how to think, talk, and act. When this is going on in our lives, we will be able to extend this same invitation to imitate.

What would make you think twice before saying, "Imitate me"?

In a single word, how would you describe your example as a Christian?

For the kingdom of God is not in word but in power. (1 Corinthians 4:20 NKJV)

A more contemporary way of putting this verse could be: God backs up what He says. In God's kingdom, promises are not made apart from follow-through. He does not halfheartedly say things without actually fulfilling them according to His power. It's important that we understand this about our Lord's nature. He always makes good on His promises.

This is a quality that the church is sorely lacking. Whether it's intentional or not, we are very good at saying things without actually doing them. Too often, Christians are characterized as those who are rich in words but poor in power, long on promises but short on follow-through. At the end of the day, all that really matters is who's actually following through on their promises. Jesus underscored this in the powerful parable of the two sons:

"A man had two sons, and he came to the first and said, 'Son, go, work today in my vineyard.' He answered and said, 'I will not,' but afterward he regretted it and went. Then he came to the second and said likewise. And he answered and said, 'I go, sir,' but he did not go. Which of the two did the will of his father?" They said to Him, "The first." (Matthew 21:28–31 NKJV)

Even the Pharisees understood that words without follow-through are worthless. God wants us to be people who back up the things we say. He wants us to be people whose lives are not filled with empty promises but with the power that makes our words realities. As citizens of God's kingdom, we need to live up to its standards, and it starts when we show up for things when we say we will and actually pray for people when we tell them we will. What if Jesus never made good on His promises toward us? Hasn't He followed through on His word in every possible way? Why should we feel the freedom to be any different?

When has someone failed to follow through on your behalf, and what impression did it have on you?

When do you fail to follow through, and how will you change this?

What do you want? Shall I come to you with a rod, or in love and a spirit of gentleness?
(1 Corinthians 4:21 NKJV)

The apostle Paul promised to revisit the church at Corinth. This could have been wonderful or woeful because there were two possible ways for the Corinthians to relate to Paul. They could know him as a disciplinarian—*shall I come with a rod*? Or they could know him as a friend—*in love and a spirit of gentleness.* If they continued on their course of spiritual shipwreck, Paul would be true to his calling by bringing them some much-needed discipline. If the church repented of its sin, Paul would come to them as an old friend. The choice was up to them.

Paul's pastoral relationship to the Corinthian church is a reflection of God's parental relationship toward us. We have a choice regarding how we can relate to God. We can know Him as either a disciplinarian or a friend. If we allow sin to dominate our lives, the Lord will be true to His parental nature toward us and chasten us as His children:

For whom the LORD loves He chastens, And scourges every son whom He receives.
(Hebrews 12:6 NKJV)

But if we choose to put off the old nature and submit to the Holy Spirit, we will find ourselves walking in holy obedience. As we live in obedience to the Lord's commands, we're given the promise of knowing Him as our friend:

"You are My friends if you do whatever I command you." (John 15:14 NKJV)

Either way, the Lord loves us and His love will cause Him to react to us in one of two ways. When we're in sin, it will prevent Him from letting us slide, and when we're living in obedience to Him, it will guarantee friendship fellowship. We can know Almighty God as a disciplinarian or as a friend. The choice is ours.

How have you experienced God as a disciplinarian, and what lasting lesson did you learn from it?

How have you experienced God as a friend, and what can you do to keep it that way?

It is actually reported that <u>there is sexual immorality among you</u>, and such sexual immorality as is not even named among the Gentiles; that a man has his father's wife! (1 Corinthians 5:1)

Sexual sin. It has been man's mortal enemy since the dawn of his existence. Genesis records the sexual sins of Sodom and Gomorrah as well as the immorality of Shechem, Reuben, and Judah, and this is only the beginning. In fact, it's difficult to find a book in the Bible that doesn't address or describe sexual sin in some form or fashion. It has hounded humanity throughout each age and across every continent. The Corinthians were no exception. There was even a man in their fellowship who was sleeping with his stepmother! Paul decided that enough was enough. It was time for the church to deal severely with the sexual sin that it had been tolerating.

Believers need to take every form of sin seriously. But sexual sin is unique because it carries some unique consequences. In addition to affecting those who are directly involved, sexual sin has a damaging effect on three other parties. First, it weakens the **church**. In a spiritual sense, every Christian is corporately connected in what the Bible refers to as the body of Christ (Romans 12:5). When one member sins, it has a negative impact on the spiritual health of the entire body. Second, it works against the unbelieving **world**. Christians have been entrusted with the task of pulling the unsaved from the fires of judgment by sharing the gospel message (Jude 1:23). Yet, when Christians commit sexual immorality, the world sees hypocrisy and it becomes easier for them to reject the message of salvation. Last, sexual sin wounds **Jesus**. When members of Christ's body engage in sexual sin, they actually expose Him to their wickedness (1 Corinthians 6:15). Without compromising His own holiness, Jesus becomes subject to the very sins from which He died to free us!

Sexual sin is never private. Like the proverbial ripple-effect, it extends outward and affects not only those who engage in it, but also those with whom they come in contact, both believer and non-believer alike. For the sake of the church, the world, and the Lord, we need to show zero tolerance when it comes to sexual sin.

Why is sexual sin unique?

How could you help a fellow Christian who is living in sexual sin?

... deliver such a one to Satan for the destruction of the flesh, that his spirit may be saved in the day of the Lord Jesus. (1 Corinthians 5:5)

It sounds harsh doesn't it? Word had gotten to Paul that a man in the Corinthian church was committing sexual sin with his stepmother. His prescription for dealing with this problem seems so extreme: *deliver such a one to Satan for the destruction of the flesh.* Is that really necessary? It was absolutely necessary because this man's sin revealed that his spirit needed to be saved. However, before he could know spiritual restoration, he needed to experience a degree of physical destruction at the hands of the enemy. Paul's prescription was based on the important reality that sometimes things need to get worse before they can get better.

The biblical examples of this truth abound. Samson had to be imprisoned, blinded, and humiliated before he could know the Spirit's anointing on his life. Shadrach, Meshach, and Abednego's conditions would get much worse before they got better. Nebuchadnezzar needed to experience seven years of shame in order to be set free from his pride. Lazarus' sickness had to get much worse before he could experience the resurrection power of Jesus. Even the cross of Christ shows us that things needed to get worse before they could get better.

In life, there will be times when things just seem to be getting worse and worse. We may experience a divine correction (like Samson), a testing (like Shadrach Meshach, and Abednego), a humiliation (like Nebuchadnezzar), or a loss of health (like Lazarus). We need to maintain our hope in moments like these because the Bible declares that God works all things for our ultimate good (Romans 8:28) and that the end of a matter is better than its beginning (Ecclesiastes 7:8). No matter what the Lord permits us to go through, we can always trust that it's for the purpose of making us better, not worse.

When was the last time that you felt like life was just getting worse and worse?

What should you do the next time you find yourself feeling this way?

In the name of our Lord Jesus Christ, when you are gathered together . . . . (1 Corinthians 5:4)

Paul is about to dish out several chapters of correction to the Corinthian church. But before he begins, he deliberately prefaces his discipline with a reference to *the name of our Lord Jesus Christ*. People's names represent their **character** and **authority**, and there is a deliberate reason why Paul couches his correction in Christ's name. Mark it well; all spiritual discipline needs to be based on the character and authority of Jesus Christ in order to be effective. He is the foundation for every aspect of the Christian life, including our ability to give and receive correction.

Christians can be preached to all day long about what they should and should not do, but if there is no acknowledgement of the standards that are founded in the character and authority of Christ Himself, then all such exhortations will prove fruitless and empty. Effective spiritual correction begins with an awareness of the Lord; it begins *in the name of our Lord Jesus Christ*. His character defines the standards of right and wrong, and His authority motivates us to live according to those standards. When we lose touch of this, we're bound to drift toward the world.

In 1912, a hunter from Maine named Leon Bean had the foresight to design a line of outdoor apparel that was superior in comfort and quality. His products became so popular that he went on to found a company that was named after him—L. L. Bean. Leon Bean passed away in 1967, but the name of his company still stands as a symbol of superior comfort and quality because its workers have stayed true to the standards established by its founder. As Christians, we serve a risen Lord whose standards are eternal and everlasting. We need to live according to these standards, and we will do so by living with an awareness of His character and authority.

Why does Paul mention the name of Jesus at this point in his epistle?

When have you been the recipient of spiritual correction, and how did you respond?

DAY 60

I wrote to you in my epistle not to keep company with sexually immoral people. Yet <u>I certainly did not mean with the sexually immoral people of this world</u>, or with the covetous, or extortioners, or idolaters, since then you would need to go out of the world. (1 Corinthians 5:9–10)

It is an interesting paradox: the Corinthian church had become just like the world while attempting to avoid all contact with it. Paul previously had warned the church against keeping company with Christians who were compromised in sin. They had misunderstood this to include the unbelieving world as well. The apostle points out the absurdity of this by stating that it is impossible to avoid the presence of sin in a fallen world. God's desire was for them to be in the world without becoming a part of the world.

Jesus described His followers as salt and light in this world (Matthew 5:13–14). This shows that He expects us to interact with non-believers on a regular basis. As Christ prayed for His disciples, He specifically prayed that they would not be removed from the world but preserved in the midst of it (John 17:15). He clearly wants us to have a presence on this planet. In the book of Acts, the church is growing because it constantly crossed paths with those who were not saved. Every spiritual success story shows us that conversion is preceded by some form of interaction. The Lord used Philip to bring the Ethiopian eunuch to faith, but it all began by the Spirit leading Philip to him (Acts 8:29).

There's a problem if we never find ourselves interacting with the unbelieving world. This is what the Corinthians were attempting to do, and it actually backfired on them. When we're on the cutting-edge of sharing Christ with the unsaved, it will have a refining effect on our faith so that when we interact with those who are in the world, we will be less like them.

What are your topics of conversation which those who are unbelievers?

How would you describe the connection between avoiding the world and disobeying God?

DAY 61

For what have I to do with judging those also who are outside? Do you not judge those who are inside? But those who are outside God judges. Therefore "put away from yourselves the evil person." (1 Corinthians 5:12–13 NKJV)

There is a familiar phrase in the business world that says, "Inspect what you expect." In other words, take the time to do an internal inspection in order to make sure that your expectations are being met. The reason there's a need for mottoes like this is because human beings have the built-in tendency to focus on the faults of others rather than focusing on their own flaws. Every social organization is prone to this danger, including the church.

Looking outside instead of looking within was one of the many traps into which the Corinthians had fallen. They had become very good at judging those who were outside the family of faith. But tragically, in making the world their focus, they failed to judge the sin that was running rampant in their midst. This produced a vicious cycle. Their own sinfulness meant that they were ineffective in their community . . . which meant that the surrounding world only got worse . . . which only inflamed their misplaced fixation. They needed to do an internal inspection to see that the problem was really with them.

We need to learn a lesson from the Corinthians' example. We need to focus on ourselves first and foremost because it is not enough simply to tell the world where they are wrong; we need to show them what is right. Many Christians make it their mission to judge the world. That's God's job, and its best to leave it to Him. Our job is to judge our own behavior within the church and to correct it. When we get this straight, we stand a much greater chance of impacting the world than we would by simply judging it. It's time for us to inspect ourselves to see if we live up to what we expect of others.

How have you been guilty of focusing on the world's faults rather than your own?

How can you ensure that you overcome this?

FAMILY FEUD
DAY 62

Dare any of you, having a matter against another, go to law before the unrighteous, and not before the saints? (1 Corinthians 6:1 NKJV)

The unthinkable had happened. The Christians at Corinth had become so much like the world that they were now going to court against one another. We, as Christians, are bound to have disagreements and disputes with one another, but it is wrong for us to allow these to escalate to the point that we go to court against one another. This should never happen because **the family of God should never be found fighting in front of the world**. This is like a double-edged blade, cutting two ways:

Internally, it is a sad denial of God's authority whenever we fight in front of the world. The civil authorities are for those who don't know God and who don't acknowledge His authority (Romans 13:1–4). Because Christians are under the Lord's authority, we are supposed to live by a code of love that exceeds any court's expectations. But when God's people go to the courts for help, they're basically telling God that His authority is insufficient and that the world's help is needed.

Externally, it presents a poor witness to the world whenever we fight in front of the world. The church is to be different and unique. It is to be a place where natural priorities and agendas give way to the supernatural order. Above all, it is a place where love for others ought to exceed love for self (John 13:34). But when believers go to court, it shows the world that deep down we are just like them, committed to preserving our self interests. Is it any wonder they won't take our words seriously when they can't take our witness seriously?

God's family should never feud in front of the world. When push comes to shove, it is better to suffer personal loss than for Christ's reputation to suffer.

What is your reaction to the statement "better to suffer personal loss than for Christ's reputation to suffer"?

What are some examples where you went against this principle? What was the outcome?

Do you not know? Paul asks the Corinthian congregation this question six times in 1 Corinthians 6:

<u>Do you not know</u> that the saints will judge the world? (v. 2)

<u>Do you not know</u> that we shall judge angels? (v. 3)

<u>Do you not know</u> that the unrighteous will not inherit the kingdom of God? (v. 9)

<u>Do you not know</u> that your bodies are members of Christ? (v. 15)

<u>Do you not know</u> that he who is joined to a harlot is one body with her? (v. 16)

<u>Do you not know</u> that your body is the temple of the Holy Spirit . . . ? (v. 19)

You don't need to be a genius to see that the apostle is trying to make a point here. By repeating this question over and over, Paul is actually making the statement that the church was woefully ignorant of truths that it should have known. He had spent several months teaching and nurturing the Corinthian church, and it is inconceivable to think that he would have spent so much time with them without covering these issues. This is the part we can't afford to miss—it shows us that **spiritual knowledge can be lost**.

Hebrews 2:1 (NKJV) exhorts us to *give the more earnest heed to the things we have heard* because, in reality, we all face the danger of forgetting what we've learned. Isn't it amazing how the things we know today can be forgotten a year, a month, or even a week from now? The way to protect what we know is to put our knowledge into practice. If we know that God desires purity, we must be pure. If we know that Christians are called to serve, we must serve. If we know that prayer is powerful, we must pray. When it comes to our spiritual knowledge, we will lose it if we don't use it, and unprotected knowledge today will become perilous ignorance tomorrow. Let us give more earnest heed to the things we have heard so that we're not embarrassed when we hear the question, *Do you not know?*

What are some spiritual truths that you have forgotten over time?

How can you practically protect what you have learned?

Now therefore, it is already an utter failure for you that you go to law against one another. <u>Why do you not rather accept wrong? Why do you not rather let yourselves be cheated</u>? (1 Corinthians 6:7 NKJV)

The believers in Corinth were so intent on "getting theirs" that they had begun to sue one another. Imagine how this sounded to Paul, a man who had dedicated his life to suffering in order to serve others. You can sense his bewilderment as he basically asks them, *Why not just suffer?*

Suffering has almost become synonymous with blasphemy these days. Most people don't want to hear, much less learn, this teaching. It may cause us to squirm, it may offend some in the body of Christ, but there is no getting around the fact that Christians are all called to suffer:

Now if we are children, then we are heirs—heirs of God and co-heirs with Christ, we share in his sufferings in order that we may also share in his glory. (Romans 8:17 NIV)

For to you it has been granted on behalf of Christ, not only to believe in Him, but also to suffer for His sake . . . . (Philippians 1:29 NKJV)

Therefore let those who suffer according to the will of God commit their souls to Him in doing good, as to a faithful Creator. (1 Peter 4:19 NKJV)

Should there be any further question on this point, it is settled by the Lord Himself:

"In the world you will have tribulation . . ." (John 16:33 NKJV)

Suffering is a badge of honor for the believer, marking maturity and dignity in the Christian life. Suffering shows that the servant is becoming more like the master and that the student is growing in the likeness of the teacher (John 15:20). Furthermore, nothing solidifies our personal relationship with God like personal suffering. It makes our dependency on Him and our intimacy with Him much more meaningful. Suffering simply works wonders for our faith. The sooner we embrace this truth, the sooner we will mature in our faith and the deeper our fellowship will be with the One who suffered in order to serve us.

What is your attitude toward suffering, and does it match up with Scripture?

What would you say to another believer who is going through a season of suffering?

DAY 65

Do you not know that <u>the unrighteous will not inherit the kingdom of God</u>? Do not be deceived. Neither fornicators, nor idolaters, nor adulterers, nor homosexuals, nor sodomites, nor thieves, nor covetous, nor drunkards, nor revilers, nor extortioners will inherit the kingdom of God. (1 Corinthians 6:9–10 NKJV)

The Corinthians had been duped. They had become so saturated with the world that they had begun to accept its sin as normal and acceptable behavior. Fornication, idolatry, adultery, etc.— these things had lost their sinful sting a long time ago as far as they were concerned. Perhaps some believers were saying to themselves as this part of Paul's epistle was being read to them, *C'mon Paul, get with it, man. It's only natural!* Natural, yes; acceptable, no!

Today, as then, people want to believe the lie that every natural desire is normal and acceptable. We live in a culture that tells us that as long as something seems right, it is right. *There are no consequences for acting on what feels good. As long as you don't hurt anyone else, who cares what you do with your life? There are no fixed absolutes that you need to live by, so go ahead and do what you want.* Really?

The problem is that absolutes do exist. Moral boundary lines have been drawn by the finger of God, and there are things in this world that will prevent a person from entering the kingdom of God. The natural man does not want to hear about them, but it doesn't change the fact that they exist. God is so in love with humanity that He reminds us of these boundaries. The unbelieving world may accusingly say, *How narrow and restrictive of God!* But we need to say, *No, how gracious of God to warn us!* Rather than justifying the things that appeal to our flesh, we need to know God's absolute standards and live by them.

There is a way that seems right to a man, But its end is the way of death. (Proverbs 14:12 NKJV)

How do you define right from wrong in your own life?

How many moral absolutes can you list?

DAY 66

And <u>such were some of you</u>. But you were washed, but you were sanctified, but you were justified in the name of the Lord Jesus and by the Spirit of our God. (1 Corinthians 6:11 NKJV)

By now we're well aware that the Corinthian church was full of flaws. Chapter after chapter, verse after verse, Paul rebukes the church for having become just like the world. Therefore, it is amazing that he separates them from those who are of the world. After listing those who will not inherit God's kingdom, he places them in a different category by saying, *such were some of you*. Wait a minute. These Christians had fallen in every possible area. How can Paul distinguish them from the world? The radical truth is that from God's perspective **they were different even though they weren't acting like it**.

When people sincerely place their faith in Jesus Christ, they are instantly covered in His righteousness. From God's vantage point, they are seen in their positional righteousness, not in their practical sinfulness. What an incredible truth! When we miserably fail here on earth, we are still accepted and loved in heaven because God sees us "in Christ." If this weren't so, then our salvation would be based on our performance, in which case none of us would enter God's kingdom. But we've been made righteous by what Christ has done for us, and by His grace, we have been declared different from the unbelieving world (Ephesians 2:8–9)

This is not a license to sin; it is a reason to flee from it. Anyone who would try to use God's grace as a blank check to sin hasn't truly received it. Saving grace brings with it the desire to be transformed from the sinful creatures that necessitated the death of God's precious Son. The one who has been made righteous in the sight of God will also desire to act righteous because of the grace of God. God sees us as holy. Let us honor Him by acting like it.

How does God see you and why?

Why should you be motivated to live a holy life?

All things are lawful for me, but all things are not helpful. All things are lawful for me, but I will not be brought under the power of any. (1 Corinthians 6:12 NKJV)

Evidently, there was a popular catch-phrase among the Corinthians: *All things are lawful for me.* Or perhaps this paraphrase: *I'm free to do whatever I want.* Where did such a view on life come from? It came from the fact that those who are "in Christ" are set free from the long list of requirements and regulations found in the Mosaic law (Romans 10:4; Ephesians 2:15). It's not hard to imagine how this newfound freedom must have produced a sense of celebration and liberation in them.

But something happened. They gradually allowed their liberty to turn into a license to fulfill their sinful desires. This is always a tragic turning point in our lives because when liberty turns into license, something happens inside our souls. We begin to surrender our power and authority over to the things to which we have been given license. As a result, many believers find themselves in bondage to things they once insisted on enjoying as "freedoms."

We're fooling ourselves if we think we have the spiritual strength to handle everything that we're free to experience. The truth is that we all have a sin nature within us that is seeking to enslave us (Romans 8:13). This is what Paul refers to by not being *brought under the power [authority] of any.* He understood that some things in life that were technically lawful could also be harmful. The apostle drew lines in his life by denying certain freedoms, and we should do the same. We must turn off the television program that defiles our mind, put down the catalog that stirs up covetousness in our heart, and end the conversation that causes us to compromise our witness. We need to master our freedoms before they master us.

For you, brethren, have been called to liberty; only do not use liberty as an opportunity for the flesh, but through love serve one another. (Galatians 5:13 NKJV)

Why didn't Paul want to experience everything that was lawful?

What are some "freedoms" that have actually enslaved you?

Now the body is not for sexual immorality but for the Lord, and the Lord for the body.
(1 Corinthians 6:13 NKJV)

Our bodies are interesting things. We certainly can't live without them, and there are times when we can hardly live with them. There is an ongoing battle to bring our bodies under control, and the first step in accomplishing this is to realize that **they are the Lord's property**. Jesus claims ownership over our entire being, including our bodies. They are for the Lord, and we simply have no right to use them to fulfill our fleeting fleshly desires.

The Lord wants us to use our bodies in ways that will have eternal and everlasting effects. He wants us to **evangelize** the lost. Our physical frames are to be tools in accomplishing Jesus' mandate to *"Go therefore and make disciples of all the nations" (Matthew 28:19 NKJV)*. It is estimated that Paul walked ten thousand miles over the course of his missionary career. That's a lot of wear and tear to put on his body for the sake of saving souls, but it was well worth it.

The Lord also wants us to use our bodies to **edify** His body. We're called to provide practical assistance to our brothers and sisters in Christ (Galatians 6:2), and our bodies are essential in accomplishing this. Whether we're making a hospital visit or standing by someone's side during an important court case, we're to use our bodies as valuable vessels of edification.

Last, we're expected to use our bodies to **experience** Him. It may sound trivial, but sometimes we allow our bodies to get in the way of deepening our relationship with the Lord. Jesus' body probably didn't always feel like rising early in the morning as He prayed to the Father (Mark 1:35). Regardless, Jesus made sure His body served its intended spiritual purposes.

Our bodies are the Lord's blood-bought property (1 Corinthians 6:20; 7:23). Far be it from us to use His property against His purposes.

On what basis does your body belong to Jesus, and how should this affect what you do with it?

How is your body not being used for the Lord's purposes?

Flee sexual immorality. Every sin that a man does is outside the body, but he who commits sexual immorality sins against his own body. Or do you not know that your body is the temple of the Holy Spirit who is in you, whom you have from God, and you are not your own?
(1 Corinthians 6:18–19 NKJV)

Great teachers understand their students' particular strengths and weaknesses. They know which lessons have been learned and which ones need to be readdressed. The fact that the Holy Spirit inspired Paul to reteach the Corinthians on the issue of sexual sin shows that they were particularly weak in this area. Great teachers also are able to instruct by explaining the "what," "why," and "how" of an issue, which is exactly what the Spirit does through Paul.

The **"what"** is the straightforward command to *flee sexual immorality*. The original Greek offers us some important insights here. The word for *flee* literally means "to escape from danger." The danger here is found in the form of sexual immorality, which is biblically defined as "any sexual activity beyond the confines of marriage" (Hebrews 13:4).

The **"why"** is because this form of sin is *against [one's] own body*. God's Word reveals to us that sexual sin is unique from all other sins in that it attacks on three levels. It not only disrupts our relationship with God spiritually and defiles our heart emotionally, but it also damages our body physically. What better reasons do we need to flee sexual immorality?

The **"how"** is accomplished by recognizing that a Christian's *body is the temple of the Holy Spirit*. The Corinthians had forgotten that God's Spirit was dwelling within each of them and that He was willing to enable them to overcome this sin. Then, as now, the Spirit's indwelling presence is how the believer becomes able to flee sexual immorality.

Great students desire to receive and apply the instruction they are given. May each of us show ourselves to be students worthy of the Spirit's instruction by taking heed to His what, why, and how.

Why does God teach us certain things several times?

What would you say to a Christian who is living in sexual immorality?

But <u>each one has his own gift from God</u>, one in this manner and another in that.
(1 Corinthians 7:7 NKJV)

The world's ways had infected many aspects of the Corinthians' lives and were spreading into the realm of their relationships, which is why Paul begins to turn his attention there. But first he focuses on the foundational fact that *each one has his own gift from God*. The Greek word for *gift* is *charisma*, and it speaks of divine gratuity or grace.

One in this manner refers to those who are single. It takes God's grace to live as a godly single person because the world puts tremendous pressure on Christians to wander outside of God's will. But those called to be single have also been promised a gracious gift that enables them to live a holy and pure life. The Scripture refers to this as the gift of celibacy, and it is to be honored just as highly as any other spiritual gift mentioned in Scripture.

Another in that [manner] refers to those who are married. It also takes God's grace in order to be a godly spouse. How wrong to assume that God's help is needed for the single life only and that it somehow becomes optional if you get married. The truth is that marriage requires just as much supernatural help as singleness, and a healthy marriage is indebted to God's gift of grace.

So what is Paul's point in all this? No matter who you are and no matter where you're at in life, God has not left you out. He has a **personal plan** for each and every one of us. He has called some to be single; others to be married. In addition, He has made **personal provision** for each and every one of us. It brings great comfort to know that the Lord's personal plan for us is always accompanied by His personal provision.

How would you explain the connection between God's plan and His provision for your life?

How is your heart affected by the fact that God is personally aware and interested in you?

SELFISHNESS DISGUISED

DAY 71

If any brother has a wife who does not believe, and she is willing to live with him, <u>let him not divorce her</u>. (1 Corinthians 7:12 NKJV)

It's staggering how many different disguises selfishness can assume. Someone can appear so spiritual on the surface, but a deeper look can reveal a flawed foundation. That's what Paul was addressing in the verse above. It was becoming a common occurrence in Corinth for people to get saved, only to come home and discover that their unsaved spouse wasn't as enthusiastic about their decision. Days, weeks, and months went by as tensions mounted. Apparently some were wondering, *What am I supposed to do now? Do I choose Jesus or my mate?* Apparently, there were many who chose Jesus.

It seems like a noble move at first, until you realize that in doing this the Corinthians were adopting the world's attitude of putting "self" first. Under the disguise of spirituality, there were selfish hearts pleading their case: *I can't grow in my newfound faith if I have to share my life with such an unspiritual spouse!* But God's will was for the saved spouses to stay connected as long as they were wanted. Was this because it would be easier? No, it was because it was right. What's more important: a Christian's comfort or a sinner's salvation? Given the eternal stakes, it was only right for the believers to stick things out for the sake of seeing their spouses saved.

Even though this passage is specifically speaking about husbands and wives, there is also a broader principle here. God's heart is that those who are saved will abide alongside of the unsaved in the hopes that they will be saved. This may not be easy, convenient, or pleasurable, but it is right. Whether it's an unsaved spouse, parent, child, or friend, we must never abandon someone to the enemy for selfish reasons. We are sacrificially to stay connected to them because the greater issue at stake is their salvation, not our comfort.

What are some spiritual ways that we disguise our selfishness?

How will you stay connected to the unbelievers that you know so that the Lord can use you in their lives?

HOW DO YOU KNOW?
DAY 72

For how do you know, O wife, whether you will save your husband? Or how do you know, O husband, whether you will save your wife? (1 Corinthians 7:16 NKJV)

How do you know? That's the question Paul poses to those at Corinth. In context, he was speaking of a non-believing spouse coming to know Christ. No doubt, there were those who were skeptical of their spouse taking such a step: *No way, not my mate!* But *how do you know* what can or cannot happen in the life of one who is lost?

From cover to cover, the Bible reveals a God who delights in doing what no human could ever expect or imagine (Ephesians 3:20). His abilities lie beyond our definition of possibilities, and those who have experience with God know this is true.

Jeremiah knew it in the midst of a perilous prophetic career that forced him into daily dependence on the Lord:

"Ah, Lord GOD! Behold, You have made the heavens and the earth by Your great power and outstretched arm. There is nothing too hard for You." (Jeremiah 32:17 NKJV)

Gabriel knew it after having spent an eternity in the presence of God:

"For with God nothing will be impossible." (Luke 1:37 NKJV)

Above all, Jesus knew it as the second person of the Godhead:

But Jesus looked at them and said to them, "With men this is impossible, but with God all things are possible." (Matthew 19:26 NKJV)

Anything is possible with God. This means that we always have reason to hold out hope for those whom He has called us to reach. No matter how critical, cynical, or adversarial a person might be, nobody's case is impossible because our God is the God of the impossible. May all we do for the sake of the unsaved be based on an unshakable confidence that our God is able to do anything.

What are some things you have given up on because of a lack of hope?

What will you do now in light of the fact that all things are possible with God?

STOP STRIVING

DAY 73

Brethren, let each one <u>remain with God in that state</u> in which he was called.
(1 Corinthians 7:24 NKJV)

There are those big sins that stand out to us—adultery, lying, stealing, etc. And then there are those subtle sins that seem to blend in with the daily scenery of life. Striving is one such sin, and the Corinthian church was steeped in it. Their pattern of worldliness even extended into wishing that their lives were different and striving to make it happen. That is why they were commanded to remain in the state in which they were called.

Let's face it; we're a lot like them in the sense that there are certain things about our lives that we want to change—perhaps our jobs, where we live, or our marital status. It takes a lot of time and energy to make these changes happen. But the critical lesson here is that **we need to stop striving to become something that we aren't and simply be who we are**.

Understand that there is nothing wrong with wanting change, but it must never be at the expense of what God wants for us. The problem begins when we look at an aspect of our lives and become so focused on it that we forget God's plan for our lives. There's a good reason why you're working at that job, residing in that neighborhood, living as a single person, or married to that mate. We can spend a lifetime striving against the almighty Creator of heaven and earth, or we can simply entrust our condition to Him and live out His will for our lives.

The key to entrusting ourselves to God is found in verse above: *remain <u>with God</u> in that state*. It is through abiding fellowship with God that we come to know Him better and trust in His character. Then we're able to rest in the changes He wants to make in our lives. And shouldn't we want what He wants for us anyway?

What are you specifically striving to change about your life, and what must you do about it?

Who are some examples of people in the Bible who entrusted their lot in life to God?

But this I say, brethren, <u>the time is short</u>, so that from now on even those who have wives should be as though they had none . . . . (1 Corinthians 7:29 NKJV)

Do you see Paul's sense of urgency in this verse? It doesn't matter if you're married or single. You need to be busy about kingdom business because *the time is short.*

Time is short in a **practical** sense. The simple fact of the matter is that we have no idea how long our lives are going to last. This planet is full of perils that can put an end to our earthly existence in a heartbeat. You don't even have the guarantee that you will finish reading this sentence. Recently, a teenager who was driving home from his friend's funeral was tragically killed in a freeway accident. One moment he was mourning someone's death; the next moment he was the one being mourned. He never imagined that would happen. We never do. We need to make the most of our time because we just don't know how much of it we have (James 4:14).

Time is also short in a **prophet** sense. Last words always carry a special significance; they are meant to convey a powerful point. The last recorded words of Jesus in the Bible are *"I am coming quickly"* (Revelation 22:20 NKJV). The prophetic time clock is ticking, and the Lord can put an end to this present age in an instant. At an unexpected and unforgettable moment, the Lord will fulfill His promise, and time as we know it will cease.

This isn't intended to inspire fear but rather action. Time is short . . . make the most of it.

So be careful how you live, not as fools but as those who are wise. Make the most of every opportunity for doing good in these evil days. (Ephesians 5:15–16 NLT)

How can you make better use of your time for God's kingdom?

What are some things that impair your sense of urgency?

LOVE AS YOU LEARN
DAY 75

Knowledge puffs up, but love edifies. (1 Corinthians 8:1 NKJV)

Certainly, we all have met one. In fact, from time to time we've probably even been one. You know, a believer who seems to know everything there is to know about God yet is lacking in His love. That's the type of person that Paul was describing for us in the passage above. The Corinthians had quite a bit of spiritual knowledge. Don't forget that Paul was their pastor for several months! They were especially "in the know" when it came to their freedoms in Christ. There was no question that they knew a lot. But there was a problem with their learning. It was not accompanied by God's love. They were Christians **academically** but not **practically**.

Loveless learning puffs up. A heart that isn't fortified with love will be easily overcome and overrun with pride, and nothing will bring spiritual progress to a screeching halt faster than this sin. Pride has more notches on its belt than we can count. It was the pride in Lucifer's heart that ultimately led to the rebellion of one-third of the angelic army (Isaiah 14:12–15; Revelation 12:3–4). It was C. S. Lewis who made the observation that pride is the great sin and that it is the launching pad for all other rebellions against God. Trace all sins back far enough and you'll find it tethered to pride. No wonder Paul warns us that pride is the silent assassin that accompanies spiritual learning.

The Bible does not exalt ignorance. Learning is not bad unless it is ungoverned by God's love. If we pride ourselves in all that we have learned in the Christian life, we have completely missed the point. Our learning must always be proportionate to our loving because only the power of God's love is greater than the power of pride. Nobody possessed more knowledge than Jesus and yet no one loved more than Him. His life shows us that those who love the most, learn the most. May we learn this lesson from the Master, and may we love as we learn.

How does God view knowledge that is lacking in love?

Ask God to help you love as you learn to avoid the sin of pride.

But beware lest somehow this liberty of yours become <u>a stumbling block to those who are weak</u>. (1 Corinthians 8:9 NKJV)

Paul has just laid the foundation that we must be filled with God's love as we learn God's truth. And the truth is that we are incredibly free in Jesus Christ. There are surprisingly few prohibitions that God places on Christians. God really has given us a great range of freedom and liberty.

But with that freedom comes responsibility. The Bible teaches that it is actually possible for our freedoms to serve as *a stumbling block to those who are weak*. The term *stumbling block* conjures up the image of a person who is running along only to have his stride broken by an unseen obstacle in his path. It represents not only a hindrance to progress but a harmful hazard. The truth is, our freedoms can have these effects on those who are weaker in the faith.

It happens all the time. Movies, television, and music are not identified in Scripture as sin, so we are technically free to enjoy them (and many of us do to unprofitable extremes). But, depending on your background before becoming a believer, some of these things might have an association with the old life of sin. Although the Bible might not forbid these things, the Holy Spirit might specifically be calling a Christian to forego such freedoms because they are stumbling blocks in his or her race of faith. Every Christian needs to respect this, and none of us should flaunt our freedoms at another's spiritual expense.

Wait a minute, isn't it really their problem if they are weak? Shouldn't we bring them up to our level rather than stoop to theirs? What if Jesus took that same line of logic with us? What if He didn't set aside His privileges in order to relate to us in our state of weakness? No, the onus is on mature Christians to forgo their freedoms when they would hinder or harm another member of God's family.

Let nothing be done through selfish ambition or conceit, but in lowliness of mind let each esteem others better than himself. (Philippians 2:3 NKJV)

What is the basis for forgoing your freedoms?

Who might you be stumbling with your liberties?

But I have used none of these things, nor have I written these things that it should be done so to me; for it would be better for me to die than that anyone should make my boasting void. (1 Corinthians 9:15 NKJV)

A bit of backdrop is needed to fully appreciate what Paul is saying here. The Corinthians had become so reckless with their freedoms that they were spiritually stumbling each other. Paul called them to put an end to this worldly "me-first" and "my-rights" mentality. And as an effective teacher will always do, he pointed to his own life as an example of what he was teaching. He does this by building the case that he had the right to receive a salary for the work he was doing (1 Corinthians 9:1–14), yet he didn't cash in on this right because he wanted to avoid even the slightest doubts about his integrity and authority.

Paul takes it even one step further by declaring that it would have been *better for me to die* than to lose the power of my testimony. Above all else, he knew that his testimony was his greatest teaching tool. It sanctioned the reality of what he spoke about. He could teach and preach all day long but in the end, people would look at his life, not his words. This led him to the conviction that not living at all was preferable to living a contradiction.

How many of us share his conviction? What are we willing to give up in order to keep our testimony for Jesus Christ vital and strong? Is it an income, a relationship, or a habit? Alan Redpath, former pastor of Moody Church in Chicago, once wrote: "What counts is not my doctrine or orthodoxy, but that my heart and life bear the brand of the cross: it has cost me something to follow Jesus." This is the same attitude of the apostle Paul, and it should be ours as well. A godly testimony is invaluable, and it won't come without cost in this world.

How do your actions compare to your verbal witness?

What do you need to give up in order to have a stronger testimony for Christ?

. . . to the weak I became as weak, that I might win the weak. I have become all things to all men, that I might by all means save some. (1 Corinthians 9:22 NKJV)

By now we know that Paul was willing to sacrifice his own freedoms for the sake of others. But we get a greater insight into his motivation in the verse above. Here's how The Message Bible paraphrases this passage: *I've become just about every sort of servant there is in my attempts to lead those I meet into a God-saved life.* Paul is saying that he sees his freedom in Christ as a tool that enables him to be an adaptable servant in every situation where salvation is needed. He was willing to do without something he enjoyed, and he was also willing to do something that he didn't enjoy. All that mattered was adapting to the environment. He had this perspective because he understood that **when it comes to a believer's role in this world, saving sinners is job one**.

When looking at life through the lens of eternity, nothing matters more than whether a person is saved. Everything else is inconsequential. The Bible teaches us that when our earthly existence is over, we will all face God's judgment (Hebrews 9:27). Those who have received Christ's sacrifice for their sins will enter into an eternity of unspeakable joy (2 Corinthians 4:17). Those who have not received Christ as their Savior will awaken to an unending torment that is horrific beyond words (Matthew 13:42).

We need to think like this when it comes to our daily interaction with those who don't know Christ. Moreover, we need to use our freedoms as Paul did to affect as many non-believers as we can. This isn't a matter of compromising our core convictions. Instead, it means that sometimes we don't do the things we're free to enjoy, and at other times, we do the things we don't enjoy. Anything else is a denial of who we are because for the Christian, job one is to see others won.

How do you typically view those who are unsaved?

Why is salvation job one, and how will you practically fulfill this today?

Now these things became <u>our examples,</u> to the intent that <u>we should not lust after evil things as</u> <u>they [the Israelites] also lusted</u>. (1 Corinthians 10:6 NKJV)

One of the keys to success is learning from other people's failures. This is exactly what the church of Corinth needed to do. They were failing to impact those in the world and were actually in the process of becoming just like them. So, Paul gives them the example of Israel's past failures in hopes of helping them toward spiritual success. Israel had started out well, but in time, they were brought to ruin. Their ruin was not due to external invasion but rather the internal infection of idolatry—the same infection that existed in Corinth.

The Bible says here that Israel had been guilty of lusting, and not just in the sexual sense. The original word for *lusted* is quite interesting. It is made up of two smaller words: *epi,* meaning "upon," and *thumeo,* meaning "to ponder." In the biblical sense, lusting after something means to be consumed or preoccupied with something at the expense of all else. This can be a good thing when the object of one's attention is God. But when it's anything other than Him, it becomes idolatry. Israel had allowed the things of this world to crowd God out of their consciousness. He had not failed or forsaken them. He just became irrelevant to them. The result was their ruin.

The Corinthians were facing the same danger, and so do we. When you consider that an idol is really anything that excludes God from being put first, the idols that we bow to on a regular basis are innumerable—cars, sports, movies, work, children, bills, food, catalogs, gadgets, relationships, compliments, theology, and even ourselves. Let's learn a history lesson from Israel's idolatry and allow the Lord His rightful place in our lives.

"But seek first the kingdom of God and His righteousness, and all these things shall be added to you." (Matthew 6:33 NKJV)

What does Israel's example show you about your own life?

What are some idols that fly under your radar screen, and how will deal with them?

. . . nor [let us] complain, as some of them also complained, and were destroyed by the destroyer. (1 Corinthians 10:10 NKJV)

Paul wrote this passage nearly two thousand years ago. A lot has changed in the world since then, but one thing that definitely hasn't is man's preoccupation with complaining. Add this to the list of problems that plagued the Corinthians and add it to ours because we live in a world consumed with complaining. An Internet search on the word *complain* reveals countless sites dedicated to teaching us how to complain effectively in today's world. No longer seen as a sin, complaining has become an art form.

There are certainly those isolated moments in life when a complaint is appropriate. That's not what the Bible is referring to here. Instead, it is drawing our attention to a general attitude where everything is wrong and where our expectations are never being met. Let's tell it like it is—complaining is a form of idolatry. It sets "self" up as an idol to which everything in life must bow, including God. Whether we want to admit it, complaining is a matter of putting ourselves first in the universe. When we complain, we're basically declaring that our own opinions and expectations are more important than God's ordered will for our lives. *My work, my wife, my world—none of it is what I deserve or want!* God has given us these things (John 3:27), so when we complain about them, aren't we saying that we are wiser than Him and could do a better job of being God than Him?

Notice what the end result was for those who had complained in Israel's past: *[they] were destroyed by the destroyer.* This is referring to the incident in Numbers 16:41–49, where God sent a plague upon those who were complaining against Moses' leadership. Complaining destroyed 14,700 Israelites that day. What is our complaining destroying today? It destroys our Christian testimony. Nothing smacks of the world more than a heart that's constantly complaining. Let's allow God to be God in our lives and be thankful for what He decrees and determines for us.

. . . giving thanks always for all things to God the Father in the name of our Lord Jesus Christ . . . . (Ephesians 5:20 NKJV)

What are you complaining about, and why do you need to quit?

What is the cure for complaining?

Therefore let him who thinks he stands <u>take heed</u> lest he fall. (1 Corinthians 10:12 NKJV)

The cuttlefish has an interesting way of catching its prey. When it spots another sea creature that it would like to eat, its skin begins to light up with strobe-like flashes of yellow, red, and turquoise. This demonstration has a hypnotizing effect on the unsuspecting victim, lulling it into a false sense of security. At just the right moment, the cuttlefish shoots out its tentacles and captures the stunned prey. Pride works the same way. It has the ability to lull its victims into a false sense that they are standing tall when, in reality, they are on the verge of falling. That's why Paul seizes the moment to warn the church of Corinth (and us) to *take heed*.

In context, Paul is reviewing Israel's corporate failure as God's people. They had been given every possible advantage, from miraculous manifestations to anointed leaders. Yet they allowed these advantages to go to their heads. They gradually prided themselves on the fact that they were a privileged people. And in doing so, they unwittingly allowed pride to hypnotize them into thinking that were standing on their own strengths and accomplishments rather than the grace of God. Their fall soon followed.

The church has also been given some amazing advantages. The Bible teaches that we have been blessed with every spiritual blessing in the heavenly places in Christ (Ephesians 1:3). We also run the risk of falling into the same trap of thinking that we are standing strong as we come closer and closer to the edge. But before we get to that point, we are called to *take heed*. We can do this by giving attention to three areas in our lives. First, we need to maintain vital contact with God through regular prayer and reading His Word. Second, we need to stay transparent and teachable with others. And third, we need to display God's love to those around us. When these three dynamics are operating in our lives, we will walk in the humility that will protect us from pride.

What is a sure sign of being under the influence of pride?

What can you do to protect yourself from pride?

PAST, PRESENT, FUTURE
DAY 82

. . . that I may know Him and the power of His resurrection . . . (Philippians 3:10 NKJV)

We serve a risen Savior. The resurrection of Jesus is the foundational reason why we can be different from the world and avoid becoming like them. Christ's resurrection makes us different in every aspect of our existence.

First, it gives us freedom from our **past**. The fact that God the Father raised Jesus from the dead (Galatians 1:1) serves to prove beyond any doubt that His sacrifice on the cross was fully accepted. This means that the sum total of man's sin is now a non-issue for those in Christ. All the things we're ashamed and embarrassed of have been utterly obliterated from our record. Having settled our past, we can now move forward in our life of faith.

It also gives us power in the **present**. Jesus' resurrection was an important demonstration of the power of the Holy Spirit. The Bible says that the same power that was able to raise Christ from the dead is also operative within each of us (Romans 8:11–12). Christians carry within them the Spirit's power to overcome sin and temptation. We know this power is real for us today because it was demonstrated in Christ when He rose from the grave.

Finally, it gives us hope for the **future**. The resurrection of Christ provides us with a glimpse into our own future resurrection. It is a preview of what each Christian will experience one day (1 Corinthians 15:23). This assures us that there is life beyond the grave, and we no longer need to be bound by the fear of death.

When we understand how Jesus' resurrection has impacted our entire existence, how can we not be different from the world? We would have to work against His work within us in order to turn out just like them.

What would your life be like if Jesus hadn't risen from the dead?

How are you living out the past, present, and future ramifications of Christ's resurrection?

NO NEUTRALITY
DAY 83

You cannot drink the cup of the Lord and the cup of demons; you cannot partake of the Lord's table and of the table of demons. (1 Corinthians 10:21 NKJV)

This verse really captures the heart behind 1 Corinthians 5–11. Paul is telling those who have become just like the world that there is no middle ground when it comes to the spiritual life. We must choose between one cause and the other. There is no such thing as a "spiritual Switzerland" where we can be neutral. We will either partake in the things of the Lord or in the things of the god of this world (2 Corinthians 4:4).

The Word gives us two sobering examples of this. The Old Testament records the tragic testimony of Balaam, who tried to maintain his neutrality between the nations of Moab and Israel. He knew enough of the truth to know that he could only bless the people of God. Yet he also knew that a profit could be made by serving Moab's wishes to curse Israel (Numbers 22). In a failed attempt to have it both ways, Balaam's life was destroyed.

The New Testament records the sad story of Judas, who made an attempt to remain neutral between the kingdom of darkness and the kingdom of God. We all know that Judas was willing to sell out to Satan. However, the fact that he expresses remorse (note that the Bible does not say repentance) after his betrayal shows us that he was conflicted inside (Matthew 27:3). He wanted it both ways, and we're all familiar with his fate.

The fact that both of these men were destroyed underscores the danger in trying to remain neutral in spiritual matters. There is no neutrality—we cannot casually link the things of this world to the things of our faith. We must be on the watch against the temptation to mingle the world's ways with God's ways.

Pure and undefiled religion before God and the Father is this: . . . to keep oneself unspotted from the world. (James 1:27 NKJV)

What do the lives of Balaam and Judas show you, and why is it significant?

What are some ways in which your faith has become spotted by the world? What will you do about it?

But every woman who prays or prophesies with her head uncovered dishonors her head . . . let her be covered. (1 Corinthians 11:5–6 NKJV)

This is one of those passages in the Bible where a little cultural explanation goes a long way in understanding what the Scriptures are saying. In the ancient world, it was a common custom for women to cover their heads in public. This covering symbolized a husband's covering over his wife's life. Women who did not cover themselves were letting the watching world know that they were not taken and even available. In a city like Corinth, which was home to a thousand temple prostitutes, it was very important to send the right message if you were a woman.

Evidently, there were some women in the Corinthian fellowship who took their newfound freedom in Christ to an unhealthy extreme. Being free from the law, they felt the freedom to uncover themselves in the church and in other social settings. They were technically free to go around uncovered, but in the process, they were violating the greater principle of maintaining their modesty.

Webster's Dictionary defines *modesty* as "freedom from vanity, boastfulness . . . regard for decency of behavior." It is the deliberate attempt not to stand out in the crowd. The women in Corinth needed to recognize that their freedom to go uncovered was not as important as the message it was sending to the watching world that was shocked by their "freedom."

Today, immodesty is measured by a different standard. An excess of makeup, a shortage of clothing, or anything else that has the effect of drawing attention to ourselves violates the principle of modesty and goes against God's will for our lives. We all need to demonstrate modesty in the church and in public by taking steps that are culturally appropriate. Otherwise, we will set up stumbling blocks in the church, which is the one place in this world that should be free of such things.

Why does God desire modesty among His people?

What would you say to someone who is exhibiting immodesty?

RETURN TO REVERENCE

Therefore when you come together in one place, it is not to eat the Lord's Supper. (1 Corinthians 11:20 NKJV)

In first-century churches, like the one in Corinth, believers would regularly come together for what were known as "love feasts" (Jude 12). These gatherings had a practical as well as a spiritual function. **Practically**, they provided an opportunity for everyone in the fellowship to enjoy a meal, which was not so common in those times. **Spiritually**, these feasts would also precede the celebration of communion. But as we have seen, the Corinthians had become just like the world in so many ways. Their love feasts were no exception.

People were pleased on a practical level to enjoy a good meal, but they were forsaking the spiritual significance found in communion. They had lost all sense of reverence for the Lord's Table by bringing a secular attitude into a sacred place. Their irreverence had gotten so extreme that they would actually cut in line in order to get first dibs and get drunk off the very wine that was to symbolize the shed blood of Jesus!

For in eating, each one takes his own supper ahead of others; and one is hungry and another is drunk. (1 Corinthians 11:21 NKJV)

There is an old adage that says, "Familiarity breeds contempt." It's true. In every aspect of our lives, we're prone to lose the awe and appreciation we initially have for things, including the things of God. There is certainly freedom and grace in our relationship with the Lord. But the sad fact is that many of us treat our bosses with more respect than we give God. Like children who grow insensitive to their privileges, we often lose the reverential respect for our Lord. God is holy and magnificent, utterly worthy to receive our most profound reverence. The mighty angels dare not look upon Him (Isaiah 6:2). How foolish to allow our familiarity with Him to breed an irreverent attitude! Let us be real with God and relevant to the world without being irreverent.

Why is reverence important?

What are some forms of irreverence in the church today and in your life?

...ine himself.... (1 Corinthians 11:28 NKJV)

Pau. ... parting words to the Corinthians because he knew that all the exhortation and instruction in the world is meaningless if your audience doesn't look within to see how it figures into their own lives. People can be the beneficiary of the best theological training, can be perfectly polished in presenting and proclaiming truth, can be respected and admired by the whole world, but they **won't grow one inch in their personal godliness if they lack the discipline of self-examination**.

God places the responsibility of self-examination squarely upon our shoulders. It is one of those things that He simply will not do for us. The original Greek word for *examine* is actually a commercial term meaning "to weight the worth." In our day and age, we might equate it with taking inventory of our stock. The idea is that we actually go through every compartment of our heart, mind, and soul to see what's actually in there. We are to pull it all out, sort it, identify it, account for it, and reconcile it with God's Word. Anything that doesn't agree with His Word must be discarded by the power of the Holy Spirit in order to protect and preserve our spiritual health. And an ounce of examination is worth a ton of pain and regret. Just imagine what would have happened if only Achan, Lot, Ahab, Ananias, Samson, and Judas had just taken the time to examine themselves before taking their final fatal steps.

In the retail world, the term *shrinkage* refers to the difference between what should be in stock and what actually is in stock. I wonder what the church's spiritual shrinkage would look like if God were to suddenly take inventory. I wonder what the difference is between what the Bible says we should have and what we actually do have. By constantly examining ourselves, we can decrease our spiritual shrinkage and avoid the consequences that come from living just like the world.

Conduct a spiritual inventory. What did you find?

What needs to be reconciled with God's Word?

I do not want you to be ignorant . . . . (1 Corinthians 12:1 NKJV)

In the first four chapters of 1 Corinthians, we saw how this first-century fellowship was just like us in many ways. We then saw in chapters 5–11 how they had become just like them, meaning the unsaved world around them. Now, in the remaining chapters, we will focus on the ways that Paul challenged and taught them to become just like the Lord.

It is interesting that Paul opens this third section with the words *I do not want you to be ignorant*. Ignorance, or a lack of proper understanding, was the root of many of this church's problems, and it was preventing them from becoming more like the Lord. Spiritual ignorance has also plagued the collective body of Christ over the course of its existence. For some inexplicable reason, there seems to be a circulating misconception that it somehow honors the Lord to be ignorant or oblivious to spiritual realities, a sort of pseudo-spirituality where the less you understand, the better. Ignorance does not enhance our walk with God nor does it improve our reputation with the watching world. God's heart wants us to be full of understanding when it comes to the things of Him:

Give me understanding, that I may learn Your commandments. (Psalm 119:73 NKJV)

And in all your getting, get understanding. (Proverbs 4:7 NKJV)

It's futile to think that we could ever attain the Lord's perfect understanding of all things. But by having an expanding understanding of the things of God, we move away from ignorance and toward being just like Him. Ask yourself these personal questions: How well do you understand the things of God? Are you always asking questions, or are you answering them? Do you cherish ignorance because it is a subtle disguise for spiritual laziness?

May the Lord fill us with a desire to understand more and more about Him so that we may become more and more like Him.

What's wrong with equating ignorance with spirituality?

How are you expanding your understanding of spiritual truth?

GOD'S GIFTS
DAY 88

The <u>manifestation of the Spirit</u> is given to each one for the profit of all . . . . (1 Corinthians 12:7 NKJV)

The word *manifestation* literally means "to express in visible form." In this case, the *manifestation of the Spirit* is a reference to the Holy Spirit expressing Himself through the spiritual gifts that He gives to believers. God's desire for us to be just like Him is seen in the fact that He expresses Himself in us through the gifts of His Spirit. It is important to understand that apart from this gifting, we would not be successful in our attempts to be like the Lord. But by the operation of God's gifting in us, we can effectively express Him in our lives.

Imagine if you were faced with the challenge of playing a game of one-on-one against Michael Jordan. In your natural-born condition, you would have absolutely no hope of ever competing with, much less beating, him. However, if you were somehow given the gifts of his leaping ability, his quickness, his coordination, his shooting touch, his determination, his drive, and his mind for the game of basketball, then you would be able to compete with, and perhaps even beat, him because you would now be like him. On an infinitely grander scale, the gifting of the Spirit works the same way in our lives. God makes us like Him by giving us His gifts. But instead of **competing** against Him, He gifts us for the purpose of **completing** the works that He has called and appointed us to accomplish.

If we want to grow in our godliness, we need to exercise the gifts He has given to us. Some think that God hasn't gifted them. This is not true because *the manifestation of the Spirit is given to each one*. God has gifts for each and every believer that are an important part of the process of becoming just like Him. We need to know what they are and allow their operation in us.

What spiritual gifts have you been given?

How do your spiritual gifts make you more like the Lord?

. . . for to one is given <u>the word of wisdom</u> through the Spirit . . . . (1 Corinthians 12:8 NKJV)

One of the specific ways that God enables us to be like Him is through the gift known as the word of wisdom. Somebody once defined wisdom as "the inspired ability to say or do the right thing at the right time in the right way." That is a good description of the way this gift works. The word of wisdom is like getting a divine download on how to handle a problem or crisis.

We see this gift operating during the reign of Solomon. In a classic case of "one word against the other," two women claimed ownership of an infant. The situation seemed hopeless to the natural mind, but Solomon had been given the word of wisdom and decreed that the baby be cut in two and each woman be given a half. The true mother sacrificed her half in order to see the child spared. Her love for the baby identified her as the real mother, and the people recognized that God's wisdom was in Solomon (1 Kings 3:16–28).

The word of wisdom was also demonstrated in the early church. As the body of believers grew, it became impossible for the apostles to keep up with the practical demands while maintaining spiritual contact with the Lord. Once again, the word of wisdom was at work as they determined to raise up another set of servants who could tend to the practical demands of the ministry while the apostles gave themselves over to prayer and the ministry of God's Word. Needs were met more effectively, servants were trained, and the church continued to grow (Acts 6:1–7).

When we're given God's wisdom, we better understand His heart and are able to see His solution in our times of need. Given the great needs that exist in our lives, may the Lord fill us with this gift and may we grow in godliness through its use.

If any of you lacks wisdom, let him ask of God, who gives to all liberally and without reproach, and it will be given to him. (James 1:5 NKJV)

When have you personally seen the word of wisdom at work?

What are some other examples of the word of wisdom in Scripture? (Hint: life of Christ)

. . . to one is given . . <u>the word of knowledge</u> through the same Spirit . . . . (1 Corinthians 12:8 NKJV)

In the summer of 1942, the world watched as the Japanese Navy swept through the Pacific, overcoming and capturing virtually everything in its path. The American Navy was still badly battered from the attack on Pearl Harbor and seemed no match for the powerful Imperial fleet. Clinging to existence, the Americans had one significant advantage over the Japanese: they had managed to break the Japanese secret code. Japan decided to mount a decisive surprise attack at Midway Island to drive the United States out of the Pacific for good. American intelligence intercepted the encoded plans, and with little resources, the United States took a strategic stand at Midway. What followed was the turning point of the war as the United States, armed with its knowledge, dealt a crippling blow to the Japanese Navy.

A little knowledge can go a long way. It can change the course of a war or the future of an entire nation. God knows the power of knowledge, and this power is the basis behind the spiritual gift of the word of knowledge. Pastor Chuck Smith defines this gift as "the divine impartation of knowledge concerning a person or situation that could not come through natural thought processes." It is similar to the divine download of the word of wisdom, but it is more specific because it deals with actual facts and pieces of information. We see it demonstrated in the life of Elijah as the Lord specifically warns him that a messenger has been sent to take his life (2 Kings 6:32). It can also be seen as Peter is made aware of the fact that Ananias has lied to him concerning the gift that he had given to the church (Acts 5:3). When God gives a word of knowledge, it can powerfully protect and even purify His people.

But the benefits of this gift don't end there because it also offers us another way of being like the Lord. It allows us to share in God's knowledge, and the more that we share with God, the more we can be just like Him.

What are the benefits of the word of knowledge?

How does this gift help us to be more like God?

TOTAL TRUST
DAY 91

. . . to another <u>faith</u> by the same Spirit . . . (1 Corinthians 12:9 NKJV)

As we have seen, there are different spiritual gifts that are given by God that, to a degree, are also reflections of God. It makes sense, therefore, that the more these gifts are operating in our lives, the more we will be like our Lord. Among these gifts is the gift of faith. The faith referred to here is not the saving faith that people exercise when they trust in Jesus as their Lord and Savior. This is a different type of faith that comes into play after salvation and during our Christian walk. It is the supernatural infusion of assurance in God's ability to work in and through us at a specific point in time in a specific situation. It could also be called a God-given sense of total trust.

There's a great example of this gift at work in Acts 3. As Peter and John were heading into the temple to offer prayers, they encountered a man who had been crippled from birth. This man's only hope of survival was to beg for alms, but when Peter and John passed by, his begging was met by something completely unexpected. The Bible tells us that Peter fixed his eyes on the man, and in a moment that must have required the infusion of supernatural confidence in God, Peter publicly called the man to rise up and walk. To the astonishment of the crowd that had gathered as well as this man, he stood up and walked. God desired to do something special in this man's life, and to the natural mind, Peter's words must have seemed insane. But when the gift of faith is given, God's people are filled with a total trust in Him, no matter how impossible a situation may seem.

Christ completely trusted in the Father in all things, even when it involved unspeakable suffering on the cross (Matthew 26:39). When the gift of faith is flowing in and through us, we echo the total trust shared within the Godhead.

Why does God give the gift of faith, and how does it make us more like Him?

What are some other biblical examples of the gift of faith?

. . . to another <u>gifts of healings</u> by the same Spirit . . . (1 Corinthians 12:9 NKJV)

The gift of healing is the supernatural outpouring of God's healing power to bring about physical restoration and wholeness. Of all the gifts, this one tends to get the most attention because it produces results that can be instantly seen through our natural senses. There's no doubt that there are those who have misrepresented and maligned this gift for the sake of personal gain. Despite this, we need to remember that God has determined for there to be a regular place for this gift within the church (James 5:16). The counterfeit does not invalidate the genuine.

This gift perfectly reflects the heart of God because from beginning to end, the Bible reveals Him to be a healing God. In the very first book of Scripture, God heals Abimelech's household (Genesis 20:17). Other Old Testament notables who received God's healing touch include Moses (Exodus 4:6), Miriam (Numbers 12:14–15), Naaman (2 Kings 5:14), and Hezekiah (2 Kings 20:6).

The Lord personally identified Himself to the Israelites as *the LORD who heals (Exodus 15:26 NKJV)*. Moving ahead to the life of Christ, we see that healings had a prominent place in His public ministry. In fact, His healing ministry was so prominent that it was frequently mentioned alongside of His preaching and teaching (Matthew 4:23). It is also interesting that out of the thirty-eight recorded miracles of Jesus, thirty were healings. In the Bible's final chapter, we see that God has placed a tree before His throne whose leaves are for *the healing of the nations (Revelation 22:2 NKJV)*. The God of the Bible is most definitely the God of healing.

When the gift of healing is **exercised**, the heart of God is **expressed**. It is one more link in the chain connecting our character to His and one more way in which we are able to be just like Him.

What does the gift of healing reflect concerning God's heart?

What are some reasons why God might choose not to give this gift? (Hint: read 2 Corinthians 12:7–10.)

. . . to another the <u>working of miracles</u> . . . . (1 Corinthians 12:10 NKJV)

The apostle Paul wrote this passage while he was living and ministering in the city of Ephesus. During this stay in Ephesus, God performed many mighty miracles through him (Acts 19:11–12). Therefore, when Paul writes here about the spiritual gift of the working of miracles, he is referring to something he had a great deal of personal experience with. He knew the reality of this gift as well as its unique ability to make us more like the Lord.

C. S. Lewis once defined a miracle as "an interference with Nature by supernatural power." *Nature* is another term for the fabric of laws that God has ordained for the purpose of governing time and space. These laws keep the created order in a constant condition that brings a degree of certainty and reliability to life. Thanks to the Law of Gravity, we know what to expect when we walk across the street each morning. But from time to time, God will violate these laws in order to accomplish His will. In many cases, He will exercise this divine prerogative over nature through His people—this is the gift of the working of miracles.

There are countless counterfeits out there when it comes to this spiritual gift. But there is also a genuine element of the miraculous among God's people so that we can reflect yet another facet of Him. Miracles mean that anything can happen. No matter how bleak or barren a situation seems in the natural, the possibility exists that the natural can be supernaturally set aside in order for God to fulfill His purposes. It means that when all else has come up empty, God can come through as only He can. When God uses us to manifest the miraculous, we are walking in the Master's footsteps. As He pours out this gift, we are given the unbelievable privilege of letting God do through us what only He is able to do.

What makes miracles possible?

What do miracles teach us about God, and why is this significant to you?

. . . to another prophecy . . . . (1 Corinthians 12:10 NKJV)

Prophecy is one of the most misunderstood topics in the Bible. People often believe that prophecy exclusively refers to the ability to predict the future. That is certainly one dimension of prophecy, but the true biblical definition goes much deeper. Prophecy is essentially "the declaration of God's will and Word." It is standing up and standing out in this world in order to communicate the truths from above. It is among the most precious of the spiritual gifts (1 Corinthians 14:1), and in a sense, it is the gift that most closely identifies us with Christ.

Some might find it surprising how often Jesus is referred to as a prophet in the New Testament. After Christ resurrected the widow's son in Nain, the townspeople there immediately referred to Him as a prophet (Luke 7:16). The multitudes in Jerusalem referred to Him as *"Jesus, the prophet from Nazareth of Galilee" (Matthew 21:11 NKJV)*. The two disciples on the road to Emmaus referred to Jesus as *"a Prophet mighty in deed and word before God" (Luke 24:19 NKJV)*. The woman at the well rightly identified Jesus as a prophet (John 4:19). So did the man who had been born blind (John 9:17). Peter identifies Jesus as the long-awaited prophet of whom Moses had foretold (Acts 3:22). Jesus even took the title of prophet for Himself (Mark 6:4; Luke 13:33), and He perfectly executed the responsibilities of this office by faithfully communicating the things of God:

"I have manifested Your name to the men whom You have given Me out of the world. . . . I have given to them the words which You have given Me." (John 17:6–8 NKJV)

Christ's prophetic ministry cannot be separated from who He is. When the gift of prophecy is practiced in the church, we are following the prophetic pattern that Jesus established for us and sharing in His commitment to communicate the things of God. The gift of prophecy profits us as we **communicate** God's Word and are **conformed** into His image.

How would you define the gift of prophecy?

In what way does exercising of the gift of prophecy make us like the Lord?

. . . to another <u>discerning of spirits</u> . . . . (1 Corinthians 12:10 NKJV)

Have you ever had a feeling in your spiritual gut that something about someone was "off"? Outwardly, everything seems fine and looks good, but inwardly, you can't escape the sense that there's a problem. If so, then there's a chance that you've received the spiritual gift of the discerning of spirits. The Greek word for *discerning* derives from another word that means "to separate something in a thorough manner." That's a vivid picture of how this gift works on a spiritual level. It takes in the overall impression of a person and then begins to break things down into spiritual realities. If there's an element of spiritual falsehood connected to someone, it raises a divine warning sign in your heart.

Imagine taking a glass and filling it with drinking water. Now imagine adding a few drops of a cyanide solution and stirring it up. To the natural senses, it would appear to be a perfectly normal glass of water, but in reality, it would be a deadly drink. However, there is a paper designed to detect the presence of cyanide in drinking water by turning a certain color. If that paper were applied to the glass of water, the real nature of it would be exposed. The discerning of spirits operates the same way because it allows us to detect the true spiritual nature of people despite their appearances.

Jesus frequently demonstrated spiritual discernment during His public ministry. On many occasions, people came pledging their undying devotion and dedication to Him. But His discernment saw past the promises and detected the spiritual falsehood deep down within them (John 2:23–24; 6:26). Jesus was very discerning, and He gives us the gift of discernment so that we can be more like Him. When properly used, the discerning of spirits helps to protect the flock of God from wolves that disguise themselves as sheep. This is a powerful way for us to imitate our Good Shepherd.

Why is this gift important, and what does it reveal about God's heart for His people?

What are some biblical examples of the discernment of spirits? (Hint: see the book of Acts.)

. . . to another different kinds of <u>tongues</u>, to another the <u>interpretation</u> of tongues.
(1 Corinthians 12:10 NKJV)

God makes sense. There is logic and reason in what He decrees and determines. Nobody understood this aspect of God's character better than the man who wrote 1 Corinthians. Paul was a unique combination of the three great cultures of the ancient world. Physically, he was **Jewish** and received thorough training in the Hebrew Scriptures. Socially, he was raised in the **Greek** culture and completely understood its way of thinking. Legally, he was a **Roman** citizen, which meant he was entitled to the legal protection of the empire. What better candidate to carry the gospel message to the ancient world? God chose Paul for this task because it simply made sense.

The common sense of God is also seen in the passage above. The spiritual gifts of tongues and interpretation are deliberately listed back to back. They are recorded this way because it is the only way that these gifts make sense. The gift of tongues is just a disconcerting distraction when separated from the gift of interpretation. By the same token, the gift of interpretation is completely pointless apart from the gift of tongues. They both complement and depend on each other, so it makes perfect sense that God placed them in this order for us. Again, we see that God makes sense.

There is no denying that the things of God carry an element of mystery about them (Isaiah 55:8; 1 Timothy 3:16). But for the most part, the Lord does not complicate things that relate to our daily lives. God's ways tend to make sense, and when the gift of tongues and the gift of interpretation are operating side by side, they reflect His order and common sense. We need to be sure that in all we do, we are making spiritual sense because in making sense, we are also being made into the Lord's likeness.

Where should you exercise more spiritual common sense in your life?

Why do you think this part of God's character is frequently overlooked?

LOVE LIFE
DAY 97

Though I speak with the tongues of men and of angels, but have not <u>love</u> . . . . it profits me nothing. (1 Corinthians 13:1–4 NKJV)

If there is one word that could be used to describe God, it is love. Love is the greatest attribute of God and is such an infused part of His nature that 1 John 4:16 tells us that *God is love.* Every other aspect of God's character is really irrelevant apart from His love; for without it, we're all hopelessly and deservedly judged for eternity. But because love is so central to God's nature, He sent His own Son to suffer judgment in our place (John 3:16).

Love is also central when it comes to the Christian life. Everything that we say, think, or do should be based on the love of God in our lives (1 Corinthians 16:14). It doesn't matter how many spiritual gifts we have been given, how many people we have impressed with our piety, or how much theological knowledge we have acquired and cataloged. If we don't have God's love, we lack everything and have nothing. Love is the instrument by which the reality of our relationship with the Lord is measured. If we are consistently spending time in His presence, we will consistently love others, not just with our words but also with our actions.

On November 24, 1963, the hearts of the American people were frozen with grief. The thirty-fifth president of the United States had just been assassinated two days earlier, and now his widow and two children publicly stood on the White House steps, awaiting the arrival of his casket. As they waited, John F. Kennedy Jr., just three-years-old at the time, twisted free of his mother's grip and began to restlessly clench his tiny right hand. It was completely natural to him, but to those looking on, it was painfully reminiscent of his fallen father's nervous habit. Little John-John was naturally imitating his dad. We do the same thing when we devote our lives to loving others. Love will naturally lead us to imitate God, and He loves when that happens!

Anyone who loves is born of God and knows God. (1 John 4:7 NLT)

Why is love primary to God's nature and our Christian lives?

How is God's love practically expressed through your life, and how can you love more?

Love <u>suffers long</u> . . . . (1 Corinthians 13:4 NKJV)

How do we get to be just like Him? As we've seen, it requires love. Now we'll look at the specific qualities that not only reflect love but also reflect God. In listing these qualities, Paul starts with longsuffering. Right away our flesh does not like the sound of this. Here we have not one but two words that don't sit well with our human nature: *long* (implying the need for patience) and *suffering* (implying the presence of pain). But we need to face up to the fact that unless we grow in the practice of suffering long, we will never grow to be like God.

Longsuffering is a very specific type of patience. It is the patience exercised toward another individual who is especially difficult. In the real world, it's that quality that enables us to rise above the annoying acquaintance, the belligerent boss, and the noisy neighbor. We all have at least one person in our lives who requires longsuffering, and if we aren't successful in this department, we're falling short of our Christian calling.

If you're starting to feel convicted or discouraged at this point, take heart and notice the fact that longsuffering is something that comes from love. The love of God comes first and then the power to suffer long follows. Sometimes, we reverse these two and invariably fail because we simply cannot suffer long with people before we love them. Love says, *I can bear with you longer than you can possibly weary me.* As the Lord fills us with His love, we are able to be patient with problematic people.

Since God is love and since love suffers long, it stands to reason that longsuffering is another way in which we can reflect His heart. How long has God suffered with each one of us? Let's be just like Him by suffering long with others.

. . . walk worthy of the calling with which you were called . . . with longsuffering, bearing with one another in love . . . . (Ephesians 4:1–2 NKJV)

Who requires an extra amount of longsuffering in your life? (Be specific and write down their names.)

How will you succeed in this aspect of your walk?

HIS KIND OF KINDNESS
DAY 99

[Love] is <u>kind</u> . . . (1 Corinthians 13:4 NKJV)

So often it is easy to pass by the homeless and the beggars who call out to us from street corners and sidewalks. We avert our eyes and pick up our pace to get out of their range a little faster. But not Jesus. As He was leaving Jericho with a great crowd following Him, He sees the interruption of a beggar man as an opportunity for a miracle.

Picture Bartimaeus, the beggar, by the side of road, listening as the crowd and the Teacher he has heard so much about pass by. His ragged clothes are covered with stains. His face is a dirty collage of smudges and bruises. His hair is a wild nest of unkempt curls. His knees are calloused, and his legs are caked with dirt as he sits by the roadside. His power to follow the passing crowd is long gone because he is blind. So, with pathetic desperation, he shouts, *"Jesus, Son of David, have mercy on me!"* As if he didn't already have his fair share of obstacles, he hears a chorus of what he has essentially heard all his life, warning him to be quiet. With a heart that's raw from years of rejection, he fires his last arrow of hope into the darkness, *"Son of David, have mercy on me!"*

Suddenly, something happens. The commotion of the crowd comes to a dead stop. He then hears a voice say, *"Rise, He is calling you."* As he slowly staggers toward the unknown, perhaps he hears hushed voices asking, *Jesus is stopping for him?* Yes, He is. The Ancient of Days wants to talk to the blind beggar who couldn't get the time of day from anyone else. The same mouth that spoke the universe into existence now asks him, *"What do you want Me to do for you?"*

Bartimaeus answers that we wants to receive his sight and then Jesus miraculously heals him (Mark 10:46–52). But that's not our focus. The kindness of Christ to stop for this man is just as impressive as His ability to heal him. In fact, if Jesus weren't so kind, there probably wouldn't have been a miracle. Scripture tells us that Bartimaeus *received his sight, and followed Jesus.* The Lord didn't see him as a loser but as someone who needed Him.

What would you have done that day? Would you have told this man to be quiet, or would you have shown him the kindness that springs from God's love? You can answer these questions by what you do today.

How has God been kind to you?

How can you follow His example?

EVADING ENVY
DAY 100

Love does not <u>envy</u> .... (1 Corinthians 13:4 NKJV)

Wise teachers know that you can effectively teach what something *is* by teaching what it is *not*. Paul employs this teaching technique as he continues to teach us about love. Having taught us what love is, he now starts with a series of pronouncements on what love is not, and envy is first on his list. The Greek word for *envy* is *zeloo*, and it's similarity to our word *zeal* is not a coincidence. The definition of *envy* is "to be zealously preoccupied with the achievements or attributes of others."

Envy was on dramatic display when the Jewish officials brought Jesus before Pontius Pilate to be crucified. Scripture tells us that they did this out of envy (Mark 15:10). To understand why they were so envious, we need to go back a couple years. For centuries, the Jewish religious establishment was the only show in town for those who wanted to know and worship God. They had given the impression to the people that in order to have any hope of being right with God, they had to go through them and strive to be like them. Jesus changed all that. Their manipulative monopoly crumbled as Jesus proclaimed the need to repent and receive the righteousness that God gives through simple and sincere faith. The impact was two-fold: the common people heard Him gladly, but the pious professionals grew envious of Him because they were losing devotees in droves. Jesus was seriously threatening their power and prestige.

Consumed with envy, they sought to eliminate the threat by delivering Jesus to the Romans. He stood before them as a man completely content and steadfastly secure. This ability came from the love that marked the Master's life. Love does not envy; it is content and secure within itself. It has been said that "the envious desire the excellence that they cannot attain." If that's the case, then we have absolutely no grounds for envy. God has given us His love so that we can exhibit His excellence and evade envy.

What are some spiritual dangers associated with envy?

What does it reveal about you when you envy others? What will you do to avoid envy?

Love does not <u>parade itself</u>, is not <u>puffed up</u> . . . (1 Corinthians 13:4 NKJV)

Running down the list of things that love is not, Paul declares that it does not *parade itself* nor is it *puffed up*. At first, it might seem like these are similar references to pride and that Paul is repeating himself. But take a closer look. There is a subtle yet significant difference here.

A parade is put on for the sake of spectators. Elaborate floats are carefully constructed and marching bands meticulously practice because they are going to be seen by the masses. The word *parade* is connected to that which is outwardly observed, and when the Bible uses this term, it is referring to the **outward** impressions we desire to give people. It's a form of pride when we desire to be a spectacle and dominate the spotlight so that others can admire us. In the original language, *parade* carries the connotation of "crossing a line" into the hearts of others.

The term *puffed up* carries **inward** implications. Puffing up is an increase of what is already present, like a lump of dough that has the ability within itself to rise. People with an inward sense of pride are madly impressed with themselves and have a difficult time admitting they are wrong and empathizing with others. They are always wondering why people are not more like them.

Pride's outward and inward pulls can move us away from the heart of God. We need not go any further than Lucifer's example in order to have a healthy respect for pride's potential (Isaiah 14:12–15). Fortunately, there is something powerful enough to pull us back to God. *Love does not parade itself.* When we demonstrate love, we don't desire to be the center of attention or the topic of conversation but we are soft-spoken and joyfully serve behind the scenes. *Love is not puffed up.* We shouldn't be self-consumed or impressed with ourselves, but we should be impressed with others and always have them on our minds. When we allow God's love to fill our hearts, it pulls us away from pride and toward becoming more like Him.

What part does pride play in your day-to-day living?

How does pride pull you away from God, and how can you protect yourself from it?

[Love] does not behave rudely . . . . (1 Corinthians 13:5 NKJV)

Jesus was always the perfect gentleman. People may have disagreed with Him theologically, but no one could ever say He was rude or unseemly. Even His most devoted enemies didn't call His character into question on this point. The One who was the perfect embodiment of love shows us that love is not rude.

What pops into your mind when you hear the word *rudeness*? Perhaps a variety of things, none of which fall under the umbrella of love. We know there is a moral line separating the appropriate from the inappropriate and that certain things are either right or wrong. Love is perfectly aware of where that line is and never even comes close to crossing it.

Some might think that social etiquette and manners don't matter. No doubt, there are even believers who will consider this a trivial point. But if something can be seen in the life of Christ, it is no longer trivial but valuable. There is tremendous spiritual value in minding our manners because it shows others in a practical way that we truly care about them. It indicates that we are willing to discipline our behavior in an effort to be considerate toward their sensibilities. Manners are a way of telling people that they matter to us, and it also shows respect for others as creations of God. If Jesus respected people this way, then how much more are we obligated to show this same respect?

Love does not violate what is right but rather upholds it. There's a problem if we're prone to outbursts of rudeness. It indicates that deep down, we have not allowed God's love behind the locked doors of our hearts. In fact, rudeness is nothing more than an expression of lovelessness. Let's be considerate toward others so they can experience the love of Christ.

What is the relationship between rudeness and an unloving heart?

How can bad manners negatively impact your witness?

[Love] does not seek its own . . . . (1 Corinthians 13:5 NKJV)

The type of love being described by Paul is no ordinary love but the *agape* love of God. *Agape* love has been defined by one Bible scholar as "a profound concern for the well being of another, without any desire to control that other or even to be thanked by that other." How fitting, therefore, that Paul should mention that love does not seek its own. At its very essence, love does not exist for itself but pursues the good of those outside of itself.

Jesus demonstrated the ultimate expression of this as He was being crucified. The Bible records seven things Christ said from the cross, and the first one is not a plea for personal protection but an act of intercession for those who were brutally executing Him:

Then Jesus said, "Father, forgive them, for they do not know what they do." (Luke 23:34 NKJV)

Some have even suggested that the tense in the original Greek indicates that He was crying this out *AS THEY WERE POUNDING THE SPIKES THROUGH HIS WRISTS!* What a slap to our selfish nature to consider that Jesus was so consumed with others that He was interceding for them at the one moment when it was least justified. If Jesus was others-centered under theses circumstances, what feeble excuses can we offer for being self-centered?

Martin Luther King said, "If a man hasn't discovered something that he will die for, he isn't fit to live." As Christians, we should be dying to self so that we can become more like Jesus and experience an abundant life. Being others-oriented is not optional in the Christian life; it *is* the Christian life (Matthew 10:38; Philippians 2:3). This call is impossible to fulfill in our flesh but is naturally fulfilled as we allow God's *agape* love to take anchor in our lives. In a world that only cares about itself, what better way to stand out than by caring for others?

How many selfish things have you already done today?

How can you do better, and what part will love play?

[Love] does not rejoice in iniquity . . . . (1 Corinthians 13:6 NKJV)

Paul concludes his description of God's love by stating that it *does not rejoice in iniquity*, which is another term for sin (1 John 5:17). Every Christian needs to understand that there is a fundamental incompatibility between sin and love. In fact, the original word in the Greek for *rejoice* is *chairo,* which was commonly used as a greeting of grace. This implies that love and sin cannot even say hello to one another.

But it goes even deeper. Love is so essentially opposed to sin that it will never turn a blind eye of toleration toward it but will seek to eliminate it. We see this consistently demonstrated in the life of Jesus. Love moved the Lord to heal a man who had been suffering from an incurable sickness for thirty-eight years. Truly, this was a time to rejoice, but notice Jesus' parting words to the man:

"See, you have been made well. <u>Sin no more</u>, lest a worse thing come upon you."
(John 5:14 NKJV)

A bit later in His ministry, Jesus lovingly defended a woman who was caught in the act of adultery. The penalty for her sin was death by stoning. Christ dramatically defended her from the malicious mob, and her life was spared. Love carried the day, yet the Lord was not silent on the issue of sin:

And Jesus said to her, "Neither do I condemn you; go and <u>sin no more</u>." (John 8:11 NKJV)

Many who flirt with sin are quick to quote the verses where Jesus fellowshiped with known sinners, but they usually fail to mention that those sinners didn't stay that way after encountering the Lord of Love. Jesus was never neutral in the presence of sin, and we shouldn't be either. We're fooling ourselves if we think that our lives can simultaneously stand for sin and love. One necessarily excludes the other. God is continually presenting us with a choice: we can sell-out to sin like the world, or we can live by His love.

Is the sin in your life getting stronger or weaker and why?

What would you say to a believer who wants to persist in something sinful?

[Love] rejoices in the truth. (1 Corinthians 13:6 NKJV)

Pilate has to be one of the most intriguing personalities in Scripture. He bears the responsibility of being the one who gave the final order to crucify Jesus. His place in history is an unenviable one to say the least. How many people have you met lately named Pilate? And yet, we cannot help but relate to this man because he asked a question that we've all asked at some point in our lives:

"What is truth?" (John 18:38 NKJV)

The tragic irony of his question is that he asked it while being eye to eye with the very incarnation of truth. Among the titles that Jesus ascribed to Himself, He proclaimed to be *"the truth"* (John 14:6). What did He mean by that?

Truth has three elements to it, the first of which is **purity**. When something is said to be pure, it has value because it is free of harmful and inferior qualities. Jesus was absolutely pure.

Truth also carries an element of **reality**. Each of us longs for what is real. We desire reality because it gives us something we can safely count on—no illusions, no surprises, no tricks. All that Christ ever said or promised was reliably rooted in reality.

Finally, truth speaks of **integrity**, which is a word that emphasizes strength. Large buildings must be designed with a certain integrity factor, which enables them to withstand the forces around them that could break and shatter them. Jesus was an immovable object amid the high winds of this world.

As the Truth, Jesus established the perfect standard for purity, reality, and integrity. The more we allow God's love to dominate our lives, the more we will attain Jesus' standard because love *rejoices in the truth*; truth and love are lifelong neighbors. In a world filled with people who are searching for truth, we can point them in the right direction by living a love-filled life.

How are love and truth connected to each other?

What will you do to project truth in your life?

COVER LOVER

[Love] <u>bears</u> all things . . . . (1 Corinthians 13:7 NKJV)

The word here for *bears* has a much deeper meaning than to simply carry something. It literally means "to cover something in silence." In this case, it is speaking of love's natural desire to cover the faults of other people. Realistically, we all have our fair share of flaws and imperfections, but the Bible tells us that God's love deliberately doesn't draw attention to them.

Jesus provides the perfect example of covering another's fault. Tradition tells us that Peter was a physically imposing man, but it's a safe bet that he was no match for the six hundred Roman soldiers who came to arrest Jesus (John 18:3). Still, when things started to get rough, Peter came out swinging and sliced an ear off a soldier who had come to seize the Savior. This was well-intentioned on Peter's part, but it was not God's will. Peter faced certain punishment for this. One person has even suggested that there would have been four crosses that day if Jesus had not stepped in and healed the soldier's ear, covering Peter's fault. Jesus did this out of love for His flawed follower. This is typical of what He constantly does for each of us (Hebrews 7:25).

President William McKinley was lovingly devoted to his wife, Ida. She was not a healthy woman and would frequently suffer from seizures that would distort her face. Rather than keeping his wife hidden away behind closed doors, McKinley proudly brought her to the most stately social functions and dinners. Inevitably, she would be seized by a fit, and it was at this point that McKinley's love would shine. He would drop whatever he was doing, quietly take his napkin, and lovingly hold it in front of her disfigured face until the fit had completely left her. His love naturally compelled him to cover her flaws. In the same way, God's love leads us to cover the faults in others.

He who covers over an offense promotes love . . . . (Proverbs 17:9 NIV)

What does it indicate if you aren't covering the faults of others?

Whose faults will you start covering? (Be specific and write them down.)

FAILURE IS NOT FINAL

[Love] <u>believes</u> *all things,* <u>hopes</u> *all things . . . (1 Corinthians 13:7 NKJV)*

Have you ever had your enthusiasm quenched by a spiritual skeptic? Have you ever been written-off by someone, knowing that deep down you had more to offer? If so, then you will appreciate the fact that both these things go against the loving grain of God's heart.

The Bible tells us that love *believes all things*. This does not mean that love accepts all things as being true (the Bible teaches that if you believe in everything, you believe in nothing). What it's saying is that love is always willing to believe the best report about someone. Love does not look at people through a pessimistic lens but has an optimistic outlook. In Jesus' parable of the prodigal son, He describes the father as seeing his son returning to him from afar (Luke 15:21). He must have had an optimistic eye turned toward his window, believing that his son would one day return to him.

We are also told that love *hopes all things*, or as one Bible commentator put it, "Love refuses to take failure as final." The nature of love is such that it does not dwell on where people are today but focuses on what they might become tomorrow. This is something Peter learned after denying the Lord three times. Rather than disqualify His denier from service for what he *had done*, Jesus lovingly restored him on the basis of what He knew Peter *would do* (John 21:15–18).

Love has an optimistic outlook on life, and it looks forward to the potential that exists in others. When it is flowing freely in our lives, we will believe that the best is just around the corner and we will see past where people are in the present as we focus on what they can become in the future.

How has Jesus believed and hoped all things in your life?

How can you do the same for others?

[Love] <u>endures</u> all things. (1 Corinthians 13:7 NKJV)

Endurance is very similar to longsuffering. But there is a basic difference between the two. Longsuffering is dealing with difficult **people**; endurance deals with difficult **circumstances**. It's the check-engine light that comes on in the middle of traffic, the fresh stain on the new shirt, and the test results that the doctor will not discuss with us over the phone. It's those things in life that tend to irritate or control us. Under those circumstances, love demonstrates the strong quality of endurance.

The Greek word for *endures* means "to stay under." Picture an Olympic weight lifter who plants his feet and locks his arms in triumph as he suspends a weight high above his head. This is what love does during the difficult circumstances of life.

Jesus always demonstrated the most remarkable endurance under pressure, but one day in particular stands out. It began with the news that John the Baptist, His cousin and co-laborer, had just died. That would have been enough to ruin anyone's day, but things got worse as the details behind John's death poured in. Herod, one of the most heathen-hearted men of the Bible, had murdered him. To add insult to injury, Herod had decapitated John and placed his head on a platter as a gift for his stepdaughter. Jesus did what any of us would have done—He sought to be alone with His grief. But His popularity was running high at the time, and a massive crowd of sick and diseased people were pursuing His healing touch. The news, the emotions, the frustration of not being able to be alone, the demands of the multitude . . . what would you have done at this moment? Look at what He did:

When Jesus went out He saw a great multitude; and He was moved with compassion for them, and healed their sick. (Matthew 14:14 NKJV)

Love does not cave in under the stressful situations of life. No matter what we experience this day, month, year, or lifetime, love will always give us the supernatural strength we need to endure every difficulty.

What does it reveal if you are easily overwhelmed by life's troubles?

Given the uncertainty of life, when is the best time to be filled with God's love?

INCREASING INTIMACY
DAY 109

For now we see in a mirror, dimly, but then face to face. (1 Corinthians 13:12 NKJV)

If you are a Christian, your destiny is intimacy. The passage above promises that one day each of us will finally be brought into the Lord's indescribable presence. It is a place so utterly heavenly that our earthly senses cannot even comprehend it. The Bible compares it to looking into a mirror, which in those days were usually just pieces of polished brass. An imperfect vessel cannot reflect a perfect image, and our imperfect minds cannot grasp the perfection of Jesus' presence. But one day we will. No barrier will exist between us and our Lord, and we will find ourselves in the ultimate intimacy of being face to face with our Creator, Savior, Master, and Friend. That is the destiny for each and every believer.

Until that glorious day, we are called to increase our intimacy with the Lord here in this life. In fact, the ultimate calling in the Christian life can be summed up with the words *that I may know Him (Philippians 3:10 NKJV)*. God desires and even commands us to draw close to Him at all times: *Draw near to God and He will draw near to you (James 4:8 NKJV)*. When we do this, we reflect His actions.

It is important to remember that when we placed our faith in Jesus, we didn't enter into a one-way relationship. As we desire closeness with Him here on earth, He exerts a corresponding desire for closeness with us in heaven. One day soon, these desires will meet face to face, and we need to aim our lives in the direction of that moment. We do this by constantly increasing our intimacy with Him through prayer and reading His Word. Nothing holds more rewards than spending time with Jesus.

How can you increase your intimacy with God?

What happens in your heart when you think about being face to face with Jesus? (Write it down and refer to it throughout the day.)

For God is not the author of <u>confusion</u> but of <u>peace</u>, as in all the churches of the saints.
(1 Corinthians 14:33 NKJV)

This single Scripture serves as the perfect summary for 1 Corinthians 14. Paul was dealing with a troubling situation that had been taking place in the church at Corinth. God had abundantly blessed them with the gift of speaking in tongues. This gift was being exercised but not within the proper guidelines. People frequently interrupted the teaching of the Word by speaking out in an unknown language. In the process, they caused a lot of confusion and chaos within the church. Paul shows them the various problems with this and reveals the root reason why it is so wrong—it goes against God's character.

God is not a God of confusion. The word here for *confusion* means "unstable, tumultuous, and unbalanced." It is a state of being that is the exact opposite of order and peace. Here's a reliable rule of thumb for Christians: when something promotes a sense of confusion rather than a sense of order, it is not of God. His order in the **natural** is seen in everything, from the arrangement of the universe (Psalm 8:3) to the cells in our bodies (Psalm 139:14). His order in the **spiritual** is seen in everything, from the way He arranges the different members of the body of Christ (1 Corinthians 12:18) to the leaders that He gives to it (Ephesians 4:11–12).

We are under orders to be in order (1 Corinthians 14:40). How unfortunate that many circles in the church have become places of confusion where spiritual gifts are exercised in unspiritual ways. We need to make certain that we aren't guilty of this. If the fruit of our lives is confusion, instability, or unrest, then we're not rightly representing the Lord. But when we are filled with a sense of order and peace, we are living just like Him.

What are some examples of confusion that take place in the church today?

Why is it so important to reflect God's sense of order and balance?

GOT GRACE?
DAY 111

But by the <u>grace</u> of God I am what I am, and His <u>grace</u> toward me was not in vain; but I labored more abundantly than they all, yet not I, but the <u>grace</u> of God which was with me. (1 Corinthians 15:10 NKJV)

It doesn't take a Bible scholar to see the key theme of this verse as Paul mentions the word *grace* three times. We, as Christians, refer to grace quite frequently, but do we understand it? What is grace, and how does it make us more like God?

First, **God is gracious**. This is clear from Paul's statement *by the grace of God*. Grace is "unmerited favor toward the infinitely ill-deserving." It is a cornerstone characteristic of God and has been called "the most important word in the New Testament." Another definition puts it in perspective: "Grace gives us dessert when we deserve hell."

Next, **God extends His grace to us**. Notice the progression of this verse—*His grace toward me*. This is where the theological becomes practical and the theoretical becomes personal. It is one thing for God to be gracious in heaven. It is quite another thing for Him to bestow it upon us here on earth where it impacts our lives. Paul had a profound understanding of this because no one needed unmerited favor more than him. Prior to serving the Lord, he ruthlessly persecuted Him (Acts 9:4).

Finally, **God's grace works through us**. Paul concludes by writing, *I labored more abundantly than they all, yet not I, but the grace of God which was with me.* When he mentions that he labored, he is referring to his apostolic ministry recorded in Acts 13–28. The one who was shown grace is now showing grace.

God is gracious, and He desires to extend His grace to us. When we allow grace to work through us, it becomes the cord that ties us closer to God's heart.

What is grace?

How have you been shown grace, and how can you show it today?

DAY 112

Now if Christ is preached that He has been raised from the dead, how do some <u>among you say that there is no resurrection of the dead</u>? (1 Corinthians 15:12 NKJV)

In the verse above, the apostle Paul tips us off to a potential danger in the Christian life—disagreeing with what God has clearly taught. As Christians, we must be absolutely clear on this point: we cannot be just like God if we are at odds with His teachings. This is what had happened at Corinth when it came to the teaching of the resurrection.

There is no question that Jesus taught the resurrection. In Matthew 22:30 and Luke 14:14, He affirmed the resurrection as a future event. And in John 5:29, Jesus even described the resurrection in dynamic detail. Moreover, Jesus even went so far as to identify Himself with the resurrection in the immortal words that have comforted countless saints over the centuries: *"I am the resurrection and the life. He who believes in Me, though he may die, he shall live" (John 11:25 NKJV).* On top of this, Jesus also foreshadowed the resurrection at the end of the age by resurrecting Jairus' daughter (Matthew 9:25), a widow's son (Luke 7:15), and Lazarus (John 11:44). We can clearly see where Jesus stands on this issue—through instruction, identification, and action, He supported the resurrection.

Yet, despite all this, there were those in Corinth who denied the reality of the resurrection. Paul asks, *How do some among you say there is no resurrection of the dead?* Now we have a situation where people have a doctrinal disagreement with God. Mark this well: whenever our view does not agree with God's view, we are wrong! But the deeper issue is that when we are at odds with God's teaching, we cannot grow in His likeness.

Each of us must give careful attention to what God has taught in His Word and make certain that we do not disagree with Him. This means believing what He believed, teaching what He taught, and preaching what He preached.

Why is it important to know what the Bible teaches?

How can you strengthen your knowledge of God's teachings?

And as we have borne the image of the man of dust, we shall also bear the image of the heavenly Man. (1 Corinthians 15:49 NKJV)

In this present life, we need to allow God's Spirit to produce changes in us that make us grow in His likeness. This is a total and complete experience for us. It will produce spiritual and even mental changes. But what about the physical? Will God leave us physically unlike Himself?

The blessed answer from God's Word is no. Scripture teaches that one day every believer in Christ will shed their old *image of the man of dust [Adam] (1 Corinthians 15:49 NKJV)*, which is the natural body we are forced to live in for now. Notice that the Bible describes our present body as dust. Dust is the barest and least-esteemed material this poor planet has to offer; it doesn't get any lower. We are dust when compared to what we will become one day.

The body awaiting us will be in the likeness of our resurrected Lord. This means no more disease. Never again will we anxiously await reports from the lab or endure the hassle of trying to secure the perfect prescriptions for our sicknesses. Our weakest moment in our resurrection body will be infinitely greater than our strongest moment in this one. This also means that there will be no more death. We will no longer shed tears of mourning, only tears of joy. We will be forever free from man's mortal enemy for *we shall also bear the image of the heavenly Man (1 Corinthians 15:49 NKJV).*

Just as the moon reflects the sun's radiant glory, we will reflect the glory of God in Christ. For now, our ability to be like the Lord is limited to the spiritual and the mental, but in the resurrection, we will be physical reflections of Him.

Beloved, now we are children of God; and it has not yet been revealed what we shall be, but we know that when He is revealed, <u>we shall be like Him</u>. (1 John 3:2–3 NKJV)

Why is it important for believers to remember that they will share in Christ's resurrection glory?

How does your understanding of your future impact your outlook today?

AND THE WINNER IS . . .

DAY 114

But thanks be to God, who gives us the <u>victory</u> through our Lord Jesus Christ.
(1 Corinthians 15:57 NKJV)

We serve a victorious God. He never loses. In every conceivable contest, He emerges as the victor. This is one of the great themes throughout the life of Christ. Consider the various victories our Lord can claim.

He was victorious over sin. Scripture shows people in the truest light of their character. In almost every case, the lives of those covered in the Bible have one feature in common—sin. But not Jesus. Even though He is referenced and written about more than any other individual, there's a striking absence of sin in all that He did and said. Hebrews 4:15 tells us that Jesus was tempted in every possible way yet never once bowed to sin.

He was also victorious over Satan. Perhaps this is most vividly depicted during Jesus' temptation in the wilderness (Matthew 4:1–11). Satan attacked Him in three different ways and was routed each time. Yet it was by His death on the cross that Jesus dealt the devil's kingdom a deathblow from which it will never recover. Colossians 2:14–15 records that the crucifixion made a public spectacle of Satan's forces because it repaired the relational gap between God and man that Satan had exploited for many a millennia.

Our Savior was also victorious over death. Nothing is more consistent in this life than the reality of death. As you may have heard, ten out of ten people die, and you may have noticed that they stay that way. But Romans 6:9 teaches that Jesus overcame the grave's grip through His resurrection. Mankind's mortal enemy was no match for Jesus.

Christ's victories are also our victories. We are given victory *through* His accomplishments because we are *in Him*. As Christians, sin no longer has the power to bind us (Romans 6:14), Satan no longer has authority over us (1 John 4:4), and death no longer is something to be feared (Hebrews 2:14). We need to walk in the victories that Christ has purchased and provided for us.

How can Jesus' victory have a practical impact on your life today?

How can you encourage another believer who is not experiencing victory through Jesus?

Now if Timothy comes, see that he may be with you without fear; for he does the <u>work</u> of the Lord, as I also do. (1 Corinthians 16:10 NKJV)

A recent survey revealed that fifty-two percent of employees wish they could change their jobs. This means that every other person who is serving in a professional capacity is not satisfied. Work is a sore subject for many of us. This is because we don't see it for what it truly is—an opportunity to be like the Lord.

The Greek word for *work* in the verse above is *ergon*, which is best defined as "one's object of employment and activity." It is one of the most popular words in the New Testament, occurring in every book except Philemon. Jesus applied this word to Himself on several occasions. In John 9:4 (NKJV), He said, *"I must work the <u>works</u> of Him who sent Me."* A few verses later, in John 10:37 (NKJV), Jesus declared, *"If I do not do the <u>works</u> of My Father, do not believe Me."* In John 17:4 (NKJV), He proclaimed in his prayer to the Father, *"I have finished the <u>work</u> which You have given Me to do."* Jesus viewed His work as all that the Father had appointed for Him to accomplish in His life. The Lord was faithful to finish His work, and when He cried, *"It is finished"* from the cross, He was speaking of His work.

According to our lead verse, Timothy and Paul were also workers in God's great plan, and we need to understand that every believer is called to this work as well. Ephesians 2:10 (NKJV) tells us, *We are His workmanship, created in Christ Jesus for good <u>works</u>, which God prepared beforehand that we should walk in them.* First Corinthians 15:58 (NKJV) commands us to *be steadfast, immovable, always abounding in the <u>work</u> of the Lord.* Our work extends far beyond our place of employment. It is the divine agenda that God has personally scripted for each of us. We are all responsible to know it, do it, and finish it.

What is God's ergon *for your life?*

How can Jesus' example in this area be helpful to you?

IDOLATRY IS . . .
DAY 116

"You shall have no other gods before Me." (Exodus 20:3 NKJV)

What is an idol? It *isn't* an ancient statue that's carved out of wood, stone, silver, or gold. An idol is far more elaborate and relevant. The verse above defines an idol as anything in a person's life that comes before God. The Hebrew word for *before* carries the connotation of "above." Whenever we allow anything to be above God in our lives, it is an idol, making us guilty of idolatry. Idols have a million different faces. Some are obvious; others, subtle. Regardless of the particular idols in our lives, we need to keep three things in mind.

First, idolatry is serious. The Bible teaches that those who persist in idolatry will have no inheritance in heaven (1 Corinthians 6:9; Ephesians 5:5) and are destined to suffer eternal torment (Revelation 21:8). These warnings are as strong as any in Scripture, showing us that God takes idolatry very seriously, and so should we!

Idolatry is also internal. We often mistakenly think of idolatry as the external act of bowing before a sculpture. In reality, idolatry is an internal condition of the heart. In Ezekiel 14, God repeatedly describes His people as having set up countless idols *in their hearts*. Outwardly, everything seemed in order, but they were inwardly broken and blind to the fact that they even had this problem. The same thing can happen to us when we fail to realize that the potential for idolatry is always as close as our own hearts.

Finally, idolatry is correctable. God does not point out our problems without graciously giving us a solution to overcome them. The prescription for correcting idolatry is given to us by Jesus when He taught, *"Seek first the kingdom of God and His righteousness" (Matthew 6:33 NKJV).* We need to make it our daily discipline to seek the Lord and to be preoccupied with His righteousness, faithfulness, and goodness. In the light of God's glory, all idols lose their luster and we find freedom from this besetting sin.

What comes between you and the Lord?

How will you correct this?

"No one can serve two masters; for either he will hate the one and love the other, or else he will be loyal to the one and despise the other. You cannot serve God and mammon." (Matthew 6:24 NKJV)

Love of money is one of the most effective ways to separate us from God. Jesus referred to this idol as *mammon*, and it has rivaled the true and living God for the love and loyalty of countless hearts. Jesus described mammon as a cruel taskmaster, and its enslaving power is dramatically displayed in an encounter that took place during Christ's ministry:

Now behold, one came and said to Him, "Good Teacher, what good thing shall I do that I may have eternal life?" (Matthew 19:16 NKJV)

Who was this man who spoke to Jesus? He was young and moral (Matthew 19:20). Luke 18:18 tells us that he was a ruler, presumably of a local synagogue, which would mean that he was also religious and powerful. This man was courageous because he publicly came to Jesus, going against the wishes of the religious establishment at that time. Despite all these things, he still feels empty and seeks Christ's help. As He always does, Jesus looked past the outward exterior and zeroed in on the real issue—mammon:

Jesus said to him, "If you want to be perfect, go, sell what you have and give to the poor, and you will have treasure in heaven; and come, follow Me." But when the young man heard that saying, he went away sorrowful, for he had great possessions. (Matthew 19:21–22 NKJV)

Because mammon kept this man from following the Lord, we know that this idol had enslaved his heart. We run the same risk whenever we allow money (whether we have it or not) to eclipse our focus and affection for the Lord. Moreover, we need to make certain that the money God blesses us with is surrendered and submitted to His purposes. Somebody once commented, "Money is a terrific servant, but a terrible master." Which will you choose?

Do you need to be rich in order to idolize money? Why or why not?

How can you protect yourself from worshiping mammon?

TRADITION
DAY 118

"All too well you reject the commandment of God, that you may keep your tradition."
(Mark 7:9 NKJV)

This was Christ's rebuke for the men of His day who were known as Pharisees. The word *Pharisees* literally means "separated ones," which is exactly what this group of ultra-strict Jews sought to do. In their minds, the Mosaic law, which God had given to Israel, was not enough in order to live a godly life. They made it their mission to separate themselves from everyone else by taking the written law and going a step further by making additions that were nothing more than man-made traditions.

Eventually, these traditions became more important to them than the God-given laws on which they were based. For example, the Lord had commanded children to honor their mother and father (Exodus 20:12), which would eventually include financial assistance. Children have a God-given duty to support their parents in their old age, but the Pharisees had devised a tradition that pressured people into giving their support money to the temple instead. Their tradition was obscuring the heart of God, and He was not pleased.

Before we're too critical of the Pharisees, we need to examine our own behavior and confess that we have our own share of traditions. For some, it can be a matter of believing that people need to fit a certain image in order for God to love them. For others, it may be the impression that God only appreciates a certain style of music. Or perhaps there are those who feel that things must always be done a certain way because "that's the way we've always done it." If we're not careful, these traditions can become idols that separate us from God's heart.

Humans are creatures of comfort, and traditions provide a degree of comfort by giving us something that is expected, fixed, and unchanging. The problem begins when we start pledging our allegiance to traditions rather than Scripture. If we are to live an idol-less life, we need to understand that the convictions of God's Word are greater than the comforts of man's traditions.

What are some traditions in your life that could separate your heart from God's?

What should be the criterion for your traditions?

God tested Abraham, and said to him, "Abraham!" And he said, "Here I am." Then He said, "Take now your son, your only son Isaac, whom you love, and go to the land of Moriah, and offer him there as a burnt offering on one of the mountains of which I shall tell you." (Genesis 22:1–2 NKJV)

This is one of those passages that ought to make us do a double take. Did God just ask Abraham to sacrifice his son, Isaac? He did, and in order to understand this command, we need to look back at Abraham's life and consider what he had been through before Isaac was born. Abraham and his wife, Sarah, had lived a long life of barrenness. The years passed, and their hopes of having a child of their own began to flicker and fade. But just as their prospects for a child were at their lowest, God promised to bless them with a son. Isaac was miraculously born to a mother of 90 and a father of 100. Their long and difficult years had given way to joy and laughter.

Abraham had great affection for Isaac; therefore, Isaac posed the greatest threat of idolatry to Abraham's heart. God's purpose for this command was to give Abraham an opportunity to prove who was truly his first love. By giving up Isaac, he would also reveal his greater love for God. It was not God's will to see Isaac's life quenched but to see Abraham's faith fanned into flame. Abraham passed the test. Notice God's response to him:

"Do not lay your hand on the lad, or do anything to him; for now I know that you fear God, since you have not withheld your son, your only son, from Me." (Genesis 22:12 NKJV)

There is a real danger for parents to give their children such priority in their hearts that they become idols to them. This is a tragedy because what children truly need are parents whose hearts are wholly surrendered to the Lord.

What lesson did you learn from the test that God gave to Abraham?

What would you have done if you were in Abraham's position?

Abram dwelt in the land of Canaan, and Lot dwelt in the cities of the plain and pitched his tent even as far as Sodom. (Genesis 13:12 NKJV)

An interesting discovery is made when we trace Lot's footprints. They start in the land of Ur when he leaves his homeland with his uncle, Abraham. They journeyed together to the edge of Canaan where they decided that it was best for them to part ways. As the verse above shows, Lot chose to head toward the heavily populated plain, under the shadow of Sodom. His tracks then take him directly into Sodom where he makes his home (Genesis 14:12). He is then described as sitting in the gate of Sodom, showing that he had become a representative of the city (Genesis 19:1).

Why was Lot pulled toward the city of Sodom? We know that he was not drawn to the sinful lifestyle in Sodom because the New Testament tells us that he was tormented by its sinfulness (2 Peter 2:7–8). Scripture seems to suggest that the buzz and excitement of society had gotten hold of Lot's heart. His love for the social life of the city became an idol that made him insensitive to the things of God. This idol was firmly embedded in Lot, even to the point that God's angels had to take him by the hand and lead him out of Sodom before its destruction. Even after all this, Lot's tracks take him right back to his idol as he begged to be allowed to go and live in another city (Genesis 19:20).

It isn't a sin to live in a city or to appreciate the fast-paced excitement of society. Paul predominately ministered in the cities of his day, and Jesus spent much of His ministry in Jerusalem. But when we neglect God and allow a love for society to become a driving desire in our lives, we are foolishly following in Lot's footsteps.

How can society be idolized in the twenty-first century?

What will you do to ensure that you don't follow in Lot's footsteps?

POPULARITY
DAY 121

"Thus speaks the LORD of hosts, the God of Israel, saying: 'I have broken the yoke of the king of Babylon. Within two full years I will bring back to this place all the vessels of the Lord's house, that Nebuchadnezzar king of Babylon took away from this place and carried to Babylon.'" *(Jeremiah 28:2–3 NKJV)*

Hananiah the prophet spoke these words as the city of Jerusalem was under siege by the Babylonian army. They were words of deliverance, encouragement, hope, and inspiration—but they were not true.

The Bible reveals that God used Babylon to punish the spiritual waywardness of the Israelites. They had become so desensitized to their sin that they failed to recognize their need for correction. Therefore, in their minds, it was unthinkable that the Lord would allow the Babylonians to win. The popular party line was that "everything is going to be okay." Repeating this proclamation and remaining popular had become so important to Hananiah that he was unable and unwilling to hear what God was saying. Bowing to the idol of popularity, he became a false prophet. But there was a man in Jerusalem whose heart had not bowed to this idol, and he delivered a message from the Lord that was unpopular but true:

"For thus says the LORD of hosts, the God of Israel: 'I have put a yoke of iron on the neck of all these nations, that they may serve Nebuchadnezzar king of Babylon; and they shall serve him.'" (Jeremiah 28:14 NKJV)

Jeremiah went on to pronounce judgment against Hananiah for falsely prophesying:

"Therefore thus says the LORD: 'Behold, I will cast you from the face of the earth. This year you shall die, because you have taught rebellion against the LORD.'" So Hananiah the prophet died the same year in the seventh month. (Jeremiah 28:16–17 NKJV)

This is a powerful lesson on how the pursuit of popularity can become an idol that leads to a person's ruin. We must carefully weigh and consider our words. Are they according to the truth of God's Word, or are we simply saying them out of a desire to be popular?

How important is popularity to you?

Why is it dangerous to pursue popularity?

Children, obey your parents in all things, for this is well pleasing to the Lord. (Colossians 3:20 NKJV)

It is God's will for children to love, honor, and obey their parents. But what about those inevitable moments in life when this conflicts with our devotion to the Lord? What happens when a parent pulls us in one direction while Christ calls us in another? We tend not to think of our parents as idols, but that is exactly what they become when they hinder or inhibit us from following the Lord. We have a perfect example of parental idolatry in an encounter that took place in the life of Christ:

Then another of His disciples said to Him, "Lord, let me first go and bury my father." But Jesus said to him, "Follow Me, and let the dead bury their own dead." (Matthew 8:21–22 NKJV)

Christ's words may sound harsh at first, but in that particular culture, it was customary for a son to care for his parents until they died. When this man said, *"Let me first go and bury my father,"* he was telling Jesus that he wanted to follow Him but that his obligations to his earthly father had priority. He wanted to serve his dad before he started serving Jesus. By saying, *"Follow me, and let the dead bury their own dead,"* Jesus was telling him to get his priorities straight and let his earthly father take care of himself. We never hear anything else from this man; therefore, by all indications, he allowed his devotion to his dad to separate him from following the Lord.

Unfortunately, this same scenario is played out in the lives of many prospective followers today. Often times, unbelieving parents will object to their child's newfound love and devotion to Jesus. Rather than encourage their child's pursuit of Him, sometimes they pull him or her in the opposite direction. If believers allow this to occur, it is nothing shy of idolatry because it keeps them from following the Lord.

If you have been guilty of choosing your parents' approval over the Lord's, the solution is to love Him with all your heart. When you do, it naturally gives Him priority and authority in your life.

"He who loves father or mother more than Me is not worthy of Me." (Matthew 10:37 NKJV)

How might your parents become an idol in your life?

What is the proper balance between loving your parents and loving God?

EXPECTATIONS
DAY 123

"And blessed is he who is not offended because of Me." (Matthew 11:6 NKJV)

An old adage says, "With no expectations, there are no disappointments." How true. Our greatest disappointments in life are typically attached to our greatest expectations. There's a spiritual parallel to this principle: the more expectations we place upon God, the more disappointed or offended we become when He doesn't deliver as expected.

This is what happened in Naaman's life. The Bible tells us that he was the commander of the Syrian army and a great and honorable man (2 Kings 5:1). There was just one problem: he suffered from leprosy. His wife's servant suggested that he seek the help of Elisha, who had performed many mighty miracles. Naaman went to Elisha bearing a small fortune of silver, gold, and fine clothing. He was also bearing the expectation that Elisha would cure him of his leprosy on the spot. But Elisha wouldn't even go to Naaman or take his treasures. Instead, he simply told him to go and wash in the Jordan seven times and he would be healed. Notice the sense of dashed expectations in Naaman's response:

But Naaman went away angry and said, "I thought that he would surely come out to me and stand and call on the name of the LORD his God, wave his hand over the spot and cure me of my leprosy." . . . So he turned and went off in a rage. (2 Kings 5:11–12 NIV)

As the story goes, Naaman got over his disappointment. He followed Elisha's orders, and God cleansed him of his leprosy. He had allowed his expectations to reach proportions that nearly kept him from experiencing the Lord's touch on his life. The same thing can happen to us. If we expect God to remove all our problems or to bless us with our every desire, our expectations can become idols that cause us to turn from God when they are unfulfilled. As we keep the Lord first in our lives, we'll find satisfaction and peace even when our expectations are not met.

What expectations do you place on God?

How can your expectations become idols in your life?

SELF-RIGHTEOUSNESS
DAY 124

And Jesus said, "For judgment I have come into this world, that those who do not see may see, and that those who see may be made blind." Then some of the Pharisees who were with Him heard these words, and said to Him, "Are we blind also?" Jesus said to them, "If you were blind, you would have no sin; but now you say, 'We see.' Therefore your sin remains." (John 9:39–41 NKJV)

We can't afford to miss what Jesus is saying here: if you think you're okay, you aren't okay. The human heart wants to believe that it has a reason to boast and that it's capable of being righteous all on its own. A self-righteous spirit will always separate us from God's presence, making it an idol in the truest sense.

Christ illustrated this in the parable of two men who went up to the temple to pray (Luke 18:9–14 NKJV). One man was a Pharisee who was respected and revered by the Jewish community; the other, a despised tax collector. As the Pharisee stood in the temple, he thanked God that he was *not like other men—extortioners, unjust, adulterers, or even as this tax collector.* Then he bragged that he fasted twice a week and tithed all his possessions. In marked contrast, the tax collector would not even dare to lift his head to heaven but beat his chest and cried, *"God, be merciful to me a sinner!"*

Outwardly, the Pharisee seemed to have his act together while the tax collector did not have a spiritual leg to stand on. However, internally, the Pharisee was bowing to the idol of self-righteousness while the tax collector was broken before the true and living God. Jesus declared that it was the broken sinner who was accepted before God, not the self-righteous Pharisee.

Our human hearts want to play the part of the Pharisee. We like recognition for the good things we do. Rather than find ourselves separated from God by the idol of self-righteousness, we need to remember that we're saved only by God's grace and we have absolutely nothing to be self-righteous about.

When do you get a self-righteous attitude, and how will you prevent it in the future?

How does God's perspective differ from ours?

INABILITY

"Come now, therefore, and I will send you to Pharaoh that you may bring My people, the children of Israel, out of Egypt." (Exodus 3:10 NKJV)

There were two ways for Moses to respond to the overwhelming task of freeing the Israelites from their slavery in Egypt. He could have embraced his divine commission, trusting God to see the Israelites successfully through. Instead, he chose to back away from his calling by focusing on his inabilities:

But Moses said to God, "Who am I that I should go to Pharaoh, and that I should bring the children of Israel out of Egypt?" (Exodus 3:11 NKJV)

It's interesting that God did not allow this argument to stand, but He repeated the calling and assured Moses that He would be with him and that victory would be achieved through His might (Exodus 3:12). This did not satisfy Moses because he had allowed his inabilities to crowd out his spiritual vision and trust in the Lord's abilities:

Then Moses said to the LORD, "O my Lord, I am not eloquent, neither before nor since You have spoken to Your servant; but I am slow of speech and slow of tongue." (Exodus 4:10 NKJV)

In a practical sense, Moses was worshiping the idol of inability rather than the Almighty God of Abraham, Isaac, and Jacob. Once again, the Lord's remedy for this was to assure Moses that He would be with him, enabling him to do what was needed (Exodus 4:11–12). In the end, God's promises proved true and He worked through Moses to accomplish the impossible.

We can make the same mistake as Moses when it comes to God's calling on our lives. If we focus on our shortcomings, it can hinder us from embracing the divine commission that has been placed upon our lives. The remedy for idolizing our own inabilities is to be fully focused on God's ability because the basis of our calling resides in what He can do—not in what we cannot do.

What can you apply to your life from Moses' example?

If God calls you to do something that you feel unqualified for, what will you do?

"Seek first the kingdom of God and His righteousness, and all these things shall be added to you." (Matthew 6:33 NKJV)

The verse above is one of the most familiar Scriptures in the Bible. We frequently see the words *"Seek first the kingdom of God"* on Christian plaques, pictures, screen savers, coffee mugs, and even afghans. We can literally surround ourselves with this passage, and it is well if we do because seeking the Lord first will prevent our hearts from being overtaken by idolatry. As a matter of fact, Jesus was addressing a specific form of idolatry as He spoke these well-known words. The idol's identity is revealed when we back up a few verses:

"Therefore I say to you, <u>do not worry</u> about your life, what you will eat or what you will drink; nor about your body, what you will put on. Is not life more than food and the body more than clothing?" (Matthew 6:25 NKJV)

When Jesus taught, *"Seek first the kingdom of God,"* He offered the perfect prescription for removing the idol of worry from our lives. An old proverb says, "Worry gives big shadows to small things." This is an apt description of how the idol of worry can overshadow our confidence in God. It is impossible to simultaneously trust the Lord and worry. At any given moment, we will be bowed down to one or the other—never both. This means that we cannot experience intimate fellowship with God when we're submitted and surrendered to our worries.

The admonition is obvious: we must steadfastly guard our hearts and never allow the worries of this world to become idols that we worship. We can only accomplish this by proactively seeking the Lord above all else and by desiring His righteousness to be displayed in and through our lives.

When has worry served as an idol in your life?

Why do you think people don't typically think of worry as being an idol?

Then the men of Israel said to Gideon, "Rule over us, both you and your son, and your grandson also; for you have delivered us from the hand of Midian." But Gideon said to them, "I will not rule over you, nor shall my son rule over you; the LORD shall rule over you." (Judges 8:22–23 NKJV)

Gideon's spiritual stock was at an all-time high. God had just used him to bring about sweeping reform and deliverance to Israel. He not only smashed his family's false idol, but also defeated and expelled the Midianites who had oppressed the Jews for seven years. The nation of Israel had such respect for Gideon that they asked him to serve as their ruler. Gideon responded by pointing the people's focus back to where it belonged—the Lord. But something happened in Gideon's heart between these verses and the very next one:

Then Gideon said to them, "I would like to make a request of you, that each of you would give me the earrings from his plunder.". . Then Gideon made it into an ephod and set it up in his city, Ophrah. And all Israel played the harlot with it there. It became a snare to Gideon and to his house. (Judges 8:24, 27 NKJV)

It seems incomprehensible that a man who had risen to such spiritual heights could sink to such a spiritual low. After all he had accomplished, how could this spiritual giant bow himself to the idol of gold? Gideon had allowed his accomplishments to lead him into idolatrous bondage. The victories of the past became more important to him than his ever-present need to abide in the Lord. Before he knew it, Gideon was miles away from the One who was truly responsible for the victory.

This is a sobering lesson about the potential dangers that come with spiritual success. If God uses us to lead someone to Christ or to teach a great Bible study, we need to be humbled that He chose us and give Him all the glory instead of turning what He has truly accomplished into an idolatrous ephod in our hearts. Our spiritual milestones will become stumbling stones unless we acknowledge that all our accomplishments come from God and that He deserves all the credit and glory.

What does Gideon's example serve as a warning against?

How does God want you to deal with your spiritual accomplishments?

". . . you shall surely set a king over you whom the LORD your God chooses; one from among your brethren you shall set as king over you; you may not set a foreigner over you, who is not your brother. . . . Neither shall he multiply wives for himself, lest his heart turn away . . . ."
(Deuteronomy 17:15, 17 NKJV)

God has a parental heart toward His people, and as a loving parent, He warns us against the spiritual pitfalls in life. This is what the Lord is doing in the verses above as He tells Israel that their king should not have multiple wives. The purpose for this prohibition was to protect the king's heart from being turned away from the true and living God by these relationships. In His infinite wisdom, the Lord knows that relationships can very easily become idols that sever our intimacy with Him.

Solomon's life stands as a tragic example of this reality. As the king of Israel, Solomon had clearly been warned against having multiple wives, and yet the Bible tells us that he had seven hundred of them (1 Kings 11:3)! By courting these wives, Solomon courted disaster, and the idolatrous effects of his relationships eventually caught up with him:

For it was so, when Solomon was old, that his wives turned his heart after other gods; and his heart was not loyal to the LORD his God, as was the heart of his father David.
(1 Kings 11:4 NKJV)

If Solomon, who surpassed all the kings of the earth in wisdom (2 Chronicles 9:22), was susceptible to serving the idol of relationships, then so are we. We are foolish to think that a relationship with a spouse, fiancé, or someone whom we feel strongly for doesn't possess the potential to steal our hearts away from the One who deserves our first love at all times. Whenever this happens, the relationship has overstepped its rightful place in our lives and we need to elevate our relationship with God above all else.

When does a relationship with another person become an idol?

What is a good guideline to determine if a relationship is pleasing to God?

REPUTATION
DAY 129

So the women sang as they danced, and said: "Saul has slain his thousands, And David his ten thousands." (1 Samuel 18:7 NKJV)

How this song must have stung Saul's ears! All his life he had been head and shoulders above the rest—literally (1 Samuel 9:2). Then along came a small shepherd boy named David who was willing to step out in faith and stand up to Goliath. His victory over the giant Philistine catapulted him to national stardom, and suddenly Saul's reputation started to suffer. Even though the Israelites were singing how he had *"slain his thousands,"* it wasn't as impressive as David's *"ten thousands."*

Being less than the best was a foreign experience for Saul. He was used to being the one whom everyone looked up to, the one whom everybody wanted an appointment with, the one with the greatest reputation. Unfortunately, as Saul's reputation had grown in Israel over the years, it had also grown in his own heart. It had achieved idolatrous proportions by the time it began to suffer, and it obscured his spiritual sight from seeing that God's hand was now upon David.

Then Saul was very angry, and the saying displeased him; and he said, "They have ascribed to David ten thousands, and to me they have ascribed only thousands. Now what more can he have but the kingdom?" So Saul eyed David from that day forward. (1 Samuel 18:8–9 NKJV)

Thomas Paine once wrote, "Reputation is what men and women think of us; character is what God and angels know of us." The truth is, you can be so preoccupied with what other people think about you that you neglect the more important issue of your own character before God. This was Saul's mistake, and it will be yours if you're not careful. If you're living for your reputation, you're bound to suffer as it suffers. If you put your relationship with God above your reputation, you will stay strong even if it happens to suffer.

How could your reputation become something that you idolize?

Why is it foolish to preoccupy yourself with what others think of you?

For many walk, of whom I have told you often, and now tell you even weeping, that they are the enemies of the cross of Christ: whose end is destruction, <u>whose god is their belly</u> . . .
(Philippians 3:18–19 NKJV)

The dictionary defines gluttony as "the act or practice of eating to excess." The verse above defines it as idolatry. Make no mistake; an uncontrolled appetite for food can be as destructive on our spirituality as any other idol that takes control of our lives. In fact, gluttony can be even more detrimental because it is so often ignored and pushed to the side in our culture of excess. The most dangerous idol is the one that is not taken seriously, and all too often, gluttony is overlooked.

We can't accuse God of not warning us. Proverbs 23:21 tells us that the glutton will come to poverty, and in Deuteronomy 21:20, gluttony is linked with stubbornness, rebellion, and disobedience. Even the Pharisees understood the negative impact of gluttony; for as they sought to slander Jesus, they falsely accused Him of being a glutton (Matthew 11:19; Luke 7:34). Scripture is clear on this point: gluttony is to be avoided at all costs, especially when our god becomes our belly.

The underlying issue when it comes to gluttony is a lack of self-control. Many of us are aware of the fact that we eat to excess, but we can't stop. God never promised us that we would be able to control ourselves in our own strength. Instead, we are told in Galatians 5:23 that self-control is something produced in us through the working of the Holy Spirit.

In order to overcome the gluttony that exists in our lives, we need to allow God's Spirit to overcome us with His presence and power. This happens when we take the time to ask the Father to fill us afresh with the One that He has promised to give us upon request:

"How much more will your heavenly Father give the Holy Spirit to those who ask Him!"
(Luke 11:13 NKJV)

How is gluttony justified in our day and age?

What would you share with a person who is worshiping the god of gluttony?

ISOLATION
DAY 131

And let us consider one another in order to stir up love and good works, <u>not forsaking the assembling of ourselves together</u>, as is the manner of some, but exhorting one another, and so much the more as you see the Day approaching. (Hebrews 10:24–25 NKJV)

As we have seen, an idol is anything that separates us from God. This includes anything that we chose to do instead of obeying God because our obedience is the basis for our fellowship with Him. God has commanded us not to forsake fellowship with other Christians; therefore, an attitude of isolation is essentially an idol because it prevents us from obeying God. When we sacrifice our fellowship with our fellow believers, we sacrifice our fellowship with Him.

Consider the precedent set for us in Scripture. In the Old Testament, God called the Israelites out of Egypt and led them through the wilderness as one corporate body. The Lord even directed them to camp together in order to give them a consistent sense of community (Numbers 2). Isolation simply was not an option. When we examine the four gospels, we see that Jesus was usually in fellowship with His disciples. He did not spend the majority of His time in isolation by Himself but placed a priority on fellowship by willingly interacting with those who believed in Him. In the book of Acts, the first generation of believers could not be separated. They were constantly around each other, drawing strength and encouragement from one another during their trials and persecutions (Acts 2:42).

We can make excuses for *forsaking the assembling of ourselves together*. In the end, these are only attempts to defend the idol of isolation that we have put before God. Our fellowship with God and other believers is connected, and we cannot expect one without the other.

Why is spiritual isolation a form of idolatry?

On a scale of one to ten, how important is fellowship to you?

LAZINESS

The way of the <u>lazy</u> man is like a hedge of thorns, But the way of the upright is a highway.
(Proverbs 15:19 NKJV)

Not all forms of idolatry are active or aggressive. Some are passive, such as laziness. Initially, it might seem like a stretch to identify laziness as idolatry, but remember that an idol is anything that causes separation from God. Believers and non-believes alike often allow laziness to get in God's way.

Jesus once shared a story that highlighted the great danger that lurks behind laziness. In the parable, a wealthy man travels to a far away country. Before he leaves, he calls three of his servants and entrusts them with different amounts of his fortune. He expects each of them to turn a profit on the treasure in his absence. When the rich man returns, he finds that two of the servants have invested his wealth and earned a return. The last servant, however, has not been industrious in earning more. Instead, the lazy servant has buried what he was given in the ground. We can hear Christ's attitude toward laziness as the wealthy man responds to the servant:

"But his lord answered and said to him, 'You wicked and <u>lazy</u> servant, you knew that I reap where I have not sown, and gather where I have not scattered seed. . . . Cast the unprofitable servant into the outer darkness. There will be weeping and gnashing of teeth.'"
(Matthew 25:26, 30 NKJV)

As a result of his laziness, the servant is cast into outer darkness. Throughout the Bible, this is also a description for hell, which is characterized by the absence of God's presence. This parable serves as a warning of how laziness can separate someone from God, and this separation can happen on two different levels. For non-believers, laziness can be an idol that prevents them from finding union with God through faith in Jesus Christ. In the life of believers, laziness can become an idol that prevents them from having communion with God. In both cases, laziness needs to be identified as the idol that it is and forsaken at all costs.

How should you view laziness in your life?

How has laziness been a barrier between you and the Lord?

For the weapons of our warfare are not carnal but mighty in God for pulling down strongholds, casting down arguments and every high thing that exalts itself against the knowledge of God, bringing every <u>thought</u> into captivity to the obedience of Christ . . . (2 Corinthians 10:4–5 NKJV)

How often do you think about your thought-life? Our minds are constantly creating a stream of thoughts, and the flow can be so steady that we forget this process is even taking place. Whether we realize it, we each have a thought-life that has a powerful impact on the rest of our lives. This thought-life is so powerful that it even possesses the ability to become an idol—and it frequently does.

All of us are guilty of allowing certain thoughts to distract us from the Lord. Perhaps God has told us to abandon some memories, yet we allow our minds to go back to them. Maybe He has declared specific fantasies about the future "off limits," yet we indulge in them anyway. If we are to grow in our walk with God, we must understand that we are choosing mental idolatry when we choose to think thoughts that lead us down the path of mental disobedience. The Bible characterizes these thoughts as rebellious renegades that need to be immediately captured and made to bow before the throne of Jesus.

You accomplish this by making Christ the supreme object of your thought-life. Scripture teaches that you are to use your thought-life to a holy advantage by setting your mind on the things above (Colossians 3:2) and thinking about those things that reflect God's character (Philippians 4:8–9). The more you do this, the more sensitive you will be to the stray thoughts that will only distance you from Him. Believers have been given the mind of Christ (1 Corinthians 2:16). Make sure your thoughts are lined up with His.

How do your thought patterns pull you toward mental idolatry? How will you stop?

How will you set your mind on the things above?

All things are lawful for me, but all things are not helpful. All things are lawful for me, but I will not be brought under the power of any. (1 Corinthians 6:12 NKJV)

Scripture is black and white when it comes to the most important matters in life. For example, we know it is always wrong to lie, steal, cheat, gossip, and covet. We also know that it is always right to be encouraging, honest, faithful, merciful, and loving. But what are we to do about the things that aren't classified as being universally right or wrong? When Scripture doesn't specifically identify something as being sinful, it is generally a freedom that believers are able to enjoy. Paul is referring to these freedoms as he declares that *all things are lawful.*

It's a wonderful fact that the Christian life is characterized more by freedoms than prohibitions. However, the Bible is warning us here that it's possible to become bound by our freedoms. We can enjoy a freedom with such excess that it controls and directs us instead of God. Rather than obey the leading of the Holy Spirit, we obey the impulse to indulge in something that we can always justify as being lawful.

When our freedoms have a higher priority in our lives than the Lord, it means that we have set them up as idols in our hearts. Many Christians place their favorite music, television shows, movies, hobbies, or sports before God. These things aren't sinful in their proper place; they are part of the freedoms we have been blessed with in Christ. They become sinful for us the moment they usurp God's authority in our lives.

The key to overcoming this potential form of idolatry is to follow Matthew 6:33 and seek God first. We are never as free as when we are bound to Christ. The closer we are to Him, the freer our hearts will be when it comes to enjoying and exercising our freedoms.

Which freedoms in your life have the ability to dominate you?

How can you protect yourself from being bound by your freedoms?

FRIENDSHIPS
DAY 135

The righteous should choose his friends carefully, For the way of the wicked leads them astray. (Proverbs 12:26 NKJV)

Friendship is a powerful force. It has the ability to bind people together for a lifetime, which can be either good or bad. A friendship based on being mutually surrendered to the lordship of Jesus Christ is more valuable than all the world's riches. However, a friendship that consistently interferes with our relationship with God is a form of spiritual idolatry. The Bible recognizes this reality and warns us to choose our friends carefully so we can protect ourselves from ungodly friendships that will lead us astray.

Ungodly friends will pressure us to please someone or something at the expense of pleasing the Lord. In addition, they will not respect our spiritual convictions. A "friend" who pushes us to redefine our Spirit-led convictions is an ungodly friend who doesn't respect the work God is doing in us. Moreover, ungodly friends never advance our discipleship but only stunt spiritual development.

Godly friends are just the opposite. They join us in our common goal to please and obey God through our words and actions, have a healthy respect for the convictions we have purposed in our hearts, and encourage us draw closer to God's throne by growing stronger in Him.

We need to heed the warning of Scripture by taking an inventory of our friendships. Our associations will impact our affections, and if we are around people who don't seek the Lord first, then we probably won't either. These "friends" will be another idol that keeps us from seeking Jesus as we should. In contrast, it's a wonderful thing to have friends in this world who encourage and enable us to live for the world to come!

Two are better than one . . . For if they fall, one will lift up his companion. (Ecclesiastes 4:9–10 NKJV)

How many godly friendships do you have in your life?

What are some changes you need to make regarding those whom you call friends?

ACCEPTANCE
DAY 136

Blessed be the God and Father of our Lord Jesus Christ, who has blessed us with every spiritual blessing in the heavenly places in Christ . . . to the praise of the glory of His grace, by which He has made us accepted in the Beloved. (Ephesians 1:3–6 NKJV)

All of us desire acceptance. From the young woman who settles for the abusive boyfriend to the college freshman who does anything to become a fraternity member, we are willing to make amazing sacrifices to gain acceptance from others. The Bible teaches that we can find true acceptance from God by placing our faith in His beloved Son, Jesus Christ. Those of us who have taken this step can attest that Jesus provides a sense of acceptance that this world cannot.

Unfortunately, we sometimes forget that our acceptance is in Christ and we start looking for it elsewhere. This search becomes idolatry when it leads us away from the Lord's heart, and even the most seasoned Christians succumb to this idol.

At one point, the apostle Peter bowed down to the idol of acceptance. It happened when he was staying with the church in Antioch, which primarily consisted of non-Jews. As a believing Jew, Peter enjoyed fellowship with these Christians until a group of Judaizers came to Antioch. With them, they brought their own brand of Christianity that included Jewish traditions and customs that appealed to Peter. In an effort to be accepted by these Judaizers, he began to distance himself from the rest of the church. In the process, he began to distort the unconditional acceptance found in Christ. When Paul came to Antioch, he saw how Peter had been misrepresenting God's grace and called him on the carpet for putting his quest for human acceptance above the One who accepts all believers equally (Galatians 2:11–13).

From whom do we derive our sense of acceptance? If it's from the people in this world, acceptance will become an idol that takes God's place in our lives, but if we constantly remind ourselves that our acceptance is found in Christ, we will steer clear of this subtle snare.

At what point does a desire to be accepted become idolatry?

From whom do you derive your sense of acceptance?

UNBELIEF

Now with whom was He angry forty years? Was it not with those who sinned, whose corpses fell in the wilderness? And to whom did He swear that they would not enter His rest, but to those who did not obey? So we see that they could not enter in because of unbelief. (Hebrews 3:17–19 NKJV)

A lot of spiritual lessons can be learned from the Israelites' example. No group of people ever had greater reasons to believe God, yet they didn't. Despite the prolific outpouring of miracles in Egypt, the parting of the Red Sea, the provision of manna, and the thunder and lightning on Mount Sinai, they failed to believe God's promise that He would give them victory in the Promised Land. Their unbelief made it impossible for them to enter into the inheritance that had been provided for them, and the Lord waited for this entire generation to die before He fulfilled His promise.

Their unbelief became an idol, which resulted in spiritual separation from the true and living God. Our unbelief may not be as significant as Israel's, but we need to recognize that it still has the effect of damaging our relationship with God. He is never blessed by an unbelieving attitude, and it will always bring about a breach in our relationship with Him. Scripture reveals this truth to us by declaring that it is impossible to please God apart from faith (Hebrews 11:6).

If we want our lives to please the Lord, we need to be free from the idol of unbelief. This means we need to **receive** all that He has declared as being true. It also means that we sanction our trust in His truths by **applying** them in our lives. It is not enough to believe that God will bring us into the Promised Land of spiritual victory; we must also step out in faith.

The more we walk by faith, the less we will bow down to the idol of unbelief. Let's learn from Israel's example and believe God for all that He has promised.

What areas of unbelief do you struggle with?

How should you perceive unbelief, and how will this help you to deal with it?

Professing to be wise, they became fools, and changed the glory of the incorruptible God into an image made like corruptible man; and birds and four-footed animals and creeping things. (Romans 1:22–23 NKJV)

From the dawn of time, people have been bowing down before the idol of their own intellect. Professing to be wise, they foolishly fall into a form of idolatry that isolates them from the all-knowing God. Whether this is expressed through the idolatrous statues of antiquity or the more modern theory of evolution, this idol has trained people to believe that all reality must be subject to the limitations of their own intellect. Therefore, when it comes to God, He, too, must be subject to their understanding in order for Him to be true.

When Paul traveled to Athens in Acts 17, he was immediately struck by the number of idols that dotted the city's landscape. At that time, it was said that there were more idols than citizens in Athens, which would have amounted to about a quarter of a million! All these idols were by-products of man's intellect, except for one dedicated TO THE UNKNOWN GOD.

Seizing the opportunity to proclaim the Gospel, Paul began to preach to the intellectual elite in Athens about the transcendent God who sent His Son to die in order to provide salvation for man. When he started to share about Christ's resurrection from the dead, they couldn't believe what they were hearing and responded by mocking him. They reacted this way because their hearts were already bowed to their intellect, and in their minds, a God who didn't operate within their limited understanding wasn't worth believing.

We are made in God's image, not vice versa. When we try to impose our intellect on Him, we fall into the idolatry that has taken countless souls captive over the centuries. When we can't understand God's ways, let's be smart enough to submit our intellect to His omniscience, knowing that His thoughts and ways are infinitely above our own (Isaiah 55:8–9).

When has your intellect gotten in the way of your relationship with God?

What would you say to people who idolize their own intellect?

"God resists the proud, But gives grace to the humble." (1 Peter 5:5 NKJV)

The idol of pride towers above all other forms of idolatry. Pride not only is the foundation for many other types of idolatry, but severs us from the Lord's presence quicker than anything else. As the verse above states, God resists those who worship this idol.

This was the painful lesson that Nebuchadnezzar learned firsthand. At the time of his rule as the king of Babylon, he was the most powerful person on the planet. His kingdom had conquered the known world, and nobody within the foreseeable future posed the slightest threat to him—except himself. In the deepest dwelling place of his heart, the idol of pride had taken root and begun to rise. It continued to ascend until one day as he gloated over the glory of Babylon, he praised himself by saying:

Is not this great Babylon, that I have built for a royal dwelling by my mighty power and for the honor of my majesty?" (Daniel 4:30 NKJV)

Before the words were even out of Nebuchadnezzar's mouth, God proclaimed that he not only would lose his kingdom but also would be humbled to the point of acting like an animal for seven years. As is always the case, the word of the Lord was fulfilled, and at the end of his seven years, Nebuchadnezzar had a different perspective on his pride:

"Now I, Nebuchadnezzar, praise and extol and honor the King of heaven, all of whose works are truth, and His ways justice. And those who walk in pride He is able to put down." (Daniel 4:37 NKJV)

God will do whatever it takes to break out devotion to pride. We don't need to be as powerful as Nebuchadnezzar to fall into this form of idolatry. Pride can turn the smallest things into the biggest obstacles in our walk with God. The power to prevent pride comes to us only when we humbly confess our own weaknesses and insufficiencies.

What causes you pride, and how should you handle it?

What are some other idols that are based on pride?

LUST
DAY 140

The righteousness of the upright will deliver them, But the unfaithful will be caught by their <u>lust</u>. (Proverbs 11:6 NKJV)

No list of idols would be complete without lust. As we look around us today, no other form of idolatry seems to be more celebrated and flaunted than lust. And this idol doesn't just claim victims who are on the "fringe" with God. As David's life shows, lust is capable of capturing those who have experienced incredible intimacy with the Lord.

David's life is a spiritual benchmark in the Old Testament. The kings that followed in his footsteps were measured according to how closely they matched up to him. God's Word pays David the rarest compliment by declaring that he was a man after God's own heart (1 Samuel 13:14). His faith in confronting Goliath is unparalleled; his passion for worship, unsurpassed. Yet, despite all this, there was an opening in David's heart for lust to come in and assert itself above the Lord:

Then it happened one evening that David arose from his bed and walked on the roof of the king's house. And from the roof he saw a woman bathing, and the woman was very beautiful to behold. . . . Then David sent messengers, and took her; and she came to him, and he lay with her . . . . (2 Samuel 11:2, 4 NKJV)

From this point forward, David began to drift further and further from the One who had faithfully shepherded him through life. He became so fixated upon his idol that the Spirit's voice became more and more distant to him. Eventually, God had to speak to David through the prophet Nathan (2 Samuel 12:1). What followed was a time of repentance and restoration, but the ripple effects of David's idolatry continued to affect him and his family.

In an age when the enticements toward lust are unrelenting, we need to be particularly vigilant in guarding ourselves against it. When lust becomes our focus, we will dangerously drift away from God like David did. If we seek Him first, we can ensure our safety against this insidious form of idolatry.

What can you learn from David's example?

What would you share with another believer who is struggling with lust?

GRUDGES

"Therefore if you bring your gift to the altar, and there remember that your brother has something against you, leave your gift there before the altar, and go your way. First be reconciled to your brother, and then come and offer your gift." (Matthew 5:23–24 NKJV)

In the midst of His immortal Sermon on the Mount, Jesus provides a prescription for a problem that has the potential to make idolaters out of us all. He describes a scenario where a man goes to offer a gift to the Lord in the temple, but in the act of bringing his offering, he remembers there is a relationship with a brother that requires reconciliation. Jesus goes on to say that in such cases, one must leave the offering and make the necessary reconciliation before the gift is acceptable to God.

The essential truth of this passage is that our relationships with others have a direct bearing on our relationship with the Lord. We cannot be wrong with others and be right with God. Notice that Jesus puts the onus on us to pursue reconciliation even if someone is guilty of holding a grudge against us. This may seem like a tall order until we remember that we are called to live as brothers and sisters; we wouldn't want someone's grudge against us to be a stumbling block in his or her life. Instead, as Christians, we need to forgive those who have wronged us and humbly seek forgiveness from those whom we may have wronged. Harboring grudges against others and allowing others to harbor grudges against us is inconsistent with what Jesus taught and with how we ought to live as His disciples.

We can stubbornly ignore Christ's words and try to plow ahead in our walk with the Lord, but we really won't get anywhere. God will peer past our offerings and see the idolatrous grudges that are inhibiting our growth in Him. Grudges simply are not worth the spiritual price tag they carry. May God's Spirit search our hearts and reveal any grudges that require reconciliation, and may He give us the strength to make those reconciliations.

Do you have any grudges in your life? Why is it so important to deal with them?

What price do you pay for hanging on to a grudge?

SERVICE
DAY 142

He entered a certain village; and a certain woman named Martha welcomed Him into her house. And she had a sister called Mary, who also sat at Jesus' feet and heard His word. But Martha was <u>distracted with much serving</u>, and she approached Him and said, "Lord, do You not care that my sister has left me to serve alone? Therefore tell her to help me." (Luke 10:38–40 NKJV)

One of the more covert forms of idolatry is spiritual service. As unbelievable as it may sound, it is actually possible for us to become so caught up in serving the Lord that it distracts us from Him. What began as an expression of love toward Jesus can become an idol that turns us away from Him.

There's a perfect portrait of this in the passage above. When Jesus came to a village, He and His disciples were welcomed into the home of a woman named Martha. Being a good hostess, she busily went about serving her guests. She soon became aware that her sister, Mary, wasn't helping her serve. Instead, Mary was at the feet of Jesus, listening intently to His words. Filled with frustration, Martha asked Jesus to tell Mary to get up and give her a hand. The Lord's response is quite amazing:

And Jesus answered and said to her, "Martha, Martha, you are worried and troubled about many things. But one thing is needed, and Mary has chosen that good part, which will not be taken away from her." (Luke 10:41–42 NKJV)

Serving the Lord should be part of every believer's life. But according to Jesus, spending time in His presence takes priority over serving Him. Spiritual service will soon turn unspiritual if we aren't being constantly refreshed by our Savior. When we grow *distracted with much serving,* we will be tempted to look around and resent those who aren't as busy as we are.

It is easier to be busy than to be still. We need to make sure our service for the Lord is balanced with being still before Him because idolatry cannot penetrate the quiet moments spent in His presence.

How much time to do you spend in God's presence, and how does it compare to the time you spend serving Him?

How can you increase the time you spend quiet before the Lord?

SPIRITUALITY
DAY 143

How is it then, brethren? Whenever you come together, each of you has a psalm, has a teaching, has a tongue, has a revelation, has an interpretation. Let all things be done for edification. (1 Corinthians 14:26 NKJV)

The church of Corinth was an amazing collection of contradictions. On one hand, they had the most dynamic demonstration of spiritual gifts recorded in the Bible. On the other hand, they had the most dysfunctional situation ever encountered in Scripture. How could a group of men and women who were so vested with the gifts of the Holy Spirit be so ungodly in their exercise of those gifts?

It comes as no surprise that the reason behind this confusing contradiction was idolatry. The Corinthians were placing more importance on spiritual experiences than on the Lord. The gifts had dethroned the Giver, and a predictable pattern of idolatry started to unfold in Corinth.

Selfishness crept into their gatherings, and soon people were using their gifts while disregarding others in the fellowship and their gifts. In time, contentions erupted because people weren't getting their turn to "be spiritual." Pride had gained a foothold, providing the occasion for spiritual grandstanding. A sense of order was lost, and spiritual gifts were being demonstrated all at once—but nobody was being edified. This was symptomatic of the fact that they had strayed from God and His governing presence over their spiritual gifts. If they had kept the Lord first, their spiritual experiences would have been truly spiritual.

The idol of spirituality looms large to this day. We, too, can exalt the manifestations of the Spirit to such a level that they transform into a type of idolatry. When this happens, God is neglected, the body of Christ is not edified, and the world looks on and is either amused or confused by our foolishness. In order to keep our spirituality spiritual, we must stay centered on the Giver rather than the gifts.

What ought to be your first priority when using your spiritual gifts?

Are you guilty of spiritual idolatry? If so, how will you put an end to it?

STUDY

"You search the Scriptures, for in them you think you have eternal life; and these are they which testify of Me." (John 5:39 NKJV)

The Pharisees of Jesus' day had elevated the study of the Scriptures to an art form. Each day they would spend hours poring over the minutest details of the Old Testament. Endless debates would ensue over the exact nuance of a certain word. Sadly, they were so consumed by their study of the Scriptures that they were unable to recognize the One whom the Scriptures had been pointing to all along. Study had become an idol that commanded their full attention, and in their preoccupation with the Word of God, they grew ignorant of the God of the Word.

The temptation to do this is just as strong today. Perhaps it's even stronger because we have much more to study. We have not only received the New Testament, but also are the beneficiaries of the invention of the printing press. Computers provide us with endless opportunities to search and study the finer points of Bible doctrine. It is very easy to study about God without ever taking the time to know Him. When we're seduced away from the Lord by the study of Him, we become guilty of idolatry.

C. H. Mackintosh once warned, "It is not life eternal to know theology or divinity. A man may sit down to the study of these, as he would study law or medicine, astronomy or geology, and all the while know nothing of God, and therefore be without divine life, and perish in the end." The study of God's Word is important, but it is not an end unto itself. It is a means to the greater end of having a personal relationship with God. If we're more enthusiastic about filling our bookcases and our brains with an academic knowledge of God than about cultivating our relationship with Him, then we are well-disguised idol worshipers at best. Let's be faithful to search the Scriptures in a way that exalts the Author above anything else.

Why isn't studying the Bible an end unto itself? What is it?

How much time do you spend studying about God versus time you spend with God?

So <u>rend your heart, and not your garments;</u> Return to the LORD your God, For He is gracious and merciful, Slow to anger, and of great kindness; And He relents from doing harm. (Joel 2:13 NKJV)

We don't use the word *piety* much these days. Many of us probably aren't even aware of its definition, which is "the dutiful demonstration of religious obligations." In other words, piety is the external evidences of the internal operation of God's Spirit. A life that's lined up with God should have a pious appearance. Unfortunately, piety can also be a source of idolatry when it is sought above God.

In the days of the prophet Joel, the Israelites had slipped into a pattern of pretentious piety. They would frequently tear their clothes in a gesture that was intended to demonstrate their religious passion and devotion. Yet, behind the scenes, they were carrying on a long-distance relationship with God in their hearts. He saw past this and told them in the verse above that instead of tearing up their clothes, they should tear up their hearts, which had developed an idolatrous preoccupation with piety.

Jesus also addressed this insidious idol when He exhorted His listeners to steer clear of the pious hypocrisy of the Pharisees. Outwardly, they seemed so connected to God. They publicly prayed on the street corners, regularly gave vast amounts of their money to the poor, and even regularly fasted. These were all commendable acts of piety and should be incorporated into the walk of every believer, but in case of the Pharisees, they were not indications of a godly life; they merely had become distractions from God's rightful place in their lives (Matthew 6:1–18).

Outward piety can be an indication of either genuine spirituality or idolatry. The difference is determined by our motivations. If we simply want to "look the part" of a godly person, we can temporarily project this image through pious acts. However, in the process, we will lose out on enjoying fellowship with God, the true and proper catalyst for piety.

When have you done something pious out of an improper motive?

At what point does our piety become idolatry?

Little children, keep yourselves from idols. Amen. (1 John 5:21 NKJV)

The short five-chapter epistle of 1 John has been referred to as "the cliff notes for Christianity" because it covers all the essential elements of the Christian life. It deals with our need to confess our sinfulness (1:8), God's ability to cleanse us (1:9), Jesus' sacrificial death on the cross (2:2), our need to stay separate from the world (2:15), God's great love for us (3:1), our duty to love one another (4:7), and the assurance of eternal life for all who believe in Jesus as the Son of God (5:13). As the best books so often do, 1 John has a surprise ending. By the inspiration of the Holy Spirit, John ends his epistle by warning his readers to keep themselves from idols.

Most Bible scholars agree that the gospels indicate that John began following Jesus as a young man and that by the time he wrote this epistle, he was probably in his late eighties or early nineties. As he put his pen to parchment, John had the benefit of being well aged in his walk with God. He had witnessed the gamut of besetting sins and stumbling blocks that had caused many to depart from the faith over the years. As the tethers to these sins were traced, they had a common source—idolatry. It is the sin that nobody thinks they have, yet everybody does to some degree. John's admonition couldn't be more relevant.

The warning against idols is also an exhortation to make the Lord your primary pursuit. All that you think, say, and do should be screened through this filtering question: how does this impact my relationship with the Lord? Your life should always be striving *to know Him,* first and foremost (Philippians 3:10). Anything that gets in the way of this will spiritually sabotage you. Starting today, make the daily commitment not only to keep yourself from idols, but also to dedicate every moment of your God-given life to knowing Him better.

How have you been guilty of idolatry?

What is the best (and only) defense against idols? (Hint: read Matthew 6:33.)

Then God said, "Let Us make man in Our image, according to Our <u>likeness</u>." (Genesis 1:26 NKJV)

There's a common misconception that it is wrong to have emotions or to be emotional. This simply is not true. In fact, God is an emotional being. The Old Testament reveals that He feels grief (Genesis 6:6), jealousy (Exodus 20:5), and even anger (Ezekiel 5:13). In the New Testament, we see Jesus expressing the emotions of grief (John 11:35) and anger (John 2:15). We also find that the Holy Spirit is equally capable of being touched by these emotions (Ephesians 4:30). What would God's Word look like apart from emotions? We would be missing most of the psalms and the entire book of Lamentations. God places value on emotions, and He has created us with the capacity to feel them.

The Scripture above tells us that God formed man in His image and likeness. The image is the outward appearance, and the likeness is the inward essence. Likeness speaks of the internal capacity of God to know and express emotions. By being made in God's likeness, we reflect His capacity to have emotions. Unique from all other works of creation, only mankind can relate to God on the higher emotional level. A mighty mountain doesn't know what it is to lose an only son, and an ocean cannot understand what it means to fall in love. While animals come close, their elementary joy, shame, and other emotional-like reactions are not nearly as complex as ours, and many of their emotions can be easily attributed to instinct.

Emotions have an important place in God's plan for our lives, but we need to know their *proper* place. They aren't bad in and of themselves because they help us relate to and understand God. But they can become bad for us if we allow them to control and consume us. Instead, we must be led by the Holy Spirit:

If we live in the Spirit, let us also walk in the Spirit. Let us not become conceited, provoking one another, envying one another. (Galatians 5:25–26 NKJV)

If your emotions aren't submitted and surrendered to the Spirit, they will soon lead you outside of the Lord's will and into sinful territory. You have been created like Him. You must also behave like Him by staying in step with His Spirit.

What are some common misconceptions when it comes to emotions?

What is the value of having emotions, and what is the danger?

WHOM DO YOU FEAR?

The fear of man brings a snare. (Proverbs 29:25 NKJV)

Herod's life is a classic example of this biblical truth. In Matthew 14, we see this ruler being ruled by his fear of man. First, he imprisoned John the Baptist because of the pressure his wife, Herodias, put on him (v. 3). She wasn't going to be satisfied until John was dead. However, Herod wouldn't kill him because he also feared the multitude that believed John was a prophet (v. 5). In the end, Herod's fear finally led him to execute John because he was afraid of looking bad in front of his party guests (v. 9). Herod is a pathetic picture of what it means to be ensnared by the fear of man.

God knows how powerful the fear of man can be and how it will inevitably lead us to make terrible choices in our lives. For this reason, the Lord calls us to put our fear in Him instead.

"And do not fear those who kill the body but cannot kill the soul. But rather fear Him who is able to destroy both soul and body in hell." (Matthew 10:28 NKJV)

It's an amazing paradox, but fearing the Lord is actually a safeguard against fearing man. If God is our primary concern in life, then we won't worry about how others perceive and criticize us. All that matters at the end of the day is whether we have been pleasing to Him. One fear pushes out the other.

In and of itself, fear is not an evil emotion, but what and whom we invest our fear in will determine what our fear does to us. If our fear is in the Lord, it will lead to a healthy reverence that will serve as the basis for a relationship with Him that will grow and flourish. But if our fear is in man, it will obscure our view of God and mercilessly lead us from one bad choice to another. God is worthy of our fear; man isn't. We must learn from Herod's example and follow Jesus' instruction by placing our fear in the Lord—not man.

Whom are you more fearful of, God or man?

What can you do to cultivate more of a God-based fear in your life?

DAY 149

Then Judas . . . was remorseful . . . . and departed, and went and hanged himself.
(Matthew 27:3–5 NKJV)

So Peter went out and wept bitterly. (Luke 22:62 NKJV)

On the night before the crucifixion, Judas betrays Jesus for thirty pieces of silver and Peter publicly denies Him three times. Both of these men were experiencing an overwhelming sense of guilt.

But things start to change from there. Judas, whose heart was self-centered and closed-off to the working of God's Spirit, deals with his guilt on his own. This leads to a sense of condemnation. Ultimately and tragically, Judas could not handle the pressure and takes his own life. Peter, on the other hand, opens his heart to the Spirit of God, who brings him to the point of conviction. As we know, Peter responds to the Spirit's work and goes on to be an important part of the early church.

Condemnation is not of God. It shows people their shortcomings and sins but does not offer a solution. Conviction is different. It points out people's flaws but also offers a way of dealing with them through repentance. This enables them to move forward in life. Condemnation is a hopeless dead-end. Conviction is a path toward progress.

When we're feeling condemnation and can't bear the burden of our guilt, we need to open our hearts to the Lord and ask Him to take the weight of condemnation from us.

There is therefore now no condemnation to those who are in Christ Jesus, who do not walk according to the flesh, but according to the Spirit. (Romans 8:1 NKJV)

When we're feeling convicted and know that there's something God is calling us to do, we need to allow the convicting power of the Holy Spirit to lead us to do what's right.

"And when He [the Holy Spirit] has come, He will convict the world of sin, and of righteousness, and of judgment. (John 16:8 NKJV)

How would you explain the difference between condemnation and conviction?

What would you say to someone who is feeling condemned?

GOD'S LAW OF E-MOTIONS

DAY 150

Now there was a famine in the land, and Abram went down to Egypt to dwell there, for the famine was severe in the land. (Genesis 12:10 NKJV)

Everyone who has taken junior high science will instantly recognize Newton's Third Law of Motion: for every action, there is an equal and opposite reaction. Basically, this means that everything in the natural world has an effect on something else. This natural Law of Motion is also a Law of the E-Motions, for the Scriptures show us that our feelings don't just impact us but that they inevitably have an effect on those around us.

When Abram went down to Egypt to avoid the famine, it probably seemed like a reasonable thing to do. The only problem was that God had not called Abram to go to Egypt but to the land that he was already in (Genesis 12:1). Abram's feeling of fear led him to move outside of God's will for his life, and God's Law of E-Motions was set into motion. On this journey, Abram acquired an Egyptian servant girl named Hagar. Eventually, Abram's wife would suggest that he conceive a child with Hagar. This child was Ishmael, who would become the father of the Arab nations that would be in constant conflict with the children of Israel (Genesis 16:12). The conflict exists to this very day. God still loved Ishmael and continues to love his descendants (John 3:16), but Abram's fear has had a painful impact on millions of people for thousands of years.

How do we apply this Law of E-Motions to our lives? We may think that our feelings are personal and private. I'm sure Abram thought the same thing when he allowed fear to have the upper hand in his heart. But the truth is, our emotions will eventually have an effect on those around us, either good or bad. The key is in how we deal with them as they come to us. When we're feeling fearful, angry, depressed, etc., we shouldn't act upon these emotions in a way that will harm others. We should submit our feelings to the Lord and set an example of sacrificial trust for others to follow.

How have your feelings had a negative impact on others in the past?

How can you ensure that your feelings will have a positive impact on others in the future?

SYMPATHETIC SAVIOR
DAY 151

Jesus wept. (John 11:35 NKJV)

This is the shortest verse in the entire Bible, yet it contains a vast volume of profound truth. At first, the two words seem like an unlikely match. **Jesus**—the epitome of power and glory, the One who created the cosmos and absolutely everything in it (Colossians 1:16), the One who holds the keys to hell and death (Revelation 1:18), and the One to whom every knee will bow and every tongue will confess "Lord!" (Philippians 2:10–11)—**wept**.

In the original Greek, *wept* carries the meaning "to tear apart." It describes an emotional tearing that leaves one weakened and in pain. We've all wept at one point or another, and we know that it can bring deep vulnerability. Our defenses are down when we weep, and in a way, it is when we're at our weakest. How could these two words possibly be connected to one another?

They're connected because they describe the indescribable. The eternally infinite Christ, who is the source of all power and authority, is also vulnerable and susceptible to the power of emotion. The One whom death itself could not defeat . . . cries. This is incomprehensible when you consider the leaders of other world religions. They are always portrayed as untouchable and stoic. Not Jesus. He really and truly feels the same emotions as His followers.

We do not have a High Priest who cannot sympathize with our weaknesses.
(Hebrews 4:15 NKJV)

The fact that Jesus makes Himself vulnerable to emotions doesn't make Him any less of a man. It makes Him a real man in the sense that He can fully identify with the human experience. No one can tell Him that He doesn't know what it's like to lose a loved one. We serve a sympathetic Savior, and we can seek His help with confidence because we know He has personally experienced the power of emotion. We need to go to Him when we're hurting and when we're overwhelmed with feelings because nobody understands what we're going through better than Him.

What does it mean to you that "Jesus wept"?

Where else in Scripture do we see Jesus exhibit strong emotion?

A LOOK AT LUST
DAY 152

. . . looking unto Jesus, the author and finisher of our faith, who for the joy that was set before Him endured the cross, despising the shame, and has sat down at the right hand of the throne of God. (Hebrews 12:2 NKJV)

Let's take a look a lust. Upon close examination, a consistent pattern emerges in the Scriptures. Lust is preceded by the act of looking. From the very outset, even before mankind had committed its first sin, we see this pattern come into play:

So when the woman <u>saw</u> that the tree was good for food, that it was pleasant to the eyes, and a tree <u>desirable</u> to make one wise, she took of its fruit and ate. (Genesis 3:6 NKJV)

Eve looked at the forbidden fruit of the tree and then began to desire (or lust after) it. Before King David lusted after Bathsheba in his heart, he looked upon her with his eyes. As the Israelites began to take possession of the Promised Land, the Lord told them not to take any spoils from their victories. Achan sinned by hoarding some of the loot and as a result, destroyed his entire family. What led him to make such a bad decision? Achan tells us:

"When I <u>saw</u> among the spoils a beautiful Babylonian garment, two hundred shekels of silver, and a wedge of gold weighing fifty shekels, I <u>coveted</u> [lusted for] them and took them. And there they are, hidden in the earth in the midst of my tent, with the silver under it." (Joshua 7:21 NKJV)

Looking leads to lusting. And if lust is something you struggle with, you can be sure it is connected to the things you allow yourself to look at. This is actually good news because you have control over the things you choose to look at. Make the decision to look away from those things that lead you into lust. Turn your eyes upon Jesus, and He will be your supreme desire in life.

Be honest, what things do you allow yourself to look at that lead you into lust?

How will you cultivate a more disciplined "look life"?

LONELINESS IS AN ILLUSION
DAY 153

"I am with you <u>always</u>, even to the end of the age." Amen. (Matthew 28:20 NKJV)

"I will <u>never</u> leave you nor forsake you." (Hebrews 13:5 NKJV)

Could the Bible make itself any clearer on this point? The Holy Spirit deliberately uses the definitive words *always* and *never* to drive a very important truth into our hearts. If you are a believer in Jesus Christ, He is *always* present and *never* absent in your life. As a human being, you are bound to feel lonely from time to time, but the fact of the matter is that you never really are. Loneliness is an emotion you cannot trust because it ultimately is not true.

Look at the long list of proofs that God has given to us. Moses was on the backside of the desert, yet the Lord appeared to him (Exodus 3:1–2). Elijah hid in a deserted cave, yet the Lord was there to meet him (1 Kings 19:9). Paul was put in solitary confinement, yet the Lord stood beside him (Acts 23:10–11). John was banished to the island of Patmos, yet the Lord revealed Himself to him (Revelation 1:9–10). Even as Jonah was in the stomach of the great fish, the Lord was with him (Jonah 2:10). If there is anything we can rely on in this life, it's that our sense of loneliness in this world is really an illusion. The Lord is always there, and He is always waiting for us to find our fulfillment in Him. F. B. Meyer once said, "Loneliness is an opportunity for Jesus to make Himself known to us."

Loneliness is something we will all experience at some point in our lives. If we're not dealing with loneliness now, we eventually will. In those times, we need to remind ourselves that loneliness is an illusion because, no matter where we go, the Lord has promised that He is always with us.

Where can I go from Your Spirit? Or where can I flee from Your presence? (Psalm 139:7 NKJV)

Why is the emotion of loneliness ultimately an illusion for Christians?

When has God personally shown you that your sense of loneliness is an illusion?

Stir up the gift of God which is in you . . . . God has not given us a spirit of fear . . . . Do not be ashamed of the testimony of our Lord . . . . (2 Timothy 1:6–8 NKJV)

As Paul begins his second letter to Timothy, he gives some very direct exhortations to his young protégé. If we read between the lines, we see that Timothy was intimidated from using his spiritual gift of teaching, was often fearful, and was even ashamed of the Gospel message. Timothy struggled with timidity, which is the emotional reaction to one's own shortcomings or inabilities.

As a young man, Timothy was probably prone to comparing his life experience to those whom he was entrusted to pastor (1 Timothy 4:12). Having less experience, he thought of himself as having less authority and worth. Paul's remedy for Timothy's timidity was to point him away from himself and toward God.

Share with me in the sufferings for the gospel according to the <u>power of God</u>, who has <u>saved</u> us and <u>called</u> us with a holy calling, not according to our works, but according to His own <u>purpose</u> and <u>grace</u> which was given to us in Christ Jesus <u>before time began</u>. (2 Timothy 1:8–9 NKJV)

Paul reminded Timothy that it wasn't about him but about the Lord's infinite resources. He could trust in God for strength, salvation, confidence in his calling, purpose, grace, and equipping. And, Paul reminded Timothy that God had determined to bestow all this in accordance with His eternal plan; it was not a mistake!

When you view yourself in light of your own weaknesses and inabilities, you will grow timid. But when you take the focus off yourself and simply see yourself as an extension of the infinite resources of an eternal God, you will have the boldness and confidence only He can give.

In what ways can you relate to Timothy's timidity?

How does self-centeredness contribute to timidity?

WHY WORRY?

DAY 155

"Therefore I say to you, <u>do not worry</u> about your life . . . " (Matthew 6:25 NKJV)

The same God who commands us not to murder, lie, and steal also orders us, with equal force and authority, not to worry. This is a tough one because these other sins are external acts while worry is an internal emotion. Worry comes so naturally to us that we often don't even realize we're doing it. The weight of worry can crush us, and if we hope to avoid this, we must make a habit of doing two things.

First, we must focus on **the faithfulness of God**. Worry is attached to a fearful uncertainty of the future, and when we worry, we're actually calling God's future faithfulness into question. Yet, if anything can be established from Scripture, it's that God is always faithful to His people. In fact, the Bible declares that it is impossible for Him to be unfaithful (2 Timothy 2:13). When do we ever see Jesus worried or questioning the faithfulness of the Father? When has God ever given us a reason to have the slightest doubt in His faithfulness? C. H. Mackintosh once observed, "Ten thousand mercies are so quickly forgotten in the face of a single difficulty." God's faithfulness in our past warrants our present trust in Him for our future.

"And you know in all your hearts and in all your souls that not one thing has failed of all the good things which the LORD your God spoke concerning you. All have come to pass for you; not one word of them has failed." (Joshua 23:14 NKJV)

Second, we need to focus on **the needs of others**. Self-centeredness is a catalyst for worry. It's amazing how quickly we forget about our own worries when we turn our attention to others. God's provision for what we worry about is often found as we help others. Don't forget that each disciples was left with a basketful of bread *after* they had served the multitudes (John 6:13).

What's got you worried, and how does God want you to deal with it?

What other emotions are connected to worry?

"This is John the Baptist; he is risen from the dead, and therefore these powers are at work in him." (Matthew 14:2 NKJV)

Herod was ruled by fear. Fear led him to imprison John the Baptist, and it also led him to kill him in horrific fashion. But it's interesting that months after the deed was done, Herod is still afraid of John. As he hears about the miraculous ministry of Christ, he rushes to the conclusion, *"This is John."* Herod's fear had led to a deep sense of guilt that wasn't about to go away. This shows us something very important about our emotions—they are closely interconnected. If we allow one emotion to have control over us, we can be sure it is going to set off a chain reaction of other emotions.

This happened to Ananias in Acts, chapter 5. He held back a portion of what he had committed to God because he had allowed greed to wedge its foot in the doorway of his heart. But he knew it was wrong, so his greed gave way to guilt for what he had done. This guilt led him to fear being found out, so he lied about the amount he had originally given. His fear was part of a chain of emotions that ultimately led to his premature death.

Our emotions are interconnected, and they feed off each another. This is why we have to keep them in check and resist the temptation to place our trust in them. Here's how to break the emotional chain reaction once it begins in our hearts. First, we must **recognize** when our emotions have taken over. Failure to recognize the problem is preparation for even greater problems. Once we recognize the problem, it enables us to **repent** for harboring certain emotions in our hearts. We need to be honest with the Lord about our weaknesses. Finally, we need to **request** spiritual assistance from the Lord. Left to ourselves, we're prone to make the same mistakes as Herod and Ananias. But in asking for the Lord's help, we can be sure that the emotional chain reaction will be broken.

What chain of emotions do you consistently see in your life?

Do some extra research. What eventually happened to Herod and Ananias?

GRAPPLING WITH GRIEF

DAY 157

So Sarah died. (Genesis 23:2 NKJV)

Grief touches all of us sooner or later; it's simply part and parcel with the human experience, and we shouldn't rush to find a "quick fix" for it (Ecclesiastes 3:4). But there is a right way to grieve, and Isaac shows us how to do this.

And Isaac went out to meditate in the field in the evening. (Genesis 24:63 NKJV)

In the midst of his mourning, Isaac meditated. The word *meditate* means "to rehearse," "to go over a matter," and "to deliberately ponder and reflect on something." And the phrase *in the evening* implies that this was a regular practice for him. The key to grappling with grief is to do as Isaac did and maintain continual communion with the Lord by meditating upon Him. If we don't focus on Jesus as we grieve, this emotion can quickly become a portal leading to guilt, bitterness, and even depression. But look what happened as Isaac meditated on the Lord.

He lifted his eyes and looked, and there, the camels were coming. Then Rebekah lifted her eyes, and when she saw Isaac she dismounted from her camel; for she had said to the servant, "Who is this man walking in the field to meet us?" The servant said, "It is my master." So she took a veil and covered herself. And the servant told Isaac all the things that he had done. Then Isaac brought her into his mother Sarah's tent; and he took Rebekah and she became his wife, and he loved her. So Isaac was comforted after his mother's death. (Genesis 24:63–67 NKJV)

Notice that it was in Isaac's time of meditation that he also discovered the Lord's provision for his grief. When we're faced with the loss of a loved one and the time comes for us to grapple with grief, we too will find God's provision of comfort as we set the time aside to meditate on Him.

Blessed are those who mourn, For they shall be comforted. (Matthew 5:4 NKJV)

What should your response to grief be?

What would you say to someone who is having a hard time dealing with grief?

THE SHAME GAME

Then the LORD God called to Adam and said to him, "Where are you?" So he said, "I heard Your voice in the garden, and I was afraid because I was naked; and I hid myself." (Genesis 3:9–10 NKJV)

This is the first time we see shame expressed in the Bible. It comes immediately after Adam and Eve sinned by eating the forbidden fruit. Through sin, they lost their innocence and were instantly aware of their nakedness. Shame works the same way in our lives. As sinners, we're know we're flawed and imperfect. We hide from God because deep down we know that we're not right. Just like our forefather, Adam, we play the shame game with God.

Shame is healthy to a certain degree because it shows us we are sinners. But God does not want us to *stay* ashamed before Him, and He proves this in His response to Adam and Eve's shame:

Also for Adam and his wife the LORD God made tunics of skin, and clothed them. (Genesis 3:21 NKJV)

God graciously covered Adam and Eve's nakedness, which was the cause of their shame. And He has done the same for you and me. All our sins, our spiritual nakedness, if you will, have been covered by the righteousness of Jesus Christ (Revelation 3:5; 19:8). If you're a Christian, you have no grounds for feeling ashamed before God because He sees you perfect and complete in Christ.

. . . to reconcile all things to Himself, by Him, whether things on earth or things in heaven, having made peace through the blood of His cross. . . . to present you holy, and blameless, and above reproach in His sight . . . . (Colossians 1:20–22 NKJV)

Shame is not to be trusted because it tells us that God doesn't want us when, in reality, He does. In fact, He has graciously gone out of His way to make us unashamed by giving us His Son. Be secure in the knowledge that you are covered in Jesus' righteousness and that there is no need to play the shame game with God.

"He who believes on Him will by no means be put to shame." (1 Peter 2:6 NKJV)

Why is it unhealthy to live with a sense of shame?

How has shame affected your relationship with God and other people?

"For I always do those things that please <u>Him</u>." (John 8:29 NKJV)

In all things, Jesus is our perfect example, even when it comes to dealing with guilt. There were a couple of occasions where people tried to place a guilt trip on Jesus in an effort to get Him to do something. The way He deals with this is powerful in showing us how we can get rid of guilt.

At a wedding feast in Cana, Jesus' mother drew His attention to the fact that the wine had run out and that the celebration was about to come to an abrupt end. Perhaps Mary's family was giving the wedding feast, and she wanted to avoid the disgrace of a wine shortage, or maybe Mary wanted to use this as an opportunity for Jesus to publicly demonstrate His power, thus vindicating her reputation. Whatever the reason, Mary seemed to play the guilt card: *"They have no wine" (John 2:3 NKJV).* Jesus miraculously met the need but only after He drew her attention to the fact that His hour had not yet come (John 2:4 NKJV). This was another way of saying that His Father's divine timeline was His first consideration.

Later on Jesus was pursued by a multitude that He had miraculously fed by multiplying bread and fish. They finally cornered Him and in a not-so-subtle way asked Him to feed them again: *"Lord, give us this bread always" (John 6:34 NKJV).* A lesser man would have bowed to the pressure of a multitude asking for food. But Jesus knew they were asking for the wrong reasons, and He refused to respond out of guilt. Instead, He told them that He hadn't come to do His own will, but the will of His Father who had sent Him (John 6:38 NKJV).

Jesus never acted or responded out of a sense of guilt. Instead, He allowed His Father's will to determine what He would do and when He would do it. The next time you feel obligated to do something out of guilt, remember Jesus' example. And before you act, pray and evaluate if it's the Father's will. If it's not, then you shouldn't be moved by the guilt trip.

When have you allowed yourself to be manipulated by guilt?

How can you apply Jesus' example to the way you respond to guilt?

Then Jesus came with them to a place called Gethsemane, and said to the disciples, "Sit here while I go and pray over there." And He took with Him Peter and the two sons of Zebedee, and He began to be <u>sorrowful and deeply distressed</u>. Then He said to them, "My soul is exceedingly sorrowful, even to death. Stay here and watch with Me." (Matthew 26:36–38 NKJV)

This is the one time in Christ's life when we see the slightest hint of fear. Fear by itself is not sin, but the way we respond to it can become sin. Jesus did not allow His fear of enduring God's wrath to lead Him into sin (1 John 3:5), but He responded the way we all need to respond whenever we face a fearful situation:

He went a little farther and fell on His face, and prayed, saying, "O My Father, if it is possible, let this cup pass from Me; nevertheless, not as I will, but as You will." (Matthew 26:39 NKJV)

Jesus does three things here that we need to emulate. First, Jesus *went a little farther*, meaning He separated Himself from Peter, James, and John. When fear hits us, the first thing we need to do is get alone with God. Getting together with others can be a great blessing, but it can also be a distraction from fellowshiping with the One we need to meet with the most. Second, Jesus *fell on His face, and prayed*. It is impossible to overestimate the importance of prayer in the Christian life. We simply cannot experience a relationship with God without prayer, and Jesus showed us that it is indispensable when it comes to facing our fears. Last, He said, *"Not as I will, but as You will."* Christ's statement expressed His complete trust in His Father's loving wisdom (which would only allow Him to do what was right and best) and in His Father's ability to control all things.

The next time you're feeling fearful, you need to get alone with God. As you open your heart in prayer to Him, remember that He is in complete control and that He will only allow what will ultimately be best for you.

How will Jesus' example affect the way you deal with your fears?

Whom do you know who needs to know this?

Therefore, my beloved brethren, be steadfast, immovable, always abounding in the work of the Lord, knowing that your labor is not in vain in the Lord. (1 Corinthians 15:58 NKJV)

Our emotions constantly change on us. A strong feeling can turn 180 degrees in an instant. David's son, Amnon, serves as a classic example of this. He desperately desired his half-sister, Tamar, and lured her into his bedroom by feigning a sickness. Driven by his desire, Amnon suddenly grabbed her and made his intentions known. You can sense the desperation in Tamar's protest:

"No, my brother, do not force me, for no such thing should be done in Israel. Do not do this disgraceful thing! . . However, he would not heed her voice; and being stronger than she, he forced her and lay with her. (2 Samuel 13:12–14 NKJV)

Amnon impulsively acted on his lustful passion for Tamar, and take careful notice of his emotional reaction toward her after he got what he wanted.

Then Amnon hated her exceedingly, so that the hatred with which he hated her was greater than the love with which he had loved her! And Amnon said to her, "Arise, be gone!" (2 Samuel 13:15 NKJV)

What a dramatic swing of emotions! Amnon's desire turned into disgust, and the one he couldn't stand to be without became someone he couldn't stand to be with. Emotions are so quick to change with the circumstances of life. They are shifty and unstable, and the same can be said of people who place their trust in them. For this reason, we need to trust in something permanent, sure, and fixed.

The entirety of Your word is truth, And every one of Your righteous judgments endures forever. (Psalm 119:160 NKJV)

Unlike our emotions, God's Word never changes (Matthew 5:18; Luke 21:33). This is valuable because the Bible is constant and consistent when our emotions are shifting. We shouldn't let the instability of our emotions characterize our lives. Instead, we need to allow the Scriptures to serve as the stabilizing force in all that we experience and encounter.

What does an unstable life indicate?

How would you explain the advantages of living by the Bible to another person?

FEELINGS VS. FACTS
DAY 162

Likewise you also, <u>reckon</u> yourselves to be dead indeed to sin, but alive to God in Christ Jesus our Lord. (Romans 6:11 NKJV)

Our emotions have the potential to dictate reality to us. We can assume that something is either true or false based on the way we feel toward it. Unfortunately, many Christians allow their emotions to dictate reality to them in the crucial area of their salvation.

The Bible never tells us that we are saved according to our feelings. But we are told over and over that our salvation is based on our faith in certain facts. In the verse above, the apostle Paul tells us to *reckon* ourselves dead to sin and alive to God. The word *reckon* is critical. It does not refer to a feeling or an emotional sensation. It is a mathematical term that means "to count upon something as being factual." We reckon that 2 + 2 = 4 because we know that it is factually true.

If you're a Christian, you should place your faith in the absolute fact that you are dead to sin and alive to God. There may be times when we don't feel this, but, again, feelings don't determine reality. You are not saved on feelings; you are saved based on absolute facts. FACT: You are a sinner. FACT: Jesus Christ died on the cross to save sinners. FACT: If you confess with a sincere heart that Jesus is Lord and believe that God raised Him from the dead, you will be saved. FACT: If you are in Christ, you are a new creation. J. Oswald Sanders once commented, "When we count on this fact, it becomes true in experience."

It feels like a bad thing whenever I receive a shot from the doctor, but the fact is that the injection is good for me in the long run. Don't allow your feelings to obscure the facts. If you have placed your faith in Christ, you belong to Him and are safe in His keeping.

"My sheep hear My voice, and I know them, and they follow Me. And I give them eternal life, and they shall never perish; neither shall anyone snatch them out of My hand." (John 10:27–28 NKJV)

When have your feelings obscured the facts?

How can you know that you are saved?

PROMISES YOU CAN TRUST

And the Philistine said, "I defy the armies of Israel this day; give me a man, that we may fight together." When Saul and all Israel heard these words of the Philistine, they were dismayed and greatly afraid. (1 Samuel 17:10–11 NKJV)

The soldiers of Israel had made the decision to put their trust in their fear of Goliath. As a result, he went unchallenged for forty days. But along came David, who didn't trust in his feelings but in the promises of God.

"Who is this uncircumcised Philistine, that he should defy the armies of the living God?" (1 Samuel 17:26 NKJV)

David knew that God had promised to be on Israel's side and that defeat was not an option. Their adversary was an uncircumcised Philistine, a man outside of the covenant relationship Israel had with the living God. Goliath wasn't just an enemy of Israel but of God Himself. David's confidence to defeat Goliath was never based on how he felt but on what he knew concerning God's promises. Notice the outcome:

So David prevailed over the Philistine with a sling and a stone, and struck the Philistine and killed him. (1 Samuel 17:50 NKJV)

Victory was the result of a single man who chose to trust in God's promises. But as long as the Israelites trusted in their feelings, they would never taste victory. In a similar sense, many Christians never taste spiritual victory because they have chosen to trust in their feelings, rather than God's promises. They never *feel* like serving others, so they don't, despite the promised blessing when we serve (John 13:17). They never *feel* like sharing the Gospel message, so they don't, despite the promised blessing when we share (Romans 10:15). They never *feel* like studying the Scriptures, so they don't, despite the promised blessing when we study (Psalm 1:1–3).

Those who trust in their feelings above God's promises will never experience spiritual victory. We need to know the promises of God concerning us and place our total trust in them.

How many of God's promises for you can you list?

How can you create a greater day-to-day awareness of these promises?

DISCOURAGEMENT'S DECEPTION

And Jacob their father said to them, "You have bereaved me: Joseph is no more, Simeon is no more, and you want to take Benjamin. <u>All these things are against me</u>." (Genesis 42:36 NKJV)

Jacob had been through some trying times. His son Joseph had been lost years earlier, his son Simeon was being held captive in Egypt, and now he faced the prospect of losing his favorite son Benjamin. It certainly seemed like everything in life, including God, was conspiring against this man, and his discouragement rises to the surface of his soul as he cries, *"All these things are against me."*

In reality, nothing was further from the truth. God was not against Jacob but was actually working on his behalf. Joseph hadn't died, but the Lord had sent him into Egypt to secure provision and protection for his family's future. Simeon's separation was only temporary, and Benjamin would return in just a couple of weeks. All this was just around the corner, but discouragement had blinded Jacob to everything that he had previously learned about his God—that He is merciful, gracious, and, above all else, for and not against him (Genesis 28:15).

Discouragement can do the same thing to us if we allow it to blind us to what we know to be true of God. When you're feeling discouraged like Jacob, remember that God is always working on your behalf; that no matter how bad the story seems, it isn't over; and that the end of a matter is better than the beginning. Take some time today to dwell on the following Scriptures and allow them to reinforce the fact that God is good and that He is for you.

For I know the thoughts that I think toward you, says the LORD, thoughts of peace and not of evil, to give you a future and a hope. (Jeremiah 29:11 NKJV)

And we know that all things work together for good to those who love God, to those who are the called according to His purpose. (Romans 8:28 NKJV)

What then shall we say to these things? If God is for us, who can be against us? (Romans 8:31 NKJV)

What does the Lord want you to do when you're feeling discouraged?

What would you say to someone who is in the depths of discouragement?

This is a faithful saying and worthy of all acceptance, that Christ Jesus came into the world to save sinners, <u>of whom I am chief</u>. (1 Timothy 1:15 NKJV)

The apostle Paul isn't exaggerating here. We tend to forget the kind of sin he brought to the cross. Before becoming the most prolific proponent for Christianity, he was Saul—a one-man militia bent on eradicating every trace of the faith. He was unrivaled when it came to the damage he did to the church. We know that he even tortured and killed a multitude of Christians (Acts 22:4; Galatians 1:13). It's reasonable to suggest that no one ever brought more guilt to the cross than Paul. Have *you* ever killed a person for the sole fact that he or she loved and followed Jesus?

If anyone had an excuse to be paralyzed by the past, it was Paul. And yet, we see that just the opposite happened. No one was more active or productive in serving the Lord than this chief sinner. How was he able to get free from guilt's grip?

The <u>grace</u> of our Lord was exceedingly abundant. (1 Timothy 1:14 NKJV)

The answer is God's grace—the only remedy for man's guilt. Grace is the free and undeserved favor of God bestowed on those who belong to Christ. Grace declares that all wrongdoing on our part has been eternally forgiven and permanently forgotten. Apart from grace, it would have been impossible for Paul to get over the guilt from what he had done. But, by God's grace, he was a new being, called to serve as a living example of just how great God's grace is.

However, for this reason I obtained mercy, that in me first Jesus Christ might show all longsuffering, as a pattern to those who are going to believe on Him for everlasting life. (1 Timothy 1:16 NKJV)

If you're allowing something from your past to keep you in a state of spiritual paralysis, remember that God's grace is infinitely greater than the sum total of your sins and that the Lord wants you to be active and productive for Him (Ephesians 2:10). Grace was able to free Paul, and it will certainly do the same for you!

Have you allowed yourself to be spiritually paralyzed by something from your past?

How would you describe the impact of God's grace upon your life?

Now there was also a man who prophesied in the name of the LORD, Urijah . . . who prophesied against this city [Jerusalem] and against this land [Israel] according to all the words of Jeremiah. (Jeremiah 26:20 NKJV)

Spiritually speaking, Urijah had a lot going for him. He prophesied in the name of the Lord, and in sharing the message of Jeremiah, he was one of the few prophets who actually told the truth. Yet, despite all this, he made a terrible decision.

And when Jehoiakim the king, with all his mighty men and all the princes, heard his words, the king sought to put him to death; but when Urijah heard it, he was afraid and fled, and went to Egypt. Then Jehoiakim the king sent men to Egypt: Elnathan the son of Achbor, and other men who went with him to Egypt. And they brought Urijah from Egypt and brought him to Jehoiakim the king, who killed him with the sword and cast his dead body into the graves of the common people. (Jeremiah 26:21–23 NKJV)

Fear is never a good motivation for action. When the heat was turned up on Urijah, he was afraid and fled, and it cost him dearly. He lost not only his testimony as an unflinching and uncompromising prophet of God, but also the very thing he had feared losing the most—his life.

Jeremiah stands in stark contrast. Though threatened with the same dangers, Jeremiah stayed put because He knew that God had planted him where he was and that flight simply was not an option (Jeremiah 1:18–19). This must have been an incredibly difficult decision, but notice how the Lord was faithful to protect His faithful servant.

Nevertheless the hand of Ahikam the son of Shaphan was with Jeremiah, so that they should not give him into the hand of the people to put him to death. (Jeremiah 26:24 NKJV)

This is a powerful lesson on the consequences of allowing fear to move us into action. When threats surround us, we shouldn't let fear move us; instead, we should stand in the center of God's will for our lives. By doing so, we'll preserve our testimony and prove God's faithfulness.

When have you allowed fear to move you to action, and what were the results?

What can you apply from Jeremiah's example?

Jesus said to him, "Assuredly, I say to you that this night, before the rooster crows, you will deny Me three times." Peter said to Him, "Even if I have to die with You, I will not deny You!" And so said all the disciples. (Matthew 26:34–35 NKJV)

I don't doubt Peter's sincerity. Nor do I doubt that any of the disciples were insincere in saying that when push came to shove, they would be there for the Lord. They all felt a sense of duty and loyalty to Jesus, and this was the reasonable response. But, in truth, they were much weaker than they realized, and their feelings for Him had blinded them to this fact. This shows us something very important about our emotions: they can be deceptive.

This is why we shouldn't put our trust in the way we feel. Even so called "good emotions" have the power to cloud the truth. In Jeremiah's day, the nation of Judah hoped that their special status with God would spare them from captivity and destruction. Their feeling was deceptive, and the judgment of which Jeremiah had prophesied eventually came (Jeremiah 39:8).

Sometimes, our "good emotions" can even cause us to get in the way of God's will. Agabus was a man who cared about others. His "concern" for Paul's safety in Jerusalem compelled him to warn the apostle against going there. His feelings were deceptive because God's will was for Paul to preach to the Jewish people, even at the expense of bodily harm (Acts 21:13).

Amid the counterfeit currency of our emotions, there is always the gold standard of God's Word. Peter and the others felt one way, but Jesus had declared otherwise. Judah felt one way, but the prophecies of God said otherwise. Agabus felt one way, but the commission of God directed otherwise. How about you? Have your feelings deceived you into thinking one way, despite the fact that God's Word declares otherwise? Don't allow your feelings to deceive you by obscuring the truth. Walk in the security and safety of what God has declared in His Word.

Your word is a lamp to my feet And a light to my path. (Psalm 119:105 NKJV)

What experience from your past proves that emotions can be deceiving?

How does God's Word play a part in the way you view truth?

And they came to John and said to him, "Rabbi, He who was with you beyond the Jordan, to whom you have testified; behold, He is baptizing, and all are coming to Him!" (John 3:26 NKJV)

Imagine for a moment that you are John the Baptist. Your ministry is a success story, to say the least. People are flocking to hear your teachings. Tears of repentance are flowing. Lives are truly being transformed. Even the religious rulers have left the comfortable confines of Jerusalem in order to witness your work firsthand. Some have suggested that you might even be "the One"—the Christ. But all this is starting to change. Your star is no longer on the rise because someone else, Jesus of Nazareth, is beginning to eclipse your glory. On top of this, He's even using your pattern for success: *"He is baptizing."* To make matters worse: *"All are coming to him!"* How would you feel at this point if you were John? Angry, depressed, envious?

Perhaps all these emotions were crouching at the door of John's heart, tempting his flesh to invite them in. But being a Spirit-filled man, John overcame this temptation. The very next verse shows us how he was able to do this:

John answered and said, "A man can receive nothing unless it has been given to him from heaven." (John 3:27 NKJV)

John overcame because of his outlook. He understood that the ministry was never really *his* to begin with. From start to finish, the work that John had been involved in was ultimately the Lord's and he had simply been given a part to play in God's plan. He had been given the awesome privilege of being a part of God's plan. What reason was there for being depressed or envious?

The next time you're tempted to be angry, depressed, or even envious over another's success, do what John did. Embrace an overcomer's outlook that sees everything as God's gracious gift.

How would you have reacted in John's place?

How can you integrate John's example into your life?

AN UNPARALLELED PROMISE
DAY 169

"Let not your heart be <u>troubled</u>; you believe in God, believe also in Me." (John 14:1 NKJV)

The Greek verb here for *troubled* means "to agitate" or "to stir up." In context, Jesus was commanding the disciples not to allow their emotions to spin out of control because He was about to be taken away from them. The same is true for us. No matter what happens in life, it is not the Lord's will for us to allow our hearts to be agitated or stirred up. He wants us to maintain control over our feelings and to have a stable and secure outlook on life. Jesus' word to the disciples back then is the same word to us today: *"Let not your heart be troubled."*

The circumstances of life are bound to challenge this. An unexpected phone call in the middle of the night, an untimely knock on the door, a "surprise" piece of mail—these are all things that have the potential to stir us up. But Jesus went on to share a promise that towers above all the real and imagined troubles of this life:

"In My Father's house are many mansions; if it were not so, I would have told you. I go to prepare a place for you. And if I go and prepare a place for you, I will come again and receive you to Myself; that where I am, there you may be also. (John 14:2–3 NKJV)

What an anchor for the soul! No matter what may happen in this life, believers can look forward to heaven and the day when Jesus returns, when the troubles of this world will fade way in the splendid light of His eternal glory. We need to take some time today to reflect on this unparalleled promise. Nothing will calm our troubled hearts quicker than dwelling on the fact that Jesus is coming back to rescue us from this world.

How does Jesus' promise encourage you in your current circumstances?

How does this promise alter your outlook on what truly matters?

So David and his men came to the city, and there it was, burned with fire; and their wives, their sons, and their daughters had been taken captive. Then David and the people who were with him lifted up their voices and wept, until they had no more power to weep.... Now David was greatly distressed, for the people spoke of stoning him, because the soul of all the people was grieved, every man for his sons and his daughters. (1 Samuel 30:3–6 NKJV)

Have you ever experienced the loneliness that occurs when everybody turns on you? That's exactly how David felt at this pivotal point in his life. The group of faithful men who had chosen to follow David just had their homes destroyed, their wives taken captive, and their children kidnapped under his leadership. They began to turn on their leader and openly planned how they would kill him. David suddenly found himself all alone in the midst of an angry mob. How did he overcome such an incredible feeling of loneliness? The next phrase gives us the answer:

But David strengthened himself in the LORD his God. (1 Samuel 30:6 NKJV)

David did something we all need to do when we're feeling lonely: he *strengthened himself in the LORD his God.* Notice what David didn't do. He didn't strengthen himself in his church or in his pastor or even in his accountability group. He went straight to the heart of the Lord, his God.

Many of us struggle with loneliness because we settle for substitutes, instead of going to the Lord Himself. As long as we settle for substitutions, we won't find fulfillment for our loneliness. Jesus *fills all in all (Ephesians 1:23 NKJV),* and only He can truly fill an empty and lonely heart. When we're feeling lonely, we shouldn't settle for anything less than the Lord's personal presence. As we go to Him, He will be faithful to fill our hearts with His love, joy, and peace, and we can be sure that He will never leave us feeling lonely.

What do you substitute for God's presence when you're feeling lonely?

How can you help ensure that you keep your focus on God when you're feeling lonely?

. . . lest anyone fall short of the grace of God; lest any root of bitterness springing up cause trouble, and by this many become defiled. (Hebrews 12:15 NKJV)

Bitterness is unresolved anger. It festers within people's hearts, and it slowly but surely poisons their souls. The Lord takes it very seriously, and He makes it clear how we're to deal with this untrustworthy emotion.

Let all <u>bitterness</u>, wrath, anger, clamor, and evil speaking be put away from you, with all malice. And be kind to one another, tenderhearted, <u>forgiving one another, just as God in Christ forgave you</u>. (Ephesians 4:31–32 NKJV)

There is only one way to break the bondage of bitterness: forgive others *just as God in Christ forgave you.* As sinners, were utterly offensive to a holy and righteous God. Yet, instead of holding this against us, He chose to forgive us by sending His Son to die for our sins. No matter what another person does to us, it can never compare to what we've done to God. But the fact remains that He has forgiven us and spared us from a fiery fate in hell. Recognizing that we've been forgiven an enormous debt makes it easy for us to forgive a small one (Matthew 18:21–35).

A Komodo dragon has an interesting way of killing its prey. Its mouth is full of small pointed teeth and toxic saliva, and when it bites another animal, it inflicts several puncture wounds into which the saliva enters. Usually, an animal is able to escape the grip of the Komodo, and it begins to run away. But before long, the poison in its bloodstream takes effect, and it drops dead in its tracks. The Komodo finds its victim by following its scent. Bitterness works the same way. We may think that it isn't hurting us to hold onto it, but if it's in our system, it will eventually bring us down spiritually. We must be careful not to let this feeling infect our hearts. If we follow God's instructions by forgiving those who have wronged us, just as He has forgiven us, we will find freedom from the bondage of bitterness.

What role has bitterness played in your life?

Whom do you need to forgive as God has forgiven you?

THE PARADOX OF IMPATIENCE

DAY 172

But the fruit of the Spirit is . . . patience . . . . (Galatians 5:22 NASB)

Webster's Dictionary defines *impatience* as "an eager desire for relief or change." It is a powerful emotion that we shouldn't trust because it will lead us into making some terrible decisions.

Just ask Esau. After a long day of hunting, he comes home famished and notices that his brother, Jacob, is cooking up a delicious pot of stew. Esau is impatient and doesn't want to wait to fix something for himself. Consequently, he exchanges his blessing as the firstborn son for a quick meal to satisfy his flesh. In the heat of the moment and under the influence of impatience, Esau makes a terrible decision (Genesis 25:29–34).

Just ask Saul. While awaiting Samuel's instructions on how to deal with the invading enemy, he grows impatient. With all eyes on him, Saul sacrifices to the Lord, which according to the law, was only to be done by a priest. Samuel returns, rebukes Saul for breaking God's law, and prophesies that the Lord will raise up another king in his place. Another terrible decision brought on by impatience (1 Samuel 13:6–14).

Just ask Achan. God brings the Israelites into Canaan and promises to eventually give them the entire land as their inheritance. But He commands them not to take any of the spoils of victory for themselves. Achan just can't wait, so he takes some of the forbidden loot. God draws this to Joshua's attention, and Achan is singled out and destroyed as a result of his impatient heart (Joshua 7).

Impatience will always cause us to lose something. Esau lost his birthright, Saul lost his kingdom, and Achan lost his life. This is the paradox of impatience: we act on it because we think that we're gaining something when, in reality, we're losing out in the long run. Impatience is natural to us, and the only way to guard against it is to be filled with the Spirit, who supernaturally produces God's patience within us. When we walk in the Spirit and allow Him to fill our hearts with His patience, we have everything to gain and nothing to lose.

What makes you impatient?

What is God's remedy for impatience?

Flee also youthful lusts. (2 Timothy 2:22 NKJV)

The Bible teaches us that we need to take lustful feelings very seriously. The Bible also tells us that there is a sure-fire way to overcome lust when we encounter it. Run! Running away from things is not looked on very highly by the world. It carries the stigma of being weak and cowardly. But the believer's goal is to live up to God's standards, not the world's, and God tells us that the best way to handle lust is to run from it.

Joseph serves as the classic example of running away from lust. As another man's wife tried to seduce him, he was faced with two choices: he could either linger in the presence of his lustful feelings, or he could put feet to his faith and simply run away. Of course, we know that he made the decision to run, and the Lord blessed his life over and above anything that he could have gained from this encounter (Genesis 39:11–12). Even though Joseph's story is familiar to most of us, his example is seldom followed.

If we were truthful, we would have to admit that we enjoy lingering with lust. The reason many of us battle with lustful feelings is because we simply don't make the willful decision to run from them. Instead, we try to negotiate with our lusts by thinking, *How long can I enjoy this without getting into too much trouble?* When we take this approach to lust, we will always walk away the loser. The simple fact is, God doesn't want us to negotiate or bargain with lust. He wants us to run away from it. It is not a question of *can we* overcome lust but *will we* overcome it by putting feet to our faith. Don't let this powerful emotion make a loser out of you. Take a courageous stand against lust by running away from it.

Why does God tell us to run from our lusts?

Who are some people in the Bible who lingered with lust, and what were the results?

Elijah was a man subject to like <u>passions</u> as we are, and he <u>prayed</u> earnestly. (James 5:17 KJV)

The Greek word for *passions* here is *pathos*, and it refers to the strong desires or lusts within a human heart. Elijah was a human being, just like the rest of us, and he had a set of emotions that he had to deal with, just as we do. But notice the connection the Bible makes between his passions and his prayers. They are mentioned together because there's a powerful principle here: our emotions can become an effective motivation for prayer.

When David was being hunted down like an animal by Saul, it angered him. However, he didn't allow his anger to fester in his heart and turn into bitterness toward Saul. Instead, David openly and honestly called out to the Lord and shared his frustrations with Him. In the process, David penned some of the most powerful passages in Scripture (Psalm 59).

When the Assyrian army surrounded the city of Jerusalem, King Hezekiah was totally discouraged. The Assyrians had decimated every other kingdom in the land, and it seemed only a matter of time before Jerusalem joined the list of casualties. But he did the right thing with his discouragement; he went to the Lord in prayer. The Lord heard and answered, and Jerusalem was miraculously spared (Isaiah 37:36).

When Peter walked on the waves to Jesus, he made the mistake of taking his eyes off the Lord and began to focus on the storm around him. Understandably, he grew afraid and uttered one of the most concise, yet sincere, prayers in Scripture: *"Lord, save me!"* Jesus reached out and rescued Peter from drowning (Matthew 14:30–31).

These examples show that our anger, discouragement, fear, and other powerful emotions can be put to good use when we turn to prayer. Make it a point today to examine your heart and identify the emotions you're dealing with. Instead of dwelling on them, allow them to prompt a time of prayer.

How is your prayer life proportionate to your passions?

What advice would you give to someone who always seems overwhelmed with emotion?

PRIDE'S PRICE
DAY 175

Those who walk in pride <u>He is able</u> to put down. (Daniel 4:37 NKJV)

These words come to us from none other than Nebuchadnezzar. As the king of the most powerful empire on earth, he knew the dangers of pride. As the object of God's love and affection, he also knew what the Lord is able and willing to do in order to break those who are consumed with pride (read Daniel 4).

Pride cannot be trusted because it downplays our own weaknesses and belittles God's greatness. The Lord knows how to cleanse us of this emotion. David's sin with Bathsheba was more than just physical; it was also emotional because he had allowed his pride to tell him that he was above the laws he enforced over his kingdom. God broke David of that pride, but it only came at the painful and precious price of his son's life (2 Samuel 12:14). Samson also knew the price of pride. It wasn't until the Lord had allowed the Philistines to blind and humiliate him that he was convinced that he was absolutely nothing apart from God (Judges 16:28). Saul of Tarsus had credentials that would have made any Jew proud (Philippians 3:5). The Lord blinded him on the road to Damascus in order to make him dependant upon others and show him the futility of his pride. God will do whatever it takes to break us of our pride, and as Nebuchadnezzar said, *He is able to put down.*

But we shouldn't lose heart over this because the Bible tells us that the Lord is also able to do something else to us:

Therefore <u>He is also able</u> to save to the uttermost those who come to God through Him, since He always lives to make intercession for them. (Hebrews 7:25 NKJV)

The One who is able to break us of the pride that plagues our hearts is the same One who is able to save us from it. Don't be too proud to call out to the Lord for help with this. It is better to break before the mercy seat of God than to be broken by Him.

How do the examples of David, Samson, and Saul compare to your own life?

What do you need to change in your life so that you're not guilty of pride?

ANGRY AT GOD?

DAY 176

And Joshua said, "Alas, Lord GOD, why have You brought this people over the Jordan at all; to deliver us into the hand of the Amorites, to destroy us? Oh, that we had been content, and dwelt on the other side of the Jordan!" (Joshua 7:7 NKJV)

Joshua was on a roll! He had finally led the Israelites into the Promised Land, and they had just experienced the dramatic victory at Jericho. Momentum was on their side. And then, Joshua's army experienced a demoralizing defeat at the city of Ai.

Joshua was angry with God. And the Bible shows that he wasn't the only saint to have ever felt this way. In several of his psalms, David cried out to God and even goes so far as to question His goodness and fairness (Psalm 13:1). Martha expressed her frustration to the Lord when she greeted Him at her brother Lazarus' tomb with the icy words, *"Lord, if You had been here, my brother would not have died" (John 11:21 NKJV)*. Chances are, we've all had moments when we've grown angry with God.

But we can't trust this emotion because our anger toward God is based on our limited view of life. Joshua thought the Lord was leading him into destruction, David saw no end in sight to his problems, and Martha was under the impression that Jesus didn't care whether her brother lived or died. They all lacked the perspective of the bigger picture. Joshua's defeat was only temporary, David's trials were preparing him for greatness, and Martha was about to witness the resurrection power of God. Had they known this from the beginning, none of them would have been angry with God.

Now what about us? Is God allowing something to take place in our lives that we're angry with Him about? The remedy is to understand that God is always for us and that just like with Joshua, David, and Martha, our circumstances are for our ultimate good. We should never allow our hearts to stay angry with God. We need to hold out for His bigger picture and remember that no one who gives Him the benefit of the doubt will ever be disappointed.

When have you gotten angry with God, and how did time prove that your anger was unfounded?

What would you say to someone who is angry with God?

DON'T BE DISCOURAGED
DAY 177

But we know that <u>when He is revealed</u>, we shall be like Him. (1 John 3:2 NKJV)

No matter how accomplished or mature we are in the Christian life, we need to understand that we are still bound to have our moments of emotional weakness. This is important to understand because when we get blindsided by our own shortcomings, we can be too hard on ourselves. The truth is that we're all human and will lack spiritual perfection until the time when the Lord calls us to be with Him.

We would all agree that Paul was about as close to spiritual perfection as one can get in this life. He wrote nearly half the books in the New Testament, worked mighty miracles, and advanced the Gospel more than anyone else. And yet, despite his accomplishments, Paul still had his moments of emotional weakness. Paul's passion was to see all of Israel converted, as he was (Romans 9:3). His moment of glory arrived as he preached the Gospel to the Jewish leaders on the steps of the temple in Jerusalem. They violently rejected it, and Paul had to be put in prison for his own safety. Alone in his cell, a tidal wave of discouragement must have washed over him because the Lord makes it a point to personally encourage Paul.

But the following night the Lord stood by him and said, "Be of good cheer, Paul."
(Acts 23:11 NKJV)

The mightiest men and women of God still have their moments of weakness. Yet, in a wonderful way that only the Lord could author, our times of weakness actually work to our advantage in three ways: they **cure** us of our pride, they **cause** us to depend more on Him, and they **create** an understanding heart in us for others when they are emotionally weak and weary. Paul's episode accomplished all of these in his life and propelled him on to even greater service for the Lord.

When this happens to you (and it will happen), don't be discouraged. Instead, go to the throne and ask God to use your time of weakness as a tool to strengthen and perfect you.

For our light and momentary troubles are achieving for us an eternal glory that far outweighs them all. (2 Corinthians 4:17 NIV)

Why is it so important to have a realistic perspective on spiritual perfection?

How does this affect the way you look at everyday life?

Jesus spoke these words, lifted up His eyes to heaven, and said: "Father, <u>the hour</u> has come. <u>Glorify Your Son</u>, that Your Son also may glorify You . . . ." (John 17:1 NKJV)

Jesus' last day of earthly ministry began with prayer. He opened by **acknowledging** that the hour had come and by **asking** the Father to glorify Him. "*The hour*" that Jesus referred to is the event that His entire life was directed toward—the cross. This means that His prayer to be glorified is a reference to the crucifixion, which, at this point, was just a few hours away.

At first, this may be difficult to accept. How could something as brutal and bloody as the crucifixion be glorious? In the physical sense, the scene at Calvary was one of shame and disgrace, but in the spiritual realm, the glory of the cross is unmatched in terms of its brilliance and beauty.

The cross shows Jesus' perfect submission and surrender to the will of the Father. The Son not only preached that we should be obedient to the will of the Father, but lived it out as well. The cross also demonstrated the Father's deep and amazing love for mankind—He would rather have His Son die on the cross, than live without us in eternity. How blessed are those who receive the message of the cross and the hope of heaven by placing their faith and truth in Jesus.

For the message of the cross is foolishness to those who are perishing, but to us who are being saved it is the power of God. (1 Corinthians 1:18 NKJV)

The natural mind cannot comprehend the glorious nature of the cross. But we who have been given spiritual life see the cross for what it truly is—an unlikely source of glory.

What is glorious about the cross?

How can you help people see the cross in a whole new light?

". . . You have given Him authority over all flesh, that He should give eternal life to as many as You have given Him." (John 17:2 NKJV)

God gave Christ the authority to give eternal life to those whom He had given Him—that's a lot of giving going on. This idea is contrary to our human model where authority is often used to take rather than give. Yet the divine purpose of position was always meant to benefit others. We see this clearly in the fall of Adam and Eve in the garden of Eden. After God confronted this couple with their sin, He immediately set into place a pecking order putting Adam in a position of authority over Eve:

To the woman he said, ". . . Your desire will be for your husband, and he will rule over you." (Genesis 3:16 NIV)

What men and women miss in this divine order is that God did not punish Eve by giving Adam authority over her. He gave authority to Adam so that Eve would be protected. Paul explains this truth:

I do not let women teach men or have authority over them. . . . For God made Adam first . . . And it was the woman, not Adam, who was deceived by Satan, and sin was the result. (1 Timothy 2:12–14 NLT)

God gave Adam authority over Eve to protect her from deception. God gave to Adam so that Adam might give to Eve. From the very beginning, the purpose of authority was to benefit those under it.

Apart from this divine understanding of God's heart, people will tend to use their authority to take, rather than give. The proof text of this selfish tendency is in the old adage, "Power corrupts and absolute power corrupts absolutely." Only in Christ can we walk in the original design where "power gives and absolute power gives absolutely."

"For God so loved the world that He gave His only begotten Son, that whoever believes in Him should not perish but have everlasting life." (John 3:16 NKJV)

Have you ever been the recipient of authority that has blessed your life?

How can you use the authority that God has given you to bless someone today?

DISCIPLE DESCRIPTION
DAY 180

"For I have given to them [the disciples] <u>the words which You have given Me</u>; and they have received them, and have known surely that <u>I came forth from You</u>; and they have believed that <u>You sent Me</u>." (John 17:8 NKJV)

Disciples do certain things. If people aren't doing these things, then it raises the question of whether they are really disciples.

First, disciples readily receive the Word of God. Just like the original disciples, there should always be an excitement in our hearts when it comes to God's Word. Something is wrong with those who profess to follow the Lord yet lack a personal passion for the Scriptures.

Second, disciples believe that Jesus came from heaven. Some people hold the popular position that Jesus was merely a man who had a unique relationship with God. According to this view, Jesus was just as earth-born and earth-bound as the rest of us. However, the Bible teaches that Jesus has a heavenly origin, and anyone who disagrees with this disagrees with Him.

Finally, disciples believe that Jesus is the representation of the Father. This means that Christ's words are the end to any argument. There is no review committee for what Jesus said; He speaks with the authority of the Godhead, and His word carries absolute authority and finality.

This ought to lead to some self-examination on our part. Do we still get excited by our quiet times in the Word or by the Bible studies we attend? Do we see Jesus as just another man or as the Lord of heaven and earth? Are Jesus' words final for our lives, or do we tend to explain away anything we disagree with? May we give earnest consideration to each of these questions, and may we act as disciples of Jesus Christ.

Are you doing what a disciple should do?

How can you grow in the disciplines that have been discussed?

"I pray for them. I do not pray for the world but for those whom You have given Me, for they are Yours." (John 17:9 NKJV).

It is hard to even imagine someone like Billy Graham taking us aside and asking for our most personal prayer needs and then committing to go to God daily on our behalf for those things. Yet, the One who sits at the right hand of our Father prays for us. Think about that for a moment. Jesus Christ—the second person in the triune Godhead; the one and only Son of God; the One through whom, by whom, and for whom the world was made; the Messiah; the King of Kings; the Lord of Lords; the Lion; the Lamb; the Savior of the world—prays for us. And it is not a fleeting fancy that He endeavors to do from time to time. The Bible tells us that He lives to pray for us:

Therefore he is able, once and forever, to save everyone who comes to God through him. He lives forever to plead with God on their behalf. (Hebrews 7:25 NLT)

In light of this startling revelation, it should be crystal clear that Christ's prayers will not be ineffective. He is omnipotent: He has the power to get us through trials. He is omniscient: He knows what we need even better than we do. He is omnipresent: there is never a time when we will face this world without Him. He is love: He will go to all lengths—even death—to save us.

As we contemplate the amazing impact of Christ's prayers on our behalf, the depth of His promise through Peter's pen becomes keenly acute:

Give all your worries and cares to God, for he cares about what happens to you. (1 Peter 5:7 NLT)

Whatever is on your plate as you read this devotion is no match for the sovereign Lord of the Universe who loves you to death!

Why do you think we fail to take our concerns and cares to God?

What can you personally bring to Christ's throne room today?

"Holy Father, <u>keep</u> through Your name those whom You have given Me . . . ." (John 17:11 NKJV)

Unfortunately, the English language sometimes comes up short in translating the original text of the New Testament. For example, the word that Jesus used for *keep* in the verse above has a much deeper meaning than the English word initially suggests. In the Greek, *keep* literally means "to guard something against injury through constant care and attention." In biblical times, this would describe a shepherd's continual watch over his flock. A more modern parallel is a bodyguard who is always on alert to ensure that his assignment is safe.

Jesus asks His Father to bestow this type of protective care on His followers. It was an important prayer given the persecution that they would encounter in the coming years. Notice that their defense was to come **exclusively** from the Father. Jesus did not devise an elaborate security network for His followers to fall back on. There was no "Plan B" prayer for their protection. The Father could be fully depended upon and fully trusted.

As modern-day disciples, we need to recognize that our protection in this world ultimately comes from our heavenly Father. He is the one who keeps our lives, and He is the one in whom we must securely rest. This is where we prove whether we truly believe in God's sovereignty. Is His control over all things just good reading, or do we confidently count on it in the real world?

Many years ago, the Christian apologist Dr. Walter Martin was about to give a lecture on Christianity to an openly hostile audience. Organizers suggested that he might want to put on a bulletproof vest before he began, but Dr. Martin replied, "Psalm 91 is my bulletproof vest!" He understood that the Father would be faithful to keep him. Do we?

He who dwells in the secret place of the Most High Shall abide under the shadow of the Almighty. I will say of the LORD, "He is my refuge and my fortress; My God, in Him I will trust." (Psalm 91:1–2 NKJV)

From whom does your protection ultimately come?

How is God's faithfulness to protect His people demonstrated in the Bible?

STRENGTHENED BY STRUGGLE
DAY 183

"I do not pray that You should take them out of the world, but that You should keep them from the evil one." (John 17:15 NKJV)

Holiness does not require isolation. In fact, it's quite the contrary. God has purposed for us to be a beacon of light and hope to the lost and dying. One of the ways we achieve this is through the trials and temptations we face as believers.

The only temptations that you have are the temptations that all people have. But you can trust God. He will not let you be tempted more than you can stand. But when you are tempted, God will also give you a way to escape that temptation. Then you will be able to stand it. (1 Corinthians 10:13 ICB)

Did you notice that God doesn't remove temptations? The way of escape has nothing to do with an exit strategy. Otherwise, this verse would not conclude *then you will be able to stand it.* Why would you need *to stand it,* if it goes away? God wants to use our lives as examples to the world around us. He wants to show the difference between a person who has the hope of Christ and one who does not. That was the crux of Christ's parable about the two houses built on two different foundations (Matthew 7). Those who built upon the rock were Christians, and those who built upon the sand were not. But notice that the storm came upon both houses. One house was able to bear up under the storm; the other was not.

When we face difficult circumstances, we may be tempted to feel fear, doubt, anxiety, and anger. God keeps us in the world because the lives of those built upon the rock of God's Word can withstand the trials of life with a heart of joy and be a witness of God's glory to a watching world:

Dear brothers and sisters, whenever trouble comes your way, let it be an opportunity for joy. (James 1:2 NLT)

Can you recall someone's faith through a trial that inspired you?

Does your life reflect the joy of God through difficult circumstances?

HIS DESIRE
DAY 184

"Father, <u>I desire</u> that they also whom You gave Me may be with Me . . . ." (John 17:24 NKJV)

At the end of Jesus' prayer for His disciples, He proclaimed His desire for them to one day be with Him. Jesus knew that the hour of His crucifixion was drawing near and that soon He would be back in heaven, sitting at the right hand of His Father. The disciples would miss the Lord's physical presence and endure persecution before they saw Him again. How gracious and merciful of our Lord to remind them that their final destination is heaven, an eternity with Him.

Deep down, many of us believe that we will somehow disqualify ourselves from making it to heaven. Or perhaps we imagine that when we make it there, God will begrudgingly let us in. We view our salvation with a sense of fearful insecurity because we don't think the Lord truly wants us. Nothing could be more unbiblical. Jesus went on the record to say that He desires for us to join Him in heaven. To suggest, or even think, that He doesn't desperately want us by His side in the kingdom is to call Him a liar and resist His prayer for us!

God wants us to be certain of our future with Him. In fact, this is what we are supposed to count on during our short stay here on earth. We need to get past our feelings of insecurity by standing on what the eternal Word of God says. Jesus lovingly looks forward to our union with Him. Let us simply receive this truth and allow it to produce a joy in us that dominates our lives and quenches any sense of insecurity we may have hidden in our hearts.

"Most assuredly, I say to you, he who believes in Me has everlasting life." (John 6:47 NKJV)

What does Jesus desire when it comes to you? How do you know?

What would you say to another Christian who is insecure about his or her salvation?

"Father, I desire that they also whom You gave Me may be with Me where I am, that <u>they may behold My glory</u> which You have given Me ..." (John 17:24 NKJV)

What will we see when we get to heaven? God has kept much of this a mystery for our eventual discovery. But in His prayer to the Father, Jesus asked that His followers join Him in heaven so that they would behold His glory. This means that when we get to heaven, one of the sights we will see is the Lord in His glorified form. When we study the Scriptures, we see three different forms of Jesus' glory.

First, we see Jesus in His **pre-incarnate** glory. This refers to the Old Testament appearances that the Lord made before His incarnation in human flesh. Daniel encountered Jesus in His pre-incarnate glory nearly six hundred years before His birth in Bethlehem:

. . . behold, a certain man clothed in linen, whose waist was girded with gold . . . . his face like the appearance of lightning, his eyes like torches of fire . . . the sound of his words like the voice of a multitude. (Daniel 10:5–6 NKJV)

We also see Christ in His **transfigured** glory during the brief moment when the veil of His human flesh was pulled back. Peter, James, and John witnessed this glory and conveyed it to Matthew, who gives this description:

His face shone like the sun, and His clothes became as white as the light. (Matthew 17:2 NKJV)

Finally, we see our Savior in His **resurrected** glory. When John was exiled on the island of Patmos, he suddenly found himself face to face with the Lord in His resurrected glory:

His head and hair were white like wool, as white as snow, and His eyes like a flame of fire; His feet were like fine brass, as if refined in a furnace, and His voice as the sound of many waters. (Revelation 1:14–15 NKJV)

These images give us an idea of what we will see in heaven. While living in a world that is dark and dismal, it is good to focus on the radiant light of our glorious Lord who is waiting for us!

What can we expect to see when we get to heaven?

How can the anticipation of heaven help you through today?

GUARD YOUR GETHSEMANE
DAY 186

When Jesus had spoken these words, He went out with His disciples over the Brook Kidron, where there was <u>a garden</u>, which He and His disciples entered. (John 18:1 NKJV)

After Jesus finished His prayer for His disciples, He led them out of Jerusalem to a garden just outside the city limits. By cross-referencing the other gospels, we discover that the name of this garden was Gethsemane (Matthew 26:26; Mark 14:32) and that it served as a frequent prayer closet for Jesus and His disciples (Luke 22:39). Immediately before Jesus' arrest and crucifixion, He retreated to this secluded and serene place in order to pray and draw close to His Father.

But only eleven of the twelve disciples went with Jesus to Gethsemane that night. Judas was not with them because he had made an earlier exit. The Bible tells us that Satan had entered into his heart and had led him to betray Jesus to the chief priests and Pharisees (John 13:27). Judas then brought a cohort of soldiers to where he knew Christ could be found—Gethsemane:

And Judas, who betrayed Him, also knew the place; for Jesus often met there with His disciples. Then Judas, having received a detachment of troops, and officers from the chief priests and Pharisees, came there with lanterns, torches, and weapons. (John 18:2–3 NKJV)

Gethsemane was the Lord's place of prayer, and that was exactly where Satan launched his assault against Him. The enemy will do the same thing to us. Watch what happens the next time you make it a point to pray. Whether it's a ringing phone, a noisy neighbor, or a lingering thought that you just can't seem to shake out of your head, there will be some sort of spiritual attack intended to disrupt your time with the Lord. The devil knows that if he can beat you in your prayer life, he can beat you in the other areas of your spiritual life. Understand the importance of prayer and guard your own Gethsemane with all your heart.

Where is your Gethsemane?

How will you protect your place of prayer?

GOING FORWARD

Jesus therefore, knowing <u>all things</u> that would come upon Him, <u>went forward</u> and said to them, "Whom are you seeking?" (John 18:4 NKJV)

What do you dread? What is the one thing that you can't bring yourself to face? No matter what it might be, it cannot compare with what Jesus faced as a band of Roman soldiers sought to seize Him. The physical aspects of the cross were horrific, but the spiritual aspects were even worse for our Lord. The sinless Son of God would soon be "made sin" so that He could receive the fullness of the Father's fury (2 Corinthians 5:21). Jesus was fully aware that all this was about to come upon Him if He allowed the soldiers to take Him. No combination of earthly horrors could ever compare to what this must have meant to Him. We must never forget this.

Jesus understood that it was His calling in life to bear the price for our sins. Before time began, He was ordained as our sacrificial Lamb (1 Peter 1:20; Revelation 13:8). In a very literal sense, Jesus was born to die. He knew this was His calling in life, and the Bible tells us that He *went forward* and faced the wrath of Almighty God on our behalf.

The Lord sets an example for us by accepting and going forward with the calling that had been placed upon His life. All too often, we, as Christians, shrink from the calling that has been placed upon our lives. We invent a variety of excuses for why we won't go forward with what God wants us to do, but in the end, they all amount to one word—disobedience.

It is sin to shrink away from the Lord's calling on our lives. Can you imagine if Jesus would have turned and run away from His captors? But the One who had the greatest reason to run away *went forward*. In comparison, our calling is an exciting adventure that is sure to end in spiritual victory (Ephesians 2:10). Let's follow the Lord's lead by going forward with the calling that God has for each of us.

What is God's calling on your life? Are you doing it?

What are some common excuses for not going forward with God's calling?

SUB-MISSION: ACCOMPLISHED
DAY 188

So Jesus said to Peter, "Put your sword into the sheath. <u>Shall I not drink the cup which My Father</u> <u>has given Me</u>?" (John 18:11 NKJV)

Peter had undergone some serious changes over the past few years. Walking with Jesus each day will do that to a person. Life had become a classroom where Christ was constantly teaching and training him for the incredible calling that lay ahead. The cross would bring this spiritual semester to a close, but this student still had one last lesson to learn—total submission to God's will.

As a cohort of Roman soldiers sought to seize Christ, Peter made a desperate attempt to save Him. Jesus responded to him with the command, *"Put your sword into the sheath,"* and the question, *"Shall I not drink the cup which My Father has given Me?"* The command is clear enough, but is the meaning behind Christ's question? According to Psalm 75:8 and Isaiah 51:17, Jesus was referring to God's wrath when He spoke of *"the cup"* that had been given to Him. This cup of wrath was given to Him because it was His calling to suffer on our behalf.

By asking this question, Jesus was telling Peter that it was not the time to swing the sword but to submit to God's will for His life and entrust Himself into His care. True safety is found in the midst of the Father's will, not in circumstances that seem safer from a worldly standpoint. Jesus was now in custody, but He was in the center of the sovereign will of the Almighty. This made an indelible impression on Peter, who would write decades later that Christ *committed Himself to Him who judges righteously (1 Peter 2:23 NKJV).*

God does not want us to try to hack our way out of circumstances that He has ordained for us. Instead, He wants us to submit our will to His and entrust ourselves into His care. Spiritual victory is not measured by **escaping** situations that we have been called to but by **enduring** them with patient confidence in our faithful Father.

What has God called you to that you're trying to escape?

What will it take for you to totally submit to the Father's will?

Now it was Caiaphas who advised the Jews that it was expedient that one man should die for the people. (John 18:14 NKJV)

In the final hours of Christ's life, He is placed on trial before the Jewish priesthood. One of these priests was named Caiaphas. The Romans had control over Israel at that time, and they had appointed him as the official high priest because he was willing to serve as their puppet to control the Jewish people. By all accounts, he was a very unspiritual man who was motivated by promises of prestige and power. This is further evidenced by the fact that he was the one who initiated Jesus' arrest and execution. In fact, earlier in John's gospel, he publicly declared that the only way to deal with Jesus is to kill Him:

And one of them, Caiaphas, being high priest that year, said to them, "You know nothing at all, nor do you consider that it is expedient for us that one man should die for the people, and not that the whole nation should perish." (John 11:49–50 NKJV)

The amazing thing about Caiaphas' statement isn't its ruthlessness but its truthfulness. The heart of the Gospel message was declared in his unwitting testimony that "*one man should die for the people.*" It *is* better for one to die for the sake of saving everyone else—which is exactly what Jesus did!

Caiaphas proved that God can use anyone to accomplish His purposes, even those who don't know Him or want anything to do with Him. From pharaoh (Exodus 7:4) to the Philippian jailer (Acts 16:23), the Bible is filled with ignorant instruments who are used to fulfill God's purposes for His people. This ought to bring comfort to us because it demonstrates that nothing is beyond the Lord's control and that He can use anyone to accomplish His will.

The king's heart is like a stream of water directed by the LORD; he turns it wherever he pleases. (Proverbs 21:1 NLT)

When have you witnessed God using a non-believer to accomplish His purposes?

How should God's ability to use non-believers affect the way you view them?

WORLDLY WARMTH
DAY 190

Now the servants and officers who had made a fire of coals stood there, for it was cold, and they warmed themselves. And Peter stood with them and warmed himself. (John 18:18 NKJV)

This was a rough night for Peter. It began with him proclaiming in the presence of his fellow disciples that he would be the one who would stick with Jesus no matter how rough things got. His promise was put to the test when a band of Roman soldiers and temple guards came to arrest Jesus. Who would have known that the opposition would be such a formidable force? In a blind rush of bravado, Peter drew a sword and went for a deathblow against the closest captor. He missed.

Surrounded by heavily armed Roman soldiers, Peter obeyed his base instinct for self-preservation and fled. At some point in the darkness of the night, he came to his senses and decided that it was better to risk death than to completely abandon his Master. He found John, and the two of them stealthily made their way to the high priest's courtyard where Christ had been taken. A young servant girl, barely in her teens, asked Peter if he is one of Jesus' men. *"I am not,"* he said without hesitation.

In the chill of the Passover night, Peter saw a group of temple servants and officers gathered around the glow of a friendly fire. It must have looked like an inviting opportunity for him to sit for a while and gather his thoughts. There was only one problem: Peter had no business warming himself at the world's fire. What at first seemed like a sanctuary of security wound up being a lions' den for Peter; for as he warmed himself, he was questioned about his identity twice and denied belonging to Jesus both times (John 18:25–26).

The lesson learned from Peter is that our associations will affect our obedience. We cannot warm ourselves by the world's fire and expect to walk in spiritual victory. The glow looks so inviting at first, but we will always wind up getting burned. We need to be found around the fire of those faithfully following the Master.

When have you tried to warm yourself at the world's fire? What happened?

What steps do you need to take to protect yourself from worldly warmth?

Jesus answered him, "I spoke openly to the world. I always taught in synagogues and in the temple, where the Jews always meet, and in secret I have said nothing." (John 18:20 NKJV)

Christ's life was an open book. There was nothing that He did or said in private that He would have been ashamed of in public. When the high priest questioned Him about His teachings, He basically replied that it was all a matter of public record and that he could check it out for himself. In our day, He might have said, *Go watch the tape!* Jesus was completely upfront, hiding nothing.

We ought to have this same quality. Our lives should be open books, and it shouldn't matter which page people turn to and read. There is a word to describe someone who is one thing in private and another in public—hypocrite. Even the unbelieving world can't stomach a hypocrite. How much worse when it happens in the family of God! If we want to live the way Jesus called us to, we need to start conducting our private lives as though they will be publicly proclaimed.

"Therefore whatever you have spoken in the dark will be heard in the light, and what you have spoken in the ear in inner rooms will be proclaimed on the housetops." (Luke 12:3 NKJV)

The Lord wants us to live like this because when we do, we stand out from the world around us. In an age where revealed secrets and scandal are common headlines, those who live open and blameless lives are scarce. The more we allow our lives to be an open book, the more access and authority we will have in pointing the world to the One who has nothing to hide.

In everything you do, stay away from complaining and arguing, so that no one can speak a word of blame against you. You are to live clean, innocent lives as children of God in a dark world full of crooked and perverse people. Let your lives shine brightly before them. (Philippians 2:14–15 NLT)

What are you doing in secret that would cause you embarrassment in public?

What needs to change in order for you to live an open-book life? How and when will you make those changes?

Then Pilate entered the Praetorium again, called Jesus, and said to Him, "<u>Are You the King of the Jews</u>?" Jesus answered him, "<u>Are you speaking for yourself about this</u>, or did others tell you this concerning Me?" (John 18:33–34 NKJV)

Shortly after the Romans took occupation of Israel, they took away the Jews' right to sentence a person to death. All decisions regarding the death penalty were approved and executed by Rome. For this reason, the Jewish leaders bound and brought Jesus before Pontius Pilate, who was the highest-ranking Roman leader in the region. He is hundreds of miles away from a superior officer, and it appears that he is in complete control when he asked Jesus, *"Are You the King of the Jews?"*

Pilate was looking for a quick confession from this humble captive, but Jesus always has the ability to turn the tables on those who assume they are in control. Rather than answering Pilate, Jesus did the unexpected and asked *Pilate* a question, *"Are you speaking for yourself about this?"* In other words, Jesus asked him, *Do you really want to know who I am for yourself, or are you repeating the party line about me?*

Throughout His earthly ministry, Jesus asked questions that challenged people to consider whether they wanted to know Him personally. He does the same thing today. The Lord does not want people to know Him on the basis of what other people say or think about Him. He is not interested in our second-hand spiritual knowledge but asks the personal question, *"But who do you say that I am?"* (Matthew 16:15 NKJV)

Danger exists in knowing the Lord through the experiences and testimonies of others. Sometimes even our favorite preachers and authors can become substitutes for our own personal discovery of who He is. Jesus challenged Pilate so long ago and He also challenges us today to know Him firsthand for ourselves.

Why did Jesus ask Pilate the question that He did?

How would you describe to another person who Jesus is to you?

Jesus answered, "<u>My kingdom is not of this world</u>. If My kingdom were of this world, My servants would fight, so that I should not be delivered to the Jews; but now My kingdom is not from here." (John 18:36 NKJV)

Pilate and Jesus stood face to face. From an earthly perspective, one was the perfect picture of power while the other seemed like an insignificant embarrassment. Wielding his earthly authority, Pilate demanded that Jesus give an account of Himself or else face the wrath of Rome. Pilate had surely seen many men whither at this point—crying, confessing, and clinging to the slightest shred of hope that they would find mercy. No doubt, this obscure Jew would do the same. As usual, Jesus did the unexpected.

Instead of defending His earthly existence, Jesus completely bypassed this world and pointed to the higher reality of His higher authority: *"My kingdom is not of this world."* Jesus does not fear the authority of this world because He possesses the almighty authority of heaven. Consider His portrait of power painted in the New Testament:

. . . Jesus is ordained of God to be the judge of all—the living and the dead. (Acts 10:42 NLT)

Now he is far above any ruler or authority or power or leader or anything else in this world or in the world to come. And God has put all things under the authority of Christ . . . . (Ephesians 1:21–22 NLT)

. . . God raised him up to the heights of heaven and gave him a name that is above every other name, so that at the name of Jesus every knee will bow, in heaven and on earth and under the earth, and every tongue will confess that Jesus Christ is Lord, to the glory of God the Father. (Philippians 2:9–11 NLT)

"I hold the keys of death and the grave." (Revelation 1:18 NLT)

All power and authority belongs to Jesus, and He is the only one you need to please. All that matters in eternity is your obedience to Him now. Are you living like it?

How would you compare Pilate and Jesus?

How can you cultivate a greater awareness of Christ's authority?

And when he [Pilate] had said this, he went out again to the Jews, and said to them, "I find <u>no fault</u> in Him at all." (John 18:38 NKJV)

As the hours of Jesus' earthly life dwindles down, the pressure on Pilate mounts. The Jewish leaders are resolute in their request to have Jesus executed, and from a political perspective, it makes all the sense in the world for Pilate to make them happy. But the Roman governor is in a difficult position because the accused does not show the slightest trace of the guilt. Pilate's judicial instincts are telling him that Jesus should not even be bound, much less put to death. Acting on those instincts, Pilate proclaims, *"I find no fault in Him at all."* He is so convinced on this point that he repeats it again and again (John 19:4, 6).

Jesus was faultless, absolutely free from the stain of sin (2 Corinthians 5:21; 1 Peter 2:22; Hebrews 4:15; 1 John 3:5). From center to circumference, Jesus was perfectly pure, and it was this perfection that enabled Him to stand as the perfect sacrifice for our sins. Logic teaches us that imperfection cannot produce perfection, and an imperfect Jesus could not have provided a sacrifice sufficient to cover and clean us from our sinful guilt.

There is a powerful picture of this as God instructed the Israelites on how they were to celebrate the Passover. He instructed them to select a faultless lamb, sacrifice it, and mark their doorframes with its blood. When God saw the blood of the faultless lamb upon their homes, He passed over them and withheld His judgment (Exodus 12). Just as the Passover lamb was faultless in the natural sense, Jesus was faultless in the spiritual sense.

It is easy for us to look at our many faults and grow discouraged and fearful before the holiness of God. We must remember that a faultless Lamb stood as our sacrifice and that we are marked with His perfectly pure blood. This assures us of our salvation.

Why was Jesus' perfect purity so important?

How can we be assured that God accepts us?

"Do you therefore want me to release to you the King of the Jews?" Then they all cried again, saying, "Not this Man, but Barabbas!" (John 18:39–40 NKJV)

Pilate found himself in the proverbial catch-22. On the one hand, he could not afford to offend the Jewish leadership that was insisting on Jesus' execution. On the other hand, he could not bring himself to violate his conscience by sentencing a man to die who was obviously innocent. It seemed like there was no way out. Then Pilate remembered the Roman custom of releasing a Jewish prisoner in honor of the Passover celebration. He thought he had his exit strategy: he would let the Jewish crowd choose who would be set free for the Passover. Surely, they would select Jesus and the matter would be settled.

A criminal in custody was needed in order to give the people a choice, and the worst one was chosen—Barabbas. Luke's gospel tells us that he had committed murder in a rebellion against the Romans, and John mentions that he was a thief, not much competition against a man like Jesus. One sought to liberate through violence and force; the other sought to liberate through peace and love. One selfishly stole; the other selflessly sacrificed. One was guilty and deserving of death; the other was guiltless and worthy of release. Matthew's gospel tells us that the Jewish leaders persuaded the crowd to choose Barabbas, forcing Pilate to release him.

Barabbas deserved death and had absolutely no hope of escape apart from Jesus. This is a powerful picture of what Christ has also done for us. Like Barabbas, we were all guilty of sin and had no hope of ever escaping its sentence of death (Romans 6:23), but Jesus received the punishment that we deserved and set us free. There's a bit of Barabbas' bio in all our lives. It's no coincidence that his name means "son of the father," which is exactly what we have become through Christ.

But when the fullness of the time had come, God sent forth His Son . . to redeem those who were under the law, that we might receive the adoption as sons. (Galatians 4:4–5 NKJV)

How does Barabbas parallel your salvation experience?

What does it mean to be a son of God, and how does this impact your life?

And the soldiers twisted a crown of thorns and put it on His head, and they put on Him a purple robe. (John 19:2 NKJV)

After Pilate consented to having Jesus scourged, the Roman soldiers who were guarding Him decided to have a bit of fun. They took a thorn branch and twisted it into the form of a crown and shoved it into His brow. Then they took a purple robe and draped it over His back, which was fresh with lacerations from the scourging. Why would God let these things to happen to His beloved Son? It seems so pointless to allow such sadistic torture, but we need to remember that there is always a deeper purpose behind the things that God allows even if we can't see it at first.

When Adam and Eve sinned in the garden of Eden, it brought about the fall of all that God had created. Not only did they suffer the consequences for their sin, but the natural world was also affected for the worse. Genesis 3:18 tells us that one by-product of their sin was that the ground would bear thorns and thistles. In a symbolic sense, Jesus' crown of thorns was testimony to His being man's sin-bearer.

Mark 15:17–20 tells us that the Roman soldiers clothed Jesus in purple, saluted Him, struck Him on the head with a reed, and spat on Him. This mocking scene, played out in the cruelest possible way, was their way of making fun of the King of the Jews. How poignant and sad that Jesus was on His way to the cross to pay for the sins that they were even now committing against Him. Jesus knew that this was not His time to reveal Himself, but we know that the day is coming when these same soldiers will bow their knees and confess Jesus as Lord.

The soldiers did not understand the significance of what they were doing, but God used their actions to bring glory and honor to His Son. After further review, the crown of cruelty is transformed into a distinguished diadem when we see that it symbolizes our sin, and the ruthless robe is a grand garment when we recognize how it represents Christ's mission.

What do you need to remember when it comes to things that seem pointless in life?

Where do you need to apply this understanding?

*Then he delivered Him to them to be crucified. So they took Jesus and led Him away.
(John 19:16 NKJV)*

The dilemma over Jesus finally ended for Pilate as he gave in to pressure from the Jewish rulers. Despite knowing that Christ was an innocent man who was being falsely accused, Pilate consented to their wishes and delivered Him for crucifixion. Even though Pilate's decision was part of God's grand plan to offer His Son for our sins, he was still responsible for his choice to reject what his heart told him about the Lord. The sense of conviction must have been intense because Matthew tells us that as Pilate sentenced Jesus, he washed his hands in water and declared, *"I am innocent of the blood of this just Person"* (Matthew 27:24 NKJV).

Pilate's act of washing his hands was an attempt to proclaim his innocence. However, no matter how much he washed his hands, the fact remained that he sentenced an innocent man to die. Pilate's efforts to make his wrongs right were futile from the start because the only way we can be cleansed from sin is by being washed *in* the very blood of Jesus that Pilate tried to wash himself *from*. As human beings, we are born into a guilty condition that only Jesus can make right.

History tells us that Pilate was removed from office three years after the cross. He then went insane and eventually committed suicide. As quickly as Pilate rose to power, he vanished into obscurity. As a matter of fact, Tacitus is the only Roman historian even to mention Pilate, and this was only because of his role in the crucifixion of Jesus. What a pathetic end to a life that had such promise! We can trace the beginning of this end to the moment in time when he rejected the testimony concerning Christ and tried to make himself righteous. May we freely admit our guilt as sinners and rely on the innocent blood of Christ to make us guiltless before God.

Where did Pilate go wrong? What should he have done differently?

How do you try to cover yourself rather than trusting in Christ's righteousness to cover you?

. . . they crucified Him . . . . Now Pilate wrote a title and put it on the cross. And the writing was: JESUS OF NAZARETH, THE KING OF THE JEWS. Then many of the Jews read this title, for the place where Jesus was crucified was near the city; and it was written in Hebrew, Greek, and Latin. (John 19:18–20 NKJV)

As Jesus was nailed to the cross, He entered the final six hours of His earthly life. God's grand plan of salvation for mankind was unfolding before the eyes of unknowing observers. Whenever Rome would crucify people, a sign was placed over them announcing their crime. The purposes for this sign were to inform the bystander, warn those who were thinking of committing the same offense, and humiliate the condemned as they helplessly hung there. Jesus' "crime" was written on His sign: "JESUS OF NAZARETH, THE KING OF THE JEWS."

It is interesting that Jesus' crime was not for something that He did but for something that He is. He is Israel's King, and they wanted nothing to do with Him. The crucifixion was the climax of Israel's rejection, bringing the end of an era. But it was also the beginning of a new era, one where this King would no longer be the exclusive hope of Jews and converts to Judaism. After having been rejected by His own, He would now become the hope of all nations, races, and tongues.

This is dramatically depicted in the sign that bore His title. The Bible tells us that it was written in the three dominant languages in that part of the ancient world: Hebrew, Greek, and Latin. These three languages represent the totality of mankind. Hebrew was the tongue of the Jewish world and the idiom of religion. Greek was the dialect of the culturally elite and the vernacular of philosophy. Latin was the language of the Gentile world and the speech of common society. God testified of His Son's identity in all three languages to indicate that the whole world is included in the knowledge of who He is. Our task is to go into all the world and point people to the cross and the sign that tells it all.

What is the extent of Jesus' authority?

How will you share this today?

DIVINE DETAILS

Then the soldiers, when they had crucified Jesus, took His garments and made four parts, to each soldier a part, and also the tunic. Now <u>the tunic was without seam</u>, woven from the top in one piece. They said therefore among themselves, "Let us not tear it, but cast lots for it, whose it shall be." (John 19:23–24 NKJV)

From time to time, the Bible provides us with certain details that seem to come out of nowhere. The passage above gives us the seemingly insignificant information that Christ's tunic was seamless. Of all the eternal mysteries that God could have revealed to us in His Word, why bother with this trivial tidbit? It seems like a waste of space and ink, but whenever something seems out of place in God's Word, it's usually a hint that something precious is buried there.

In Exodus 28:32, God gave specific instructions that Israel's high priest needed to wear a seamless robe. The purpose behind this divine design was so that it would not tear apart. Can you see the connection? Jesus wore a tunic like the high priest's, which was spared from being torn as the Roman soldiers cast lots for it. Through these subtle details, the Spirit is highlighting the fact that Jesus is our high priest.

In Old Testament times, the high priest had the awesome responsibility of entering into God's presence once a year to offer intercession for the people's sin by taking the blood from the sin sacrifice and sprinkling it on the mercy seat of the ark (Leviticus 16). The high priest represented the people to God, which was exactly what Jesus did as He hung on the cross. Rather than bringing the blood of an imperfect sacrifice, Jesus brought Himself as the perfect sacrifice for our sins. As our high priest, Christ made intercession for us by His blood and secured our favor and forgiveness.

Seeing then that we have a great High Priest who has passed through the heavens, Jesus the Son of God, let us hold fast our confession. (Hebrews 4:14 NKJV)

Why is every detail in the Bible important?

How can you increase your ability to dig deeper into God's Word?

Then the soldiers, when they had crucified Jesus, took His garments and made four parts, to each soldier a part, and also the tunic. (John 19:23 NKJV)

In many ways, the last twenty-four hours of Christ's life summarize the rest of His life. One aspect of His earthly existence that we cannot escape is that He never placed much value in material possessions. This is because Jesus understood that His life was about saving us, not acquiring things. The One who preached the way of self-denial was the living example of it from cradle to grave.

During His lifetime, Jesus borrowed even the most basic necessities of life. He borrowed a motel's manger for His nursery (Luke 2:7), transportation for His royal entry into Jerusalem (Matthew 21:3), a place to celebrate His last night with the disciples (Matthew 26:18), and a coin in order to illustrate His teaching (Matthew 22:19). Jesus was even buried in a borrowed tomb (Matthew 27:60). The only material possessions that Christ had in life were the clothes on His back. The verse above tells us that He even surrendered these for the sake of saving us. Jesus was willing to hang in humiliation so we could have the honor of entering heaven.

God is pleased to bless His children with the things of this world (1 Timothy 6:17), but somehow we seem to forget that Jesus always looked past the things of this world and focused on the matters of the world to come. He used self-denial as a tool to accomplish the objectives of His eternal kingdom, and so will we if we're wise. Each day there are opportunities for us to invest either in this world or in the one to come. Will we buy into society's materialistic mindset that "he who dies with the most toys wins"? Or, will we devote ourselves to the things that transcend death by following the example of our immaterial Immanuel.

How does materialism pull one further and further away from Christ's example?

How have you been materialistically minded? What are you going to do about it?

GAMBLING AT GOLGOTHA
DAY 201

Then the soldiers, when they had crucified Jesus, took His garments and made four parts, to each soldier a part, and also the tunic. Now the tunic was without seam, woven from the top in one piece. They said therefore among themselves, "Let us not tear it, but cast lots for it, whose it shall be," that the Scripture might be fulfilled . . . . (John 19:23–24 NKJV)

Typically, four Roman soldiers were needed in order to crucify someone. Two would take hold of each arm, one would secure the legs, and one would drive in the securing spikes. It was an unenviable task, but the perk was that they could claim the personal possessions of their prisoners. After each soldier had taken an article of Jesus' clothing, His tunic was still left over. In order to determine who should claim it, they gambled under the shadow of the cross.

Some things never change. People do the same thing whenever they come face to face with the message of the cross and fail to take refuge under it. God's Word is crystal clear when it comes to the cosmic stakes: everyone will experience either the eternal pleasures of heaven or an eternal horror that human language cannot adequately describe. The difference lies in our disposition to the cross of Jesus Christ. We can either accept the covering that it provides or stand alone as the penalty for our sin is poured out upon us.

It's amazing that there are those who are willing to gamble at the foot of the cross! *I'll look into the Jesus thing a little later. There's always time to get right with God. One of these days . . . .* What an incredible gamble! What a risk to take with one's eternity! Tomorrow is promised to no one. How many have gone to hell wishing they had taken advantage of the time that God had given to them?

Perhaps you are gambling at Golgotha or know someone who is. Whether it's through personal surrender or sharing a word of warning in love, do what you can to make the gambling stop.

What do people risk who do not put their faith in Jesus' work on the cross?

Who do you know that is gambling at the cross? How can you help them?

CROSS ACCOMPLISHMENTS
DAY 202

After this, Jesus, knowing that <u>all things were now accomplished</u> . . . . (John 19:28 NKJV)

The final twenty-four hours of Jesus' life were coming to a close. As He hung on the cross, He knew that *all things were now accomplished.* As the word *all* implies, the accomplishments of the cross were countless, but here are seven that rise above the rest.

1) **The prophetic Scriptures were fulfilled.** Daniel had long ago prophesied that the Messiah would be *cut off, but not for Himself (Daniel 9:26 NKJV)*. The sacrificial death of Christ perfectly fulfills the prophetic word and also establishes His identity.

2) **The power of Satan and death were destroyed.** Jesus' death on the cross destroyed the devil's power over death (Hebrews 2:14).

3) **Man was set free from the law.** Christ's death released us from having to live according to the impossible requirements of the law of Moses (Colossians 2:14).

4) **Jews and Gentiles were reconciled to one another.** The Lord's death brought a cease-fire to the long-standing hostility between Jews and Gentiles. In Him, they are no longer enemies but fellow members of the same body (Ephesians 2:14).

5) **The penalty for man's sin was satisfied.** John wrote that Jesus was the propitiation (or satisfaction) for our sins (1 John 2:2). The fire of God's fury has been quenched for sinners who take refuge in the cross.

6) **God and man were restored in their relationship.** The spiritual chasm between a sinful race and a holy God was bridged by Christ's crucifixion (2 Corinthians 5:19 NKJV), and we can now refer to the Almighty as our Father.

7) **God's love was demonstrated.** We know that God loves us because He sent His beloved Son to die on our behalf (Romans 5:8 NKJV).

How many accomplishments of the cross can you list?

What has the cross accomplished for you on a personal level?

So when Jesus had received the sour wine, He said, "<u>It is finished</u>!" And bowing His head, He gave up His spirit. (John 19:30 NKJV)

In the concluding moments of His life, Jesus triumphantly cried out, *"It is finished!"* This undoubtedly caught the surrounding crowd off-guard. Imagine what those who were within earshot must have thought: *What's finished? What's He talking about?*

In the original Greek, *"It is finished"* is one word, *teleo*. We can better appreciate its definition by seeing how it is used elsewhere in God's Word. *Teleo* is used to describe the completion of Jesus' commissioning of the disciples (Matthew 11:1). It is used to describe the payment of one's taxes (Matthew 17:24; Romans 13:6). It is used to describe the expiration of the thousand-year reign of Christ (Revelation 20:7). *Teleo* is also used to describe the way that love fulfills the royal law (James 2:8). This word does not just mean to finish something but to do something perfectly and in such a way that cannot be improved.

When the Lord does something, He does it to perfection, including the work of making us right with God. This is what He had in view as He cried out, *"It is finished!"* From start to finish, Christ's life-work was to die so that we could be reconciled to God. He did this as He did all else—to perfection. Man's reconciliation to God isn't 99.9 percent complete but absolutely and perfectly finished, lacking nothing. Moreover, it cannot be improved upon by anything that we could ever do or imagine. To try and do so would be a denial of Christ's cry that it is already finished.

The practical impact of this cannot be overestimated. Many times, we strive to please God for the wrong reasons. Rather than simply wanting to bless Him for who He is, we try to earn our way into His favor. We must remember that *"It is finished!"* and we are loved and accepted by Him no matter what. This should be our motivation for living a life that pleases Him. It is finished. Let's live like it!

What is finished?

What is your motivation for pleasing God?

BOUGHT AND WASHED
DAY 204

One of the soldiers pierced His side with a spear, and immediately <u>blood and water</u> came out. (John 19:34 NKJV)

The pericardium sac surrounds the human heart. It has an inner and outer layer with a small amount of fluid between them. Under extreme stress, the watery fluid between these layers increases until the heart is constricted and unable to beat. When one of the soldiers at the foot of the cross thrust his spear into Jesus' heart, blood *and* water came out, revealing that His heart had suffered from extreme stress. This is significant because it proves the humanity and frailty of Christ. Jesus was a real man, and He really died. There is also a spiritual significance behind the blood and water.

The **blood** speaks of Christ's ministry of **redemption**. When something is redeemed, it is purchased back by its original owner. God originally created mankind for fellowship. However, through the fall of man, we were enslaved to the power of sin and only Jesus' sinless blood held the necessary value to redeem us (purchase us back) to our original owner.

He has delivered us from the power of darkness and conveyed us into the kingdom of the Son of His love, in whom <u>we have redemption</u> through His blood, the forgiveness of sins. (Colossians 1:13–14 NKJV)

The **water** speaks of Christ's ministry of **purification**. Jesus has not only purchased us but also maintains us by continually cleansing us from our day-to-day sins. When we fail and fall, He does not shake His head in disgust and wonder why He bothered redeeming us. He treasures us and is always there to kneel down and wash away our sinful stains.

If we confess our sins, He is faithful and just to forgive us our sins and to <u>cleanse us</u> from all unrighteousness. (1 John 1:9 NKJV)

The blood and water signify the Lord's right to redeem us and His compassion to cleanse us. These ministries are always connected to each other, for Jesus cannot cleanse without first redeeming, and He will not redeem without also cleansing. Let's thank Him today for the blood that bought us and the water that washed us.

What is Christ's response to your failures?

What step should you take when you sin (hint: 1 John 1:9)?

After this, Joseph of Arimathea, being a disciple of Jesus, but secretly, for fear of the Jews, asked Pilate that he might take away the body of Jesus; and Pilate gave him permission. So he came and took the body of Jesus. (John 19:38 NKJV)

When the earthly life of Christ expired, there was a silence in the hearts of those who had loved and followed Him over the past few years. Some followers had been bolder than others. Joseph of Arimathea had kept his devotion a secret for fear of the conflict that it would have brought into his professional life. Mark and Luke tell us that he was a member of the Sanhedrin, which was comprised of the rulers who had demanded that Christ be crucified. Imagine how guilty he must have felt for being an "undercover believer."

It's in moments of loss that a person's character is truly defined, and in the hour that saw the end of Christ's life, Joseph proved his character as a faithful follower. He courageously asked Pilate for the Lord's body, took it, and buried it in his very own tomb. By doing this, Joseph made sacrifices that pertained to his past, present, and future.

First, he sacrificed his standing among his peers in the Sanhedrin. No doubt his actions would bring ridicule and perhaps even excommunication from the ruling class of Jewish society. Joseph also sacrificed his ability to celebrate the Passover Feast because he had defiled himself by touching a dead body. Last, he sacrificed his own tomb so that Jesus could be buried there. By caring for our Lord's body, Joseph gave up his past associations, his present celebration, and his future security.

Sacrifice breeds sacrifice. Christ's sacrifice on the cross led Joseph to sacrifice for Him. This is the way it should be in the Christian life. We should be moved to give ourselves to the Lord after considering how He gave Himself for us. This is the perfect ending to the last day of Christ's life because where His sacrificial life ends, ours begins.

Why should you sacrifice for Christ?

Based on Christ's gift to you, what are you willing to give Him today?

. . . praying always with all prayer and supplication <u>in the Spirit</u>, being watchful to this end with all perseverance and supplication for all the saints . . . . (Ephesians 6:18 NKJV)

A prominent pastor once said, "We need to stop groaning about our adversaries and begin glorying in our allies." What an awesome ally we have in the Holy Spirit! Too often we think that the Holy Spirit is optional in the Christian life. But even a light reading of the New Testament reveals that we need the Spirit just as much as we need Jesus, especially when it comes to spiritual warfare.

When we tend to forget just how powerful an ally the Holy Spirit is, here are three helpful reminders. First, the Spirit's power is seen in the work of **creation**. Genesis 1:2 tells us that at the time of creation, the Spirit hovered over the waters. The original Hebrew word for *hover* indicates a wave-like pattern of motion. Today, thousands of years later, scientists tell us that all energy moves in wave-like patterns. The material universe is still feeling the effects of the Spirit's powerful outpouring! His power is also seen in the work of **conversion**. Regardless of what we know about diamonds, the human heart can be the hardest substance on earth when it is closed off and calloused to the things of God. In fact, only one thing is powerful enough to penetrate even the hardest heart. The Holy Spirit alone can break through its fortifications with the saving truth of Jesus Christ. Last, the Spirit's power is seen in the work of **communion**. Nothing is more powerful than spending time in God's presence. These moments of communion are made possible through the Spirit as He links our hearts to God.

Some historians have said that Sir Winston Churchill danced the day that Japan attacked Pearl Harbor. He wasn't happy about the lives lost in the attack. Churchill was filled with joy because he knew that as a result of America being attacked, he had gained a powerful ally that would make victory a certainty. We, as believers, should be dancing for joy over the fact that we have the Holy Spirit as our abiding ally when we wage war with the enemy.

How does the Holy Spirit's presence impact your perspective of spiritual warfare?

How would you describe your dependence on the Holy Spirit?

AN INTERNAL ATTACK
DAY 207

. . . for he was numbered with us and obtained a part in this ministry. (Acts 1:17 NKJV)

The fallout rate for disciples was significant. They had lost many in their group because Jesus had spoken about eating His flesh and drinking His blood. They were always being asked to leave towns because of Christ's ministry. Some had even lost their families because they had followed Christ, but now the unthinkable had happened. One of the original twelve had left them.

Judas had been there from the beginning. Although we knew all along that he would betray Jesus, it wasn't that way for the disciples. They had all co-labored side by side in ministry. They had witnessed the miracles. They had traveled together for a year-and-a-half, enduring rejection, correction, and training. They had been down the road of discipleship through thick and thin. But they had no clue that Judas' heart was not really with them, as evidenced by the fact that when Jesus said that one of them would betray Him, they immediately began to question who on earth it would be.

Certainly, every believer is subject to the wiles of the enemy, and this can often produce fear. Could we be the next Judas? Could we walk with Christ, taste and see His goodness, experience His miracles, co-labor with His disciples, and still find ourselves one day down the road selling Him out for some worldly wage? This area of Scripture serves as a strong admonishment for us to be on guard against the devil's schemes in our lives and to heed Peter's warning:

Likewise you younger people, submit yourselves to your elders. Yes, all of you be submissive to one another, and be clothed with humility, for "God resists the proud, But gives grace to the humble." (1 Peter 5:5 NKJV)

Humility is the shield of faith against the fiery dart of pride; humility can keep us from following in the footsteps of Judas.

Why does the enemy want to attack God's kingdom from within?

What can you learn from Judas' mistakes?

No one engaged in warfare entangles himself with the affairs of this life, that he may please him who enlisted him as a soldier. (2 Timothy 2:4 NKJV)

Battle brings out the best in the believer. The Lord understands this, and in a spiritual sense, He's built us for war. Wartime helps us to refine our motives, priorities, and appetites. Without war, we start to entangle ourselves in the affairs of this life and become spiritual wimps instead of warriors.

We're not alone, either. Abraham was a mighty man of faith as he went to war against the coalition of kings who had enslaved his nephew, Lot (Genesis 14:14–16). But after the battle ended, Abraham's faith faltered as he followed his wife's suggestion to have a son through her servant. This decision was contrary to God's will, and it plagued Abraham for years to come. Gideon was a mighty man of valor as the Lord led him into battle against the Midianites. But shortly after the fighting was over, Gideon fell into the subtle sin of idolatry (Judges 8:29). And David, perhaps the greatest warrior that the world has ever seen, had an adulterous relationship with Bathsheba and then planned her husband's death when she became pregnant. It's no coincidence that this was made possible because David stayed behind when he would have normally been in battle (2 Samuel 11:1). The lives of Abraham, Gideon, and David show us that we're spiritually safer in battle than out of it.

C. S. Lewis wrote his most influential books, including *Mere Christianity* and *The Screwtape Letters*, as World War II was raging all around him. Lewis was at his best when he felt the pressure of war. In the same sense, we're at our best when we're under the pressure of spiritual battle. We need to understand and embrace this when we step onto the battlefield.

How do battles bring out the best in us?

What is to be expected when we're not busy in spiritual battle?

CONFESSING CHRIST
DAY 209

And the servant girl saw him again, and began to say to those who stood by, "This is one of them." But he denied it again. And a little later those who stood by said to Peter again, "Surely you are one of them; for you are a Galilean, and your speech shows it." (Mark 14:69–70 NKJV)

Peter's cover was blown. As the number of pointing fingers grew, Peter painted himself into an ever-diminishing corner. With each assertion of his disassociation, the distance between Peter and his Savior also grew until he found himself totally focused on the accusers rather than on his Advocate.

How many times do we find ourselves in the same proverbial corner as Peter? We have a secret that we think is hidden, an unconfessed sin. But the enemy comes and begins to question our association with Jesus: *Aren't you supposed to be a Christian?* the devil might rail. *Your speech sounds like a Christian,* the enemy continues, *but you are here in our camp. What's up with that?* And the more we backpedal, the smaller the corner becomes until we find ourselves face to face with the pointing finger of condemnation that disassociates us from the Savior.

I wonder what would have happened if Peter had proclaimed the profound and self-denying truth that he was a disciple in desperate need of Jesus. Would he have found the God-given grace to take his stand next to Christ and die for Him as his heart had so wanted to do? In Peter's case, we know that he repented and gave his life so completely over to Christ that he preached one of the most compelling sermons in the Bible; followed Christ for the rest of his life; and was crucified upside-down as a martyr.

When you have failed and are harboring the secret of your sin, all you need to do is confess with your mouth that Jesus is Lord and believe in your heart that God raised Him from the dead. Then you will be saved, not only from the accusations and condemnations of hell, but also from the secret sins that separate you from your precious Savior. Having been released from the burden of sin, you will then be able to follow Christ with all your heart, like Peter did.

How does Satan exploit your secret sins?

Why is a clean "sin slate" so essential when it comes to combating the enemy?

CONFLICT IS INEVITABLE

Finally, my brethren, be strong in the Lord and in the power of His might. (Ephesians 6:10 NKJV)

It's interesting to note that as Paul started to teach on the subject of spiritual warfare, he deliberately said, *my brethren*. He didn't say, "my apostles" or "my pastors" or "my missionaries." He says, *my brethren* because he understood that spiritual warfare comes to every Christian, not just to those who hold a special place or position within the church. For the believer, spiritual battle is not optional; it is inevitable.

There are three things to keep in mind as we consider this reality. First, it shows us that spiritual warfare is **universal** and that it occurs worldwide. Whether we're Christians living in Paris or Paraguay, Brooklyn or Brussels, we all share in a common conflict and are united in the same fight against the same enemy. This is important because it reminds us that no matter how we might feel in the thick of the battle, we are never alone and are shoulder to shoulder with our brothers and sisters in Christ.

This truth also shows us that warfare is **normal** and common in the Christian life. The enemy would love to get us to think that we're strange or unusual as we wage war against him. Such thinking is unhealthy and untrue and leads to isolation. We need to counter this tendency within each of us by recognizing that it's completely normal to come under the enemy's fire. When we do so, we'll be more open and honest with each other about our struggles.

Finally, we must keep in mind that our warfare is **temporal**. Just as David brought victory for the entire army of Israel when he defeated Goliath, the army of God will share in Jesus' ultimate victory over our common adversary.

Our faith and our fight are inseparable. Instead of feeling depressed or defeated by the inevitability of spiritual warfare, we should fight all the more effectively by recognizing that the battle is universal, normal, and temporal.

Why is it so important to understand that spiritual warfare is inevitable in the Christian life?

How can this be applied in your life today?

TRULY SECURE
DAY 211

Stand therefore, having <u>girded your waist with truth</u> . . . (Ephesians 6:14 NKJV)

Earlier, in Ephesians 6:11, Paul made reference to the whole armor of God. Here, in Ephesians 6:14, he begins to specifically list six pieces of armor that were common to the Roman soldier in biblical times. Perhaps Paul's inspiration for this had something to do with the fact that he was under Roman guard at the time he was writing this epistle to the Ephesians (6:20). Some have even suggested that he was physically chained on either side to a Roman soldier in battle gear. Whatever his circumstances, Paul seized upon this as the perfect parallel to our spiritual warfare.

The first element of armor that he describes is a strip of leather that a Roman soldier would use to gird his waist. *To gird* means "to gather or to fasten to oneself." We refer to this piece as a belt. Belts are extremely practical and extremely important. For the Roman soldier, the belt performed two key functions. First, it would be buckled around his tunic to fasten all the loose material to his body so that his range of motion was free from obstruction. Second, it would be used to secure various weapons and tools to his side so these would be close at hand when needed. In particular, his sword's sheath would be attached firmly to this belt.

Belts usually weren't glamorous or flashy, but they were absolutely essential for soldiers. The same can be said for God's truth. It doesn't always attract a lot of show-stopping attention, but it is an absolute must in the throes of spiritual battle. Truth helps to keep soldiers of God free from the spiritual obstruction of false teaching. Truth also keeps believers' tools and weapons secure.

Truth is central to all we do and all we are as Christians. Jesus identified Himself as the Truth in John 14:6, and when we're bound in truth, we are bound ever so tightly to our Lord and Savior. The more secure we are in God's truth, the more secure we will be in the heat of battle.

"And you shall know the truth, and the truth shall make you free." (John 8:32 NKJV)

How does God's truth secure you in life? (Write down a specific example.)

Is there someone in your life who needs to know about the securing power of God's truth?

Put on the whole armor of God, that you may be able to stand against <u>the wiles of the devil</u>.
(Ephesians 6:11 NKJV)

The Bible gives us a "heads up" when it comes to Satan's style of attack. We're clearly warned about *the wiles of the devil*. The original Greek word for *wiles* is *methodeia,* and it means "to follow an orderly and methodical procedure with the intent to deceive." Another rendering of this word could be "art form." Satan has crafted deception into an art because he knows that it is the most effective way to destroy us.

The first time we see Satan in Scripture is in the garden of Eden. It's interesting to note that the enemy approached Eve when she was alone. God had told Adam of His prohibition against eating the fruit from the tree of the knowledge of good and evil. Adam passed the information on to Eve. Her second-hand knowledge of the prohibition created an opportunity for Satan to subtlety cast doubt when he said: *"Has God indeed said, 'You shall not eat of every tree of the garden?'" (Genesis 3:1 NKJV)* The devil didn't try to overwhelm her with brute force but came in deceptively and undefended. We all know what happened. Eve was deceived and humanity has been suffering ever since. When we first see Satan in the New Testament, he was approaching Jesus in the wilderness. Again, it is shocking to see that even when dealing with the Son of God, Satan tried to deceptively attack Him through temptation.

Both of these events had dramatically different results. One ended in misery; the other, in victory. Eve was blindsided because she didn't expect the enemy to deceive her. But when we simply expect the unexpected, we can defend ourselves as Jesus did against the wiles of the devil.

When Hitler rose to power in war-torn Germany, he did so through the art of cleverly deceiving governments about his true intentions. Years of deception had bought him the time he needed to build the most powerful army the world had ever seen. Through the art of deception, Hitler duped the entire world and brought it to its knees. Satan can do the same to us unless we recognize that he is the deceiver and that his attacks seldom come in the forms that are obvious or expected.

Why is Satan so effective in deceiving people, particularly Christians?

What is the best defense against deception?

DIVERSITY AND UNITY

DAY 213

For we do not wrestle against flesh and blood, but <u>against principalities, against powers, against the rulers of the darkness of this age, against spiritual hosts of wickedness in the heavenly places</u>. (Ephesians 6:12 NKJV)

Have you ever wondered why the Bible uses so many different words to describe Satan's army? Paul lists for us principalities, powers, rulers, and spiritual hosts. Many Bible scholars believe these words actually refer to different ranks that exist in the enemy's camp. If this is true, then it sheds some interesting light on the kingdom of darkness. Satan's army is diverse in the sense that there are different ranks of power and authority, and it is united because every rank is pointed toward the same cause and purpose—darkness and wickedness. The enemy's army is highly effective because it contains diversity and unity.

The same can be said of God's army because the Bible teaches that we are all different parts of a single body. Two key passages in the New Testament describe this truth:

For as we have many members in one body, but all the members do not have the same function . . . . (Romans 12:4 NKJV)

For as the body is one and has many members, but all the members of that one body, being many, are one body, so also is Christ. (1 Corinthians 12:12 NKJV)

The passage in Romans focuses on the diversity of the members of the body of Christ, while the passage in 1 Corinthians focuses on the essential unity of the members of the body of Christ. We see that both diversity and unity are important components in Christ's body. God doesn't want His army to be one-dimensional or divided. He desires for us to be a flexible force with skills and abilities that are varied and complementary. God also desires for us to be governed by a unity of purpose, passion, and priority because an army divided against itself cannot be victorious (Matthew 12:25). As we go to war with the enemy, we need to remember that when we embrace the differences in our fellow Christians, it plays to our overall strength and helps us to have victory in our common cause.

How is the unity of the body of Christ demonstrated?

Why are both unity and diversity so important to the body of Christ?

Therefore take up the whole armor of God, that you may be able to withstand in the evil day, and having done all, to stand. (Ephesians 6:13 NKJV)

Evil isn't a word we hear much these days. It seems that everywhere we look, we see evil things happening, but we also hear people proclaiming a positive message about the times we live in. The reality is, the day we live in is evil, and this is due largely to the fact that we're fighting against an evil adversary. As long as we're living on this side of heaven and Jesus' return, there's going to be spiritual warfare, which means there's going to be evil.

It's so important for us to recognize that the day is evil. When we look at life this way, it will have three positive effects in our lives. First, it will protect us from being **shocked** to the point of inactivity. Too many believers are so surprised by what's happening around them that they curse the darkness instead allowing the Lord to shine through them. When we're expecting evil, we won't be intimidated or rendered ineffective by it. Expecting evil will also help to keep us **sharp** as we maintain our cutting edge. Someone has compared the believer in this evil world to a deep sea diver who needs to constantly remember that he's in a hostile environment. We simply can't afford to be careless with our Christianity when confronted by evil. Last, knowing that the day is evil will prompt us to **share** the Gospel with those who are lost. Dante once wrote that the hottest places in hell are reserved for those who in a period of moral crisis maintain their neutrality. Although this doesn't express a teaching from Scripture, it does drive home the urgency for sharing the Good News of Jesus Christ in this evil day.

Someone once said, "Laws are becoming more just, rulers more humane, music sweeter, and books wiser; homes are happier and the individual heart more just and gentle." Shortly thereafter came the First World War! As spiritual warriors, we need to remember that the days are evil and live accordingly.

Why is it so important to know that we're living in evil days?

How can we counteract the effects of evil in the world today?

RELIABLE RIGHTEOUSNESS

DAY 215

Stand therefore . . . having put on the breastplate of righteousness . . . . (Ephesians 6:14 NKJV)

The devil is not interested in merely wounding us. His objective is to score the fatal "kill shot" and to take us out (1 Peter 5:8). He knows exactly where we are weakest, and he will take deliberate aim at these vital points. This means we need special protection over areas that are crucial to our spiritual life. God has graciously provided this protection for us in the form of the breastplate of righteousness.

Breastplates were usually fashioned out of leather, metal, or a combination of both. They would extend from the neck all the way down to the thighs in order to provide maximum protection to the heart and other vital organs. With a breastplate in place, a soldier might sustain several shots in the "kill zone" and yet continue to wreak havoc on his enemy. This piece of armor provided life for the warrior when he should have known death.

So it is with the righteousness of Jesus Christ. The Bible teaches that all humanity is under the curse of sin and utterly incapable of escaping eternal destruction in the lake of fire (Romans 6:23, Revelation 20:12–14). As members of a sinful and rebellious race, this is what we have earned. But there was one man who escaped the stain of sin—Jesus Christ. By being conceived by the Holy Spirit, He bypassed the sinful transmission of Adam's guilt, and by living a perfectly holy life, He maintained His guiltlessness. In every possible way, He is righteous. On the cross, Jesus made it possible for us to share in His righteousness. When we believe the simple message of the Gospel, our sins are covered by His holy perfection (Romans 5:17–18). We who should have been clothed in the filthy rags of our sin are now clothed in the spotless righteousness of Christ. The Christian's identity is no longer in Adam but in Christ.

In Adam, we have given our accuser an arsenal of ammunition to launch against us. In Christ, we have His righteousness as the perfect protection against every attack aimed our way. The breastplate of Jesus' unfailing and unending righteousness is our layer of protection between spiritual life and death.

How does Christ's righteousness protect you during the devil's attacks?

What could you share with another Christian who feels unworthy or unacceptable before God?

. . . praying always with all prayer and supplication in the Spirit, being watchful to this end <u>with all perseverance</u> and supplication for all the saints . . . . (Ephesians 6:18 NKJV)

We live in an age where perseverance is becoming less and less of an actual experience. Our culture has devalued the meaning of finishing what we start. How many offers have you received in the mail this week to start a new program or buy a new product with an "easy out" if you're not fully satisfied? Finishing has become a lost art for most of us. But God calls us to be good finishers and to persevere in every aspect of our lives. Spiritual warfare is no exception.

The sad truth is that we can fight for a long time and still fail if we don't persevere to the very end. Daniel prayed and fasted for twenty-one days and received an important prophecy concerning the kingdoms of the world (Daniel 10:2–21). He also received an angelic announcement that his prayers had triggered a conflict in the spiritual realm. It took twenty-one days for God's messenger to get through to Daniel as the kingdom of darkness did its best to block the prophetic word. It's interesting to note that Daniel kept praying and fasting until he was told that the battle was over and that the mission had been accomplished. I wonder what would have happened if he had quit on day twenty. Perhaps this important prophecy never would have gotten through to Daniel. Perhaps we quit on certain battles without realizing that we're just days, hours, or minutes away from victory.

In general, endings are more important than beginnings. Stories are remembered for their climaxes. In the world of sports, the final score is what separates winners from losers. When it comes to our relationships, the last encounter we have with someone defines our ultimate impression of him or her. And when it comes to wars, all that really matters is who won in the end. This is an important truth to keep in mind as we wage war in the spirit.

Why is perseverance so important when it comes to spiritual warfare?

What are some battles that you're close to quitting on, and what should you do about it?

<u>Finally</u>, my brethren, be strong in the Lord and in the power of His might. (Ephesians 6:10 NKJV)

Have you ever noticed that the Holy Spirit inspired Paul to place his teaching on spiritual warfare at the end of the book of Ephesians, instead of the beginning? There's a purpose behind this placement, and it becomes clear when we consider what precedes this passage.

In Ephesians 1–3, Paul concentrates on all that God has done for those who are in Christ. Then in Ephesians 4–5:21, he focuses on each believer's responsibility to walk in personal godliness. Finally, in Ephesians 5:22–6:9, the apostle instructs believers on how to have godly relationships. It's only after these subjects have been addressed that we move on to waging war with the enemy. It's as if the Lord is showing us that certain things need to be in place before we can begin to fight effectively in the spiritual realm.

If we are to be "battle ready," we must have a complete understanding of the spiritual resources that are ours in Christ. We won't understand how to use our spiritual resources unless we know what they are. We also need to cultivate personal godliness into our daily lives. Our lives need to be marked by obedience if we are to have any true victory in our spirituality. Last, there must be spiritual order in our relationships with each other. This includes the way we relate to our spouses, children, parents, employees, and employers. Then and only then, can we expect to experience success when it comes to spiritual warfare.

Which led me to consider the question, Why do we fail so often? Could it be that we just haven't put first things first? How grounded are we in our understanding of who we are and what we possess in Christ? Are our lives marked by godly behavior, or is our Christianity just in the showroom, not the stockroom? Are our God-given relationships lined up with His holy standards? If not, then it's time to follow the scriptural pattern of putting first things first. This is the only way to develop godliness and the only way to truly be ready for spiritual warfare.

How does the placement of Paul's teaching on spiritual warfare affect your understanding of spiritual warfare?

Why is this understanding significant?

MOBILITY AND STABILITY
DAY 218

And having <u>shod your feet with the preparation of the gospel of peace</u> . . . . (Ephesians 6:15 NKJV)

History tells us that Alexander the Great did not command the largest or even the most fortified armies. Yet, history also tells us that Alexander's armies rose to conquer the known world. One of the keys to their success was the design of their sandals. Alexander was a natural-born innovator, and he recognized that his troops could gain two decisive advantages if their sandals were fitted with cleats.

First, these sandals gave his soldiers the advantage of **mobility**. They were able to traverse the rough terrain of the ancient world in record time, surprising their enemies and catching them off guard. Second, they gave his men superior **stability**. When push came to shove in the heat of hand-to-hand combat, Alexander's men were able to keep their ground and push back the enemy one step at a time. These advantages were not lost on the Romans, who also studded their sandal soles with sharp nails.

Needless to say, a soldier's sandals were an important part of his armor. Paul ties the imagery of these sandals to the Gospel of peace. The Gospel message is many things, but in this passage, special emphasis is placed on the fact that it brings peace to the believer. It is so important for spiritual soldiers to be constantly reminded of the fact that they are at peace with God. The war against heaven has ended, and now there is eternal peace with the Prince of Peace. The power of the peace that the Gospel brings ought to have two effects on our faith.

The peace of God should give us mobility. Having received the peace of God for ourselves, we should become naturally motivated to move out and share it with others, even to the ends of the earth (Matthew 28:19). The peace of God should also bring us stability. Satan's forces are constantly trying to push us back in our faith with an onslaught of discouragement and doubt. But the knowledge that we are at peace with God keeps us firmly planted and prevents us from giving up our spiritual ground (Colossians 1:20). Let us remember that the Gospel of peace gives us the motivation to move and the stability to stand.

What effects has the Gospel message produced in your life?

How can you display a greater degree of spiritual mobility and stability?

And it happened . . . that Paul, having passed through the upper regions, came to Ephesus. (Acts 19:1 NKJV)

I can only imagine how this must have infuriated the enemy's camp. Prior to Paul's visit to Ephesus, Satan had held the citizens of this prominent city captive. This is underscored by the fact that Ephesus was the home to one of the seven wonders of the ancient world, the temple of Diana. The worship of this pagan deity was a part of daily life for the Ephesians, and the demonic presence in this city must have been incalculable.

But something happened when Paul came to town; he brought the message of the cross with him and began to establish a beachhead of believers within this cradle of the occult. The message of the cross continued to spread, and the enemy began to mount an attack to exterminate the Gospel from Ephesus. Spiritual warfare had been declared.

There were even those whom the Bible refers to as "itinerant Jewish exorcists." These men saw the **results** that Jesus produced but lacked a **relationship** with Him and attempted to exorcise a demoniac in His name. Knowing that they lacked the relational power found in Christ, the enemy taught them a painful lesson.

Then the man in whom the evil spirit was leaped on them, overpowered them, and prevailed against them, so that they fled out of that house naked and wounded. (Acts 19:16 NKJV)

Score one for the kingdom of darkness, right? Wrong! By showing his true nature to the Ephesians, the enemy actually drove people to repentance and a relationship with the Lord.

This became known both to all Jews and Greeks dwelling in Ephesus; and fear fell on them all, and the name of the Lord Jesus was magnified. (Acts 19:17 NKJV)

As he often does, Satan made the mistake of going too far and suffered a major loss as a result. Let's not be deceived; we're no match for the devil on our own. But when we follow Christ, we will always have a tactical advantage over the enemy.

If you were the enemy, how would you attack the army of God?

Why can we follow Christ's orders with full confidence?

IDENTIFYING THE ENEMY

DAY 220

For <u>we do not wrestle against flesh and blood</u>, but against principalities, against powers, against the rulers of the darkness of this age, against spiritual hosts of wickedness in the heavenly places. (Ephesians 6:12 NKJV)

It's no coincidence that as Paul warns us about the deceptive wiles of the enemy, he immediately draws our attention to the fact that *we do not wrestle against flesh and blood*. I believe that one of the enemy's favorite wiles is to confuse our understanding about his true identity. Satan's plan is to get us to think that the people in our daily lives (the flesh and blood) are our real enemies. If he can accomplish this, then we're beaten before we're out of the gate because we can't defeat an enemy we can't identify.

When we focus on the flesh, we do two things that are detrimental to us. We encourage our own carnality because we stay subject to the worldly level instead of seeing things through the spiritual perspective. We also ensure the world's captivity because when we see our fellow man as the enemy, we certainly won't be inclined to share the saving message of the Gospel with them. They stay bound in their captivity, and we stay bound in our carnality.

There are three things we can do to help us stop focusing on the flesh and start identifying the real enemy. First, we need to love those who we're tempted to call our enemy. Second, we need to pray for people who rub us the wrong way, especially those who don't know the Lord. The more we pray for people, the more we will desire what's best for them. Last, we need to share the Gospel with them, understanding their spiritual condition and need. When we do these things, we will see people in a much different light and we will also see our real enemy for who he is.

It's a terrible tragedy whenever friendly fire occurs on the battlefield. We need to remember that God calls us to befriend people in our lives whom we have mistakenly identified as our enemies.

How have you been guilty of "friendly fire"?

What steps will you take to ensure that this does not happen in the future?

And when He had fasted forty days and forty nights, afterward He was hungry. Now when the tempter came to Him, he said, "If You are the Son of God, command that these stones become bread." But He answered and said, "It is written, 'Man shall not live by bread alone, but by every word that proceeds from the mouth of God.'" (Matthew 4:2–4 NKJV)

Not all small packages contain good things. In fact, within the confines of the tiny word *if* lies the deadliest poison known to mankind. In this one little word, temptation is planted, and Satan strategically, stealthily, and shrewdly uses it to plant the seed of doubt. He drudges up this temptation from the deepest, darkest depths of hell and uses it to call into question the very Word of God.

Just before Jesus had gone into the wilderness, after he was baptized by John, the sky opened and God declared, *"This is My beloved Son, in whom I am well pleased" (Matthew 3:1 NKJV)*. And now, forty hungry, lonely, exhausted days later, the devil calls this into question. But in the fashion of the finest fencer, Jesus cuts right to the quick of the lie. Without hesitation, He clarifies the issue. Life is not about physical food or the here and now but about the spiritual food of God's Word and the kingdom to come.

The same temptation faces us day-in and day-out in every decision we make. The enemy waits patiently for the right set of circumstances, for our weakest moment, before he throws his fiery darts of doubt at the Word which God has given us. It is inescapable. When life's "if's" confront us, they are pivotal points where we must choose between God's truth and the devil's lie. We can either believe the lie and tumble head-first into the anxiety-ridden existence of worry and death or stand firmly upon the steadfast and trustworthy Word of God and enter the realm of peace found in God's abundant life.

How can you equip yourself for your battles with the enemy?

Where do you derive your definition of who you are?

And the evil spirit answered and said, "Jesus I know, and Paul I know; but who are you?"
(Acts 19:15 NKJV)

Every so often, we get a glimpse of Satan's intelligence report. In confronting a group of men who were impressed with the power of Jesus' name but who didn't have any real connection with Him, an evil spirit tips his cards just enough to teach us three important things.

First, the enemy tells us that he knows Jesus. The original Greek word here for *know* implies an experiential knowledge, and the Bible shows us that there's a long battle-torn history between the adversary and our Lord. The devil's camp knows Jesus all too well, and from Genesis to Revelation, we see that he's completely devoted to preventing God's plans and persecuting God's people.

We also see that the enemy knows Paul. We need to understand that when we come to Christ, we become a threat to the other side. Satan turns his attack on us and does so intelligently. Have you ever considered how much the enemy knows about your personal life? He knows the things that our parents and closest friends don't even know about us. He knows the areas where we are personally weak and prone to failure. We're naive to think that he won't press the buttons that are specifically problematic for us. Satan's spiritual attack isn't generic but personal, and he'll base it on the details he has acquired on us. I shudder to think of what the devil has on file against me—all the more reason to rest in the fact that Jesus has completely covered my sins!

Last, we see that the enemy doesn't really know those who aren't connected to Christ. The evil spirit was basically saying, *You mean nothing to me.* Those who don't belong to the Lord are nothing to the devil. They pose no threat to his plans and have no hope of escaping his spiritual grip apart from the Gospel. They are nothing more than slaves to be used and abused by their tyrannical taskmaster.

It's actually an honor to be known by the enemy because it shows that we're a real threat to him. We need to keep this in mind and make it our mission to rescue those who need to know Jesus.

Where do you think you fit in when it comes to the enemy's plans?

What should our attitude be toward spiritual warfare?

. . . praying always with all prayer and supplication in the Spirit, being watchful to this end with all perseverance and supplication for <u>all the saints</u> . . . (Ephesians 6:18 NKJV)

As Paul brings his teaching on spiritual warfare to a close, he makes it a point to remind us that we are to pray for *all the saints*. This shows that even in the context of spiritual warfare, we are responsible for one another.

God wants us to be others-oriented as we take on the enemy because He knows that it will do three things to make us more effective fighters. First, it will free us from focusing on ourselves. There's no better remedy for selfishness than seeing and meeting another person's need. When we're responding to the needs of others through prayer or acts of service, we prevent selfishness from controlling us. Second, being responsible for others in battle helps boost our confidence in our cause. It's part of our human nature to think in individual terms and to feel that we're the only ones fighting the good fight of faith. Elijah is a classic reminder that this can happen to even the most seasoned saints (1 Kings 19:10). But as we interact with the needs of other saints, we're reminded that our cause is bigger than we thought and that the fight involves the entire family of God. Finally, being responsible for others ensures that we will receive help in our own hour of need. It's such a blessing to be able to help those who have helped me in the past. Being responsible for other saints today sets us up to receive help in the future.

During World War II, a young American pilot was shot down over the Japanese island of Chi Chi Jima. Seconds before his bomber crashed into the Pacific Ocean, he bailed out into the water. Without question, he would have drowned or been taken captive by the enemy. But another plane saw the entire incident and dropped an inflatable life raft to the struggling pilot. That life raft enabled him to stay afloat long enough to be picked up by an American submarine that was nearby. That pilot's name was George Herbert Walker Bush! By being others-oriented, we can have an amazing impact for the kingdom of God!

How does the responsibility for others help us in our spiritual combat?

What saints are you responsible for in your circle of life?

. . . praying always with all prayer and supplication in the Spirit, being watchful to this end with all perseverance and supplication for all the saints . . . . (Ephesians 6:18 NKJV)

Victory in any form of warfare depends on keeping channels of communication clear with headquarters. When a fighting force is cut off from its source of supply and leadership, it's only a matter of time before it folds. This is why it is critical for us to be *praying always with all prayer and supplication* as we engage the enemy in spiritual battle.

Satan understands this principle, and that's why he relentlessly attacks our prayer life. Among the many descriptions of Satan in Scripture, he is compared to a lion (1 Peter 5:8). I find this fascinating because in the natural world, a lion will clamp down its powerful jaws on its victim's mouth in order to keep it from crying out to the rest of the herd. This is very descriptive of what the enemy wants to do to us in order to keep us from crying out for heavenly help in prayer. If we allow him to keep us from prayer, we're bound to go through the stages of isolation, then desperation, and finally resignation. When the devil interrupts our prayer life, it may seem insignificant at the time, but it is just the thin edge of the wedge that drives us further and further from the Lord and spiritual victory.

After decades of faithfully following the Lord, Dr. Martyn Lloyd-Jones, former British preacher, concluded, "Everything we do in the Christian life is easier than prayer." I would have to agree, and I believe that a big reason for this can be traced back to Satan's efforts to disrupt our prayer life. When Jesus faced perhaps the most intense spiritual battle of His existence in the garden of Gethsemane, He was busy praying. We need to follow our Lord's example. We need to be *praying always with all prayer and supplication*, especially when warfare is at its worst.

What practical ways does the enemy use to attack your prayer life, and what can you do about it?

How would you comment on Martyn Lloyd-Jones' statement about prayer?

Put on the whole armor of God, that you may be able to stand against the wiles of the devil. (Ephesians 6:11 NKJV)

Have you ever wondered why the Lord doesn't do it all for us? I mean, if God is so concerned with our spiritual safety, why does He leave it up to us to put on His armor? Most of us, if not all, would prefer not to have this responsibility placed upon us. However, we need to understand that responsibility is essentially healthy and that God created us to be responsible beings.

In the beginning of the book of Genesis, one of the first things God does is give Adam the responsibility of tending and keeping the garden of Eden (Genesis 2:15). Everywhere you look in the Bible, God is assigning responsibility to man. Earlier in Ephesians, we learn that husbands are responsible to their wives, wives are responsible to their husbands, children are responsible to their parents, employers are responsible to their employees, and so on.

God has designed life to be this way because He understands that responsibilities can cause our relationships with others to thrive. With responsibility comes expectation, and as expectations are fulfilled and met, a history of trust and confidence is built between people. It's true between husband and wife, and it is equally true between us and the Lord. When we're responsible to do what God tells us to do, which in this case means putting on His armor, we can expect victory in return. When we see victory take place in our lives as a result of obeying His Word, a history is built and our trust and confidence in Him increases with each and every battle.

Now think back to the original question, Why doesn't God do it all for us? If the Lord did everything for us, then we might be safe, but we would also have a pathetically weak relationship with Him. By commanding us to put on His armor, God has given us a built-in way of building up our relationship with Him, and those who are responsible to put on His armor tend to be those who are also closest to Him.

How do your responsibilities in life affect your relationships?

How can this principle help us understand God and what He calls us to do?

SEEING ISN'T BELIEVING

For we do not wrestle against flesh and blood, but against principalities, against powers, against the rulers of the darkness of this age, against spiritual hosts of wickedness <u>in the heavenly places</u>. (Ephesians 6:12 NKJV)

Maybe you've asked yourself the same question that I have, *Why doesn't God allow us to see what's happening in the spiritual realm?* When it comes to spiritual warfare, wouldn't it be a lot easier to fight the enemy if we were able to visibly witness the results of our efforts against him? Yet the fact remains that our battleground is spiritual, and it remains in the heavenly places, not here on earth.

This tends to frustrate us because we often assume that seeing is believing, and we mistakenly think it would make us better spiritual soldiers if we could just see what we're fighting against with our natural eyes. However, when you read through the Bible, you will find that seeing does not necessarily mean believing. Whether it's the Jews who wandered in the wilderness, the people who witnessed the miracles of Jesus, or those who will endure the terrible tribulation period, miraculous manifestations don't make people more spiritual. In fact, heavenly manifestations often distract hearts from drawing close to God.

God knows this, and He doesn't want us to be people driven by sight. Instead, He desires for us to be faith-based believers because lives founded on faith stand strong long after visions and miracles have passed away. It takes faith to believe that there is an unseen war taking place all around us. It takes faith to believe that there is spiritual armor that will protect us if we put it on. When you think about it, everything about spiritual warfare is faith-based because it's all based on believing in what you can't see. God has designed it to be this way because He knows the very nature of spiritual warfare, the fact that we can't see it, serves to make us into people of faith. Being made into people of faith serves the Lord's ultimate purpose and our ultimate good.

What are the advantages of being faith-based as opposed to being sight-driven?

What makes you a strong spiritual soldier?

SIFTED AS WHEAT

But Peter followed Him at a distance, right into the courtyard of the high priest. And he sat with the servants and warmed himself at the fire. (Mark 14:54 NKJV)

What a depiction of a courageous man turned coward. Yet, you have to admire Peter's determination and drive to follow Christ. From boldly cutting off an ear to stealthily sneaking into the enemy's camp, Peter attempted to carry out his rash proclamation to stay till the bitter end. It could have been this reliance on self that set him up to be sideswiped by the devil. As he warmed himself at that fire, I wonder if Peter's thoughts wandered to the words of Jesus that had elicited his emotional pledge of faithfulness unto death:

And the Lord said, "Simon, Simon! Indeed, Satan has asked for you, that he may sift you as wheat. But I have prayed for you, that your faith should not fail; and when you have returned to Me, strengthen your brethren." But he said to Him, "Lord, I am ready to go with You, both to prison and to death." (Luke 22:31–33 NKJV)

Like many of us, Peter had underestimated the cunning and craftiness of the enemy. He made two fatal mistakes. First, he thought he could stand in the enemy's camp without being affected by the enemy's servants. Second, he thought that his separation from Christ would not impair his ability to be ready for the battle, as long as he still could see Jesus from a distance.

No matter how ready we feel in our own flesh for the day ahead of us, we must remember that apart from Christ, we can do nothing. We need to stay in step with Him, not following at a distance, and avoid the camp of the enemy with its temptations to warm ourselves. In this life, there is only black and white, right and wrong, good and evil. If we are going to make every decision count for Christ, we must be close enough to hear what He tells us to do.

In what ways can you identify with Peter?

What can we learn from Peter's two fatal mistakes?

Put on the whole armor of God, that you may be able to <u>stand</u> against the wiles of the devil. (Ephesians 6:11 NKJV)

It's interesting that the Bible prescribes only one position for spiritual warfare. The soldier for Christ is never called to sit or lie down but is always called to stand. In fact, throughout this section of Scripture, the Holy Spirit deliberately used the word *stand* three times and the word *withstand* once when describing our position before the enemy. Why is standing so important to the Lord? I believe He wants us to stand because He knows what it can accomplish.

First, when we **stand up**, we are making a conscious decision to identify with a particular cause. Standing up requires us to forsake the comfort of neutrality and anonymity. There's a story of a soldier during the Civil War who tried to play it safe by wearing a Union jacket and Confederate trousers. As it turned out, he was fired upon by both sides because he was unwilling to take a stand. When we stand up, it strengthens our fighting spirit.

When we stand up, we also **stand out**. God doesn't want our lives to blend in with the scenery of this world. He desires for us to stand out because then, and only then, will the world take notice of the fact that there is something different about us. Jesus describes us as salt and light (Matthew 5:13–16), and as we stand against the enemy, we stand out against the worldly backdrop of blandness and darkness.

As our lives stand out, we show others that there is something in this world to **stand for**. God created man to stand for something. From politics to sports, people are looking for a cause to adopt and embrace. But only the cause of Christ can truly fulfill this divinely designed desire within the human heart. When we stand against Satan, we help people see the ultimate cause worth standing for.

The world record for standing in one place is sixty-one hours; this shows us that standing is not a natural position for us. It isn't always easy, but with God's help, we can take our stand against the enemy and even help others in the process.

What are a few of the risks involved with standing up for something?

What are the benefits of standing up for Christ?

Finally, my brethren, <u>be strong in the Lord and in the power of His might</u>. (Ephesians 6:10 NKJV)

From the very outset, Paul reminds us that Jesus needs to be the source of our strength as we wage war against the enemy. If we're to be effective in our fighting, we must learn to rely on the Lord's resources instead of our own. We see this principle presented to us throughout the Scriptures.

As Paul goes on to list the various articles of armor, he shows us that their value is in their association with the Lord. The belt is *His* truth, the breastplate is *His* imparted righteousness, our feet are shod with the proclamation of *His* Gospel, the shield is our faith in *Him*, the helmet is *His* salvation, and our sword is *His* Word. In Acts 16:18, Paul comes face to face with the enemy and in the name of Jesus Christ, he commands an evil spirit to come out of a slave girl. A name represents authority and reputation, and the apostle knew better than to confront the enemy on the basis of his own name, and that it was far wiser to stand behind the all-powerful name of Jesus. As if Paul's exhortation and example weren't enough to convince us of our need, the book of Jude tells us that Michael, the archangel, fought against Satan and specifically said, *"The Lord rebuke you!" (v. 9)* If the mighty archangel found it necessary to fight in the Lord's power, then how much more should we?

Unfortunately, we frequently forget this fact and try to fight the enemy in the power of our own strength. In my life, I've noticed that my pride leads me to turn from depending on Jesus' strength to relying on my own limited powers and abilities. I want to believe that I'm really stronger than the Bible says and that I can do battle all on my own. Yet each time I meet the enemy in my own strength, I meet with failure. The sooner I simply accept my own weakness, the sooner I become strong in Christ and the victory instantly becomes mine. How important for us to understand that our strength lies in Jesus and no one else.

How has your own strength gotten in the way of experiencing Christ's?

List some extreme examples of mismatches. How do these compare to the mismatch of our strength compared to Christ's?

Put on the <u>whole</u> armor of God, that you may be able to stand against the wiles of the devil. (Ephesians 6:11 NKJV)

It's part of our fallen human nature to settle for half-measures in order to just get by. Instead of striving for perfection and excellence, we frequently settle for what is "good enough." When it comes to spiritual warfare, however, half-measures are never "good enough." For this reason, Paul exhorts us to put on the **whole** armor of God, not just the particular piece that most suits us. In essence, we are called to take full advantage of God's provision.

We can learn a lesson from the enemy when it comes to this principle. Not only do we wrestle against Satan's kingdom of darkness, but we also fight against the worldly system that surrounds us (Romans 12:2; 1 John 2:15) and our fleshly nature that still dwells within us (Romans 8:13). The devil doesn't give us a free pass or let up on us when it comes to the world or the flesh. Instead, he relentlessly utilizes them against us. He makes full, or **whole,** use of these things that wound us. Because of this, we need to make full use of the things that God has given to us in order to overcome Satan. This means putting on the **whole** armor of God. We simply can't afford to go into battle with anything less.

If we find ourselves failing when it comes to spiritual warfare, we need to remember that the deficiency is not on God's part to give but on our part to receive. We need to determine if we've neglected a certain aspect of our spiritual armor, and if so, we need to take full advantage of all that the Lord has provided for us.

What are some things that keep us from taking full advantage of what God has provided for us?

What aspects of God's armor do you tend to neglect, and how can you correct this?

. . . and for me, that utterance may be given to me, that I may open my mouth boldly to make known the mystery of the gospel . . . (Ephesians 6:19 NKJV)

The three little words *and for me* link Paul's theology with Paul's personality. Up to this point, the apostle has instructed us about the various aspects of spiritual warfare. He has told us of our need to put on God's armor, of our need to know who the enemy really is, and of the importance of praying for each other. But it isn't until he says *and for me* that Paul shows himself to be an active participant in the truths he has taught.

I've learned it is very easy to look at spiritual truths and doctrines and view them from the outside without fully entering into them. Our human nature seems to want to insulate rather than participate in spiritual things. Paul was an active participant in the truths he taught. He fully believed in the power of intercessory prayer, and this is evidenced by the amount of times he asked for it (e.g., Colossians 4:3; 1 Thessalonians 5:25; 2 Thessalonians 3:1).

In John 13:17, Jesus stressed that His disciples would experience spiritual blessing if they actually *did* what they knew. In the Sermon on the Mount, Christ closed this definitive discourse on the Christian life by sharing a story about two men who built on two different foundations. One foundation was faulty, while the other was firm. One house fell, while the other stood. The foundational difference wasn't based on information but on participation:

"Therefore whoever hears these sayings of Mine, and <u>does them</u>, I will liken him to a wise man who built his house on the rock: and the rain descended, the floods came, and the winds blew and beat on that house; and it did not fall, for it was founded on the rock. But everyone who hears these sayings of Mine, and <u>does not do them</u>, will be like a foolish man who built his house on the sand . . ." (Matthew 7:24–26 NKJV)

Knowledge of the truth doesn't guarantee spiritual stability or victory; application of the truth does. What we know about spiritual warfare is useless unless it is linked to our daily lives through practical participation.

What are some areas of your life where you insulate when you should participate?

How can you ensure that you apply what you know about spiritual warfare?

. . . and for me, that utterance may be given to me, that <u>I may open my mouth boldly to make known the mystery of the gospel</u> . . . . (Ephesians 6:19 NKJV)

So what's the point? Why do we even bother dealing with this thing called spiritual warfare? Why do we willingly clash with celestial beings that are bent on making our lives downright miserable? What are we thinking when we take a stand against Satan and invite his attacks upon our lives? What's the underlying motivation in all this? The Bible tells us that it is *to make known the mystery of the gospel.* In context, Paul is asking for "prayer reinforcements" so he can effectively share the Gospel with those who are lost.

The Gospel—the message that people can be made righteous in God's sight by simply believing that Jesus Christ fully paid the price for their sins on the cross—is at the heart of every aspect of the Christian life, including spiritual warfare. The Gospel is the reason we go to war against the enemy, and the Gospel is the reason the enemy goes to war against us. We must understand that our adversary will do everything within his power to prevent this message from getting out because it is a unique threat to him. The Bible describes those who don't believe in Jesus as being spiritually blinded and bound by Satan (Acts 26:18; 2 Corinthians 4:4). The enemy hates it when we share the Gospel because it has the potential set people **free,** and as people are set free, they become able to **fight** against him. When we see the Gospel in this light, it's all the more motivating for us to make it known.

It's a proven fact that an army's effectiveness is directly proportionate to its belief in its cause. Over the centuries, men have fought and given their lives for causes that were foolish at best and false at worst. As part of the army of the Lord, we have the privilege of fighting for the greatest cause that time and eternity have ever witnessed—the cross of Jesus Christ. The Gospel message makes the warfare worthwhile.

How would you describe the connection between sharing the Gospel and spiritual warfare?

How would you describe the Gospel from Satan's perspective?

. . . and for <u>me</u>, that utterance may be given to me, that I may open my mouth boldly to make known the mystery of the gospel . . . . (Ephesians 6:19 NKJV)

How would you like to have Bill Gates show you how to use your computer? How would you like to have Emeril Lagasse show you how to make a meal? Or how would you like to have Tiger Woods show you how to play golf? Of course, we would love lessons from each of these men because we understand that they are proven experts in their fields. Paul was no less of an expert when it came to the subject of spiritual warfare. When he wrote *me* at the end of this teaching, he had already tested and proven these truths in the trenches of life for several years.

Paul had to deal with an amazing amount of spiritual warfare on his very first missionary journey. On his first stop on the island of Cyprus, an agent of the enemy **verbally** attacked him (Acts 13:6–11). A few verses later, when he was in Iconium, the adversary incited people to try to **physically** attack him (Acts 14:4–5). Paul fled to the city of Lystra where the enemy attacked him **spiritually** by appealing to his pride (Acts 14:8–13). All this happened to Paul before his first missionary journey had even ended! The Lord allowed this to take place in Paul's life because He knew that one day Paul would be able to teach on the subject of spiritual warfare from a position of experience and authority.

During World War I, British pilots were facing a crisis because their airplanes kept falling into deadly tailspins while in combat. A physicist named Frederick Lindemann devised a mathematical formula that would, in theory, help pilots pull out. Everyone scoffed, *What does a physicist know about flying airplanes?* To demonstrate the reliability of his formula, Lindemann got into an airplane, intentionally took it into a deadly tailspin, and successfully pulled out of it. Pilots started listening to professor Lindemann that day because his advice was now trench-tested. When we read Paul's teaching on spiritual warfare, we would do well to remember that it isn't theoretical but trench-tested truth.

What are the advantages of following truths that have been trench-tested?

Why do you think Paul was met with such strong opposition at the very beginning of his missionary ministry?

THE ENEMY'S END
DAY 234

The devil, who deceived them, was cast into the lake of fire and brimstone where the beast and the false prophet are. And they will be tormented day and night forever and ever. (Revelation 20:10 NKJV)

It has been estimated that since 3600 B.C., the world has known only 292 years of peace! This statistic shows that this world certainly has seen its fair share of warfare. Every war has something in common—no one can be declared the victor or loser until the dust has settled and the battle is finally over; that is, with the sole exception of our ongoing war with the enemy. As the army of God, we have the distinct advantage of knowing the final outcome of the fight we're engaged in.

According to the verse above, Satan will be seized and thrown into the lake of fire to be tormented for all eternity. For him, there is absolutely no alternative ending. It's critical to understand that this is not a **probability** but a **certainty** according to the Holy Scriptures. To suggest anything else is a denial of the written Word and equates to calling God a liar.

The natural world shows us that a soldier's motivation to fight is directly connected to his belief in his ability to win. Whenever ultimate victory seems lost, hope fades and a soldier will invariably lose his heart to fight. If any fighting force ever had a reason to fight with the utmost zeal, it's us. We're enlisted in a war that cannot be lost. We may lose our ground when it comes to the day-to-day battles of life, but the eventual outcome is fixed—there's no changing the fact that our foe is defeated. The only thing standing between the devil and his destiny is time, the time that God has ordained for him. What encouragement this is to the Christian warrior! It has been well stated, "Whenever the devil reminds you of your past, remind him of his future."

What encouragement do you get from the fact that Satan's defeat is sure?

How can this truth serve to encourage you as you fight your day-to-day battles?

. . . praying always with all prayer and supplication in the Spirit, <u>being watchful</u> to this end with all perseverance and supplication for all the saints . . . (Ephesians 6:18 NKJV)

God wants us to be watchful warriors. Being watchful is important to the heart of God because it reflects an aspect of His character. The Bible tells us that God is constantly watching over those who belong to Him (Psalm 1:6) as well as those who are His enemies (Psalm 66:7). We need to recognize that the Lord isn't pleased by ignorance or by being caught off guard. He expects us to be watchful and aware of what the enemy is up to.

When God was preparing Gideon to go to war against the Midianites, He deliberately chose watchful warriors to go with him. Gideon began at a great natural disadvantage because his army of ten thousand was outnumbered by a ratio of over ten to one! Despite this fact, the Lord trimmed down Gideon's army even more by establishing an interesting criterion:

". . bring them down to the water, and I will test them for you there. . . ." So he brought the people down to the water. And the LORD said to Gideon, "Everyone who laps from the water with his tongue, as a dog laps, you shall set apart by himself; likewise everyone who gets down on his knees to drink." And the number of those who lapped, putting their hand to their mouth, was three hundred men; but all the rest of the people got down on their knees to drink water. Then the LORD said to Gideon, "By the three hundred men who lapped I will save you, and deliver the Midianites into your hand. Let all the other people go, every man to his place." (Judges 7:4–7 NKJV)

Everyone who took their eyes off the horizon to satisfy their thirst was sent home. Gideon was left with only three hundred warriors, but they were all watchful warriors—men who drank in a way that allowed them to survey their surroundings. These men went on to victory, and the Lord was able to do more with a few watchful warriors than with a multitude of men.

As spiritual warriors, we need to be watchful, not just for Satan's schemes, but also for our neighbor's needs (Galatians 6:2) and for Christ's coming (Titus 2:13).

How does being unwatchful play to our enemy's advantage?

What are some practical ways that you can be watchful?

Above all, taking <u>the shield of faith</u> with which you will be able to quench all the fiery darts of the wicked one. (Ephesians 6:16 NKJV)

The Romans had two types of shields they took into battle. One was a small disk that was fastened to a soldier's forearm so he could defend himself in close hand-to-hand combat. The other shield was larger and door-shaped. Its function was to protect the entire body of an infantryman as he would advance in ranks upon the enemy line. This is the type of shield that Paul is envisioning as he wrote about our shield of faith.

Try to imagine what this shield meant to a Roman soldier when he marched into hostile territory. This was the only barrier to defend him from the avalanche of fire-tipped arrows, spears, and other deadly projectiles that would rain down upon him. Shields would often resemble deadly pincushions once the fighting finally stopped. A shield took the full brunt of the enemy's wrath, and without it, a warrior would have absolutely no hope of even getting close to his foe. A fighter in the Roman Legion would never dare enter battle without his shield in front of him.

Through the pen of the apostle Paul, the Holy Spirit is showing us that our shield of faith is equally important to us in our spiritual struggle against Satan. Faith is the hand that stretches out to lay hold of God's guarantees; it is the persistently stubborn trust that the Lord is all who He has proclaimed to be and that He will accomplish all that He has promised to do. Faith is the shield that protects God's army against the fiery darts launched by the devil. Faith quenched the dart of disappointment and allowed Joseph to continue to trust in God despite his circumstances. Faith extinguished the dart of doubt as David boldly went out to meet Goliath. Faith smothered the dart of depression as Paul and Silas sang praises after being beaten in jail.

And the shield of faith can sustain you as well. Every weapon of the enemy is powerless against the power of your childlike trust in the goodness of your heavenly Father. May the Lord fuel your faith in Him as you press forward against your foe.

How can you increase your personal faith in God? (Hint: read Romans 10:17.)

Who needs to hear this and when will you share it?

And take <u>the helmet of salvation</u> . . . . (Ephesians 6:17 NKJV)

As the mind goes, so goes the rest of the person. The mind is a powerful engine, directing and driving our lives in one of two directions. It can lead us in the ways of the Lord as we set our minds on the things above (Colossians 3:2) and think upon the things that reflect Him (Philippians 4:8). But it can also lead us down the path of destruction when we allow our thoughts to be influenced and infiltrated by the enemy. Satan attacked Eve's mind when he deceived her, and he wants to do the same thing to us:

But I fear, lest somehow, as the serpent deceived Eve by his craftiness, so your <u>minds</u> may be corrupted from the simplicity that is in Christ. (2 Corinthians 11:3 NKJV)

Our minds need protection from the serpent's subtle persuasions. And just as a soldier protects his head by wearing a helmet, we, as spiritual soldiers, are called to protect our minds by putting on the helmet of salvation. This piece of armor serves as a mental safeguard for us. Through constant awareness and contemplation of God's salvation, our thoughts become safe and secure from Satan's mental attacks.

Salvation impacts us on three levels. First, our salvation releases us from the penalty of our **past** sins. Second, our salvation frees us from power over sin in this **present** life. Last, our salvation guarantees our **future** in heaven. Paul eloquently presented this three-fold salvation for us in the following verses:

Yes, we had the sentence of death in ourselves, that we should not trust in ourselves but in God who raises the dead, who <u>delivered</u> [past] us from so great a death, and <u>does deliver</u> [present] us; in whom we trust that He <u>will still deliver</u> [future] us . . . . (2 Corinthians 1:9–10 NKJV)

Before going out to fight, a Roman soldier received a helmet that was chosen and given to him by the steward of the armory. So, too, before we go forward into spiritual battle, we must reach out and accept the salvation that God has extended to us. With so great a salvation, our minds can be protected from the enemy and brought under the control of the Lord.

How has God's saving work changed your life?

How would you explain to a non-believer what it means to be saved?

And take . . . the sword of the Spirit, which is the word of God . . . . (Ephesians 6:17 NKJV)

Paul has painted a powerful picture for us. We have seen how the spiritual soldier is kept secure by the belt of truth; how the breastplate of Christ's righteousness protects him from spiritual death and preserves him for spiritual life; and how his feet are fitted with the Gospel of peace, making him mobile and stable. We also have watched his faith in God act as a protective shield against the flaming arrows of the enemy and how God's salvation acts as a helmet to protect him from the satanic attacks against his mind. But there is still something missing—the spiritual soldier's weapon.

The most effective armor won't do us any good if we don't have a weapon that allows us to go on the offensive. Without a weapon, we're merely moving targets, destined to be destroyed sooner or later. But God has not left us in such a sorry state. He has given us an unstoppable sword that the kingdom of Satan cannot resist or endure. It is the mighty Word of God against which there is no possible defense or counterattack. Paul likened its efficiency to the short sword that enabled Romans to take control of conflicts at close range. This weapon gave maximum results with minimal effort. When a foe approached with his larger, heavier, and clumsier blade, a Roman soldier would draw his "machaira" and be ready to plunge it into his adversary with deadly accuracy.

What a perfect description of the Word of God! It produces maximum results without a great effort on our part. There is such power in God's Word that when we declare it in the presence of our enemy, he is forced to flee in defeat. When unleashed, it cuts to the core in the unseen realm:

For the word of God is living and powerful, and sharper than any two-edged sword, piercing even to the division of soul and spirit, and of joints and marrow, and is a discerner of the thoughts and intents of the heart. (Hebrews 4:12 NKJV)

If we aren't experiencing spiritual victory, it could mean that we aren't taking hold of God's Word and wielding it in the way a spiritual warrior should. Let us bring the sword into the spiritual battles of life and allow it to bring us the victory that is both desired and required by God.

How well do you know God's Word, and how can you prepare yourself to know it more?

How will you use the sword of the Spirit before this day is over?

"Sin will be rampant everywhere, and the love of many will grow cold. But those who endure to the end will be saved." (Matthew 24:12–13 NLT)

Pick up a newspaper or turn on the television, and you'll be forced to conclude that this world is waxing worse and worse. A recent study revealed that violent crimes in homes is up twelve percent. Our homes are no longer havens for harmony and happiness but haunts of hostility and hatred.

But what's happening in our homes reflects what's happening on a larger scale in our hearts. As a society, we're becoming more and more insensitive to sin, and this is reflected in the laws of our land. There are a lot of things that our courts consider legal that God considers sinful. Pornography is legal, but it destroys families. Gratuitous violence on the big screen is legal, but it's hurting people in real life. Obscene lyrics in today's hottest hits are legal, but they've trained society to be crueler, not more compassionate. Without question, the world we're living in is getting worse.

At this point, you're probably saying, *Thanks a lot, pastor! My life was tough enough before you painted such a bleak picture.* I'll agree that the outlook for this world is bleak, but take courage, Christian, because this sets the stage for the great and glorious truth that Jesus is coming back. Again, Jesus is coming back! God's Word couldn't get any clearer on this precious point. In fact, the New Testament draws attention to this single event over three hundred times! What we're seeing today won't last forever. Soon and very soon, the King of Righteousness will return, and under His rule, sin won't be tolerated and grace and goodness will be enforced.

As the world gets worse and worse, our longing for Christ's return grows greater and greater and the promise of His soon return grows more and more glorious.

He who is the faithful witness to all these things says, "Yes, I am coming soon!" Amen! Come, Lord Jesus! (Revelation 22:20 NLT)

How often do you dwell on the fact that Jesus is coming?

Whom can you share this truth with today?

CRITICAL CONDITION

First, I want to remind you that in the last days there will be scoffers who will laugh at the truth and do every evil thing they desire. This will be their argument: "Jesus promised to come back, did he? Then where is he? Why, as far back as anyone can remember, everything has remained exactly the same since the world was first created." (2 Peter 3:3–4 NLT)

If you haven't heard it yet, you eventually will. It's the skeptical scoffer who rises up in a spirit of sarcasm and says, *Do you really believe in this thing called the rapture? Are you seriously expecting Jesus to show up one day and suddenly snatch you up from planet earth? You can't be serious!*

If we know the Word of God, we **can** be serious because the Bible teaches that a day is coming when Jesus will do just that (John 14:3; 1 Corinthians 15:51–53; 1 Thessalonians 4:16–17). We also know that criticism and sarcasm from this world are nothing new. For as long as God has made promises, there have been those who have mocked them.

God promised Noah that a great rain would come and flood the face of the earth. In preparation, he built an ark to withstand the rainfall. Interestingly enough, the Bible indicates that the earth had never experienced rainfall up to that point but was continuously watered by a mist that came up from the earth (Genesis 2:5–6). Noah faithfully went to work, but imagine the amount of criticism he must have endured by those who watched him prepare for something that no one had ever seen (Hebrews 11:7). We all know what happened, and it wasn't very long before the skeptics were silenced.

Just as there was rain, there will be a rapture, and the sarcasm will cease. God always keeps His promises, no matter how foolish or improbable they seem to the skeptics.

The Lord isn't really being slow about his promise to return, as some people think. No, he is being patient for your sake. He does not want anyone to perish, so he is giving more time for everyone to repent. (2 Peter 3:9 NLT)

How have you been skeptical concerning God's promises?

What verses can you share that substantiate the rapture?

. . . we look forward to that wonderful event when the glory of our great God and Savior, Jesus Christ, will be revealed. (Titus 2:13 NLT)

What's so wonderful about the rapture, and why should we take the time to study and understand it? One of the reasons the rapture is so wonderful is because it's so practical. An attitude of awareness about the rapture has the ability to produce the following effects in our spiritual lives.

First, the rapture can purify our walk. What do you want to be doing when Jesus comes back for you? Do you want to be saying something you shouldn't say, drinking something you shouldn't drink, or seeing something you shouldn't see? Of course not! None of us wants to be doing something sinful when we finally see Jesus face to face. And knowing this can happen at any moment does something in our hearts so that we begin to order our lives in a way that's pure and presentable to God (1 John 2:28).

The rapture also brings a sense of urgency to our mission. The Bible teaches that we're living in an age of grace where those who choose to trust in Jesus Christ will have their sins instantly forgiven (Ephesians 3:2) and become children of God (John 1:12). But this age of grace will come to an end once Christ raptures His church, which means we have a limited time to share the Gospel of grace with those who have yet to trust in Christ as their Savior. What an incentive to share!

Last, the rapture is also an encouragement during tough times. No matter what you are going through in life, it can all literally come to an end *in the twinkling of an eye (1 Corinthians 15:52 NKJV)*. This understanding will give you just what you need in order to make it through another minute, hour, or day of whatever you're going through.

You need to believe, understand, and anticipate the rapture so that your heart is continually becoming prepared for that wonderful day.

How will your understanding of the rapture affect your daily choices?

Whom do you know who needs to hear the Gospel? Take some time to pray for them and then share the Gospel with them.

"Nor is there salvation in any other, for <u>there is no other name</u> under heaven given among men by which we must be saved." (Acts 4:12 NKJV)

It's not a popular message, it's not a politically correct message, but it's a message that must be shared in this day and age: if you don't have Jesus, you aren't going to heaven. The Bible tells us in many places that there is one and only one way to heaven—through faith in Christ. There are no other avenues or options open to humanity. A person is either one-hundred percent saved by Jesus or not saved at all.

Jesus said to him, "I am the way, the truth, and the life. <u>No one</u> comes to the Father except through Me." (John 14:6 NKJV)

I know this is bound to rub a lot of people the wrong way because I've found there are many who think they can have heaven without having Jesus. They want the good promises of glory, but they don't want to be bothered by the cross, much less the One who hung and died there for their sins. They don't want to accept Jesus as the only way and are determined to find another path to paradise. But Christ warned that no such path exists and the consequences for not trusting in Him are eternal:

"He who believes in the Son has everlasting life; and he who does not believe the Son shall not see life, but the wrath of God abides on him." (John 3:36 NKJV)

Some will argue that it's extremely narrow-minded of God to provide only one way to heaven. But I believe that in light of mankind's rebellious rejection of God, it's extremely broad-minded for Him to provide us with **any** way to heaven. We deserved judgment and instead He gave us a way of escape by sending His only begotten Son to die for our sins. Whether someone sees this as narrow or broad doesn't change the fact that it's true. We need to maintain the message that the way to heaven is just Jesus.

What are you counting on in order to get into heaven?

Whom would the Lord have you share this with?

You say, "I am allowed to do anything"—but not everything is helpful. You say, "I am allowed to do anything"—but not everything is beneficial. (1 Corinthians 10:23 NLT)

According to scriptural authority, some things are always right (love and honesty) and some things are always wrong (hatred and dishonesty). But according to subjective morality, there are certain things that can be both right and wrong. For example, it's considered impolite **not** to belch after a meal in India. So is belching after a meal right or wrong? It's all subjective to the moral standards of the culture and day. When we don't have the scriptural authority on something, we need to look at it through the lens of subjective morality to determine if it is right or wrong for us.

Paul shares in the verse above that just because something might be allowed (because Scripture doesn't prohibit it) doesn't make it right. In his day, the issue was meat that had been sacrificed to idols. After animals were sacrificed in pagan temples, the leftovers were commonly put on sale. What's a Christian to do? Is it wrong to eat this meat, or is it right to take advantage of a good deal? Notice what Paul writes:

If someone who isn't a Christian asks you home for dinner, go ahead; accept the invitation if you want to. Eat whatever is offered to you and don't ask any questions about it. Your conscience should not be bothered by this. But suppose someone warns you that this meat has been offered to an idol. <u>Don't eat it</u>, out of consideration for the conscience of the one who told you. (1 Corinthians 10:27–28 NLT)

Christians are to avoid being yoked with the world and even *appearing* to be yoked with the world. It sends a bad message to those watching our lives when we allow ourselves to be identified with the things of the world. It may not be a matter of meat for us, but it might be a matter of movies, hobbies, etc. Some will argue, *But I'm free in Christ!* We are free, but something is wrong if our freedoms make us look more like the world than our Lord.

What freedoms do you have difficulty surrendering?

What do people see when they look at your walk?

If you need wisdom—if you want to know what God wants you to do—ask him, and he will gladly tell you. He will not resent your asking. (James 1:5 NLT)

Several centuries ago, someone asked Saint Augustine a question that most of us have asked ourselves at one point, "How can I know God's will for my life." I find Augustine's answer very interesting, "Love God with all of your heart . . . and then do whatever you want." Don't make the mistake of focusing on the second half of his answer because the key to knowing God's will for our lives is by being madly in love with Him.

Wait a second, you might say, *I don't need to do that. I know God's will by reading my Bible.* In most cases, we can know God's will through His Word, but there are also many issues that the Scriptures don't provide a black-and-white answer for. These gray areas give us an opportunity to mature in our relationship with the Lord.

Which job opportunity should I accept? What school should I send my children to? Where am I supposed to serve in the body of Christ? Which friendships should I invest in? These are all questions that have different answers for different people, and it takes the personal direction of the Holy Spirit in order to reveal God's will in each case. And when we seek a closer connection to the Spirit of God, we will also grow in our love for Him. This sets up a spiritual cycle where our need for God leads to our love for Him, which, in turn, fills us with a sense of confidence when it comes to His will for our lives.

"In those days when you pray, I will listen. If you look for me in earnest, you will find me when you seek me." (Jeremiah 29:12–13 NLT)

Are you confused regarding God's will for your life? How can you clear up the confusion?

Do you know people who are confused about God's will for their lives? What will you encourage them to do?

MIRACULOUS MESSAGES
DAY 245

This miraculous sign at Cana in Galilee was Jesus' first display of his glory. And his disciples believed in him. (John 2:11 NLT)

We all have a longing for the miraculous. Our ears perk up at the mere mention of the word *miracle*, and the prospect of experiencing the miraculous fills our hearts with a heavenly hope that transcends this world. Yet, even with all our fascination and fondness for miracles, there's still a lot of confusion about them. I'm convinced our understanding of miracles will improve when we understand the messages they convey.

First, a miracle sends a message of **validation**. This is especially true in the case of Jesus' miracles when He walked this earth. Christ made some serious claims about Himself, and the miracles He performed substantiated these claims. In fact, He even pointed to His miracles as a witness of the fact that He was who He said He was:

"But I have a greater witness . . . my teachings and my miracles. They have been assigned to me by the Father, and they testify that the Father has sent me." (John 5:36 NLT)

A miracle also sends a message of **revelation**, for it reveals God's gracious character to mankind. Have you ever noticed how miracles are always impacting and benefiting the lives of those in need? Jesus didn't exercise His miraculous power for His own benefit, not even when He was being tortured and crucified. Instead, He lavished His miraculous power on other people. We serve an others-centered God, and His mighty miracles reveal this to us.

Last, a miracle sends a message of **declaration**, for whenever a material miracle was manifested, a spiritual statement was also being made. When Jesus restored sight to the blind, it declared His ability to open mankind's spiritual eyes. As Christ made lepers clean, it pronounced His power to cleanse humanity of sin. And when Jesus stilled the Sea of Galilee, it showed how He can bring peace to the stormiest seasons of our lives (Philippians 4:7).

By understanding these miraculous messages, we can better appreciate God's miracles and their place in our lives.

What miracles have you experienced in your own life?

What spiritual lessons has God taught you through His miraculous working in your life?

CONCEALING THE HEALING
DAY 246

And Jesus went about all Galilee, <u>teaching</u> in their synagogues, <u>preaching</u> the gospel of the kingdom, and <u>healing</u> all kinds of sickness and all kinds of disease among the people. (Matthew 4:23 NKJV)

Miraculous healing has a high priority in God's heart. As the verse above shows us, healing formed one of the three major components of Christ's earthly ministry. In fact, it has been calculated that Jesus performed thirty-eight miracles in the gospels, thirty of them physical healings. Healing is also identified as one of the gifts given to the church by the Holy Spirit (1 Corinthians 12:9), and we're even given the proper prescription for healing to happen in the church (James 5:14–15).

But if miraculous healings are so important to God, why don't we see more of them in our lives? Paul asked the very same question. He asked the Lord to heal him from a physical infirmity on three separate occasions (2 Corinthians 12:8). Surely this man who had the ability to heal others would be healed himself. However, each time God chose to withhold His healing touch from Paul, and each time He gave the reason for withholding the healing:

Each time he said, "My gracious favor is all you need. My power works best in your weakness." So now I am glad to boast about my weaknesses, so that the power of Christ may work through me. (2 Corinthians 12:9 NLT)

God had a greater purpose in mind by **not** performing a miracle in Paul's life. The Lord knew it was actually good for Paul to suffer because it led him to grow more in his spiritual relationship with Him. Sometimes the condition we're in is also the condition that keeps us close to God, and we would suffer spiritually if we were healed physically. Miracles are important to God, but they aren't more important than our relationship with Him. He will withhold a healing if He knows it will keep us closer to Him.

When has the Lord used physical suffering in your life for your spiritual good?

What will you do if you ask the Lord to miraculously heal you and it doesn't happen?

THE MIRACULOUS IS GLORIOUS

As Pharaoh and his army approached, the people of Israel could see them in the distance, marching toward them. The people began to panic, and they cried out to the LORD for help. (Exodus 14:10 NLT)

With the Red Sea behind them and Pharaoh's army before them, there seemed to be no escape for the children of Israel. There was absolutely no way out of this death trap . . . or was there? Those familiar with this passage of Scripture know that there actually was:

Then Moses raised his hand over the sea, and the LORD opened up a path through the water with a strong east wind. The wind blew all that night, turning the seabed into dry land. So the people of Israel walked through the sea on dry ground, with walls of water on each side! . . . The waters covered all the chariots and charioteers—the entire army of Pharaoh. . . . not a single one survived. (Exodus 14:21–22, 28 NLT)

This certainly ranks as one of the most moving and memorable miracles in the Bible, but we frequently forget an important detail that is given a few verses prior when God speaks to Moses:

"I will receive <u>great glory</u> at the expense of Pharaoh and his armies, chariots, and charioteers. When I am finished with Pharaoh and his army, all Egypt will know that I am the LORD!" (Exodus 14:17 NLT)

Miracles are about the Lord gaining glory. In one way or another, every miracle points to the greatness, goodness, and grandeur of God. But a subtle shift can occur in hearts when we actually begin to look past the Lord as we look for Him to move in the miraculous. When we pray for miracles, our motives need to be born from a desire to see His glorious reputation increased. This attitude of heart is often the difference between shallow and deep faith. The spiritual giants in this world are those who understand that miraculous events are all about God being glorified, not their own level of comfort or convenience, and they're even willing to go without miracles if God can receive more glory from their lives.

How important is it to you to see God glorified?

How can you glorify Him today?

FORSAKING FORMULAS
DAY 248

"This man certainly performs many miraculous signs." (John 11:47 NLT)

Just as miracles are similar in the sense that they glorify God, they're also very different when it comes to the means by which they are accomplished. Consider the various methods that Jesus used in healing the blind:

In Matthew 9:27–29, He meets two blind men who confess that He is the *"Son of David,"* which is another way of declaring that He is the Messiah. He touches their eyes and pronounces them healed according to their faith.

In Matthew 12:22, Jesus cures a man who is demon-possessed, blind, and mute without any apparent compliance on the man's part.

In Matthew 15:30, He heals the lame, the blind, the crippled, the mute, and many others. The Greek text implies that they are instantaneously healed as they are brought before Him.

In Mark 8:22–25, Christ spits on a blind man's eyes, and he receives partial vision. Christ then places His hands on the man's eyes and completely restores his sight.

In John 9:1–7, He seeks out a man who has been blind from birth. He spits on the ground and makes clay that He rubs on the man's eyes. Then the Lord tells him to go and wash the clay out of his eyes in the pool of Siloam, at which point he is healed.

Each miracle was accomplished by a different means. We may naturally wonder, *Why didn't the Lord just have a method of healing that was always the same?* I'm convinced that He did things so differently to protect us from falling into the trap of formulizing the miraculous. We tend to put things into boxes so we can pull them out at our convenience. When the occasion calls, we love to be able to say, *Here's how it always works.* But God's miraculous touch requires us to place our trust in Him, instead of formulas, because the One who can fit the universe in the span of His hand will never fit into any of our man-made boxes.

When has the Lord defied your attempts to put Him in a box?

What in your life do you need to surrender to Him?

And when John had heard in prison about the works of Christ, he sent two of his disciples and said to Him, "Are You the Coming One, or do we look for another?" (Matthew 11:2–3 NKJV)

All of us have been disappointed with God at some point in our lives. Perhaps you were passed over for a promotion at work or hit with an unexpected bill or devastated by the loss of a loved one. Even John the Baptist was disappointed with Jesus for not exercising His power to put an end to unrighteousness. Having been imprisoned, John began to have his doubts about Jesus, so he sent two of his disciples to ask Him, *"Are You the Coming One, or do we look for another?"* In other words, *Are you the One we've been looking for, or should we hang our hopes on someone else?* Jesus' answer provides insight into how we should deal with our disappointments with God:

"Go and tell John the things which you hear and see: The blind see and the lame walk; the lepers are cleansed and the deaf hear; the dead are raised up and the poor have the gospel preached to them." (Matthew 11:4–5 NKJV)

Jesus pointed John to the fact that He was fulfilling the prophecies that the Messiah would heal the blind, lame, and deaf and raise the dead (Isaiah 35:5–6; 61:1). What was Jesus doing here? He was forcing John to base his judgment on the fulfillment of God's Word, not on his own expectations.

Where there are no expectations, there are no disappointments, and our disappointments with God come from expectations that we have imposed on Him. We have no right to expect something that God has never promised in His Word, but by the same token, we should expect what He has promised in His Word. So what has He promised?

"Here on earth you will have many trials and sorrows. But take heart, because I have overcome the world." (John 16:33 NLT)

According to Jesus, we should expect life on earth to be full of trials and sorrows, so we shouldn't be disappointed with God when this happens. But we must also remember that we can overcome these trials because Christ in us has overcome the world.

How have you imposed your expectations on God?

How will you respond to the temptation to be disappointed with God?

DESIGNER GENES
DAY 250

Let your women keep silent in the churches, for they are not permitted to speak; but they are to be submissive, as the law also says. And if they want to learn something, let them ask their own husbands at home. (1 Corinthians 14:34–35 NKJV)

Not a month goes by that someone doesn't ask, *Pastor Bob, can a woman serve as a pastor in the church?* God's Word has the answer, but first we need to take note of a simple fact that is absolutely necessary in order to understand God's heart on this important issue: men and women are different. Check out the chart that secular science has put together listing the different types of energies typically expressed by women and men:

Female Energy		Male Energy	
cares	intuitive	accepts	rational
understands	nurturing	appreciates	efficient
respected	idealistic	trusted	practical
feeling	vulnerable	analytical	aggressive
emotional		logical	

Even beyond this, we know that men and women aren't the same because God's Word declares that they were designed to be different:

So God created man in His own image; in the image of God He created him; male and female He created them. (Genesis 1:27 NKJV)

We need to agree on this because once we acknowledge the natural differences in men and women, it makes sense that their roles in the church shouldn't be the same. The Bible tells us that men have been called to be the leaders in the home and the house of God (1 Corinthians 11:3; 1 Timothy 2:11). Scripture also teaches that women are called to support and follow their leadership (Ephesians 5:22; 1 Timothy 2:12).

God reserves the pastoral position within the body of Christ for men because even though men and women are equal in their importance, they are different in their performance. His heart is that both would be blessed as they embrace their divinely designed differences.

How does this truth impact your life?

How would you answer the question, Can a woman be a pastor?

WHAT'S A WOMAN TO DO?

DAY 251

Help these women, for they worked hard with me in telling others the Good News.
(Philippians 4:3 NLT)

As we've seen, God has created important differences between men and women and these are carried over into their roles in the church. Men have been given the responsibility to pastor and lead the church, and women have not. Unfortunately, some misunderstand this to mean that women are relegated to sitting around idly as the men do all the ministry work. Nothing could be further from the truth. For as Scripture shows, women have always played a critical role within the body of Christ.

Matthew 28:7 tells us that the first evangelists in church history were women. When Mary Magdalene and "the other Mary" came at an early hour to Christ's tomb, they were met by an angel who commissioned them to preach the Good News of the Risen Savior to the disciples. Women continued to have an important role in sharing the Gospel as shown in the verse above, where Paul makes reference to women who had worked hard in sharing the Good News.

In Romans 16:1, we're introduced to a woman named Phoebe, and the Scriptures describe her as *a servant*. This word for *servant* in the Greek language is *diakonos* from which we derive the English word *deacon*. As a deaconess, Phoebe was a critical servant in the day-to-day operations of the church, and her example sets a powerful precedent for sacrificial service.

First Corinthians 11:5 indicates that it was a regular practice for women to pray and prophesy in the early church, and in Acts 21:9, we are told that Philip had four daughters who all prophesied. This shows us that women were regularly sharing the Word of God in a way that edified and encouraged the family of faith.

So what's a woman to do when it comes to ministry? There is very little that women *can't* do, and the church is at its healthiest when women are sharing, serving, praying, and prophesying.

What is your understanding on this issue?

How can you help to dispel some of this misunderstanding?

HEAVENLY MINDED
DAY 252

"Let not your heart be troubled; you believe in God, believe also in Me." (John 14:1 NKJV)

What's "got you"? What is it that's bugging your brain and hassling your heart? For some, it's a relationship, and that special someone just doesn't seem to be on the same page. For others, it's a job because they sense their efforts are unappreciated at their workplace. Still others face a financial dilemma, worn out from phone conversations with the credit consolidators. Some have legal difficulties and are anticipating going before a judge and jury. And there are those who are facing physical afflictions that just aren't getting better or going away.

Wait a second, pastor, you might say, *I'm reading this to find some encouragement, not to be reminded about my problems.* Hang in there, for we serve a sympathetic Savior who understands our hardships even better than we do, and He has given us a way to gain the upper hand when it comes to life's struggles. We see it as He speaks to the disciples on the night before the crucifixion. He had just told them about the coming calamity that would separate them from His side. Knowing they were greatly troubled by the prospect of losing Him, Jesus gives them a timeless tool:

"In My Father's house are many mansions; if it were not so, I would have told you. I go to prepare a place for you. And if I go and prepare a place for you, I will come again and receive you to Myself; that where I am, there you may be also." (John 14:2–3 NKJV)

Notice what Jesus does. He gives the disciples a spiritual solution by reminding them of the heavenly perspective. Yes, they would be separated from Him, but this trial was only temporary. The same applies to whatever we're going through. When we're troubled by the trials of life, the Lord wants us to focus on the fact that we're headed for heaven—where all our relationships will be perfect, our work will be worship, our riches in glory will abound, Jesus will be our just judge, and our pain and suffering will be a distant memory.

What's your first response to trouble?

What can you do to be more heavenly minded?

"And I will ask the Father, and he will give you another Counselor, who will never leave you."
(John 14:16 NLT)

Trials are inevitable in this life. It doesn't matter where we live, what we have, or who we are, there will always be things that produce the proverbial pit in our stomachs. But God has graciously given us several tools for dealing with these trials, not the least of which is the presence of the Holy Spirit in our hearts. There are countless benefits to this blessing, but let's focus on one in particular:

"And when he [Holy Spirit] comes, he will convince the world of its sin, and of God's righteousness, and of the coming judgment." (John 16:8 NLT)

What does this mean, exactly? It means that the Spirit teaches people the difference between right and wrong. By the impressions that He places upon our hearts, He gives us a spiritual sense about what is sin and what is not. This is priceless, especially as we go through trials, **because sin only makes our trials worse, and it takes us deeper into trouble**. But with the Spirit acting as our godly gauge for sin, we can avoid making sinful choices and, instead, find ourselves on God's path, which takes us **through** the trials of life.

I recently ran into a friend as I was running a few errands. We started talking, and I discovered that he was really struggling in an area of his life. It became apparent to me that he was struggling because he was doing something that went against God's will for his life. Had he simply heeded the Spirit's warning as he began to struggle, it would have spared him a lot of heartache and hardship.

Sin only makes our trials more difficult than they already are. As the Spirit convicts us, let's open our hearts so we can hear Him and overcome the sins that would ensnare us as we are led from glory to glory and victory to victory .

When have you sensed the Spirit's conviction about something sinful? What did you do, and what were the results?

How can you be more sensitive to the Spirit's leading?

PROTECTIVE PEACE
DAY 254

"I am leaving you with a gift—peace of mind and heart. And the peace I give isn't like the peace the world gives. So don't be troubled or afraid." (John 14:27 NLT)

Webster's Dictionary defines the word *peace* as "freedom from civil disturbance; freedom from disquieting or oppressive thoughts or emotions; harmony in personal relations; a pact or agreement to end hostilities between those who have been at war or in a state of enmity." Different shades of definition, but do you see the common thread? In each case, peace is predicated on external circumstances. According to the world, our lives need to be a certain way in order for there to be peace.

This is not the case when it comes to the peace that the Lord promises to us. His peace is unlike the world's because it doesn't depend on what's happening here on planet earth. Despite the circumstances swirling around us, we can know a calm that transcends our trials. It comes from heaven, where the conditions are always perfectly peaceful.

I've seen this peace produce serenity in the lives of those who've lost their financial security in an instant through an unforeseen tragedy. I've also seen this peace sustain people after being told that they don't have long to live. And I've watched in wonder as this peace has supernaturally supported parents as they've had to lay a beloved child to rest. By the world's definition, peace would be impossible under these conditions, but praise God that His peace can invade even the most turbulent and tearful trials that this world can throw at us.

You will experience God's peace, which is far more wonderful than the human mind can understand. His peace will guard your hearts and minds as you live in Christ Jesus. (Philippians 4:7 NLT)

When have you personally experienced the Lord's peace, and how did it affect those who were watching you?

Whom do you know that is going through a difficult time? Take a couple of minutes and pray that they would experience God's peace.

Thomas said to Him, "Lord, we do not know where You are going, and how can we know the way?" (John 14:5 NKJV)

Thomas' question came at a very trying time. Jesus had just told the disciples that He would be leaving them. He promised that their separation would just be temporary and that they would eventually be reunited (John 14:1–3), but Thomas still had a couple of questions: *Where are you going, and how can we get there?* Jesus answers:

"<u>I am the way</u>, the truth, and the life. No one comes to the Father except through Me."
(John 14:6 NKJV)

In other words, *Thomas, don't fret about finding your way to me. I am the way!* Jesus promises to personally direct us through the trials of this life and get us to the place where our hearts long to be . . . with Him in heaven. He doesn't send us a message or a map so we can find our way through this life. He becomes our way.

Imagine for a moment that my 8-year-old daughter and I are in my office, and she says, *Daddy, I need a drink of water.* I could tell her, *Okay, Caitlyn, here's how you get there. Go out this door and then go down the hallway. When you come to the double doors, take a left, and then proceed down the other hallway until you come to another set of double doors. Go through those and make your way into the main corridor. Then make a sharp right, and you'll see the water fountain. If that door is locked, turn around and . . . .* Ahhh! Can you imagine how frustrating and inadequate this would be? If I really want to make sure my daughter gets to where she needs to go, I'll lift her up onto my shoulders and personally take her there. Rather than **telling** her the way, I'll **be** the way. This is a picture of what Jesus does as He carries us through the trials of this life and becomes our way to Him.

He will feed his flock like a shepherd. He will carry the lambs in his arms, holding them close to his heart. (Isaiah 40:11 NLT)

Are you allowing Jesus to be your way?

How would you answer the question, "How do I get to heaven?"

God is love. (1 John 4:8 NKJV)

Have you ever had someone question your character? Maybe it was an employer who didn't give you the benefit of the doubt. Or perhaps someone saw you doing something from afar, assumed the worst, and then got the rumor mill going. It's very painful when we discover that our integrity has been called into question. So just imagine what it does to God's heart when people challenge His character by asking, *How could a loving God create such an evil world?*

In the beginning God created the heavens and the earth (Genesis 1:1 NKJV), but He didn't create the world in the evil condition as we now know it. The Bible tells us that God created the angels, and there was one who was especially glorious (Ezekiel 28:13–19). But something happened. Isaiah tells us that at some point, this angel decided to exalt himself above the Lord with five "I will" statements:

For you have said in your heart: "<u>I will</u> ascend into heaven, <u>I will</u> exalt my throne above the stars of God; <u>I will</u> also sit on the mount of the congregation On the farthest sides of the north; <u>I will</u> ascend above the heights of the clouds, <u>I will</u> be like the Most High." (Isaiah 14:13–14 NKJV)

As the expression *I will* suggests, this angel possessed a free will, and he used it to defy God. He was cast out of heaven and became Satan (Luke 10:18; Revelation 12:9). Satan then tempted Adam and Eve to use their God-given will to disobey Him. As a result, all creation was corrupted by their sin (Genesis 3:1–6). Ever since, the earth has been an evil place and man has paid dearly for what he has done to himself.

God didn't create the mess we're in today, and He's done everything needed (with the exception of violating our will) to save us from our situation. He gave His Son to die for our sins, He sent His Spirit to guide us, and He has prepared a place in heaven for those who have placed their trust in His character.

How does your life affirm God's character?

How would you answer the question, "How could a loving God create such an evil world?"

TONGUE TRUTHS

To one there is given through the Spirit . . . speaking in different kinds of tongues . . . .
(1 Corinthians 12:8–10 NIV)

What kind of Christian are you? That's the question commonly asked in church circles. *Are you a liberal Christian, a conservative Christian, a traditional Christian, or a moderate Christian? Are you a Baptist, a Methodist, a Lutheran, a Presbyterian, or an Episcopalian?* Good questions, but I've found that they're often just smokescreens for the bigger question of whether someone is a Spirit-filled Christian. *And if you are, are you one of those Christians who talks in tongues?* Let's face it, tongues is a touchy topic because there's so much confusion about it. Let's allow God's Word to settle our heart on three truths when it comes to tongues.

There is a **proper place** for tongues. The gift of tongues isn't a recent invention of the church. We see that it was promised by Jesus Himself in Mark 16:17. It is then demonstrated on several occasions in the book of Acts (2:4; 10:46; 19:6). In addition, the apostle Paul expounded extensively on tongues in 1 Corinthians 12 and 14. God has certainly set His stamp of approval on this spiritual gift.

There is a **proper purpose** for tongues. First Corinthians 14:2 tells us that the gift of tongues is for the purpose of communicating with God. This can occur in either a public (1 Corinthians 14:27) or private setting (1 Corinthians 14:28). Either way, it reinforces the fact that we are the beneficiaries of a supernatural relationship God and that this relationship is completely unique from all others.

There is a **proper procedure** for tongues. Just as there is a place and purpose for tongues, there is also a procedure governing its use. In public, it is to be accompanied by an interpretation so others can be edified by the meaning (1 Corinthians 14:27). It's also to be expressed in a way that is under control (1 Corinthians 14:32) and orderly (1 Corinthians 14:40).

So what kind of Christian are you? No matter what denomination you belong to, I pray that you're a Christian who understands and appreciates the place, purpose, and procedure for the gift of tongues.

What opinions on tongues have you had in the past?

How can you help to dispel some of the misunderstandings about tongues?

OPPOSITE EXTREMES
DAY 258

But the fruit of the Spirit is . . . <u>self-control</u>. (Galatians 5:22–23 NKJV)

I've found there tend to be two extreme groups when it comes to the gift of tongues. There are those who are so enthusiastic about this gift that they make it the centerpiece of their Christianity. All their spiritual expression and experience seem to rely on them talking in tongues, and in many cases, it's also blamed for bizarre behavior. *Something took me over, and I suddenly had to speak in tongues!*

Then there's another group of people who are so intimidated by what they see from the first group that they want nothing to do with tongues. They're afraid that if they ask God for this gift, they'll suddenly "break loose" in the bank line or some other public place. No wonder they shy away from it!

Neither of these extremes are what God wants nor are they an accurate reflection of this gift. The Lord desires for the gifts of the Holy Spirit to operate in perfect harmony with the fruit of the Holy Spirit. The verse above teaches us that self-control is something that the Spirit imparts to us, and 1 Corinthians 14:32 tells us that spiritual gifts are under the control of those who exercise them. This means that a person who can speak in tongues won't suddenly lose control and act crazy.

Both groups need to recognize this because in one case, there should be more self-control, and in the other case, there should be more trust that God isn't into embarrassing His people. Many in the body of Christ are using this spiritual gift in an unspiritual way, and many others are so afraid that they wind up missing the blessing that tongues is intended to be. May we all meet God's Spirit in the middle where we experience His gifts, fruits, and leading.

Therefore, brethren, desire earnestly to prophesy, and do not forbid to speak with tongues. Let all things be done decently and in order. (1 Corinthians 14:39–40 NKJV)

Which extreme do you tend to lean closer to and why?

How does the Lord want you to look at the gift of tongues? How will you?

For you were buried with Christ when you were <u>baptized</u>. And with him you were raised to a new life because you trusted the mighty power of God, who raised Christ from the dead. (Colossians 2:12 NLT)

What exactly is baptism? For a physical description, we can turn to the dictionary, which defines it as "submersion for religious purposes." Imagine an empty drinking glass that's plunged into a sink full of water, and you get the idea. It speaks of an overflowing influence in and upon an object. This might help us when it comes to the material manner of baptism, but we need to dig into God's Word if we want to understand its spiritual significance.

For starters, water baptism is an **ordinance**—a direct command or charge from a ranking official, such as a captain or king. The Bible refers to Jesus not only as the "King of Kings" (Revelation 19:16), but also as the "Captain of our Salvation" (Hebrews 2:10). Any command from Christ is backed by the highest authority, and at the end of Matthew's gospel, our heavenly Captain and King orders us to baptize:

"Therefore, go and make disciples of all the nations, baptizing them in the name of the Father and the Son and the Holy Spirit." (Matthew 28:19 NLT)

Baptism is also a **sacrament**. Originally, the word *sacrament* was associated with a soldier's oath to fulfill and obey his orders. Before going into battle, a soldier pledged his allegiance to carry out the will of his commanding officers, no matter what the battle brought. An ordinance reflects authority; a sacrament reflects obedience.

Baptism is both God's ordinance and our sacrament. He has given us a command, and we are called to faithfully obey it. And as we obey His order to baptize all nations in the name of the Father, Son, and Holy Spirit, we demonstrate His authority over us as our Captain and King.

What's the connection between baptism and your obedience to God?

How can you better demonstrate God's authority over your life?

DUNKED, DRIZZLED, OR DIPPED?
DAY 260

Then there arose a dispute between some of John's disciples and the Jews about purification.
(John 3:25 NKJV)

Isn't it interesting to see what the religious leaders were arguing about almost two thousand years ago? John the Baptist had begun his ministry of baptizing people, and He had a certain way of doing things. The Jewish officials had a definite idea about how people should be purified, and it wasn't long before the Jewish officials took notice of John and raised a ruckus with some of his disciples.

Some things never change. Today the body of Christ baptizes in a variety of ways. In certain circles, the acceptable practice is to completely dunk people under water until they are fully submerged. Other churches want to see people sprinkled, so they drizzle them with water. And there are those who want to be somewhere in between, so they dip people until they are almost completely covered with water. Each camp believes that its way is the correct way, and in many cases, people are willing to turn it into an item of debate. So how should people be baptized? Should they be dunked, drizzled, or dipped?

I believe there is a proper procedure for water baptism, but I don't believe this debate deserves the amount of attention it gets; it certainly doesn't warrant the division it often causes. The real issue when it comes to baptism isn't the external activity but the internal attitude:

Baptism is not a removal of dirt from your body; <u>it is an appeal to God from a clean</u> <u>conscience.</u> (1 Peter 3:21 NLT)

In essence, baptism is a person's response to the fact that God has cleansed him or her of sin. It's a wonderful way to say "thank you" for the greatest gift imaginable—salvation. We need to stop arguing about the technique of a person's baptism and start rejoicing over the work that God has done in each person's heart.

What should you do if someone wants to debate this issue with you?

Is there a particular person or issue that draws you into debates? Ask the Lord to help you rise above it.

WHAT MUST YOU DO?
DAY 261

While they were traveling down the road, they came to some water. The officer said, "Look! Here is water! <u>What is stopping me from being baptized?</u>" (Acts 8:36 ICB)

"What is stopping me from being baptized?" That's a question well worth asking. There's a lot of confusion about what someone needs to do before he or she can be baptized, and the Scriptures show us two things that need to be present in a person's life.

First, there needs to be a **relationship**. In Luke 3:7, many people were coming to John the Baptist because they wanted to be baptized by him. Yet there were many in the crowd who were relying on their Jewish heritage as their means of being right with God. They assumed they were okay because they were ancestors of Abraham. John warned them that being children of Abraham didn't guarantee that they were children of God. Each and every person needs to have a personal relationship with God, which only comes through faith in Jesus Christ. When a person recognizes that his or her sins caused Jesus to die on the cross and then personally owns Him as his or her sin-sacrifice, he or she will experience a relationship with God. In other words, if you're not related to God, then you have no reason to be baptized.

Second, there needs to be **repentance**. John's warning got the attention of the Jews. They asked what they needed to do in order to have the type of relationship that he was describing. He answers them in Luke 3:10–14 by telling them that a personal relationship with God looks like repentance. In other words, there needs to be a lifestyle that demonstrates a change of heart. When people are in a relationship with God, they won't let people go unclothed or unfed, they won't rip people off, and they won't intimidate or falsely accuse anyone. In other words, unless you have repented of your old life of sin, you shouldn't be baptized because baptism represents the burial of the old life (Romans 6:2–4).

Baptism is a true blessing that every Christian ought to experience, but we should also remember that it's meaningless apart from a relationship and repentance.

Does your life demonstrate repentance? Why or why not?

What questions would you ask those who want to know if they can be baptized?

FOLLOW THE LEADER
DAY 262

Those who say they live in God should live their lives as Christ did. (1 John 2:6 NLT)

Every now and then, I'll encounter people who say they love the Lord but argue they don't need to be baptized. *What's the big deal? Does God really care whether I get baptized?* Yes, He does. Baptism is not only a command that Christ has given **to us** (Matthew 28:19), but it's also something that He has demonstrated **for us**:

Then Jesus went from Galilee to the Jordan River to be baptized by John. But John didn't want to baptize him. "I am the one who needs to be baptized by you," he said, "so why are you coming to me?" But Jesus said, "It must be done, because we must do everything that is right." So then John baptized him. (Matthew 3:13–15 NLT)

Jesus certainly didn't need to be baptized out of a personal need. He had no reason to repent of any sin because He had no sin (1 John 3:5; 2 Corinthians 5:21; 1 Peter 1:19). If anyone ever had an excuse to forego baptism, it was Jesus. Why then did He make it a point to be publicly baptized? One reason was so that He could provide us with an example to follow.

The Lord never commands us to do something that He hasn't already lived out in His own life. Jesus teaches us to love our enemies (Matthew 5:44), and He is also the ultimate example of this (Luke 23:34). Christ tells us to pray (Matthew 6:5), and we see that prayer has priority in His own life (Luke 6:12). The Lord instructs us to live for the next world (Matthew 6:20), and that's exactly how He lived out His existence on earth (John 18:36).

As Christians, we need to view baptism as not only an opportunity to obey the Lord's command, but also a chance to follow in His example, which will always have us following His Word.

Whose example do you tend to follow during difficult times?

How would you respond to Christians who think they don't need to be baptized?

SPIRITUAL SOBRIETY TEST

For I say, through the grace given to me, to everyone who is among you, not to think of himself more highly than he ought to think, but to <u>think soberly</u>, as God has dealt to each one a measure of faith. (Romans 12:3 NKJV)

How should we react when someone gives us a compliment? Perhaps we're commended for leading worship or a Bible study, sharing Christ with a non-believer, or serving at a ministry outreach. I've found that we tend to make two common mistakes when it comes to compliments.

The first is to think **too highly** of ourselves. It's a wonderful thing when the Lord does something powerful through our lives, but we must always remember that He is the one who is doing the work. The moment we begin to put our ownership on His works, we start down the path of pride that ultimately makes us unusable in the Master's hands:

When pride comes, then comes shame. (Proverbs 11:2 NKJV)

The next mistake we make is to think **too lowly** of ourselves. *Wait a minute, pastor! Where's the danger in that?* If God is working in a person's life, it needs to be recognized and appreciated. Sadly, some Christians walk around with their heads down, believing they are good for nothing. They're just biding their time on earth until the Lord comes. This is wrong because it's just as dishonoring to God to say that He isn't working in us as it is to take credit for His work.

So what should we do? Once again, the wisdom of the Word is clear. As Romans 12:3 (NKJV) tells us, we are to *think soberly*. The word *sober* means "to base one's outlook on facts." The fact is that the Lord is responsible for the good works that occur in and through our lives. When a compliment comes our way, we need to maintain this outlook and be grateful that our lives are being used for good.

For we are God's masterpiece. He has created us anew in Christ Jesus, so that we can do the good things he planned for us long ago. (Ephesians 2:10 NLT)

When and how have you made these mistakes?

How will you handle your next compliment?

BETTING ON BONDAGE
DAY 264

A greedy person tries to get rich quick, but it only leads to poverty. (Proverbs 28:22 NLT)

What are you willing to bet on? Are you willing to take chances when it comes to the weather? How about getting a table at your favorite restaurant without making a reservation? Some bets in life are harmless; others are not. Although our culture has done a good job of glorifying gambling, we need to understand that the Lord doesn't approve of it. He doesn't see it as innocent fun or recreation but as a snare that has the power to enslave us.

Studies have shown that one out of every ten adults who have gambled becomes addicted and that number jumps to one out of every seven with teenagers. The Bible teaches us that it's sin to be addicted to anything other than the Lord (1 Corinthians 6:12). Christians should be dominated and directed by Him, and this becomes impossible when they get pulled deeper and deeper into the bondage of betting.

Beyond this, gambling also oppresses the less-fortunate. Statistically, those who are the most addicted to gambling are also the most financially distressed. Billy Graham once said, "For every kick, there's a kickback." The kickback for those who play is that they ultimately pay. There's no telling how many mortgage payments, child-support checks, and college tuitions have been sacrificed to the god of gambling, but we do know that the industry takes in about forty billion dollars each year. A day of reckoning is coming because God promises to oppress those who oppress the poor (Proverbs 22:22–23).

From owning a luxury casino in Las Vegas to buying a lottery ticket at the gas station on the corner, it all supports an industry that fosters addiction and oppresses the poor. God calls us to be wise stewards of the resources He has entrusted to us (1 Corinthians 4:2). We can accomplish this by investing our money in His kingdom, not throwing our money into something that goes against His heart. You can bet on it.

Do you agree with God when it comes to gambling? Why or why not?

What Scriptures can you memorize in order to protect yourself from the bondage of betting?

WILL WORK FOR FOOD

Even while we were with you, we gave you this rule: "Whoever does not work should not eat."
(2 Thessalonians 3:10 NLT)

Gambling goes against several biblical principles. One principle in particular is God's will for people to be industrious with their lives. The allure of gambling is that you can suddenly posses what you haven't worked for. What's more, if you win enough, you can actually amass enough wealth to last a lifetime. The ultimate carrot of gambling is that you'll never need to work another day in your life!

The problem with this is that God wants man to work for his living. Notice what He declared to Adam immediately after the fall in the garden of Eden:

And to Adam he said, "Because you listened to your wife and ate the fruit I told you not to eat, I have placed a curse on the ground. All your life you will struggle to scratch a living from it. It will grow thorns and thistles for you, though you will eat of its grains. All your life you will sweat to produce food, until your dying day. Then you will return to the ground from which you came. For you were made from dust, and to the dust you will return." (Genesis 3:17–19 NLT)

When man fell, God arranged life so man would have to labor in order to survive. From that point forward, Adam was forced to spend his life working in order to live. A lot has changed since then, but the general principle remains the same. We meet our needs for survival (food and shelter) through the proverbial sweat of our brow. This is part and parcel with the curse that sin has brought upon us.

Gambling is an attempt to avoid the consequences of the curse. It offers a substitute for the way of work. But we will never find fulfillment by avoiding work. It is only when we discover the work that God has called us to that we will find true contentment and purpose for our lives.

Is work something you try to avoid, or is it something you look forward to?

How can you make sure you're doing the work that God wants for you?

A MIGHTY MESSAGE

He said to them, "Go into all the world and preach the gospel to every creature." (Mark 16:15 NKJV)

A recent survey revealed some startling statistics on the subject of salvation:

- 53% of those polled believe that you will go to heaven if you're a good person.
- 45% believe that you will go to heaven regardless of your religious beliefs.
- 93% believe in heaven while only 39% believe in hell.
- 30% have no idea what *the Gospel* is.
- 63% have no idea what John 3:16 says, much less what it means.

My heart broke as I read these numbers because God has entrusted us, His church, with the responsibility of informing and educating the world about His message of salvation. The numbers tell us something we can't afford to ignore: we need to do a better job. I'm convinced that we can and will if we stick to His model for His message, which is given to us in John 3:16:

"For God so loved the world that He gave His only begotten Son, that whoever believes in Him should not perish but have everlasting life." (NKJV)

In just twenty-five words, God tells us how to bridge the gap between heaven and hell. Whenever we ask for some form of information in twenty-five words or less, it usually means that we need it to be clear and concise. God knew that we needed the message of salvation to be simple because He understands our tendency to make things complicated. Unfortunately, we have done exactly that in many cases, and that is why we aren't being as effective as we should be.

We need to share the message of salvation in its simplicity (2 Corinthians 11:3), just as it is given to us in the Word of God. When we do so, confusion will turn into confidence as we come across with a mighty message that is clear and concise.

How do your own views compare to the survey listed above?

Who are three people that you can share the Gospel with before the end of the month?

TEMPTATION IS A DEMONSTRATION
DAY 267

Now when <u>the tempter</u> came to Him, he said, "If You are the Son of God, command that these stones become bread." (Matthew 4:3 NKJV)

Did you ever wonder why the Lord lets Satan do his thing? If God is all-powerful and cares so much about us, why doesn't He just wipe out the devil along with all of the temptations he throws our way? Wouldn't this world be a wonderful place if there were nothing out there to draw us away from God and if He were the only thing we could possibly love?

Think of what that type of love would look like. If God were all there was to love, then our love for Him would be forced love, which really isn't love at all. Love can only be proven true when it is challenged by other choices. Imagine a food menu with only a single item on it. Ordering that item doesn't prove that a person likes it. But if someone goes to a restaurant with a twenty-six page menu and orders a roast-beef sandwich, we can conclude it's something he or she really enjoys eating. This is because true love can only be proven in light of other choices.

God wants our love for Him to work the same way. He doesn't create temptations, but He allows them because they test our love for Him. We're tempted to steal, but God tells us not to. We're tempted to hate, but God tells us not to. We're tempted to lie, but God tells us not to. Which way will our love go, toward the temptation or toward the Lord's will for our lives?

When we make the choice to obey God, it proves that our love for Him goes beyond the sinful enticements of this world. God allows temptation because it gives us the opportunity to demonstrate our obedience and love for Him.

What are some temptations that compete with your love for God?

How will you prove your love for God today?

"For God so loved the world that He gave His only begotten Son, that <u>whoever believes</u> in Him should not perish but have everlasting life." (John 3:16 NKJV)

If a person doesn't understand salvation, then everything else is irrelevant. The words *whosoever* and *believes* go a long way in helping us tackle this potentially tough topic.

The word *whosoever* means "whole, any, and all." The Bible teaches that everyone has the opportunity to be saved. Being saved isn't something that the Lord has determined to be "off limits" to anyone. Just the opposite, it remains available to everyone because God loves us and wants us to be with Him in heaven.

The Lord is not slack concerning His promise, as some count slackness, but is longsuffering toward us, not willing that any should perish but that all should come to repentance. (2 Peter 3:9 NKJV)

The original Greek word for *believe* is an interesting one. It means "to lean upon something with all of one's weight." When we apply it to this passage, it means taking the full weight of our lives and placing it on Jesus. Not so long ago, I went outside to relax, and as I sat down on one of my lawn chairs, it unexpectedly collapsed. A few of the stress points had rusted, causing it to give way under my weight. You can imagine how hesitant I am now when I go to sit on one of the other chairs. That's not a picture of belief. True belief means that we're willing to take the full weight of our lives and rest it all on Jesus without hesitation.

So if we truly believe in Jesus, we will receive the salvation He extends to us as we extend our hearts and lives to Him. The result is a rest for our souls that is literally out of this world!

Then Jesus said, "Come to me, all of you who are weary and carry heavy burdens, and I will give you <u>rest</u>. Take my yoke upon you. Let me teach you, because I am humble and gentle, and you will find <u>rest</u> for your souls." (Matthew 11:28–29 NLT)

How rested are you in Jesus?

What can you do to increase your spiritual rest?

"I am the vine, you are the branches. He who abides in Me, and I in him, bears much fruit; for without Me you can do nothing." (John 15:5 NKJV)

These words of Jesus ring true in every aspect of our lives, especially when it comes to our relationships. If a person's relationship with Jesus isn't right, if he or she isn't abiding in Him, then none of the other relationships in his or her life will function properly. If a husband isn't close to the Lord, then his relationship with his wife will suffer, and vice versa. And the same can be said for every other type of relationship under the sun. Our relationship with Jesus must come first because it's through Him that we receive the love, patience, understanding, forgiveness, and other things we need in order to be rightly related to others.

So how do we keep our relationship with Christ intact? How do we abide in Him? Every strong relationship must have a strong sense of communication, and our relationship with the Lord is no different. Communication is a two-way street, where both parties have a chance to speak and listen to each other. When it comes to our relationship with God, we do this through prayer and the Word. Prayer is the primary way for us to talk to the Lord. It's our opportunity to share and express our hearts with Him. But this is only half the equation. In order to have a relationship with God, we need to hear Him speaking to us. He achieves this through His Word, a living and active instrument by which He communicates to us (Hebrews 4:12). So often I find myself in a situation where I need to hear from God and then suddenly a verse of Scripture will pop off the page and speak to my heart. That's God's way of speaking to us.

When we consistently use this two-way communication (prayer and the Word), our relationship with the Lord will be strong and vibrant. We'll also have success in the other relationships in our lives because we're correctly connected to Christ.

How can you ensure that you're correctly connected to Christ?

What can you do to improve your communication with God?

THE ROLE OF RELATIONSHIPS
DAY 270

Two are better than one, Because they have a good reward for their labor. For if they fall, one will lift up his companion. But woe to him who is alone when he falls, For he has no one to help him up.... Though one may be overpowered by another, two can withstand him.
(Ecclesiastes 4:9–10, 12 NKJV)

Relationships are valuable on a practical level. Solomon summarizes this truth in the book of Ecclesiastes as he writes that *two are better than one.* Through our relationships, we can increase what we accomplish, receive a helping hand in time of need, and withstand opposition and adversity. But the value of our relationships doesn't end on the practical plane.

Our relationships challenge us to change who we are spiritually. Every Christian is a work in progress. God's love for us is everlasting, but He won't be satisfied with who we are until we bear the perfect reflection of His Son (Philippians 1:6). The interaction that takes place in our relationships is an important part of His process in achieving this work. This is especially true of marriage; spouses bring their respective differences into a union, only to find that each one has grown a little bit like the other over the years. The lasting effect produces a more complete character in both.

Relationships also offer us the opportunity to give. Christians are called to be others-oriented (Galatians 6:2). We're to give of ourselves just as Jesus did, but this becomes impossible if our lives are empty. As our relationships become more meaningful, we'll have more opportunities to be others-oriented.

Last, relationships serve to safeguard us from going astray. Many mistakes can be avoided by allowing others to observe and speak up concerning our lives. Proverbs tells us that the *Wounds from a friend can be trusted (Proverbs 27:6 NIV).* Each of us should have a handful of people who can shoot straight with us whenever we need to be corrected or rebuked. It might sting for a season, but the value of these relationships is beyond worldly wealth.

Let's safeguard and grow relationships with those who can help us in our spiritual development. For without the help of our faithful friends, we can't expect to grow.

List some key relationships that have impacted your spiritual life.

Who can "shoot straight" with you and vice versa?

TRUTHFUL TOOL

In those days there was no king in Israel; everyone did what was right in his own eyes.
(Judges 17:6 NKJV)

A reoccurring theme appears as you read through the book of Judges. God delivers the Israelites from their enemies, they eventually backslide into sin, God uses their enemies as His rod of correction, they repent and cry out for forgiveness, God again delivers them from their enemies, and on and on it goes. The reason for this sinful cycle is given in the verse above: *everyone did what was right in his own eyes.* The people were not living according to a standard of straight but were allowing their hearts to lead and direct them instead. The results were painful and devastating.

Sadly, I see the same thing happening today when it comes to the way many people handle their relationships. Rather than seek a straight standard, many are willing to settle for less by following the feelings and desires of their hearts. But take note of what the Bible says about our hearts:

"The heart is deceitful above all things, And desperately wicked; Who can know it?"
(Jeremiah 17:9 NKJV)

We need something more reliable than our hearts to lead us in our relationships, and God has made perfect provision for us by giving us His Word as a tool for truth. The Bible enables us to discern what can and can't be done in a relationship. Because we're completely incapable of doing our relationships right without the Word, we need to give it a regular place in our day.

A compass' needle always points north, a ruler always helps to make an accurate measurement, and a plumb line always provides a perfect perpendicular line. Similarly, the Bible always points you to what's right, always helps you to see how things measure up, and always keeps your heart on the straight and narrow path of God's will for your relationships.

Are you willing to allow God's Word to determine what you can and can't do in your relationships?

How can you put this plan into action?

SPLIT DECISION

Now to the married I command, yet not I but the Lord: A wife is not to depart from her husband. (1 Corinthians 7:10 NKJV)

Imagine for a moment that you're living back in the days when Paul wrote the preceding passage. You've lived a fairly good life, never committed any major crimes, but you sense an emptiness in your soul that never finds fulfillment. Then one day you hear about a man called Jesus, who came into the world to touch and heal the brokenhearted. You're willing to see if it's true, so you open your heart to Jesus and make Him Lord of your life. But you're married, and your mate doesn't see things in quite the same light. What should you do? Does your newfound relationship with Jesus mean that you now need to end your marriage? Is it time for you to get a divorce?

A lot of Christians were confused about this point. Notice that the Word couldn't be clearer: *A wife [or husband] is not to depart (1 Corinthians 7:10 NKJV),* and *He [God] hates divorce (Malachi 2:16 NKJV).* And there's a blessing for those who are obedient and stay put with an unbelieving spouse:

For the unbelieving husband is sanctified by the wife, and the unbelieving wife is sanctified by the husband . . . . (1 Corinthians 7:14 NKJV)

Paul is instructing married couples to stay together in the hope that salvation will come to the unbelieving husband or wife. By God's divine design, an unsaved spouse has been singled out and chosen for evangelism through the most powerful instrument possible—his or her mate.

Salvation ought to enhance a marriage relationship, not end it. This principle goes beyond marriage; for if we really are the salt and light of the earth, then our lives should have a positive impact on **all** our relationships. May God give us the grace to be an instrument of influence for His holy name's sake.

What impact has your salvation had on your relationships with others?

What can you cut out of your life in order to be a brighter light to those who are watching your witness?

COMPLETELY CONTENT
DAY 273

Not that I speak in regard to need, for I have learned in whatever state I am, to be content . . .
(Philippians 4:11 NKJV)

What's the perfect state to live in? If sunshine is important to you, then you might say Florida. But if you're the type of person who enjoys having plenty of "elbow room," then perhaps the Carolinas are what you're looking for. Or Michigan might be the place for you if you want to get the best house for your buck. And if unlimited opportunity is what moves and motivates you, then you can't beat California. However, hurricanes come along with the sunshine, "elbow room" means higher rent, a bigger home requires more care and maintenance, and more opportunity brings more stress. There really isn't a perfect state to live in.

Well, then, what's the perfect state to be in? If you're a single person, you might long for marriage. Or, on the other hand, if you're married, you might wish you were once again single. Maybe you can't wait to have children. Or, if you were honest, you might confess that there are moments when you wish that you didn't have children. In each of these states, there's a potential burden to go along with the blessing. So there really isn't a perfect state to be in.

In reality, there is only one perfect state—the state of contentment. If your heart is content, then it doesn't matter if you're a married person living in Michigan or a single person in the Sunshine State. Contentment makes us complete wherever we live geographically and whoever we are relationally.

Unfortunately, we often wish for more from the relationships that God has given to us. We wait for something to be added to them when we should be pursuing the contentment that comes from being connected to Christ. The sooner we see our need to dwell in a state of contentment, the sooner we'll find fulfillment in our relationships with others.

How content are you on a scale of one to ten?

How can contentment be practically demonstrated in your life?

FATHER KNOWS BEST
DAY 274

So Abraham said to the oldest servant of his house, who ruled over all that he had, ". . I will make you swear by the LORD, the God of heaven and the God of the earth, that you will not take a wife for my son from the daughters of the Canaanites, among whom I dwell; but <u>you shall go to my country and to my family, and take a wife for my son Isaac</u>." (Genesis 24:2–4 NKJV)

Every godly dad wants the best for his children, and Abraham was no exception. When his son, Isaac, reached the age for marriage, Abraham went all out to secure the very best bride for him. Abraham sent his chief servant on a long journey to bring back a bride from among his own people. He wasn't willing to settle for a local Canaanite wife because that would mean spiritual compromise. Instead, Abraham was willing to go the distance to do what was in his son's best interest.

This is a perfect picture of how our heavenly Father operates in our own lives. He wants only the very best for His children, especially when it comes to the relationships that most influence us. For this reason, He has graciously given us His guidelines for the type of people we should allow ourselves to become close to.

Do not be unequally yoked together with unbelievers. For what fellowship has righteousness with lawlessness? And what communion has light with darkness? (2 Corinthians 6:14 NKJV)

The Lord warns us against becoming intimately entangled with unbelievers because He knows this will inevitably lead to spiritual compromise. As with Abraham, God loves His kids too much to settle for what's convenient. He has a higher standard for us that includes:

. . . love, joy, peace, longsuffering, kindness, goodness, faithfulness, gentleness, self-control. (Galatians 5:22–23 NKJV)

He wants to bless us with relationships with those who have these spiritual qualities. If a person isn't a believer, then he or she isn't God's choice for us. We would be wise to wait on Him because our heavenly Father knows best.

When have you settled for less than God's best, and what were the consequences?

How can you prevent this from happening again?

He who is unmarried cares for the things of the Lord; how he may please the Lord. But he who is married cares about the things of the world; how he may please his wife.
(1 Corinthians 7:32–33 NKJV)

We can't afford to miss what the apostle Paul is telling us here. He's showing us that there are realities connected to our relationships. They carry a certain cost, and they take work. Paul illustrates this by pointing to the marriage relationship, and he explains how it requires time and energy that were formerly being offered to the Lord's service. But he isn't condemning marriage or implying that those who are single are more spiritual. Not at all, because he goes on to acknowledge that spouses are expected to devote a degree of their time and attention toward one another:

There is a difference between a wife and a virgin. The unmarried woman cares about the things of the Lord, that she may be holy both in body and in spirit. But she who is married cares about the things of the world; how she may please her husband. (1 Corinthians 7:34 NKJV)

Scripture is acknowledging the reality that our relationships can take away from the time and energy we spend working for the Lord. This doesn't mean we should put an end to all our relationships. Instead, it should remind us to be wise when it comes to the relationships we choose to pursue due to the fact that they cost us something.

In reality, we can't fill our lives with countless relationships and still have time to invest in our relationship with God. Realistically, we need to know where to draw the line. We need to give priority to our relationship with the Lord so that we're free to enjoy the relationships that He has called us to.

How well do you consider the reality of what a relationship costs?

Ask the Lord to show you if there are any relationships that are cutting into your relationship with Him. If so, ask Him to show you the next step you should take.

RELATE-INABILITY
DAY 276

Now it happened, as Jesus sat at the table in the house, that behold, many tax collectors and sinners came and sat down with Him and His disciples. (Matthew 9:10 NKJV)

This verse is often a favorite for those who like to dress up their desire for sin in the disguise of "relatability." I commonly hear, *Well, Jesus hung out with sinners. He met them right where they were. So why can't I do the same for my unsaved buddies at the local bar? Come to think of it, those waitresses seem so lonely. If only I could show them God's love and . . . .* Stop it! Jesus *was* willing to relate to sinners, but watch what He did after He used relatability to establish a relationship with them:

And when the Pharisees saw it, they said to His disciples, "Why does your Teacher eat with tax collectors and sinners?" When Jesus heard that, He said to them, "Those who are well have no need of a physician, but those who are sick. . . . For I did not come to call the righteous, but sinners, <u>to repentance</u>." (Matthew 9:11–13 NKJV)

Notice that Jesus didn't just "pal around" with sinners and tax collectors. He didn't settle down and get comfortable where they were. Instead, Christ called sinners out of their lifestyle and into an attitude of repentance. He was willing to relate to sinners, but He was also effective in changing sinners into saints.

We need to follow Christ's example and use our relatability as a means to lead sinners away from their sin and to God's holiness. Otherwise, we're bound to be blindsided by their sin, and before we know it, rather than having an effect on the world, it's having an effect on us. This is a pathetic place for Christians to be because they've basically traded in their **ability** to rightly represent Christ for **relatabilty** with the world. Beware of relationships that depend on the ability to relate to something that Christ died to set us free from.

When has being relatable backfired on you?

Examine your relationships and deal with any that might be based on being relatable.

MIMIC THE MASTER
DAY 277

Therefore be <u>imitators of God</u> as dear children. And walk in love, as Christ also has loved us and given Himself for us, an offering and a sacrifice to God for a sweet-smelling aroma. (Ephesians 5:1–2 NKJV)

It has been said that "imitation is the sincerest form of flattery." There's a lot of truth in this statement, but be careful, Christian, because it's not the whole truth. In reality, imitation is much more than mere flattery.

Actually, imitation is a form of agreement. Each time we choose to imitate people, we're essentially agreeing to be like them. In a sense, we're saying that we approve, applaud, and agree with who and what they are.

Imitation also decreases individualism. Every time we imitate people, we are not only doing what they would do, but also not doing what we would do. It's really a matter of sacrificing who we are in favor of someone else. It makes me wonder what we fail to accomplish when we stop marching to the beat of our own drummer.

Finally, imitation sets us up for comparison. When it becomes clear to others that we're imitating somebody else, they will naturally compare us to that person. Whenever you see an Elvis impersonator, you automatically compare him to "the king" (notice the lowercase "k" here). But no matter how good an impersonator may be, he can only be a second-place Elvis. In the same way, we shouldn't settle for second place, imitating those whom God has not called us to be. Instead, we should strive to be imitators of God, which will result in a unique identity that fully realizes our potential in Christ Jesus.

It's so important to bring this understanding into the realm of our relationships, for there is always the temptation and tendency for us to imitate our closest companions. Unless we're imitating a Christ-like example in them, we'll always settle for second best and sell our identity in Christ short. Let's set our sights on Jesus because He's the only one worthy of our adoration and imitation.

When has imitating another person gotten you into trouble?

What are some ways you can more effectively mimic the Master?

Oh, don't worry; I wouldn't dare say that I am as wonderful as these other men who tell you how important they are! But <u>they are only comparing themselves with each other</u>, and measuring themselves by themselves. What foolishness! (2 Corinthians 10:12 NLT)

Perhaps you've noticed that the more you form a friendship with someone, the more you compare yourself to him or her. As you draw closer to another life, it's easy to allow yourself to become preoccupied with the differences in your personalities and characters instead of focusing on who God wants you to be. It's human nature to assume we are supposed to measure up to the stature of others. But our supernatural connection to God means that we have a personal calling on our lives that requires our obedience. But we won't be obedient to this customized call if we're constantly making comparisons.

Let's say you have a friend and she happens to share with you that she prays five times each day. The natural tendency is to think, *Wow, if she prays five times a day, then I need to start praying five times a day.* This may seem like a noble resolution, but what if God wants you to pray ten times a day? Or what if He wants you to pray once a day because you're supposed to serve Him in some other form or fashion? You could obey a standard you've learned by comparing yourself to someone else and miss out on the personal plan the Lord has for you.

Even the most spiritual saints have a sinful nature, which means that on their very best days, they're still an imperfect guide to compare ourselves to. As our closeness to others increases, our comparing ourselves to them needs to decrease. Christ must always be the standard we compare ourselves to. When we're faithful in this area, our relationships will have more spiritual substance by virtue of our growing personal relationship with God.

Whom do you tend to compare yourself to, and what should you do about it?

How can you discourage others from comparing themselves to you?

WOUNDS THAT HEAL
DAY 279

Faithful are the wounds of a friend . . . . (Proverbs 27:6 NKJV)

Here's something to try out the next time you're in a conversation with an acquaintance, friend, or family member. As you open your mouth to talk, make mental note of how many times you use the words *I, me, my,* and *mine.* If you're like most people, you'll be startled to discover just how frequently you use these personal pronouns. We're on our minds a lot more than we care to admit, and I've found that God will frequently use a friendship to reveal this to us.

An idol is anything that has first place in a person's heart, and believe it or not, we can actually be our own idol if we're always our first consideration. *What do I want to eat? How does something benefit me? When will it be my turn? How long before I can make something mine?* These are all tell-tale signs that we've become preoccupied with ourselves. And we need to see that being in this condition isn't trivial . . it's idolatry.

One of the great dangers of this type of idolatry is that we get so focused on ourselves that we don't notice the proverbial warning signs. But in His great grace, God has given us relationships with those who are often the mirror He uses to show us the ugliness of our self-centeredness. Because others see us from a different angle, they not only see when we've strayed into self-centeredness, but also bring it to our attention in a way that's undeniable and unavoidable. *Hey, bro, I can't help but notice that you seem really consumed by your own agenda lately. Can I remind you, as a friend, that it's not about you?* Sound harsh? Not at all when spoken by a faithful friend who wants to help us avoid the spiritual self-destruction of idolatry.

There's a dual responsibility here. If our role is the faithful friend, then we need to be bold enough to speak up, and if we're the one in sin, we need to be humble enough to receive these healing wounds.

How often do you put your own considerations first?

How can you protect yourself from making an idol out of yourself?

PROFANE PAIN

For the lips of an immoral woman drip honey, And her mouth is smoother than oil; But in the end she is bitter as wormwood, Sharp as a two-edged sword. Her feet go down to death, Her steps lay hold of hell. (Proverbs 5:3–5 NKJV)

We are strangely drawn to forbidden things, and the immoral woman described in Proverbs 5 is the perfect example of this declaration. This two-edged sword cuts both ways, for both men and women can have immoral characters. The emphasis isn't on gender but on immorality.

The Hebrew word here for *immoral* carries the connotation of something that is profane, which is the way God sees immorality. Unfortunately, we don't always share His perspective. Satan knows this and will do all he can to disguise sexual sin. He is also cunning enough to package the profane as something that seems to satisfy a need or want. Things might seem fine at first, but don't fail to notice that the steps of the immoral go down to hell and death.

As the one who sits behind the pastor's desk, I have personally seen the devastation, destruction, and death that immoral men and women leave in their wake. In practically every case, they chose to establish and nurture a relationship with someone outside of the marriage relationship. Had the relationship been avoided, then the sin never would have happened.

The Lord wants us to avoid this profane pain and, therefore, He pleads with us to never allow these types of relationships to take root in our hearts. He has made it clear that we need to be diligent in our duty to monitor the relationships we voluntarily invite in. This will keep our relationships pure and preserve our hearts for the relationship with the one whom the Lord has called us to love for a lifetime.

But fornication and all uncleanness or covetousness, let it not even be named among you, as is fitting for saints . . . . (Ephesians 5:3 NKJV)

Are there any questionable relationships in your life? Ask the opinion of someone who knows you well.

Ask God to help you from being drawn to relationships that are forbidden.

Lest . . . your reputation be ruined. (Proverbs 25:10 NKJV)

Suppose one of our 4-star generals stood behind a lectern and confessed that he had swapped national secrets with the enemy. Would you trust him again in the same way? Imagine you have the good fortune of owning a classic Rolls Royce. Unfortunately, after a head-on collision, a mechanic tells you that due to your car's rarity, it can't be properly repaired. Would you feel the same way about it? In both cases, you would have to answer no. Something was lost that couldn't be regained, which is what happens when our reputation is ruined.

A person's **reputation** is a representation of his or her character. It captures his or her value and virtue. A righteous reputation is a powerful tool that can accomplish incredible feats for God's kingdom. But once a person's reputation is ruined, it sets off a chain reaction of loss in his or her relationships.

When we lose our reputation, we lose the **respect** of others. Respect is directly connected to reputation. If one is strong, the same will hold true for the other. Conversely, when you weaken the one, you will destroy the other.

When we lose the respect of others, we also lose the **right** to speak into their lives. The value of our input in others' lives is based on how much they value our character. When we're respected, people will listen to us, and then we will have the ability to impact them in positive ways.

When we lose the right to speak into others' lives, we inevitably lose **rewards** that we might have earned by fulfilling the function of a faithful friend.

If more people treated their reputation like gold, there would be a lot less problems in our relationships. Let's make it a point to invest in our reputations, and God will make it a point to enrich our relationships.

How would you summarize your reputation in a single word?

Ask at least five friends for their take on your reputation.

In a perfect world, there would be no sin. Our lives would have spotless records, and all our past relationships would be pure and presentable before a holy and righteous God. But this isn't a perfect world, we aren't perfect people, and none of us can point to a perfect past. In fact, most of us have a profound sense of shame when it comes to our past relationships. Perhaps we've made so many mistakes that we've never felt fully forgiven or completely cleansed. But instead of dwelling on what we've done, let's look at what God's Word tells us in the midst of our imperfection. Allow these verses to hit your heart and watch as God's Spirit empowers you to push past your past.

He has not dealt with us according to our sins, Nor punished us according to our iniquities. For as the heavens are high above the earth, So great is His mercy toward those who fear Him; As far as the east is from the west, So far has He removed our transgressions from us. As a father pities his children, So the LORD pities those who fear Him. For He knows our frame; He remembers that we are dust. (Psalm 103:10–14 NKJV)

Who is a God like You, Pardoning iniquity And passing over the transgression of the remnant of His heritage? He does not retain His anger forever, Because He delights in mercy. He will again have compassion on us, And will subdue our iniquities. You will cast all our sins Into the depths of the sea. (Micah 7:18–19 NKJV)

For I am persuaded that neither death nor life, nor angels nor principalities nor powers, nor things present nor things to come, nor height nor depth, nor any other created thing, shall be able to separate us from the love of God which is in Christ Jesus our Lord. (Romans 8:38–39 NKJV)

Therefore, if anyone is in Christ, he is a new creation; old things have passed away; behold, all things have become new. (2 Corinthians 5:17 NKJV)

If we confess our sins, He is faithful and just to forgive us our sins and to cleanse us from all unrighteousness. (1 John 1:9 NKJV)

Which verse ministers to you the most? Why?

Whom will you share this with?

WHAT'S IT WORTH?
DAY 283

"Greater love has no one than this, than to lay down one's life for his friends." (John 15:13 NKJV)

If something has no cost attached to it, what is it really worth? What is a home or car worth that doesn't cost anything? The answer is nothing because where there is no cost, there is no worth. By the same token, if a relationship has value and worth, there is an element of cost attached to it. Show me a relationship steeped in sacrifice, and I'll show you a relationship that is worth more than any amount of worldly wealth.

This is an important principle when it comes to our relationship with God. Jesus declares in the verse above that the greatest expression of love is *"to lay down one's life for his friends."* That's because laying down one's life is the greatest sacrifice that can be made in this life. When Jesus chose to sacrifice and surrender everything for us, it gave birth to a relationship that is worth everything. Nothing compares to the price Christ paid for us, and nothing is more precious and valuable than our relationship with Him. That was Paul's perspective when he wrote:

I once thought all these things were so very important, but now I consider them worthless because of what Christ has done. Yes, everything else is worthless when compared with the priceless gain of knowing Christ Jesus my Lord. I have discarded everything else, counting it all as garbage, so that I may have Christ and become one with him. (Philippians 3:7–9 NLT)

Life shows us that the relationships worth the most are also the ones steeped in sacrifice. If we want relationships that are worth something, then we need to be willing to sacrifice something. Let's move beyond just **knowing this** and begin **doing this** in the relationships that God has blessed us with.

When was the last time you made a personal sacrifice for a friend, and how did it impact your relationship?

How can you practically apply this principle?

And so you became a <u>model</u> to all the believers . . . . (1 Thessalonians 1:7 NIV)

As a kid growing up in the Motor City, I was also quite the model maker. I learned some important lessons as I sat and assembled various vehicles. First, I found that I needed to read the instructions. If I skipped this step, I was bound to get off track and make some major mistakes. I also learned that before building, I had to examine all the parts and pieces to make sure that everything was there. Last, I needed to have the type of glue that was especially designed for making models.

If any of these steps were skipped, the model would end up as a humiliating pile of plastic. But when they were patiently and properly followed, the results were something worth celebrating. The same principles apply when it comes to our relationships; for if we don't carefully read the instructions, examine if we have all the necessary parts, and have the right type of glue, our relationships will be a source of humiliation rather than celebration.

Our instructions are provided for us in God's Word. The Scriptures are capable of equipping us for every need in life (2 Timothy 2:16–17)—this includes our relational needs. When we take the time to read through God's Word, we find a set of instructions, showing us the "what," "when," "why," and "how" for our relationships. There also needs to be a bit of self-examination as we check ourselves to see if we have the love, joy, peace, patience, kindness, and gentleness that are necessary in order for us to build. And we've got to have the right type of glue to hold everything together. In this case, God's Spirit is the glue that holds hearts together when the pressure and stress of life would normally break relationships apart.

When we follow these steps, we won't be ashamed or frustrated by our relationships. Instead, we will literally have model relationships.

What do you use as a source of instruction for your life in general and for your relationships in particular?

Which relationships need some "model work"?

LUST OR LOVE?
DAY 285

Let us walk properly, as in the day, not in revelry and drunkenness, not in lewdness and <u>lust</u>, not in strife and envy. But put on the Lord Jesus Christ, and make no provision for the flesh, to fulfill its <u>lusts</u>. (Romans 13:13–14 NKJV)

The dictionary defines the word *lust* as "an intense and unrestrained craving, an overwhelming desire." Synonyms include *obsession*, *longing*, *yearning*, *hunger*, and *thirst*. There isn't any specific mention of sexuality because lust is much bigger than the sexual sin we usually associate with it. Lust can be found in fans who never miss their favorite team's games. We witness lust in the shopping sprees that only meet desires, not needs. And we can see lust in those who pursue relationships for the sole sake of filling a sense of emptiness that only God can fill. Sadly, many relationships (even non-sexual ones) are built on lust.

We can also see lust by looking at what it isn't. If lust has an exact opposite, it's God's love, and this is how God defines it in His Word:

Love suffers long and is kind; love does not envy; love does not parade itself, is not puffed up; does not behave rudely, does not seek its own, is not provoked, thinks no evil; does not rejoice in iniquity, but rejoices in the truth; bears all things, believes all things, hopes all things, endures all things. (1 Corinthians 13:4–7 NKJV)

What a divine difference between lust and love! So let me ask you a few questions as you form your friendships and relationships: Would you rather have lust or love as your foundation? Is it better to have demonstrative, unruly, selfish, mean, and false relationships, or patient, considerate, hospitable, and true relationships? Do you want to connect yourself to people who will cut and run once they get what they want, or would you rather have relationships with those who will stay by your side through thick and thin, demonstrating a love that never fails? The answers are obvious, and so is the need to build our relationships on God's love instead of our lust.

Are there any relationships in your life that are lust-based? How do you know?

Take time today and ask God to exchange your lust for His love.

LEARN TO LISTEN

Where there is no counsel, the people fall; But in the multitude of counselors there is safety.
(Proverbs 11:14 NKJV)

From time to time, I'll run into a starry-eyed couple who would like me to perform their wedding ceremony. As a pastor, this places me in an awkward position because our church requires our couples go through a seven-week course designed to educate and ensure that it's God's will for them to wed. In many cases, they take advantage of these classes, but sometimes a couple will say, *Well, that's great for other people. But we know that we're in love, and we want to get married as soon as possible. So we're going to pass on the premarital counseling.* They go ahead and get married by some other means, and I'll bump into them after the fact. But now, just a few months later, the twinkle in their eyes is gone as they relate how difficult life has been since they forsook counsel and decided to do things their way.

I'll also encounter people who are on the brink of beginning a business relationship that sounds a little shady. It usually requires them to invest some money that isn't theirs to begin with. They plan to take out a loan they can't afford in hopes of hitting the jackpot. I'll warn them against spending money that isn't theirs, no matter what the potential payoff might be. Yet, more often than not, my counsel is unheeded, and they begin a disastrous business relationship that will take them years to recover from.

The point I'm making is the same one that Solomon makes in the verse above. The proverb tells us that wise counsel is a safeguard against making mistakes. No matter how sure we may feel about a relationship, we need to seek the counsel of people we trust and, this is the key, **listen to them**. It doesn't do any good to ask for an opinion if we aren't willing to listen to it. Heed the counsel of your friends, parents, and pastors, especially when it concerns romantic and business relationships.

When has a word of wise counsel spared you from making a bad decision?

Designate two or three people in your life as counselors whom you will truly listen to, even if you don't like what they have to say.

BIRD BEHAVIOR

Do not be misled: "Bad company corrupts good character." (1 Corinthians 15:33 NIV)

It has been said that "birds of a feather flock together." If you visit a zoo, you'll see that this saying is true. There you will see penguins gathered with other penguins, vultures gathered with other vultures, and flamingos gathered with other flamingos. This is so they can be safe and survive.

As the flock of God (1 Peter 5:2), Christians should also be found flocking together. The Bible tells us that *"bad company corrupts good character."* The Greek word here for *bad* is quite interesting. It comes from another word that means "to give back, to recede, to retire, or to retreat in battle." It's a type of badness that produces the effect of giving ground, and Christians will always surrender their spiritual territory when they start to flock around those who aren't a part of God's flock. If you're always hanging out with people who ignore the things of God, it's only a matter of time before you will find yourself held back in your spiritual walk. Carnality in them will produce carnality in you, anger in them will produce anger in you, and the list goes on and on.

But if bad company corrupts good character, then the reverse must also be true: **holy company hinders bad behavior**. If you're constantly surrounding yourself with those who are spiritual, then it will produce spirituality in you. Their patience will birth patience in you; their peace will generate peace in you, etc. You won't find yourself succumbing to the same old sins but will be encouraged and pushed forward in your walk with Jesus.

Let's seek out the spiritual strength and safety that is found in the midst of God's flock instead of letting bad company corrupt our character. It may require you to align your priorities differently, but you will see the rewards in this life and the next.

How has a godly relationship positively impacted you?

Ask God to reveal if your character is being corrupted through some bad company.

[King Jehoram] went and sent to Jehoshaphat king of Judah, saying, "The king of Moab has rebelled against me. Will you go with me to fight against Moab?" And he said, "I will go up; I am as you are, my people as your people, my horses as your horses." (2 Kings 3:7 NKJV)

Jehoram was the newly crowned king of Israel, and there were those who weren't willing to submit to his leadership. Specifically, Israel's archrivals, the Moabites, raised a rebellion against Jehoram. There was only one person he could turn to in his hour of need—Jehoshaphat, the king of Judah, Israel's sister-nation, and a man who walked in the ways of the Lord (1 Kings 22:43). He had heard Jehoram's cry for help and was willing to establish an alliance with him.

Interestingly, Jehoram's father, Ahab, had been in a similar situation and had also asked Jehoshaphat for help (1 Kings 22:4). This union between Ahab and Jehoshaphat ended in disaster. But even though Jehoshaphat had been burned through this alliance, he was still willing to help Ahab's son with virtually the same request.

From time to time, we enter into relationships that leave us burned. As a result, we could promise ourselves not to make the same mistake twice, allowing our hearts to grow calloused. *My last neighbor never returned my stepladder, so I'm through with the nice neighbor thing! My co-worker made fun of the fact that I offered to pray for him, so that's it for letting my light shine!* As long as we're in this world, we'll find ourselves getting burned by others. But God calls us to get past what people have done and remain open to the relationships He has for our future:

"But I say to you, love your enemies, bless those who curse you, do good to those who hate you, and pray for those who spitefully use you and persecute you . . . ." (Matthew 5:44 NKJV)

We definitely need to be wise in choosing our relationships, but at the same time, we can't be afraid to reach out to others.

When have you been burned by a relationship, and how did you handle it?

How well are you living Matthew 5:44?

But it happened, when Ahab died, that the king of Moab rebelled against the king of Israel. So King Jehoram went out of Samaria at that time and mustered all Israel. Then he went and sent to Jehoshaphat king of Judah, saying, "The king of Moab has rebelled against me. Will you go with me to fight against Moab?" And he said, "I will go up; I am as you are, my people as your people, my horses as your horses." (2 Kings 3:5–7 NKJV)

Sometimes the trials of life seem absolutely unbearable. Our troubles can add up until we're brought to our breaking point. This is what happened in the life of Jehoram. Two tragic tidal waves have come crashing down on him. The first is that his father, Ahab, has just been killed in battle, leaving Jehoram to occupy the throne. This would have been a heavy enough burden to bear, but then the second wave hits him in the form of a rebellion. The nation of Moab, which had submitted to his father, is now ready to rebel against him. Imagine the effect this mixture of grief and insecurity must have produced.

But just as the world seems to close in around him, Jehoram breaks down and begs Jehoshaphat for help. This is a desperate step, but it is in the right direction. The Bible describes Jehoshaphat as a man who constantly did what was right in the Lord's eyes (1 Kings 22:43). Jehoram was the polar opposite. He is described as one who did evil in the sight of the Lord (2 Kings 3:2). Ordinarily, Jehoram probably wouldn't have had anything to do with Jehoshaphat, but through his trials, he was driven to pursue a relationship with this righteous man.

Sometimes our trials are designed to direct us. God wants to connect "Jehorams" with "Jehoshaphats" because He knows that "Jehorams" need a godly presence in their lives. Their problems are the means that God uses to connect them to someone who will be a witness in their lives. We need to remember this when people, especially non-believers, come to us for help.

What did you learn from the example of Jehoram and Jehoshaphat?

How can you apply this in your own life?

VERY VALUABLE

DAY 290

"Do not lay up for yourselves treasures on earth, where moth and rust destroy and where thieves break in and steal; but lay up for yourselves treasures in heaven, where neither moth nor rust destroys and where thieves do not break in and steal." (Matthew 6:19–20 NKJV)

In the automotive industry, value is determined by longevity. If a certain make or model has the good reputation of lasting longer, then it's going to have a higher price tag. The same thing goes for dishwashers, refrigerators, toasters, wristwatches, televisions, batteries, ink pens, and even deodorants. The value of something is linked to its enduring qualities.

This should cause us to consider how much value we place on our relationships. Fewer things in life have the ability to influence us more than our relationships. And if these relationships are influencing us to live our lives for God's greater glory, then we know that our spiritual bank account in heaven is being bolstered (1 Corinthians 3:12–14). We also know that these heavenly riches are beyond the reach of this world's devices. They are permanently eternal, unable to be touched by the corrosive laws of nature or even the corrupted nature of man. And as such, the relationships that motivate and push us to attain these riches are beyond any earthly value.

When fellow Christians challenge you to go further in your faith, they are leading you to reap an eternal reward. Or when a spouse encourages you to press on when you feel like quitting and giving up in your service to God, it is more precious than the entire material universe. God-based relationships are far more valuable than we give them credit for. Let's appreciate what they're worth by virtue of what they allow us to accomplish, and let's thank the Lord for blessing us with these very valuable relationships.

How much value do you place on your relationships?

How can you show an important person in your life that you consider your relationship with him or her to be very valuable?

FATHER FACTOR

"I will be his <u>Father</u>, and he shall be My son." (2 Samuel 7:14 NKJV)

He shall cry to Me, "You are my <u>Father</u>, My God, and the rock of my salvation." (Psalm 89:26 NKJV)

".. For I am a Father . . . ." (Jeremiah 31:9 NKJV)

God employs many means to reveal Himself. Romans 1:20–21 tells us that His eternal power is revealed to us through the wonders of the natural world. Romans 2:14–15 says that His moral absolutes are imprinted on the conscience of every human being. And Hebrews 1:1–2 teaches us that He has declared Himself through the life of His Son. But there is still one more way that God reveals Himself.

Have you ever noticed how frequently God refers to Himself as *Father*? He draws this comparison because He wants to get a point across to us. As humans, we're limited in what we can understand about Him. He has provided the paternal example for us on the earthly plane so that we can comprehend His heart for us on the heavenly plane. The dynamic of the father-child relationship is a gateway for our understanding of God.

Many people who've had poor or non-existent relationships with their fathers also have a hard time coming to God. When they hear the words *heavenly Father*, they are immediately turned off by recollections of a faulty fatherly relationship that they were subjected to as children. Some were berated, some were beaten, and others were simply ignored.

This was never God's intention. He wants earthly fathers to demonstrate His qualities to their children because then it will be an easy transition for children to take their own step of faith toward God. If you are a father, understand the awesome power you wield when it comes to your relationship with your children. And if you have been bruised through your relationship with your earthly father, remember that it is a distorted picture of the perfect paternal heart that beats for you in heaven . . even now.

"Your Father in heaven is perfect." (Matthew 5:48 NKJV)

How has your relationship with your father impacted your relationship with God?

Take some time today and ask God to show you the depth of His Father's heart toward you.

All things are <u>lawful for me, but not all things are helpful</u>; all things are lawful for me, but not all things edify. (1 Corinthians 10:23 NKJV)

Imagine if we ran into each other at the local video store. We exchange a few polite words and then you notice that I'm holding three R-rated movies in my hand. How would that impact our relationship? Would it cause you to have a hard time receiving spiritual instruction from me the next time I preach on living a pure and holy life? Of course it would because my relationship to you, as a pastor, carries the expectation that I am keeping my eyes and heart pure. And so to ensure that this scenario never happens, I don't watch R-rated movies as a general rule.

Some would say, *But wait a minute, pastor, there's no "thou shalt not watch an R-rated movie" commandment in the Bible. You're free to see those types of films if you want to.* I know this, but just because I'm free to do something doesn't mean it's going to be good for the relationships in my life. It would be penny wise and pound foolish to enjoy an R-rated movie if it stumbles a brother or sister who struggles in this area.

It is good neither to eat meat nor drink wine nor do anything by which your brother stumbles or is offended or is made weak. (Romans 14:21 NKJV)

Our relationships ought to be more important than the fleeting enjoyment of a freedom that carries the potential to stumble others. It's not worth running the risk of ruining a relationship over something so trivial. If we aren't willing to give up certain "rights," then it says a lot about how little our brothers and sisters really mean to us. All things are lawful but not all things are helpful. Let's be bold enough to ask the Lord to show us when our insistence upon a right is damaging a relationship.

When has a freedom damaged a relationship in your life, and is it possible for you to fix it?

Ask the Lord to give you a heart that always puts the considerations of others before yours (Philippians 2:4).

CHANGE THE CHANNEL
DAY 293

" . . . sin lies at the door. And its desire is for you, but you should rule over it." (Genesis 4:7 NKJV)

Sin is not passive; it is prolific. Scripture describes it as crouching just outside the door of our hearts, waiting for an opportune time to attack and subdue us. The very nature of sin is to grow and spread itself in as many lives and situations as possible. And whether we like it or not, our relationships can serve as channels through which our own sin can pass and infect others.

Here's one example of how this works. Let's pretend that you know something really juicy about a man with an addiction. A Christian is supposed to cover another person's shame (Proverbs 17:9), but your flesh is having a difficult time keeping this quiet. So, in a moment of weakness, you find yourself picking up the phone and dialing the number of one of your friends. It's just a matter of time before you start to discuss this man's dirt. This is bad enough, but it doesn't stop there because now this friend feels the need to pick up the phone, and on and on it goes until word gets back to the one with the addiction and now he's devastated! What happened? Not only did you sin but there's now a trail of sin winding its way through many hearts.

Again, sin is not passive; it is prolific. And when it isn't dealt with in your heart by the power of the Holy Spirit, it will seize the opportunity to infect others via your relationships with your spouse, parents, children, employers, and friends. Your relationships should serve as channels for blessing, not sin. If you're guilty of letting a relationship be used for sin, ask God's Spirit to change your heart and help you change the channel.

So I advise you to live according to your new life in the Holy Spirit. Then you won't be doing what your sinful nature craves. (Galatians 5:16 NLT)

When have you allowed a relationship to serve as a channel of blessing or of sin?

What can you do to "change the channel"? (Hint: read Galatians 5:16–26.)

BUSY BUT BELOVED

<u>Greet</u> Priscilla and Aquila, my fellow workers in Christ Jesus, who risked their own necks for my life, to whom not only I give thanks, but also all the churches of the Gentiles. Likewise <u>greet</u> the church that is in their house. <u>Greet</u> my beloved Epaenetus, who is the firstfruits of Achaia to Christ. <u>Greet</u> Mary, who labored much for us. <u>Greet</u> Andronicus and Junia, my countrymen and my fellow prisoners, who are of note among the apostles, who also were in Christ before me. <u>Greet</u> Amplias, my beloved in the Lord. <u>Greet</u> Urbanus, our fellow worker in Christ, and Stachys, my beloved. <u>Greet</u> Apelles, approved in Christ. <u>Greet</u> those who are of the household of Aristobulus. <u>Greet</u> Herodion, my countryman. <u>Greet</u> those who are of the household of Narcissus who are in the Lord. <u>Greet</u> Tryphena and Tryphosa, who have labored in the Lord. <u>Greet</u> the beloved Persis, who labored much in the Lord. (Romans 16:3–12 NKJV)

As Paul wraps up his epistle to the church in Rome, he commands them to greet many people. The Greek word for *greet* means "to enfold with one's arms." It describes the warmth and love between two close friends. This gives us an interesting insight into Paul's life because it reveals that he had a lot of friends in Rome. And this was just one of the many churches he was involved with. Imagine how long the list would be if we could chronicle every friend from every church!

This is all the more amazing when you consider how busy Paul was. Based on the information we have in the New Testament, it has been estimated that during his ministry career, Paul traveled over ten thousand miles, mostly on foot. That's roughly the equivalent of walking from Los Angeles to Chicago five times! Even though he was a man on the move, ministering to others wherever he went, he also understood that his devotion to God had to be nurtured by spending a healthy amount of alone time with the Lord. One wonders how Paul had any time to establish all these friendships, yet he did because it was important to him.

Those who don't have healthy friendships commonly complain that they're just too busy. There are errands, work, the need to sleep, and don't forget the alone time with God. But if Paul wasn't too busy to make friends, then **nobody** can use that as an excuse. Our lives are bound to be busy, but this is not an excuse for not building beloved friendships.

Why should we do our best to follow Paul's example?

How can you delegate more time toward relationship building? Write it down and stick to it.

TIMOTHY-TYPE
DAY 295

But I trust in the Lord Jesus to send <u>Timothy</u> to you shortly, that I also may be encouraged when I know your state. For I have no one <u>like-minded</u>, who will sincerely care for your state. (Philippians 2:19–20 NKJV)

Our relationships with some people are so special that they belong at the top of the list. These are the ones who come through when all others fail, the ones who are still standing when the rest of the world seems to fall apart. This describes the type of relationship between Paul and Timothy.

Paul probably encounters Timothy for the first time on his initial missionary journey to the city of Lystra. Bible scholars suggest that Timothy was in his mid to late teens at this point. When Paul revisits Lystra on his second journey, he decides to take Timothy with him as a traveling companion (Acts 16:3). This partnership becomes a blessing to both, as Paul needs a young back to truck his supplies across Asia Minor and Timothy seems to lack a father figure in his life (2 Timothy 1:5). From this point on, the two are practically inseparable, except when Paul has a special task for Timothy (Acts 19:22; 1 Corinthians 4:17).

Over the next several years, they log many miles, face numerous persecutions, and together witness the miraculous moving of God. These experiences further deepen this unique relationship, which becomes increasingly important as time goes on. Toward the end of his ministry, Paul refers to Timothy as *a true son in the faith (1 Timothy 1:2 NKJV)*, and when the apostle finds himself abandoned by virtually everyone, Timothy is still standing by his side (2 Timothy 4:11–13).

In the verse above, Paul describes Timothy as being uniquely *like-minded*, which is another way of saying that they really understood each other. No wonder, when we consider all they had been through as Christian brothers. What about you? Is there a Timothy in your life whom you can count on when it's "crunch time," someone who really understands you? If so, thank the Lord for this gift. If not, ask the Lord for this gift.

Who comes the closest to being a Timothy in your life?

How can you enrich and improve your relationship with this person?

WHO'S HUSHAI?
DAY 296

And Hushai the Archite was the king's companion. (1 Chronicles 27:33 NKJV)

I'm willing to guess that you haven't given much thought to Hushai the Archite lately. His name only shows up thirteen times in Scripture, and he certainly isn't among the more popular Bible characters (have you ever met someone named Hushai?). As far as we know, he didn't perform any mighty miracles, inspire any revivals of repentance, or deliver any powerful prophecies. Hushai did not go down in history as a notable prophet, priest, or king. But take note of who he was—*the king's companion.*

The king referenced here is none other than David, the most powerful man who ever sat on Israel's throne. There are more verses devoted to David's life than to any other Old Testament figure. His name is mentioned over eight hundred times in the Old Testament and over sixty times in the New Testament. Jesus is rarely given a title that includes another person's name, and yet the Son of God is also identified as the Son of David. A strong case can even be made that one cannot fully appreciate Jesus' life without understanding David's because Christ's coming was the fulfillment of a personal promise that God had given to David (2 Samuel 7:16).

There's no questioning David's importance, and Hushai played an important role in his life. He served as *the king's companion,* which could also be translated as "friend and confidant." He was the man behind the man, never dominating the spotlight but always there for David when he needed a friend. There's a certain beauty in the way the Bible simply identifies Hushai as a friend, and it also shows us how important friendships are from God's perspective.

Our lives might not make the front page, but this doesn't mean they aren't important. Hushai shows us that we can fulfill an important function by simply being a faithful friend. This may not seem like a big deal in the world's eyes, but if friendship is important enough for God to highlight it in His Word, then it ought to be important to us.

How do you think your view of friendship compares with God's?

Take the time today to tell those closest to you how much you appreciate their friendship.

A man who has friends must himself be friendly . . . . (Proverbs 18:24 NKJV)

A person who sits in front of the television all day can *know* every last detail about a celebrity, but he or she will never be *known* by the celebrity. A father who neglects his children throughout the course of their childhood may have a biological relationship *to* them, but he will never have a meaningful relationship *with* them. A married couple that never talks to each other may have a relationship on *paper*, but they won't have one in *practice*.

The reason for this is because real relationships are reciprocal; they require two-way interaction in order to exist and develop. They also require effort and investment; they do not "just happen" on their own. The proverb above spells this out by telling us that if someone wants to have friends, then he or she must be friendly. It's the age-old principle of reaping and sowing; what we get out of our relationships really depends on what we put into them.

Don't be misled. . . . You will always reap what you sow! (Galatians 6:7 NLT)

Sometimes we are prone to wonder why we don't have great relationships with our parents, children, neighbors, friends, colleagues, etc. The natural tendency is to look at others and assume that the problem lies somewhere within their hearts when, in reality, the problem is really with us. All too often we want the intimacy without wanting to make the investment. We want to be surrounded with friends, but we aren't willing to go the distance to be friendly. In essence, we want to reap the harvest without having to sow the seed. That harvest will never come.

God's Word teaches us to take personal responsibility for our relationships if we hope to see any change in them. It only makes sense that we need to be a friend before we can expect to be befriended.

Have you ever been involved in a one-way relationship? What happened and why?

How can you do better at sowing into your relationships?

. . . you do not know what will happen tomorrow. For what is your life? It is even a vapor that appears for a little time and then vanishes away. (James 4:14 NKJV)

Jesus has promised to give everlasting life to those who trust in Him as their Lord and Savior (Romans 10:9–10). When it comes to life here on earth, it is just a passing vapor. It can end in an instant, and God calls us to make the most of today because we don't know if there will be a tomorrow. By the same token, we need to make the most of our relationships today because there's no guarantee they will be here tomorrow. This isn't meant to be fatalistic but realistic. For we cannot escape the fact that each of our earthly relationships will eventually come to an end.

When we look at Jesus' relationship with His disciples, we see that He always had an eye on the fact that He was going to leave them. Christ didn't squander any of His time with the Twelve because He understood that it was limited:

"Little children, I shall be with you a little while longer. You will seek Me; and as I said to the Jews, 'Where I am going, you cannot come,' so now I say to you." (John 13:33 NKJV)

A part of our fallen nature prefers procrastination to being proactive. We tend to put things off by telling ourselves that there's always going to be plenty of time down the road. This type of thinking goes against the way God wants us to look at life (James 4:14). Often we make the tragic mistake of assuming we will always have plenty of time to enjoy our relationships with our family and friends. But distance or death may take us by surprise, and we will find ourselves regretting the time that was lost. May we make the most of the relationships we have today because there's no guarantee they will be here tomorrow.

Which relationships have you neglected, and what can you do to change that?

Pray that God will give you the proper perspective on life and that He will help you to be more proactive.

WE'RE AT WAR
DAY 299

For we do not wrestle against flesh and blood, but against principalities, against powers, against the rulers of the darkness of this age, against spiritual hosts of wickedness in the heavenly places. (Ephesians 6:12 NKJV)

There's a spiritual war going on. Unseen to the naked eye, but real nonetheless, there's a cosmic clash taking place between the kingdom of heaven and the kingdom of darkness. As a defeated foe, the devil is desperate to take as many with him to his doom as he possibly can. And that's where we come in. Satan's mission is to harass and hinder us from following the Lord. He is a master strategist with a vast array of weapons in his arsenal. And one has proven particularly effective for him over the ages . . . relationships.

Not every relationship is a gift from God. Occasionally, they can be a tool of attack. Let's say that you have been living the life of a compromised Christian. You've known for a while that you need to make some serious changes if you're going to get closer to God. So, in the process of pressing forward, you've decided to end a relationship that constantly causes you to compromise. You put an end to things, and all seems to be just fine until you come home one night after a hard day's work to find a familiar voice on the answering machine. It's that old relationship begging to be let back into your life. What do you do? If you're wise, you'll recognize that this relationship is a tool of attack intended to take you down.

Most of our relationships are blessings from above, but a few are from below. May we never forget that we're at war with the enemy, and may we make it our mission to monitor our relationships well enough to know when we're being attacked.

When has the enemy used a relationship to attack you? What did you do?

Make it a point to monitor your relationships and determine which ones are drawing you toward and which ones are pulling you away from Jesus.

IT'S ALL HIS
DAY 300

The earth is the Lord's, and all its fullness, The world and those who dwell therein. (Psalm 24:1 NKJV)

Everything we have ultimately belongs to God. The psalmist reminds us of this as he writes, *The earth is the Lord's, and all its fullness.* In other words, there's nothing worth having in this world that doesn't already belong to God. John the Baptist had the same perspective on life as he announced:

"A man can receive nothing unless it has been given to him from heaven." (John 3:27 NKJV)

And even James, the Lord's brother, writes in his epistle:

Every good gift and every perfect gift is from above, and comes down from the Father of lights, with whom there is no variation or shadow of turning. (James 1:17 NKJV)

The Bible couldn't be clearer; everything of value in our lives belongs to God. And this doesn't just mean our possessions; it also includes our abilities that enable us to earn our possessions. If you have the ability to close a deal in the corporate world, or if you can throw a ball with pin-point accuracy, or whatever it is that you're best at, God is the one who has gifted you with that ability. It makes me cringe whenever I hear a person refer to himself or herself as a "self-made" man or woman. There's no such thing because success is something that's graciously given by God. The Bible says that promotion doesn't come from the east or west but from the Lord (Psalm 75:6–7).

It's so important for us to look at life this way because if we don't acknowledge the Lord's ownership over all we hold dear, then we'll be tempted to hoard it for ourselves. But if we see that it's all His to begin with, we'll be ready to respond to what He wants us to do with it. We need to disown what we've come to claim as "ours," acknowledge that it's really God's, and ask Him how He wants us to use it.

Why do you think it's so hard to acknowledge God's ownership over our lives?

What are some things you need to "disown"?

TALENT SHOW

"For the kingdom of heaven is like a man traveling to a far country, who called his own servants and delivered his goods to them. And to one he gave five <u>talents</u>, to another two, and to another one, to each according to his own ability; and immediately he went on a journey." *(Matthew 25:14–15 NKJV)*

In biblical times, a *talent* was a term for monetary measurement. It represented a certain weight and worth. Jesus referred to this form of currency in the parable where a master entrusts various amounts of talents to three of his servants, who responded quite differently:

"Then he who had received the five talents went and traded with them, and made another five talents. And likewise he who had received two gained two more also. But he who had received one went and dug in the ground, and <u>hid his lord's money</u>." (Matthew 25:16–18 NKJV)

The first two servants did something productive with the talents entrusted to them, but the third servant basically did nothing with what he had been given. When their master returned to see what they had done, he commended the first two but had some hard words for the third:

"But his lord answered and said to him, 'You wicked and lazy servant . . . . So take the talent from him, and give it to him who has ten talents. For to everyone who has, more will be given, and he will have abundance; but from him who does not have, even what he has will be taken away.'" (Matthew 25:26–29 NKJV)

This parable proves an important point: as God looks at what He has given to us, He also expects us to do something with it. Whether we find ourselves with five talents, two talents, or one talent, we need to be busy about our Lord's business, making the most with what we've been given. Our talents can't be buried; they need to grow, and in order for them to do this, we need to put them to good use for God's kingdom.

What talents have you been entrusted with?

How can you do a better job of putting them to good use?

YOUR GRASS IS GREEN
DAY 302

"For everyone to whom much is given, from him much will be required; and to whom much has been committed, of him they will ask the more." (Luke 12:48 NKJV)

We're all familiar with the phrase, The grass is always greener on the other side of the fence. It seems true. A part of the human heart wants to focus on what others have, and before long we completely lose sight of what we have. Even as the issue of generosity is raised, there's bound to be those who say to themselves, *But I don't have anything to be generous with.*

The reality is that many of us have been abundantly blessed. For example, if you woke up this morning, you're ahead of the one million people who didn't survive the past week. If you are able to sit down, read the paper, and drink a cup of coffee, you're better off than the five hundred million men, women, and children around the world who are presently experiencing the horrors of war, the loneliness of imprisonment, the agony of torture, and the pangs of starvation. If you can attend church without the threat of persecution, then you have a freedom envied by two billion others who have never been inside a church. If you have food, clothes, and a roof over your head, you're richer than seventy-five percent of the earth's inhabitants. If you have money in your purse, wallet, or bank, you're in the world's top eighth percentile of wealth. If you own a Bible, you're better off than the one-and-a-half-billion people who have never seen one. If you can read this devotion, you're ahead of one-third of the people on the planet who are illiterate.

Regardless of what we do for a living or the income we earn, almost all of us fall into the category of those *to whom much is given.* After putting this in perspective, we see that we simply don't have the excuse of not having anything to share with others. It's time to stop looking at what others have, appreciate what we have, and start asking God what He requires of us.

Take inventory of your life and make a list of how God has blessed you.

Whom can you share your blessings with?

SENIOR STATUS
DAY 303

Brethren, do not be children in understanding . . but in understanding be mature.
(1 Corinthians 14:20 NKJV)

In context, Paul is exhorting the Corinthians to grow up in their understanding of spiritual gifts, but this principle can also apply to giving. As in life, there are different stages of growth for giving, and God wants us to grow up when it comes to sharing what He has given us.

Infant stage. This describes those who are brand new in their faith. Babes in Christ typically have a hard time sharing because they're still getting a grip on the basics of Christianity. They need to be fed the milk of the Word (Hebrews 5:13) so they can continue to grow.

Toddler stage. Have you ever noticed how toddlers are wired to act on their impulses? They don't ponder anything. They instantly respond to whatever is in front of them. Believers at this spiritual stage are moved to give based on emotions. This is good, but just as with a toddler, they still expect some sort of applause in return.

Teenage stage. We've all been through those teenage years, and who can forget how we found it so necessary to question everything? The same thing happens with some Christians when it comes to the subject of sharing. *Why does God want me to share with others? What's in it for me?* In the end, they do the right thing, but it often comes with a heavy grip attached.

Adult stage. This is when Christians go from *having* to share to sincerely *wanting* to. Sharing is no longer the big deal that it once was because they've come to understand its value, and now it's a natural part of who they are in Christ.

Senior stage. Finally, there are the "senior saints" who've watched God work over the years. They've experienced so much joy in giving and sharing that they don't want to hold anything back if they don't have to.

The way we share shows where we're at in our spiritual growth. Let's strive for senior status as we allow God's Spirit to make us more mature.

What stage are you in when it comes to your sharing?

What steps can you take to move to the next stage of growth?

ADVENTUROUS INVESTMENTS
DAY 304

"So he who had received five talents came and brought five other talents, saying, 'Lord, you delivered to me five talents; <u>look</u>, I have gained five more talents besides them.' His lord said to him, 'Well done, good and faithful servant; you were faithful over a few things, I will make you ruler over many things. Enter into the joy of your lord.' He also who had received two talents came and said, 'Lord, you delivered to me two talents; <u>look</u>, I have gained two more talents besides them.'" (Matthew 25:20–22 NKJV)

Can you sense the excitement in each of these servants? *Look, Lord, look what I was able to do with what you gave me!* There's a spirit of enthusiasm and excitement here, and for good reason. For when we use the resources that God has given us for His purposes, there's always an atmosphere of adventure.

I'll confess that there are a lot of things in life that I'm just not excited to spend money on. For example, I don't get a thrill when I buy gas for my car. It goes in the tank, and for the most part, I don't think about it again. Paying for my car insurance doesn't generate a lot of excitement in me either. The same goes for the water and electric bills. All these are necessary, but they don't stimulate a spirit of adventure.

But if you want to have a lot of fun spending your resources, find a new mother and drop off a pack of diapers on her front porch or get some groceries together for a family that's having a hard time making ends meet. I've also found that there's nothing like helping people who need some support to go on a mission trip. I can't wait for them to get back and tell me what happened because I've made an investment in them and I now have a share in their story.

Sometimes people will ask me why their walk seems to have gotten a bit boring. I'll typically ask how they've been spending the resources that God has given them because nothing is more thrilling than making investments in His kingdom.

When was the last time you made a kingdom investment in someone's life?

When and how will you make the next one?

Jesus said to him, "If you want to be perfect, go, sell what you have and give to the poor, and you will have treasure in heaven; and come, follow Me." But when the young man heard that saying, he went away sorrowful, for he had great possessions. (Matthew 19:21–22 NKJV)

I used to think this passage meant that in order to be spiritual you had to go through life without having any possessions. But after taking a closer look at this exchange between Jesus and this man whom we know as the rich young ruler, we find something more special and specific in these instructions.

The Bible tells us that Jesus knew the condition of each person's heart (John 2:24), and as He came face to face with this man, He knew there was something in his heart that was holding him back. He was harboring an attitude of fear when it came to letting go of his possessions. As a matter of fact, he had become possessed by his possessions. That's why Jesus challenged him so dramatically in this area. But a striking contrast is seen when we look at another encounter with Christ:

Now behold, there was a man named Zacchaeus who was a chief tax collector, and he was rich. . . . And when Jesus came to the place, He looked up and saw him, and said to him, "Zacchaeus, make haste and come down, for today I must stay at your house." (Luke 19:2, 5 NKJV)

Here's another wealthy man, but notice that Jesus doesn't call him to give away his riches; instead, He invites Himself to Zacchaeus' home. Something happens in Zacchaeus' heart as he plays host to the Lord of Hosts because at one point, he suddenly stands up and says:

"Look, Lord, I give half of my goods to the poor; and if I have taken anything from anyone by false accusation, I restore fourfold." (Luke 19:8 NKJV)

We can be like the rich young ruler and have a fearful attitude about our possessions, or we can emulate Zacchaeus and spend time in Christ's presence, allowing Him to turn our greed into generosity.

When have you been afraid to let go of something? Be specific.

How can you follow Zacchaeus' example by having Christ in your home?

Moreover it is required in <u>stewards</u> that one be found faithful. (1 Corinthians 4:2 NKJV)

We don't use the word *steward* very much these days. But it's important for Christians to have an understanding of what a steward is because that's what we are. The Greek word used in Scripture for *steward* is a combination of the words *house* and *administrator*. In biblical times, a steward was entrusted with the responsibility of making sure that a household was running according to the owner's wishes. All purchases pertaining to home life went through the steward, including the ingredients for the meals that the owner wanted.

Yet, at the end of the day, a steward was not an owner. He was simply a servant who had been trusted to make decisions on behalf of his master. That's essentially what we do. Whether we realize it, we're constantly making stewardship decisions. With every single cent we spend, we're acting as stewards of our God-given resources. Just think of the ramifications of this. The beds we sleep in, the water we use, the cereal we eat, the clothes we wear, the gas we buy—all of these have a certain dollar amount attached to them. And these are just a few of our stewardship decisions. The list goes on and on, and so does our stewardship role in life. With each spending decision, we'll be stewards who are either faithful or unfaithful to our Lord.

So what does a faithful steward look like? Again, a steward was trusted to spend on the *master's* behalf. He needed to know what the master wanted in order to do his job properly. A faithful stewards knows his master's will and makes sure there's enough to go around to fulfill it. As stewards for Jesus, we know He wants us to help those in need (1 John 3:17), which means we need to spend in a way that allows us to have something set aside to share.

How are you doing as a steward of God's resources?

How can you re-order your spending to allow for more giving?

Not that I seek the gift, but I seek the fruit that abounds to <u>your account</u>. (Philippians 4:17 NKJV)

All of us have a kingdom account. It reflects what we've done during our lifetime with what God has given us. And when we finally see our Savior face to face, our balance will be revealed to us. One of two possible scenarios will occur when this happens.

The first scenario is that we will experience **reward**. The Bible teaches that we will be rewarded in heaven for our faithfulness to God (1 Corinthians 3:11–15; 2 Corinthians 5:10). Our stewardship over the resources that He has entrusted to us is certainly a factor in our faithfulness. In other words, the way we spend what we have here will affect what we're rewarded with up there. When we align our purchase priorities with God's purposes, we're assured an abundance of heavenly reward:

"Do not lay up for yourselves treasures on earth, where moth and rust destroy and where thieves break in and steal; but lay up for yourselves treasures in heaven, where neither moth nor rust destroys and where thieves do not break in and steal." (Matthew 6:19–20 NKJV)

The other scenario isn't so exciting. For if we aren't being spiritual in our spending, we will experience **regret** when we realize we don't have any rewards in heaven. Please don't misunderstand what I'm saying. Heaven is going to be magnificent, no matter what. But at the same time, there will be a difference when it comes to the scale of reward that people receive. Those who have spent for the kingdom will inherit much while those who have spent God's resources on nothing but their own wants will be disappointed to find a low balance awaiting them in their kingdom account.

Rather than wasting God's riches on the passing pleasures of this world, let's spend it on causes that are close to His heart and that will result in heavenly rewards and riches.

How does our stewardship have an eternal impact? What are some causes that are close to God's heart?

Do you think you're going to experience reward or regret? What do you need to change?

"Behold, I send you out as sheep in the midst of wolves. Therefore be wise as serpents and harmless as doves." (Matthew 10:16 NKJV)

I love these parting instructions that Jesus gave to His disciples as He sent them out to preach the message of the kingdom. They were to be *"wise as serpents and harmless as doves."* In other words, they were to be discerning but not overly judgmental. Jesus was basically telling them that it was important for them to have a balanced approach to life, and this truth also applies to the way we look at money.

I see two extremes in the body of Christ when it comes to finances. On one side, financial prosperity seems to take center stage and virtually everything in life goes back to money and wealth. This is a matter of **materialism**, which *Webster's Dictionary* defines as "looking at the physical with great good and high value." It's lusting after the things of this world rather than placing priority on the world to come.

On the other side of the spectrum, absolute poverty is equated with spirituality and all material goods are renounced. This is an attitude of **asceticism**, which teaches that you can reach a higher spiritual state by rigorous self-denial.

Both views are out of balance because they both give money a lot more credit than it deserves. One assumes money can make people more spiritual while the other supposes that it can make them less spiritual. But if this were true, why do we see godly people in Scripture with a lot of wealth (Abraham and Nicodemus) and also with very little (Mary and Joseph)? Money is just a tool. Twenty dollars can either buy a bottle of booze or a box of Bibles. We need to see the value in money without making it our supreme desire. That place belongs to Jesus, and when we're right with Him, we'll have a balanced view of money.

What are some experiences you've had with an unbalanced view of money?

Which extreme do you tend to be closer to, and how can you move closer to the middle?

MIGHTY MITES

Now Jesus sat opposite the treasury and saw how the people put money into the treasury. And many who were rich put in much. Then one poor widow came and threw in two mites, which make a quadrans. (Mark 12:41–42 NKJV)

People often believe that you can't give to others unless you have a lot of wealth already and that riches equal generosity. Nothing could be further from the truth. I happen to know there are a lot of wealthy people who aren't generous at all. And on the flip side, I know people who have not been blessed with much in the way of monetary wealth who are among the most generous people who walk the planet. Generosity does not depend on one's income.

The passage above is a perfect illustration of this fact. Jesus calls our attention to a poor widow who came to the temple to give an offering to God. It must have been intimidating for her to shuffle in and wait in line beside the rich and wealthy with their obvious offerings, but she did it anyway. The Bible says that she gave two mites, which by today's standards would be worth about an eighth of a penny, practically nothing in man's eyes, and yet notice how Jesus commends her:

So He called His disciples to Himself and said to them, "Assuredly, I say to you that this poor widow has put in more than all those who have given to the treasury; for they all put in out of their abundance, but she out of her poverty put in all that she had, her whole livelihood." (Mark 12:43–44 NKJV)

Of all that was given that day, the Lord was most impressed with these two mites. I love how this woman was generous with what little she had. She didn't wait until she had more before she gave to God's purposes, which is what we tend to do. I've learned that if we aren't generous when we have little, we won't be generous when we have a lot. Generosity can begin for anyone at any time with any income, even if it amounts to two mites.

How generous are you in proportion to what God has given you?

How will you apply this lesson?

SELFISH GIVING

"Two men went up to the temple to pray, one a Pharisee and the other a tax collector. The Pharisee stood and prayed thus with himself, 'God, I thank You that I am not like other men; extortioners, unjust, adulterers, or even as this tax collector. I fast twice a week; <u>I give tithes of all that I possess.</u>'" (Luke 18:10–12 NKJV)

Generosity is defined by attitude, not amount. A person who donates large sums of money to charitable causes isn't necessarily generous. And it's possible to turn something as pure and positive as giving into something selfish.

The Pharisee in the preceding parable is a classic example of selfish giving. As a Pharisee, he didn't just give God a ten-percent tithe of his money but of all his possessions. Some Pharisees were even known to tithe on the herbs they cooked with (Luke 11:42)! If generosity were measured according to amounts, this man would have been the cream of the crop. But despite the amazing amount he had given away, his attitude was all wrong. He was a selfish giver because he saw giving as a way of gaining.

Notice how he made his tithing record the basis for his righteousness before God. *Why should God accept me? Well, isn't it obvious? Look at how much I give!* He made the mistake of thinking that his giving was a way to gain favor with God. He was attempting to buy God's grace, which is impossible because grace cannot be bought or even earned. It's a free and priceless gift that's available to even the most sin-stained soul. The parable goes on to reveal that a lifetime of selfish giving did absolutely nothing to help this Pharisee's relationship with the Lord (Luke 18:14).

The attitude we give with is more important than the amount we give. If there's a spirit of selfishness attached to our giving, then we may as well not give at all. Giving isn't a way to "score points" with God; it's the response of a heart that has already received the greatest gift of all—God's grace.

When have you given something with a selfish motive? What was the outcome?

Dwell on God's grace before you give your next gift.

SHARING IS SHINING

Do all things without complaining and disputing, that you may become blameless and harmless, children of God without fault in the midst of a crooked and perverse generation, among whom <u>*you shine as lights in the world*</u> *.... (Philippians 2:14–15 NKJV)*

Here's a breakdown on how average Americans spend their money.
- 24% on housing related expenses, such as the mortgage, rent, and utilities
- 19% on healthcare expenses, such as insurance, prescriptions, and co-pays
- 23% on various personal needs
- 15% on food
- 17% on automobiles

And the remaining two percent? Well, that's the amount that the average American gives toward charitable causes.

Perhaps at this point you're pretty disappointed with the world. You might even be thinking, *I can't believe that the typical person only gives two cents on every dollar toward the needs of others. It's a good thing the church is here to pick up their slack. Pastor Bob, share how different us Christians are when it comes to what we give to others. We're a lot different from the world. Right?* Actually, we aren't. When it comes to the family of God, the average amount of charitable giving goes from two to three percent. Put another way, we're only outpacing the world by a single percentage point.

I can't help but connect these numbers with the fact that the church seems to be losing its influence on our society. Christians are supposed to stand out and *shine as lights in the world*, but in many cases, we've lost our brilliance and brightness. Could it be that we're not shining because we're not sharing? What would happen if Christians started to live so generously that they outpaced the world's giving by ten to twenty percent? The world would have more respect than ridicule for the body of Christ, and we would be all the more effective in our mission (Matthew 28:19–20). If we want to shine, we need to share.

How does your personal giving compare to the world's standard of giving?

How can you increase the amount you share?

The borrower is servant to the lender. (Proverbs 22:7 NKJV)

Owe no one anything except to love one another ... (Romans 13:8 NKJV)

The Bible calls us to live a debt-free life because debt essentially brings us under the bondage of the person or institution that we borrow from. With debt hanging over our heads, we lose the freedom to be generous with the Lord's resources. Instead, we're forced to give money that could have gone toward God's work to lenders and agencies.

I feel the need to address this because debt has become an epidemic, both inside and outside the church. A recent survey revealed that Americans have now racked up 2.1 trillion dollars in consumer debt, most of which was spent on things that weren't even legitimate needs. This has happened because our cultural mindset has grown accustomed to the idea of borrowing what you don't have so you can have something that you can't afford. It's the "buy-now, pay-later" mentality. The problem is that we wind up paying a lot more than we ever realize or expect.

For example, if a person borrows $10,000 on credit cards at an 18 percent interest rate and makes the minimum payment of $200 per month, it will take more than six years to pay it off. What's worse, when all is said and done, he or she will have paid out $6,200 in interest. It doesn't make sense for a Christian to pay $16,200 of God's money for things that could have bought for $10,000 if he or she had just exercised good stewardship and discipline to begin with.

Some forms of debt, like a mortgage, are necessary in this day and age, but a lot are not. In most cases, it's just a matter of saying no to the latest line of clothing, the four-star restaurants, and the things of this world that are simply beyond our financial reach. As God's people, we need to live as debt-free as possible because debt hinders our ability to be faithful stewards.

Is there any financial debt in your life? If so, how will you work toward eliminating it?

What are some lifestyle changes you can implement to protect you from debt?

For you died, and your life is <u>hidden</u> with Christ in God. When Christ who is our life appears, then you also will appear with Him in <u>glory</u>. (Colossians 3:3–4 NKJV)

Two words stand out to me in the preceding passage of Scripture. The first is the word *hidden*, which describes the spiritual condition of those of us who've surrendered our lives to Jesus. As we hand the reins of control over to God, an exchange happens where we become concealed, covered, and hidden in Him.

The second word of note is *glory*, which is what we share in once our lives are *hidden with Christ*. The Greek word for glory is *doxa*, and it literally means "substance, weight, fruitfulness." It represents a value that we could never produce or attain on our own. When we put these two key words together, we see an important principle: God can take us much further than we can get on our own when our lives are hidden in Him.

A while back, my schedule required me to leave Florida and travel to Washington D.C. for a couple days. From there I had to take a short trip to Atlanta and then back to Florida. That was a lot of mileage to pack into a few days. I'm so thankful that I flew the entire distance, and I was able to do so because the people flying the planes I was on had their pilot's license. My driver's license only would have gotten me so far. In fact, on my own, I would never have been able to tackle the trip. But by being "covered" by the pilot's license, I was able to go a lot farther, a lot faster.

The same is true once we're covered by Christ. In God, we can do what we could never do on our own. This especially applies to the area of giving. For once we're covered in Christ, we're given great opportunities to glorify God through giving that we never would have had on our own. Let's seize these opportunities, and in so doing, we'll find that we accomplish our goal to glorify God.

How has God taken you further and faster in Him?

What opportunity has He opened up for you to give on His behalf?

SATISFIED OR SPENT?
DAY 314

Then the word of the LORD came by Haggai the prophet, saying, "Is it time for you yourselves to dwell in your paneled houses, and this temple to lie in ruins?" Now therefore, thus says the LORD of hosts: "Consider your ways!" (Haggai 1:3–5 NKJV)

The prophet Haggai stepped onto a scene that we can relate to. The Israelites had gained their freedom from captivity and were starting to return to their native land. Jerusalem was in ruins, and the temple was torn apart. The people began to reclaim what they had lost as they rebuilt their homes. Unfortunately, everyone was so busy spending their time and resources on themselves that the temple, God's house, was neglected. Notice Haggai's commentary on this condition:

"You have sown much, and bring in little; You eat, but do not have enough; You drink, but you are not filled with drink; You clothe yourselves, but no one is warm; And he who earns wages, Earns wages to put into a bag with holes." Thus says the LORD of hosts: "Consider your ways!" (Haggai 1:6–7 NKJV)

No matter how much they ate, they were still hungry. No matter how much they drank, they were still thirsty. No matter how much money they made, they were still broke. That's because they were spending everything on themselves rather than responding to their responsibility to give toward God's purposes.

A lot of us are frustrated by the fact that we're living paycheck to paycheck. Now I understand that there are special situations where finances are going to be tight. But I also know that many of us go through this because we spend everything on ourselves rather than respond to our responsibility to give toward kingdom causes. God's Word says that His purposes need to be our priorities:

"Your heavenly Father already knows all your needs, and he will give you all you need from day to day if you live for him and make the Kingdom of God your primary concern." (Matthew 6:32–33 NLT)

If the Lord's work isn't a priority in our lives, we'll simply spend and spend, only to find in the end that our pockets and our souls are empty.

Are God's purposes your priorities?

How can you ensure a greater degree of satisfaction in your life?

SPIRITUAL SPENDING
DAY 315

I say then: <u>Walk in the Spirit</u>, and you shall not fulfill the lust of the flesh. (Galatians 5:16 NKJV)

During a recent trip to California, I was unexpectedly invited to preach at a church that has had a profound impact on my life. It was an honor to accept, but later on it occurred to me that I hadn't packed anything appropriate enough to wear for the occasion. I needed to buy a jacket and a tie, so I went to a discount department store and found what I considered to be a great deal. But when I took a closer look at my purchase, I realized it really wasn't a good deal because it wasn't something I wanted to wear.

So I went to another store that was a bit more upscale, and for a few dollars more, I was able to find something that was perfect. But in the back of my mind, a voice said, *You know, if you really want to look great, you can always go to that high-end store, spend a lot more and . . . .* You know something, I could have, but I didn't. I stuck with what I already had because I was sure it was what the Lord wanted me to wear and what He wanted me to spend.

Please don't mistake this to mean that we need to hold a prayer vigil for every decision we make in life. At the same time, however, I do believe that the Holy Spirit wants to direct and guide us when it comes to our spending. The Bible tells us that we are to *walk in the Spirit* and allow Him to lead us in every aspect of our lives. Why should an area as important as stewardship be any different?

The next time you're at the check-out counter, ask yourself, *What is the Spirit saying at this point of purchase? Is it a go or a no?* When we involve Him in this part of our lives, our spending becomes a way to build our spirituality. And if there's something we could all use in our credit-casual, debt-driven society, it's spiritual accountability.

When have you paid the price for ignoring the Spirit's voice concerning a purchase?

What are you considering buying for yourself? Ask God if this is what He wants for you.

The LORD Almighty says to the priests: "A son honors his father, and a servant respects his master. I am your father and master, but <u>where are the honor and respect I deserve</u>? You have despised my name! But you ask, 'How have we ever despised your name?'" (Malachi 1:6 NLT)

God sent Malachi to the children of Israel with a corrective call, *Stop disrespecting me!* The people were confused: *Lord, nobody disrespects you. We all love you. You mean so much to us. We even give you offerings to prove it.* But that was the problem. Their offerings had become a pathetic picture of giving God their leftovers:

"You have despised my name by offering defiled sacrifices on my altar. Then you ask, 'How have we defiled the sacrifices?' You defile them by saying the altar of the LORD deserves no respect. When you give <u>blind animals</u> as sacrifices, isn't that wrong? And isn't it wrong to offer animals that are <u>crippled and diseased</u>? Try giving gifts like that to your governor, and see how pleased he is!" says the LORD Almighty. (Malachi 1:7–8 NLT)

Rather than giving God their best, the Israelites were disrespecting Him by offering their worst. Have you ever noticed we do the same thing? When a church announces that its taking in donations to help clothe and feed people, it often ends up with wrinkled and ripped clothes and plenty of cans of okra and olives. Is this what we really want to give to God for His purpose of helping people? Would we offer the same to our governor or to *anyone else* for that matter? The sad truth is, we'll do a lot more for people than we will for the Lord.

This is upside-down giving. God deserves our best, not our worst. When we give toward the Lord's purposes, let's be sure to give Him our best because, as we see from Israel's example, anything less is a sign of disrespect.

When have you been guilty of giving God less than your best?

How can you improve in terms of the type of things that you offer to God?

GOD ISN'T BROKE

"Hear, O My people, and I will speak, O Israel, and I will testify against you; I am God, your God! I will not rebuke you for your sacrifices Or your burnt offerings, Which are continually before Me. I will not take a bull from your house, Nor goats out of your folds. For every beast of the forest is Mine, And the cattle on a thousand hills. I know all the birds of the mountains, And the wild beasts of the field are Mine. If I were hungry, I would not tell you; <u>For the world is Mine, and all its fullness</u>." (Psalm 50:7–12 NKJV)

There is a gross misrepresentation of God these days. It's spread by those who give off the impression He is in a financial bind and literally helpless to do anything unless you and I get out our checkbooks and cut Him a big check. What an insult! God isn't broke, and He doesn't *need* our money. He is the sovereign Creator of the Cosmos. He is above needing man. In this psalm, He declares that He wouldn't even let us know if He *was* hungry. He owns the entire world and everything that has ever existed, or ever will exist, in it. Let's be perfectly clear on this point: God doesn't *need* our money.

So why does He want us to give? The reason God calls us to give is for our sake, not His. He knows the way we're wired: our character is covetous, and our hearts can be more tight-fisted than a toddler with a toy. He knows that this selfishness is self-destructive and that we're in bondage unless we find freedom through giving. When we loosen our grip and give, we let go of the old nature, which constantly gets in the way of the work that God is doing in us. Giving is the catalyst for cultivating a relationship with the One who gave all.

God isn't broke; we are. And giving is the way He has ordained to fix our problem.

Why does God want you to be a giver?

How does this change your perspective on giving?

"For what will it profit a man if he gains the whole world, and loses his own soul?" (Mark 8:36 NKJV)

When John D. Rockefeller died in 1937, it was generally accepted that he was the richest man in the world. An enormous amount of people were at his funeral, including family, friends, and employees from his many companies. A large gathering of photographers, journalists, and newspaper reporters were also there. One young journalist caught sight of Rockefeller's chief accountant and asked him after the funeral, "Weren't you Mr. Rockefeller's accountant?" "Yes, I was," he responded. "Tell me," the journalist continued, "how much did he leave?" To which the accountant wryly responded, "All of it."

The accountant's answer proves an important point when it comes to our material possessions: whatever we gain here stays here. As the saying goes, You can't take it with you. A person can have all of the world's wealth and riches, but it's only temporary. Life is rapidly passing away, and no matter how big the bank account or how valuable the vault, none of it will count in the eternal world to come.

And yet so much of our lifetime can be wasted by trying to accumulate and keep wealth. When we get caught up in what we can lay our hands on here, it's easy to let go of the eternal truths we need to steer us through this life and lead us into the next. What an unwise decision to invest in the temporal rather than the eternal. The late missionary Jim Elliot profoundly pointed out, "He is no fool who gives what he cannot keep to gain that which he cannot lose." You can't take earthly wealth with you, but you can send it ahead by sharing and giving toward kingdom causes that have eternal value.

"But God said to him, 'Fool! This night your soul will be required of you; then whose will those things be which you have provided?' So is he who lays up treasure for himself, and is not rich toward God." (Luke 12:20–21 NKJV)

How important is worldly wealth to you?

What would you say to someone who's investing everything in this world?

THE FATHER FACTOR

"And I have led you forty years in the wilderness. Your clothes have not worn out on you, and your sandals have not worn out on your feet. . . that you may know that I am the LORD your God." (Deuteronomy 29:5–6 NKJV)

We tend to forget what was involved when God delivered the Israelites out of Egypt. Conservative estimates place the number of Hebrews who left in the exodus at two million! That's the equivalent of the entire city of Houston, Texas. We also tend to forget that these people were on the move for nearly forty years. Imagine the needs that must have accompanied this massive migration!

And yet, we never read about an Israelite dying for lack of provision. Disobedience, yes, but not lack of provision. That's because they enjoyed the "Father factor." As this multitude trudged through the wilderness year after year, they were always accompanied by God, who presided over them as a faithful father. He saw that all their needs were met, and in the verses above, we're told that part of His provision was to keep their clothes and sandals from falling apart!

I love this about God. He can cover our needs by stretching out the lifespan on things that we already have. My brother-in-law knows this firsthand. He has a truck with well over 200,000 miles. The thing just won't quit, not because of the manufacturer, but because God's hand is on that vehicle and it's going to run as long as He wants it to . . . period.

But you also need to know that my brother-in-law is a faithful giver, and I believe the two are connected. For when we do our part to give, even if it means sacrificing something new for ourselves, God often keeps us from needing new things. It's important we understand this because it helps to free us up when God calls us to give. And if He can handle the needs of two million Israelites over the course of forty years, as well as run the universe at the same time, I think He's got our needs more than covered.

When have you experienced the "Father factor" with regard to your possessions?

How can your understanding of this truth increase your generosity?

Honor the LORD with your possessions, And with the firstfruits of all your increase; So your barns will be filled with plenty, And your vats will overflow with new wine. (Proverbs 3:9–10 NKJV)

Did you catch the "what," "how," and "why" contained in these two verses? When it comes to the subject of stewardship and generous giving, these elements are always present. Allow me to elaborate.

The Hebrew word used here for *honor* is *kavad*, which means "to be heavy, be weighty; to be numerous; to be honored, be renowned, be esteemed, be glorious." This act of *kavad* is **what** we're supposed to do in life. It carries with it a sense of gravity and seriousness: we need to bring honor and glory to the Lord by giving what costs us something.

How we do this is defined for us next: *with your possessions, And with the firstfruits of all your increase*. The word *firstfruits* was a Hebrew term that referred to the first ripe crops at harvest time. In that society and culture, it represented a person's livelihood. God had instructed the Israelites to bring their firstfruits to the altar of the tabernacle as an offering to Him (Deuteronomy 26:1–4). God's Word is telling us that He receives *kavad* when a person's livelihood is offered to Him. When we do this, it demonstrates to God that we know He will be faithful in the future; we're so confident in God's goodness that we thank Him even before He provides. That is what it means to *kavad* the Lord.

The **why** is given in the next verse: *your vats will overflow with new wine*. Let's be clear: giving is not based on greed. Yet here God tells us that when we honor Him with our livelihood, He will take what's left over and cause it to abound and overflow so that all our needs are met.

In God's economy, we find our provision and satisfaction as we fulfill our function of glorifying Him through our giving.

How would you define your firstfruits?

Are you offering your firstfruits to the Lord?

THE UNFORESEEABLE FUTURE
DAY 321

And he blessed him and said: "Blessed be Abram of God Most High, Possessor of heaven and earth; And blessed be God Most High, Who has delivered your enemies into your hand." <u>And he gave him a tithe of all</u>. (Genesis 14:19–20 NKJV)

Abram was fresh from the battlefield. He, along with more than three hundred of his servants, had just defeated a coalition of kings that had kidnapped his nephew, Lot. To acknowledge God's deliverance, Abram gave a tithe, or ten percent, of his possessions to Him. God continued to bless Abram (who was later named Abraham) over the next several years, giving him a vast amount of wealth, even by today's standards. God certainly gave back to Abraham what he had given to Him. Then one day the Lord spoke to Abraham and asked for the unthinkable:

"Take now your son, your only son Isaac, whom you love, and go to the land of Moriah, and offer him there as a burnt offering on one of the mountains of which I shall tell you." (Genesis 22:2 NKJV)

God did something absolutely amazing. He asked Abraham to offer up his son as a sacrifice. But Abraham did something even more amazing—he obeyed:

So Abraham rose early in the morning and saddled his donkey, and took two of his young men with him, and Isaac his son; and he split the wood for the burnt offering, and arose and went to the place of which God had told him. (Genesis 22:3 NKJV)

How was Abraham able to have such an obedient heart when it came to such a difficult command? I submit that Abraham had learned an important lesson back in the beginning when he tithed. God had given Abraham back what he had given to Him. If this was true when it came to his *stuff*, then it must also be true when it came to his *son*. In the end, God spared Abraham from sacrificing his son; and in a symbolic sense, He gave Abraham back his son.

Abraham's tithe to God wasn't an isolated incident. It set the stage for an act of obedience that was the ultimate demonstration of faith. By the same token, we can't see how our giving today will impact our faith tomorrow, but in reality, it's building our faith for greater tests in the unforeseeable future.

How can giving today prepare you for tomorrow?

Whom can you share this principle with?

Once you were dead, doomed forever because of your many sins. You used to live just like the rest of the world, full of sin, obeying Satan, the mighty prince of the power of the air. He is the spirit at work in the hearts of those who refuse to obey God. All of us used to live that way, following the passions and desires of our evil nature. We were born with an evil nature, and we were under God's anger just like everyone else. (Ephesians 2:1–3 NLT)

We all possess a gratitude gauge, a thankfulness thermometer, a means-a-lot meter. It internally instructs us that the greater the gift, the greater the gratitude. For example, how do you react when someone gives you a card? Probably the same way I do: *Oh, thank you. How nice. How special.* But what if someone gives you a car? That's a bit more significant: *I can't believe you just gave me a . . . wow! No one has ever given me a . . . wow!* Now imagine that you have a terminal disease and someone comes along and gives you the cure. You'd be absolutely speechless because the greater the gift, the greater the gratitude.

Let me draw your attention to the gift that God has given us. The Bible tells us that we were all doomed forever because of our many sins. Whether we realized it or not, we were obeying Satan and we even became enemies of God. But the Bible also tells us that God stepped in and rescued us from this condition:

But God is so rich in mercy, and he loved us so very much, that even while we were dead because of our sins, he gave us life when he raised Christ from the dead. (It is only by God's special favor that you have been saved!) (Ephesians 2:4–5 NLT)

This needs to register on our gratitude gauge because there's a direct link between our gratitude and our giving. The more we see what God has done for us, the more we'll want to give of ourselves because a grateful heart is also a generous heart.

How does God's gift of salvation register on your gratitude gauge?

Let God's gift to you inspire you to give.

"I have shown you in every way, by laboring like this, that you must support the weak. And remember the words of the Lord Jesus, that He said, 'It is more blessed to give than to receive.'" (Acts 20:35 NKJV)

This is one of those Bible verses that everybody knows by heart. Even those who aren't Christians know that *"it is more blessed to give than to receive."* But knowing this is not the same as living by it. In fact, I've noticed there tend to be three different types of people in life. There are scrooges, there are those who are stuffed, and then there are stewards.

Scrooges are people who live with their fists clenched. They're convinced that their satisfaction in life will come from keeping all their stuff as close to their hearts as possible. Scrooges are so bound to their possessions that they won't even *lend* anything to a person in need, much less give.

Then there are those who are **stuffed**. They're the people who are open to giving to others in theory. You won't hear them argue when it comes to giving being better than receiving. But in actual practice, they still stuff themselves with things they desire, and in the process, they prevent themselves from being a clear conduit for God to pour His blessing through.

Last, there are the **stewards**. They understand that God has given them everything they have, and they're responsible to use His resources in ways He would approve of. They understand God's heart is to help those in need, and their checkbooks reflect this. Moreover, they live by the principle that *"it is more blessed to give than to receive"* because they've learned that giving opens the door to the unparalleled joy found in God's presence.

So which one are you? If you're a scrooge, ask the Lord to help you let go of the it's-my-stuff mindset. If you're stuffed, pray that God will clean you out so you can give to your fullest potential. And if you're a steward, stay that way by being filled and led by the Spirit.

Which category do you fall into?

What should you do based on your category?

He who has pity on the poor lends to the LORD, And He will pay back what he has given. (Proverbs 19:17 NKJV)

Does the object of your giving affect whether you give? Are you more open and enthusiastic to help out those whom you respect, admire, or appreciate? Are you hesitant to share your stuff with those whom you don't know or just don't like the looks of? If you've ever found yourself using these as excuses for not giving, then consider that *he who has pity on the poor lends to the LORD.*

Imagine for just a moment, hypothetically, that Jesus decided to spend some personal time with you here on planet earth. After spending the better part of the day together, He turns to you and says, *Hey, I don't happen to have any money with me. Do you think you could give me some to get by on today?* What would you do? I wouldn't be able to reach into my pocket quick enough to give Him whatever He needed. I'd even sacrifice what I was going to spend on myself if it meant giving Him what He needed. Who wouldn't? Because after all, it's the Lord!

But according to the Bible, it's the Lord whenever we see single parents struggling to make ends meet. It's the Lord when we're aware of colleagues who get laid off and don't know how they're going to get by. It's even the Lord when we come across people on a street corner who are just looking for their next meal. Understand that the people here on planet earth are just an extension of our opportunity to give to the Lord.

Why do we have such a hard time seeing it this way? Why are we so prone to look at people, size them up, and then decide if we want to help them or not? Let's make it a point to remember this verse and see the Savior when we see someone in need.

How will this truth impact how you give?

Make it your mission to memorize Proverbs 19:17 and then do it.

GOD-OLOGIC CYCLE

DAY 325

And this same God who takes care of me will supply all your needs from his glorious riches, which have been given to us in Christ Jesus. (Philippians 4:19 NLT)

Perhaps you've heard of the Hydrologic Cycle that God has put in place. Here's how it works: water is poured out on the earth's surface in the form of rain, this water eventually evaporates, the evaporated water then condenses and forms clouds, the clouds reach a point of saturation and then release rain back onto the earth's surface, and the cycle begins again. I find it fascinating how this process so efficiently meets the needs here on planet earth.

God has another cycle set up to meet needs, but this time we move from the *natural* to the *financial*. I call it the God-ologic Cycle, and here's how it works: God pours out His provision on our lives, we receive and recognize His goodness with a heart of gratitude, we offer it back to up to Him, He sees that we can be trusted to give what we're given and then He pours out more and more of His provision on our lives. In the process, we learn to be more like Him and all our needs are met.

The apostle Paul had a strong understanding of this God-ologic Cycle and shared with the church in Philippi that the same God who took care of his needs would also cover theirs. He said this with confidence because they had been the ones who had given toward his needs as a missionary (Philippians 4:14–15). Knowing that God gives to givers, it became a foregone conclusion that He would pour out His provision to meet all their needs.

What was true for the Philippians is also true for us. When we give back a portion of what God has given to us, He will be faithful to pour out His provision upon our lives. Like rain returning to the ground, so are God's resources in the lives of those who are willing to offer them back up to Him.

Is the God-ologic Cycle at work in your life?

How can you put the reliability of this cycle to the test?

Can two walk together, unless they are agreed? (Amos 3:3 NKJV)

I have a dog named Spot (really). She's a fairly young dog, and she's at the stage where everything in life is an adventure, which makes taking her for a walk an adventure. If I want to go right, you can be sure that she will want to go left, straight, or even backward. She has her own agenda, and while I appreciate her enthusiasm for everything, it makes it difficult to walk her.

For that reason, I appreciate Amos' question, *Can two walk together, unless they are agreed?* This is really a statement on the importance of communication. In order to make progress together, two parties need to have a strong sense of communication and be in agreement. If they don't agree, then they will always be drawn in different directions. And this is never more evident than when it comes to finances within marriage.

A couple that can't communicate on how to handle their finances is in for a very difficult walk through life. Unfortunately, there are a lot of marriages like this; one spouse only wants to save while the other only wants to spend. The result is a lot of resentment and division, which is why it's so important for couples to agree on what they should spend, save, and share.

Early in our marriage, Diane and I decided we would never spend more than $25 without talking about it. This was one of the wisest decisions we ever made because the more we communicated about a purchase, the more we agreed that it was or wasn't something we should get. We found that good communication about our finances was a great way to know how to spend God's money because it caused us to really examine what we bought. We also found that it was a great way to save God's money, which allowed us to share it with others.

How would you paraphrase Amos 3:3 in your own words?

How can you apply the essential truth of this verse?

Therefore He said: "A certain nobleman went into a far country to receive for himself a kingdom and to return. So he called ten of his servants, delivered to them ten minas, and said to them, 'Do business till I come.' <u>But his citizens hated him, and sent a delegation after him, saying, 'We will not have this man to reign over us.'</u> And so it was that when he returned, having received the kingdom, he then commanded these servants, to whom he had given the money, to be called to him, that he might know how much every man had gained by trading." (Luke 19:12–15 NKJV)

The underlined portion in the preceding passage is where we're all at as stewards right now. We're living in between our Master's departure and His return. We have been charged with the responsibility to manage His money according to His will. In essence, we're doing kingdom business until He comes.

One day we will all be face to face with the Lord, and He will have some questions for us. We will have to give an account of how we handled His resources. Did we keep it all to ourselves, squandering it selfishly? Or did we invest it wisely by sharing with those in need and by giving to kingdom causes? If you're anything like me, you'll want to be able to say that you lived a generous life, using what He gave you just the way He wanted you to. I don't even want to think of what it would be like to answer the Lord any other way.

It's important we think this through because it's easy for us to *talk* about living generously without actually letting it get into our lives. We can be enthused about giving to God today, only to let our resolve slip away over the next several days. But when we recognize that the Master *is* coming, that there *will* be a day of reckoning accounts, we will find the motivation we need to be spiritual stewards.

When He comes, we all want to hear those glorious words:

"Well done, good and faithful servant . . . . Enter into the joy of your lord."
(Matthew 25:21 NKJV)

How are you handling the Lord's money until He returns?

How will you stay motivated to live generously?

For <u>Jews request a sign</u>, and <u>Greeks seek after wisdom</u>; but we preach Christ crucified, to the Jews a stumbling block and to the Greeks foolishness . . . . (1 Corinthians 1:22–23 NKJV)

The apostle Paul turns his attention to the cross of Jesus Christ as he begins his first letter to the Corinthian church. In proclaiming the power of the cross, he mentions two different reactions people can have toward the message of the cross.

The Jewish community reacted to the cross in a way that requested (or more literally, required) a sign. They were so accustomed to walking by sight that they couldn't handle the concept of the cross without personally seeing and touching all it represented. They wanted God's salvation to appear to them on their own tangible terms. But Jesus rebuked the Jewish leaders for their insistence on seeing signs (Matthew 12:39).

The Greeks generally reacted in an entirely different way. Rather than getting caught up in external signs, they were preoccupied with an internal struggle to have the cross all figured out before believing in it. Have you ever met people who are never satisfied with your answers to their questions? No matter how much time and energy you spend on clearing up a matter for them, they always have another one lined up for you. It becomes an unending search for a perfect understanding of the unfathomable ways of God (Isaiah 55:8–9).

Two different reactions . . two different hearts. One says I must *see* it all before I can believe; the other says I must *understand* it all before I can believe. The cross doesn't cater to either but requires a measure of faith in order to be effective in a person's life. In our attempts to share the Gospel with others, we need to anticipate these two reactions from people and then point them to their need for faith.

Why do you think people tend to react to the Gospel in these two ways?

How can you use this understanding when sharing the cross with others?

REASONS FOR REJECTION
DAY 329

We preach Christ crucified, <u>to the Jews a stumbling block</u> and <u>to the Greeks foolishness</u>....
(1 Corinthians 1:23 NKJV)

Yesterday we looked at the different reactions that the Jews and Greeks had to the message of the cross, and today we'll take a closer look at the reasons underlying those reactions. In so doing, we can get a glimpse as to why some people respond the way they do when we share Jesus with them.

The Bible says that the Jews were stumbled by the cross. That's because every Jew in the first century had a preconceived idea of what the Christ would look like and do. According to their sacred Scriptures, He would enjoy national notoriety (Isaiah 9:6), would rule and reign righteously (Isaiah 9:7), and would be mighty militarily (Isaiah 30:30). How could He possibly suffer and die on a detestable cross? They were stumbled by the very thought of their Christ being crucified because it didn't match their expectations of Him. Although those expectations were correct, they were incomplete—for the Scriptures also declare that the Christ would suffer and be sacrificed for our sins (Isaiah 53:4–5).

The Greeks saw the cross as a colossal exercise in foolishness: *So, let me get this straight. This Jesus, this Christ, this Savior, He comes to earth, gets arrested, and then gets executed? You're telling me that I need His help? It sounds like He needed my help!* To the natural-minded man, the cross makes no sense: *how can life come from death?* But God has a way of doing things that seem impossible. Because the Greeks were outside of God's covenant, they didn't know Him and thus didn't appreciate His power.

When we put these two together, we see that some reject the cross because they have an incomplete knowledge of God's Word, while others reject it because they don't understand God's power. Jesus addressed both of these spiritual symptoms (Matthew 22:29). We need to help those who have rejected the cross see it in its completeness so they can accept the truth of the Gospel.

Do you have enough understanding of God's Word and His power to share it with those who don't know Him?

What can you do to strengthen your understanding in these areas?

For Jews request a sign, and Greeks seek after wisdom; but <u>we preach Christ crucified</u>, to the Jews a stumbling block and to the Greeks foolishness . . . (1 Corinthians 1:22–23 NKJV)

We've looked at two reasons people reject the cross. We know the *problems*, but what about the *prescription*? What are we supposed to do when people won't receive the Gospel? The prescription is to keep on preaching Christ crucified. There are two important components to this.

First, there is the **message** of Christ crucified. Our lives should be constantly pointing to the essential truth that *"God so loved the world that He gave His only begotten Son, that whoever believes in Him should not perish but have everlasting life" (John 3:16 NKJV).* The heart of the Gospel message is that God loves you so much that He deliberately died for you. This message is perfect, profound, and permanent. There's no need to twist, tweak, or tamper with the message of Christ crucified. In fact, the Bible warns that anyone who messes with this message is accursed (Galatians 1:9)!

But there's also a **manner** by which we are to communicate this message. Notice that the Bible says we are to preach the cross. We aren't told to whisper Christ crucified, we aren't commanded to chant Christ crucified, we aren't called to whimper or whine that Christ was crucified, nor should we yell at people that Christ was crucified. Paul preached the cross, and so should we. *But, pastor, I don't know how to preach!* Preaching simply means to tell the truth with a sense of urgency, sharing the cross with people in a way that's real and relevant.

Remember to share the Gospel message in a manner that gets people's attention, preaching Christ crucified and with a sense of unashamed urgency. It is both simple and powerful enough to break the hardest heart.

How have you miscommunicated the message?

Make a list of practical do's and don'ts for sharing the Gospel. Keep it handy for when you have an opportunity to share.

For <u>Jews</u> request a sign, and <u>Greeks</u> seek after wisdom; but we preach Christ crucified, to the <u>Jews</u> a stumbling block and to the <u>Greeks</u> foolishness, but to those who are called, both <u>Jews</u> and <u>Greeks</u>, Christ the power of God and the wisdom of God. (1 Corinthians 1:22–24 NKJV)

You don't have to be a Bible scholar to notice a pattern in the preceding passage. As the apostle Paul starts to share about Christ crucified, he repeatedly refers to the Jews and Greeks. Why does he single out these two people-groups? And why does he feel the need to mention them over and over?

Keep in mind that God had established a special covenant with the Jewish people in the Old Testament. Of all the nations on the face of the earth, they were the ones favored with a unique relationship with God. They were in a class of their own, and everyone else fell into a different category known as Gentiles. When the New Testament was being written, Greek influence on civilization had become so dominant that they came to represent the Gentile (non-Jewish) world. So when Paul refers to Jews and Greeks, he's really referring to all humanity.

The need to hear the message of the cross is universal because everyone has sinned:

For we have previously charged both Jews and Greeks that they are all under sin. As it is written: "There is none righteous, no, not one; There is none who understands; There is none who seeks after God. They have all turned aside; They have together become unprofitable; There is none who does good, no, not one." (Romans 3:9–12 NKJV)

Regardless of your nationality or pedigree, if you're human, you're a sinner deserving of punishment—punishment that can only be avoided through responding to the message of the Gospel. This needs to settle deep into our hearts because when we recognize that everyone needs Jesus, we'll find the motivation to share Him.

How do you react to the statement, "Everyone is a sinner"?

What impact should Romans 3:9–12 have on your interaction with others?

And when Jesus went out He saw a great multitude; and He was moved with compassion for them, and healed their sick. When it was evening, <u>His disciples came to Him, saying, "This is a deserted place, and the hour is already late. Send the multitudes away, that they may go into the villages and buy themselves food."</u> (Matthew 14:14–15 NKJV)

We tend to imagine the disciples as gracious, godly, and gallant, not quite as holy as Jesus but certainly the next best thing. But this isn't the picture the Bible paints for us. As we read in the verses above, there was actually a time when the Twelve wanted to get rid of those for whom Jesus had compassion.

Think this was an isolated incident? Think again:

And behold, a woman of Canaan came from that region and cried out to Him, saying, "Have mercy on me, O Lord, Son of David! My daughter is severely demon-possessed." But He answered her not a word. And <u>His disciples came and urged Him, saying, "Send her away, for she cries out after us."</u> (Matthew 15:22–23 NKJV)

Then little children were brought to Him that He might put His hands on them and pray, <u>but the disciples rebuked them.</u> But Jesus said, "Let the little children come to Me, and do not forbid them; for of such is the kingdom of heaven." (Matthew 19:13–14 NKJV)

We know very few details about the disciples, but we do know that they were prone to pushing away the very people whom Jesus was drawing! At this point, we might want to snicker and start to judge the Twelve. But the sobering truth is, we do the same thing. Something happens in the human heart where we lose compassion once we're "in." When our unsaved acquaintances start to anger or annoy us, how often do we start praying for God to get rid of them rather than save them?

The disciples didn't intend to be callous; they just forgot how it felt when *their* lives first connected to Christ. Let's avoid making the same mistake by remembering the joy that Jesus brought us and by desiring the same for others.

When have you been guilty of doing the same thing?

How can you prevent this from happening again?

PRAYER'S PLACE
DAY 333

. . . praying always with all prayer and supplication in the Spirit, being watchful to this end with all perseverance and supplication for all the saints; and for me, that utterance may be given to me, that I may open my mouth boldly to make known the mystery of the gospel. (Ephesians 6:18–19 NKJV)

Your ability to witness in the world is directly connected to the time you spend in your prayer closet. For some reason, we tend to forget this. We pray for our health, our finances, our future, our friends, and even our food. But what about praying for the ability to be a faithful witness of the Gospel in both word and deed?

The most powerful and prolific evangelist the world has ever seen had a profound understanding of this. In writing to the church of Ephesus, Paul concludes his epistle by imploring them to pray for him (not just in a general or generic sense) so that he could be faithful in making the Gospel known. This powerful apostle understood that he was a witnessing weakling apart from the empowerment of prayer.

We see the same principle at work throughout the book of Acts as the first few followers of Christ were constantly praying along with their witnessing. One activity didn't take place without the other close by its side, and we can be certain that the early church would not have grown as it did apart from the act of prayer.

When our attempts to witness aren't preceded by prayer, our words come off as rash and brash. But with prayer paving the way, our words seem to hit the mark. We find that we're able to strike the perfect balance of truthfulness and tactfulness, sensitivity and seriousness. May we be wise enough to follow the proven pattern, not only praying for our own witnessing opportunities, but also asking for prayer from others.

How have you seen this dynamic demonstrated in your own life?

Make it a priority in your prayer life to ask for more opportunities to share the Gospel.

. . . praying always with all prayer and supplication in the Spirit, being watchful to this end with all perseverance and supplication for all the saints; and for me, that utterance may be given to me, <u>that I may open my mouth</u> boldly to make known the mystery of the gospel . . . (Ephesians 6:18–19 NKJV)

Have you ever been part of a small group meeting or home fellowship where there's someone who does most of the talking? A Scripture will be shared, a question asked, and there's always one person who is first to say something. But then, out of the shadowy corner of the room, a reluctant and uncertain hand goes up, and that brother or sister who usually sits silent shares something that carries a ton of spiritual weight.

I love those moments because it proves a powerful point that is also indicated in Paul's prayer request to the Ephesians. There are times when we (no matter how introverted or shy) need to open our mouths in order to be the witnesses we've been called to be. Sadly, many of us keep our mouths shut when God wants them open.

Even our heroes in the faith have been guilty of this. Moses basically refused to serve as God's spokesman (Exodus 4:10–13), Jeremiah bottled up the word of the Lord until it burned inside him like a fire in his bones (Jeremiah 20:9), and we can't forget Peter's failure to speak up when the world was asking him about his relationship with Jesus (Matthew 26:69–75). Keeping quiet when it counts is nothing new for God's people.

But on the flip side, we see that great things happen when we fight the temptation to stay silent and, instead, open our mouths. That's because this step of faith is backed by God's promise to fill our words with weight and wisdom when He calls us to witness:

"Do not worry about how or what you should speak. For it will be given to you in that hour what you should speak; for it is not you who speak, but the Spirit of your Father who speaks in you." (Matthew 10:19–20 NKJV)

How obedient are you to open your mouth when you're supposed to?

How can memorizing Matthew 10:19–20 help you when the time comes to open your mouth?

ANSWERING MACHINES
DAY 335

Jesus said to him, "'You shall love the LORD your God with all your heart, with all your soul, and with all your <u>mind</u>.'" (Matthew 22:37 NKJV)

Before I became a believer, I was always annoyed by Christians who spoke of love and peace but weren't able to answer any of my questions. I'm not talking about the type of questions that are just smokescreens for unbelief. I'm talking about sincere questions, such as, *What makes Christianity different from all other religions in this world? How do you know Jesus was a real person? Why do you trust what the Bible says?*

Sadly, these questions went unanswered a lot longer than they should have. I believe there are a lot of people out there who are turned off to the church because they aren't getting good answers to their questions. Just think how much stronger the church's witness in this world would be if every Christian were capable of answering those three questions. Imagine what could happen if every believer were able to share how Christianity is the only belief system where God is the one reaching out to man instead of man reaching out to God; how secular history corroborates the life, death, and resurrection of Jesus of Nazareth; and how there is an inexhaustible amount of prophetic, archeological, and scientific evidence to prove that the Bible is God's inerrant Word.

Jesus told us that we're supposed to love God with all our minds. And I believe we can do this by dedicating our minds to the task of educating ourselves on these issues. Buy a few books, take a few classes, or invest in getting information you can use when the questions start coming your way. Become an answering machine for Jesus and watch what He's able to do with your witness.

Always be ready to give a defense to everyone who asks you a reason for the hope that is in you, with meekness and fear . . . (1 Peter 3:15 NKJV)

How well can you answer the three questions listed in the first paragraph?

How are you equipping yourself to become an answering machine for Jesus?

THE RESULTS OF RELATIONSHIP
DAY 336

Jacob's well was there; and Jesus, tired from the long walk, sat wearily beside the well about noontime. Soon a Samaritan woman came to draw water, and <u>Jesus said to her</u>, "Please give me a drink." (John 4:6–7 NLT)

Effective evangelism requires relationship. It's true; the numbers don't lie. According to a recent survey, here's how those polled were won to Christ:

1% A 12-step program	5% Evangelistic event
2% Birth of a child	6% Experienced physical healing
3% Independently reading the Bible	10% Conversing with a friend
3% Christian television	14% Church service
4% Sunday school	14% Upbringing in a Christian home
4% Death of a loved one	24% Conversing with family

Notice how the numbers jump when personal relationships become more prominent. People are more likely to accept Jesus after talking to their friends, going to church, or spending time with their families. This shouldn't surprise us because Jesus was the first to show us how effective evangelism requires relationship.

The fourth chapter of John's gospel tells us how Christ took a cynical Samaritan woman of low morals and changed her into a devoted worshiper of God. It's a true glory story, but it was only possible because Jesus initiated a relationship with her by asking her for a drink of water. It didn't seem like much initially, but it became the first link in the chain that anchored a wayward heart to God.

We can be guilty of underestimating the importance of relationships when we witness. Often we share Christ out of a sense of duty and obligation rather than out of genuine interest and compassion, and people pick up on it. No wonder they don't respond when we tell them what they should do with their lives. But the results are different when there's a real effort to invest relationally. So much so that even the simple act of asking for a drink of water can lead to a converted life.

How were relationships instrumental in your own salvation experience?

Read the rest of John 4 to see how Jesus used relationship in evangelizing.

THE WITNESS WITHIN

DAY 337

"And when He has come, <u>He will convict the world of sin</u>, and of righteousness, and of judgment: of sin, because they do not believe in Me; of righteousness, because I go to My Father and you see Me no more; of judgment, because the ruler of this world is judged." (John 16:8–11 NKJV)

Every week I have the privilege of presenting the Gospel to those who attend our church. I'll typically conclude our services by inviting those who haven't received Jesus into their hearts to come forward and do so. And every week I have the honor of seeing dozens of people respond as they publicly profess Christ as their Lord and Savior. And yet I can honestly say that I have not led a single soul to Christ.

Hold on, Pastor Bob, how can you preach the gospel, invite people forward, see so many respond, and still say that you've never led a person to Christ? Aren't you contradicting yourself? No, I'm not because although I may be *an* instrument that God is using to proclaim His message, I'm not *the* instrument that actually convicts a person's heart to the point of repentance.

That task belongs to the Holy Spirit, who is described in John's gospel as the One who convinces the unbelieving world of their sin and need for Jesus. As we witness to people on the outside, He witnesses to them inside their heart, touching places where no human can ever see or approach.

I love this truth because it means I'm never alone when I witness to someone. As I do my part on the outside, I know the Spirit is doing His part on the inside, and because He's the one at work, wonderful things are bound to happen:

"'Ah, Lord GOD! Behold, You have made the heavens and the earth by Your great power and outstretched arm. There is nothing too hard for You.'" (Jeremiah 32:17 NKJV)

How did you experience the Spirit's witness within you when you accepted Jesus?

Why should you remind yourself of the Spirit's work in salvation as you do your part in sharing the Gospel?

Now an angel of the Lord spoke to Philip, saying, "Arise and go toward the south along the road which goes down from Jerusalem to Gaza." This is desert. So he arose and went. And behold, a man of Ethiopia, a eunuch of great authority under Candace the queen of the Ethiopians, who had charge of all her treasury, and had come to Jerusalem to worship, was returning. And sitting in his chariot, he was reading Isaiah the prophet. (Acts 8:26–28 NKJV)

God set the stage for a wonderful work. He had maneuvered Philip into position to intercept a man who was seeking and searching. This high-ranking official from Egypt had just worshiped in the temple, but for some reason, he still had a sense of emptiness and disconnectedness from the God whom he longed after. What follows is an excellent example of what should happen when we witness to those who are seeking:

Then the Spirit said to Philip, "Go near and overtake this chariot." So Philip ran to him, and heard him reading the prophet Isaiah, and said, "Do you understand what you are reading?" (Acts 8:29–30 NKJV)

Philip did three things that enabled him to be an effective evangelist. First, he was led by the Spirit. Rather than randomly run around, Philip was in the right place at the right time because he was sensitive and obedient to the Spirit's voice. Next, as he came alongside the man's chariot, he took the time to listen to him. Instead of hastily interrupting the scene, Philip surveyed the situation. Last, he asked a good question. Philip noticed that the man was reading from Isaiah and asked a question designed to draw him deeper into the written Word. Notice the result:

And he said, "How can I, unless someone guides me?" And he asked Philip to come up and sit with him. . . . Then Philip opened his mouth, and beginning at this Scripture, preached Jesus to him. . . . And he answered and said, "I believe that Jesus Christ is the Son of God." (Acts 8:31, 35, 37 NKJV)

Philip's example serves as a Witnessing 101 class. It shows us the importance of being led by the Spirit, listening to those we're witnessing to, and asking strategic questions designed to draw their attention toward God. May we keep this in mind as we walk in the works the Lord has in store for us (Ephesians 2:10).

What three things did Philip do?

How can you better incorporate all three into your witnessing opportunities?

HOW'S YOUR CONNECTION?

And both Philip and the eunuch went down into the water, and he baptized him. Now when they came up out of the water, the Spirit of the Lord caught Philip away, so that the eunuch saw him no more; and he went on his way rejoicing. (Acts 8:38–39 NKJV)

Some incredible things happen in these two verses. A eunuch from Ethiopia is baptized as a brand-new believer, and Philip is miraculously whisked away by the Spirit of the Lord. But what I find most fascinating is the eunuch's reaction after Philip has been taken away from him. The Bible says that *he went on his way rejoicing.*

Put yourself in the eunuch's position for a moment. You've been searching and seeking for God all your life. Then one day a man meets you in the desert and by divine appointment, he opens your understanding of the Scriptures that have always left you confused. Everything makes sense now because he shares Jesus with you, and your life will never be the same. Just think of all the questions this man must have had, and then suddenly his only earthly link to his newfound faith is gone! If it were us, we probably would have been a bit bummed (if not frightened) by the fact that Philip was taken out of our lives so abruptly.

But in their short time together, Philip had managed to do something worth noting. Philip connected the eunuch to God, not himself. Consequently, the eunuch was able to rejoice when Philip left him because his connection was with God and not man.

It's wonderful when God allows us to play a part in people's conversions and be involved in their lives as they begin their spiritual journey. But we must be careful that we aren't so connected to them that they don't connect to the Lord. Our ultimate goal is to connect people to Jesus, not us. If we fail in this, then their walk will be as weak as the earthly relationship that it's founded on.

Are you pointing people to the Lord or to yourself?

Identify three people in your life and make a conscious effort to increase their connection with God.

"<u>You are the salt of the earth</u>; but if the salt loses its flavor, how shall it be seasoned?"
(Matthew 5:13 NKJV)

The United States has become a place of great religious diversity. Practically every religion is represented here, and they all seem to be thriving. Americans are showing an increased interest in Buddhism, Hinduism, and Paganism. The religious landscape is getting increasingly crowded, and the cross of Christ is becoming harder and harder to find. It hasn't always been this way. There was a time when American society was synonymous with the Christian faith. Just read what some of our founding fathers went on record as saying:

> The general principles on which the fathers achieved independence were . . . the general principles of Christianity . . . I will avow that I then believed and now believe that those general principles of Christianity are as eternal and immutable as the existence and attributes of God.—John Adams in a letter written on the day the Declaration of Independence was approved by Congress

> We recognize no Sovereign but God, and no King but Jesus!—Rev. Jonas Clarke or one in his company on April 18, 1775, on the eve of the Revolutionary War, after a British major ordered John Adams, John Hancock, and those with them to disperse in "the name of George the Sovereign King of England."

> It cannot be emphasized too strongly or too often that this great nation was founded, not by religionists, but by Christians; not on religion, but on the Gospel of Jesus Christ.—Patrick Henry in a speech to the House of Burgesses in May 1765

The list goes on, and it shows how far our nation has drifted from the Christian Gospel. Now our children aren't permitted to pray in school, and the Ten Commandments can't be displayed in our halls of justice. Jesus declared that we're the salt of the earth. I pray we would take our call seriously and act with a sense of urgency before we see all semblance of the Gospel vanish from our society.

What attitudinal changes have you seen toward Christianity over the past few years?

How will this affect the way you live?

SALTY SAINTS

"You are the salt of the earth; but if the salt loses its flavor, how shall it be seasoned?"
(Matthew 5:13 NKJV)

Of all the things Jesus could have compared His people to, He specifically and selectively associates them with salt. *Salt?* It doesn't sound very spiritual, does it? But did you know that salt is one of the most valuable substances the world has ever known? In fact, there are over fourteen thousand known uses for salt. It can be used to drip proof candles, remove soot, kill poison ivy, deodorize shoes, clean coffee pots, extinguish grease fires, remove dry skin, and even keep windows frost free.

Salt can also be used as a **preservative**. Before the days of refrigeration, meats were packed in salt to prevent spoiling. We live in a world that's full of moral corruption and decay, and the Christian church has been placed in the midst of this mess to preserve God's standard of righteousness. As bad as this world is, just imagine what it would be like apart from our presence.

Salt is also a **healing agent**. Soldiers used to carry a chunk of salt with them into battle because it possessed antiseptic qualities. If they were wounded, they would rub salt into their wound in order to kill bacteria and prevent infection. Even today salt is used to alleviate sore throats and skin irritations. The believer is a source of spiritual healing for those who have been broken and burned by the effects of sin. We don't have the ability to heal them on our own, but we are able to direct them heavenward into the Healer's hands.

Finally, salt is **flavorful**. Have you ever noticed that the right amount of salt makes everything taste better? What else could you put on peanuts, broccoli, popcorn, fish, potatoes, and corn? By the same token, Christians in this world should be enhancing the flavor of those they come into contact with. We should attract people to us, and people ought to want to be around us when given the choice.

As saints, we're supposed to be salty, not in an irritating way, but in a way that preserves the world around us, heals those who are hurting, and makes life more palatable.

How was a salty saint used in your coming to Christ?

Ask God to help you to be as salty as you're supposed to be.

"You are the light of the world." *(Matthew 5:14 NKJV)*

Jesus not only likens His followers to salt, but also declares that we *"are the light of the world."* By making this statement, the Lord is declaring that there is a standard of expectation for how we, as Christians, should live our lives. The world should see in our lives three things that light does.

First, light guides. If you've ever stumbled your way through the dark, you know how valuable light is as a guide. The Christian has access to God's Word, which is described in Psalm 119:105 as a lamp unto our feet and a light unto our path. We have an amazing advantage as we walk in this world. The Scriptures are there to guide us in our decisions, giving us a sense of confidence as we course through life, and non-believers notice this. When they see that we have a real sense of guidance and want it for themselves, we can, in turn, guide them to God.

Light also defines. Darkness conceals truth, but light defines and reveals it. John 3:19–21 tells us that those who love evil will walk in the darkness because they don't want their wickedness exposed. But believers enjoy dwelling in the light, and as we do, our lives help to define for others what's right and what's wrong. That's why when there's a moral dilemma in the workplace, people frequently say, *Let's ask the Christian!*

Last, light inspires. Light has a way of motivating and moving a person in the right direction. I can think of no better example of this than the Lord Himself. In John 8:12, He proclaimed Himself to be the light of the world, and as the light of the world, His inspirational influence is unmatched in human history.

So now we need to turn the spotlight on ourselves and honestly answer whether we're shining as we should. Are we guiding, defining, and inspiring? I pray that the Lord will continue to shine His light on us so we can say yes to that question.

How bright is your light?

Ask the Lord to show you how you can shine even brighter.

KEEPING THE CONNECTION

"You are the light of the world. A city that is set on a hill cannot be hidden." (Matthew 5:14 NKJV)

Remember how Christmas lights used to go out when one of the bulbs burned out? Before you could get them to light up again, you had to check every one of those tiny twinkle lights until you found and replaced the culprit. One burnt-out bulb would cut the electrical current to the rest of the line, and without that connection, there couldn't be any light.

A similar principle exists in the spiritual world. We need to have a strong connection to God if we're to have any hope of being a bright light in this world. Some Christians never make an impact on their surroundings because they don't do what it takes to stay connected to Christ. Jesus Himself warned us that our witness would wither if we didn't abide in Him:

"I am the vine, you are the branches. He who abides in Me, and I in him, bears much fruit; for without Me you can do nothing." (John 15:5 NKJV)

So how do we keep this spiritual connection that enables our light to shine? I don't want to turn our relationship with God into a fleshly formula for doing this or that. At the same time, there are spiritual disciplines that will keep us connected when exercised from a pure and sincere heart—a regular and reliable time of prayer; reading, studying, and meditating on God's Word; worship; and even being still and quiet before the Lord.

If these things aren't happening with regularity, our connection will be weak, which means our life will look a lot like those Christmas lights did. But as we do what's necessary to maintain a connection with God, His power will flow to us, through us, and into the hearts of those who need to know Him.

How do you keep your connection to God?

Is there something you need to include in your spiritual disciplines? How would this impact your walk and your witness?

For it is <u>the God who commanded light to shine out of darkness, who has shone in our hearts to give the light of the knowledge of the glory of God in the face of Jesus Christ</u>. (2 Corinthians 4:6 NKJV)

But <u>we have this treasure in earthen vessels</u>, that the excellence of the power may be of God and not of us. (2 Corinthians 4:7 NKJV)

The Bible describes God as shining His light into our hearts so that it can shine out from us and into the lives of others. It also describes our bodies as earthen vessels that contain the treasure of God's light.

At this point, you might be thinking, *Wait a second, how is light supposed to shine out through a clay jar? God may have made a mistake here.* Actually, God hasn't made a mistake, for He does have a way of letting His light shine forth from our earthen vessels:

<u>*We are hard pressed on every side, yet not crushed*</u>. *(2 Corinthians 4:8–10 NKJV)*

Notice that Scripture says our earthen vessels are hard pressed. That's a polite way of saying that we will experience a degree of brokenness. From time to time, God will allow circumstances in life to bring us to the breaking point. It might be a matter of our finances, our family, or even our freedom. It's in our times of trial that we can shine brightest. I know of countless occasions where people came to Christ because they saw His glory shine in the life of a loved one who was suffering in some form or fashion. God allows everything to happen for a reason, but He doesn't allow us to be crushed to the point of wrecking or ruining us.

Spiritual maturity occurs once we recognize that our trials aren't our enemies but rather opportunities that enable us to show off the surpassing greatness of God. His molding is always followed by His blessing, and nothing is more blessed than leading the lost to Him.

What trials are you going through now? Why is God allowing them?

What should your perspective be on your trials?

CAPTIVE AUDIENCE
DAY 345

. . . and the magistrates tore off their clothes and commanded them [Paul and Silas] to be beaten with rods. And when they had laid many stripes on them, they threw them into prison, commanding the jailer to keep them securely. Having received such a charge, he put them into the inner prison and fastened their feet in the stocks. (Acts 16:22–24 NKJV)

I wonder how you and I would have felt if we had been Paul and Silas. Here we are faithfully sharing the Gospel of Jesus Christ on the mission field when all of the sudden we're seized by the authorities, beaten with rods, and thrown into prison. We would probably come to the conclusion that we had failed miserably in our witness for Christ. People not only rejected what we had to say, but humiliated us and then put us in lock down.

But there's more to the story. As God would have it, Paul and Silas' imprisonment actually presented them with a captive audience (literally):

But at midnight Paul and Silas were praying and singing hymns to God, <u>and the prisoners were listening to them</u>. (Acts 16:25 NKJV)

There were other prisoners dwelling in that dark and dismal dungeon. There's no telling how long they had been bound, but it had probably been long enough for them to have surrendered any sense of hope and joy. Then something strange and heavenly happened—they heard Paul and Silas singing, not just any songs but songs declaring the goodness and glory of God. It must have sounded like a foreign language to these men who had been driven to the depths of despair and depression. But there, in the still blackness, the Scriptures say that *the prisoners were listening to them*. The prison door had closed shut, but the witnessing door had swung wide open.

Sometimes it may seem like we've failed in our evangelistic attempts. But this story shows us that whenever one door closes, another opens. And whether we realize it, there's bound to be a captive audience waiting and willing to hear what we have to say.

When have you been rejected for your witness?

What should you remember when you run the risk of being rejected for the sake of the Gospel?

SACRIFICE SAVES
DAY 346

But at midnight Paul and Silas were praying and singing hymns to God, and the prisoners were listening to them. Suddenly there was a great earthquake, so that the foundations of the prison were shaken; and immediately all the doors were opened and everyone's chains were loosed. (Acts 16:25–26 NKJV)

It seemed like the perfect opportunity—a divine jail break. In the middle of the night, an earthquake struck the prison where Paul and Silas had been wrongfully incarcerated and there was no one around to prevent their escape. Had they been preoccupied with their own agendas, they surely would have snuck away under cover of night. However, Paul and Silas sensed there was a greater work of deliverance at hand, so they stayed put.

And the keeper of the prison, awaking from sleep and seeing the prison doors open, supposing the prisoners had fled, drew his sword and was about to kill himself. But Paul called with a loud voice, saying, "Do yourself no harm, for we are all here." (Acts 16:27–28 NKJV)

In that culture, a jailer faced the humiliation of execution if his prisoners escaped. Rather than have his life taken from him, Paul and Silas' jailer drew his sword and prepared to take it himself. Just then, Paul's voice rang out from the rubble, *"We are all here."* Instead of saving themselves by leaving, they saved the jailer by staying. What follows is a powerful picture of what happens when we set aside our own self-interests.

And he brought them out and said, "Sirs, what must I do to be saved?" So they said, "Believe on the Lord Jesus Christ, and you will be saved, you and your household." (Acts 16:30–31 NKJV)

Something special happens when we're willing to sacrifice what might be most beneficial for ourselves. It lends credibility to our creed and gets the attention of those watching our lives. Just as the jailer was won over because Paul and Silas sacrificed themselves for his sake, there are those in our lives who would do the same as the jailer if we would do the same as Paul and Silas.

Is selfishness hindering your witness toward others? If so, how?

How can you use sacrifice as a witnessing tool in the future?

MISSION CONTROL
DAY 347

"Go therefore and make disciples of all the nations, baptizing them in the name of the Father and of the Son and of the Holy Spirit, teaching them to observe all things that I have commanded you; and lo, I am with you always, even to the end of the age." Amen. (Matthew 28:19–20 NKJV)

These two verses comprise what we commonly refer to as the Great Commission. Shortly before ascending into heaven to take His place at the right hand of the Father, Jesus gave the church these marching orders. It is our mission to make disciples of all nations by sharing the Gospel, baptizing those who respond, and instructing them in the words and ways of Christ. Our faith isn't something to be hoarded or kept to ourselves; it must be given away in order to be worth having.

I believe that most of us know this is our mission, yet we frequently fail in it because we lack proper **motivation**. That motivation is given to us by Jesus, who is with us always. Sharing the cross of Christ is our mission, but our motivation comes from Christ dwelling in us.

Have you ever noticed the behavior of a love-struck couple? They're practically inseparable, always doing things together. The more they are together, the more they try to please and bless each other because that's the way a loving relationship works. When we recognize Jesus as our constant companion, we will grow in our desire to please Him, and what pleases Him more than being involved in the saving of souls?

The Lord . . . is longsuffering toward us, not willing that any should perish but that all should come to repentance. (2 Peter 3:9 NKJV)

If you know your mission as a Christian yet have a hard time finding the right motivation to do it, you need to allow the Lord's presence inside you to control and compel you. The more in love you are with Him, the more in love you'll be with the mission He's given us.

How does it make you feel to know that Christ is with you always?

How can you be more motivated by the fact that Christ is in you?

MAY I HAVE YOUR ATTENTION PLEASE?
DAY 348

"A new commandment I give to you, that you love one another; as I have loved you, that you also love one another. <u>By this all will know that you are My disciples, if you have love for one another</u>." (John 13:34–35 NKJV)

What gets a person's attention? Is it a beautiful face, a mountain of material possessions, an impressive physique, an extensive education, or a winsome wit? All these things have the power to capture attention, but over time the fixation will fade. What gets a person's attention and keeps it?

As usual, Jesus has the answer. It's love. Christ's love. When His love is actively expressed through the life of a believer, it becomes the most powerful force that planet earth has ever witnessed. The love of Jesus is the one point that has no counterpoint. It ends all arguments, accomplishes the unimaginable, and opens hearts that have been cynically sealed up for a lifetime.

Knowing this, Jesus told the disciples on the night before His crucifixion that if they were to have an impact on this world, they had to love one another. What wisdom! For as the world watches this thing called the church, where the love of God is exchanged and expressed, it sees something that gets its attention . . . and keeps it. When God's love is flowing freely within the family of faith, all lines of separation are erased:

There is neither Jew nor Greek, there is neither slave nor free, there is neither male nor female; for you are all one in Christ Jesus. (Galatians 3:28 NKJV)

The world is drawn to this because it cannot find it within itself. It longs to experience the peace, harmony, and oneness that is ours, found exclusively in Christ. When our love level for one another is at its highest, our witness to the world is at its strongest. May the Lord make us mindful of this, and may He fill our hearts with His love for our brothers and sisters.

What role did love play in your own conversion experience?

Whom haven't you been loving toward in the body of Christ? Go out of your way to change that!

IT'S BEING . . . NOT DOING
DAY 349

"But you shall receive power when the Holy Spirit has come upon you; and you shall <u>be witnesses</u> to Me in Jerusalem, and in all Judea and Samaria, and to the end of the earth." (Acts 1:8 NKJV)

Mere moments before He ascended into heaven, Jesus told His disciples they would receive the power of the Holy Spirit, which would enable them to be witnesses to Him. Note that He said they would *be* witnesses and not that they would *do* witnessing. It's a subtle difference, but it's important because it shows us that when it comes to witnessing, it's not just something we do, but it's a part of who we are.

If we were in Jesus' original audience, His words would have hit us a bit differently. The Greek word that Christ used for *witnesses* is *martus*, from which we derive our English word *martyr*. Connect these dots with me. A martyr is someone who has died for something, and as God apprehends people's hearts, He produces a want within them to die to their self-centered and selfish nature:

I have been crucified with Christ; it is no longer I who live, but Christ lives in me; and the life which I now live in the flesh I live by faith in the Son of God, who loved me and gave Himself for me. (Galatians 2:20 NKJV)

It's a well-known fact that ten of the twelve disciples (except Judas and John) died as martyrs proclaiming the Gospel. We might look at their devotion and wonder how they were capable of such sacrifice. But the fact is that they had all died years before their physical deaths as their selfish natures were put to death. They were totally committed to doing the Lord's will because they martyred their own wills.

If we haven't really died to self, we will be reluctant to witness. But when we fully understand that Christ died for us, it makes us want to die to self and be His witnesses, willing to go anywhere and do anything He tells us.

How have your own wants gotten in the way of your becoming the witness you could be?

Ask God to help you die to your own desires and agendas.

OUTCASTS ARE INCLUDED

DAY 350

But He needed to go through Samaria. (John 4:4 NKJV)

This is an odd little verse. It comes in the middle of one of the Master's missions as He travels from the southern area of Israel to the northern region of Galilee. There's a strong sense of urgency in Him to go through Samaria, which was a detour from His destination. What could be important enough to cause the King of the Cosmos to go out of His way?

So He came to a city of Samaria which is called Sychar, near the plot of ground that Jacob gave to his son Joseph. Now Jacob's well was there. Jesus therefore, being wearied from His journey, sat thus by the well. It was about the sixth hour. A woman of Samaria came to draw water. Jesus said to her, "Give Me a drink." (John 4:5–7 NKJV)

Did you see the divine appointment? Jesus went through Samaria for the sake of saving this woman. This is all the more amazing because in that culture men looked at women as possessions, not people. Another social strike against her was that she was a Samaritan. Jews despised Samaritans because of something that happened centuries earlier. The Assyrians had conquered that particular region of Israel, carried away most of the Israelites, and replaced them with people from foreign lands. These people intermarried, and the Samaritans were the by-products of those mixed relationships. The Jews saw them as spiritual half-breeds, unfit and unworthy of God. To make matters worse, this woman was living with a man to whom she wasn't married (John 4:18).

If you were a Jewish man in that day, as Jesus was, you'd have a hard time finding a more unlikely person to talk to. Yet Jesus not only talked to her but changed His itinerary for her. That's the way He is. He goes out of His way to reach the most despised and dejected people of this world because He has a huge heart for the outcast (Isaiah 66:2).

Do you know someone who is looked down on? Is there someone at work or school who bears the brunt of all the jokes? That's the very person with whom Jesus wants you to share the Gospel. And in many cases, that's the person who is going to be most receptive to the message of God's love.

How can you follow Jesus' example?

Make it a point to befriend someone the world despises.

A RIGHTEOUS REPUTATION?
DAY 351

. . . having your conduct honorable among the Gentiles, that when they speak against you as evildoers, they may, by your good works which they observe, glorify God in the day of visitation. (1 Peter 2:12 NKJV)

Imagine for a moment that you're listening in on a conversation among the movers and shakers in Hollywood. They get together and decide that a movie needs a Christian character. *Oh, yeah, that would be perfect! We need a Christian so that we can punch up the humor, a real buffoon who doesn't have a clue. Great idea! After all, everybody knows at least one "born-againer" like that.*

Right about now our hearts should break because deep down we know they're right. We have given the world most of the ammunition they fire at us. When the church makes the headlines, it's usually for the wrong reasons, and when people hear the name of Christ, they're often turned off because of what they've come to expect from Christians.

It shouldn't be this way, and it certainly doesn't have to be. As damaging as our deeds can be against us, they can work all the more for us. For when we live the type of lives that we've been called to, when we shine with the humility and compassion of Christ, and when we exhibit the fruit of the Holy Spirit, it will build a reputation that will cause a studio exec to say, *Wait a minute, bad idea. My neighbor is a Christian, and he just helped me through a really tough time. Let's come up with something else.* Sound far fetched? If so, it's only because our conduct isn't more honorable these days.

Our witnessing words need to be preceded by a righteous reputation. When people hear the word *Christ* or *Christian*, it ought to evoke a sense of respect and reverence. But that won't *collectively* happen until we *personally* commit ourselves to walk the way we're supposed to. We can't wait around for someone else to create a favorable impression of what it means to be a believer. It starts with you and me. When we live honorable lives, we'll earn the world's respect and then the right to share the Gospel with them.

Do you fit this stereotype? Why or why not?

How can you enhance your righteous reputation among those you're called to witness to?

When he saw Jesus from afar, he ran and worshiped Him. And he cried out with a loud voice and said, "What have I to do with You, Jesus, Son of the Most High God? I implore You by God that You do not torment me." For He said to him, "Come out of the man, unclean spirit!" (Mark 5:6–8 NKJV)

It was an unbelievable scene. Just as Jesus steps out of a boat and onto the Galilean shoreline, a crazed demoniac suddenly charges up to Him. The gospels tell us that the demons inhabiting him made him mutilate himself with sharp stones and howl all day and night (Mark 5:5). He was so detached from civility that his life consisted of running around in naked misery and dwelling amid the tombs of the dead (Luke 8:27). I don't think life can get much worse than that!

But here comes Jesus, and as this spiritual exchange between light and darkness takes place, He exerts His authority. Christ commands the evil spirits to depart, and when the dust settles, we see the former demoniac clothed, seated, and in his right mind (Mark 5:15). His gratitude was so great that he begs to follow Jesus:

And when He got into the boat, he who had been demon-possessed begged Him that he might be with Him. However, Jesus did not permit him, but said to him, "<u>Go home to your friends, and tell them what great things the Lord has done for you, and how He has had compassion on you</u>." (Mark 5:18–19 NKJV)

Jesus immediately enlists this man as a missionary by sending him back to his old friends. Notice how simple His message was: *"Tell them what great things the Lord has done for you, and how He has had compassion on you."* Sometimes we think that in order to be an effective witness, we need to have a theological degree under our belt. Not true. All that's necessary is a personal encounter with Jesus and a willingness to share the good things He has done in our lives. It's just that simple, and if a former demoniac can do it, we can too.

What are some of the good things the Lord has done for you?

Whom can you share this with over the next couple days?

CHAIN OF COMMAND

And they called them and commanded them not to speak at all nor teach in the name of Jesus. But Peter and John answered and said to them, "Whether it is right in the sight of God to listen to you more than to God, you judge. <u>For we cannot but speak the things which we have seen and heard</u>." (Acts 4:18–20 NKJV)

I wish I could say that everyone will want to hear the Gospel, but it just isn't true. Even as we look to the Scriptures, we see instances, like the one above, where people not only rejected the Gospel but also threatened God's messengers to keep quiet about it. More likely than not, we eventually will face situations like this as we're faithful to fulfill our commission (Matthew 28:19–20). So what are we supposed to do? Do we stop sharing when people put pressure on us to stay silent?

There is a proper time to stop witnessing with our words, and it's when we sense people are moving further and further away, becoming more resistant to the Gospel. We shouldn't be annoying or obnoxious by continuing to speak; instead, we need to allow our actions to affirm what we have already shared. Such seasons of silence stem from a desire to invest in the long-term harvest of a heart, not taking the quick and easy route to fruitlessness.

But we should never stop sharing the Gospel because we fear man. Peter and John understood this when they stood up to the authorities of their day and declared that they were bound to share the Good News. God had told them to do something that man had told them not to do, but they reasoned that His will should be obeyed above man's (Matthew 28:19–20). Their chain of command began and ended with Christ.

When we refer to Jesus as our Lord, it's saying something pretty powerful. It's saying we should be concerned with obeying Him above everyone else. He's the only one we need to worry about pleasing, and He's pleased when we share what He's done for mankind, even when mankind isn't.

When have you had to choose between pleasing God and man? What did you do?

Write Acts 4:18–20 down and have it handy for those situations where you're tempted to fear man before God.

And the common people heard Him gladly. (Mark 12:37 NKJV)

Jesus is the champion of the common man. When He walked this earth, He did not shut Himself up in an ivory tower. He walked the back roads and city streets of Israel just like everyone else. He didn't run in the A-list social circles. He was willing to rub shoulders with the lowest of the low, the world's Z-list. And He didn't talk in terms that only exceptionally educated people could understand; He spoke in the plain street language of His day. The religious elite had done an excellent job of distancing the average man from God, so you can imagine how refreshing it was as Jesus entered the scene, turning the religious system upside-down and putting God back within reach of the common folks. No wonder they heard Him gladly.

He was relatable to those He came into contact with, and we should follow His example. There are some Christians who feel their effectiveness as a witness is in direct proportion to their weirdness. They speak in King James English, carry around one of those mammoth coffee-table Bibles, and frequently incorporate references to "the blood of the Lamb" and "crucifying the flesh" into their casual conversations. That's not being a witness; that's being weird!

Effective Christians know all of those aforementioned things but also that the average person in this day and age isn't going to respond or identify with such things. They recognize that people need to know Christians who are holy but still relatable. And when they see the word *relatable*, they don't view it as a license to compromise their convictions but as a tool for building a bridge to those who desperately need God.

Let's be on guard against getting weird and remember where those in the world are so that we can better relate to them and ultimately help them.

How well do you maintain a balance between holiness and relatability?

Ask a couple of trustworthy and respected Christians how relatable your life is.

POINT OUT THE POSITIVE

Philip found Nathanael and said to him, "We have found Him of whom Moses in the law, and also the prophets, wrote; Jesus of Nazareth, the son of Joseph." And Nathanael said to him, "Can anything good come out of Nazareth?" Philip said to him, "Come and see." Jesus saw Nathanael coming toward Him, and said of him, "Behold, an Israelite indeed, in whom is no deceit!" (John 1:45–47 NKJV)

Nathanael was a serious student of the Scriptures. Philip indicates that he was very familiar with all the Old Testament Scriptures concerning the coming of the Messiah. He was well-up on the Word, which is why he was skeptical about the Messiah coming out of Nazareth. Micah 5:2 indicates that He would be born in Bethlehem, but nothing was written about Nazareth.

With reluctance, Nathanael approaches Jesus, and as they meet, the first thing Jesus says is that Nathanael is a man without deceit. The Greek word for *deceit* is a very interesting one. It literally means "to bait the hook," and it speaks of deception or a quality of falseness that's frequently found in people. Jesus is basically saying, *I know that you are a "straight-shooter," and that's admirable.*

I find this fascinating because Jesus could have scolded Nathanael for his unbelief or for his arrogance in thinking that the Christ couldn't have a connection with the town of Nazareth (for further study, compare this with Matthew 2:23). But rather than note the negative, Jesus points out the positive in Nathanael's character. Watch what happened:

Nathanael said to Him, "How do You know me?" Jesus answered and said to him, "Before Philip called you, when you were under the fig tree, I saw you." Nathanael answered and said to Him, "Rabbi, You are the Son of God! You are the King of Israel!" (John 1:48–49 NKJV)

By complimenting Nathanael on an aspect of his character, Jesus opened a door of dialogue that led to salvation. When we encounter the "Nathanaels" in our lives, we should edify and encourage them in what they're doing well instead of hammering away at their faults and flaws. Our words will go a lot further.

How can you use Christ's example as a tool in your everyday evangelism?

Compliment the positive traits in those you're trying to reach.

"Judge not, that you be not judged. For with what judgment you judge, you will be judged; and with the measure you use, it will be measured back to you." (Matthew 7:1–2 NKJV)

Anyone who has been saved for a season of time knows that there's enormous spiritual pressure for us to grow judgmental toward the unsaved. It starts so subtly, but like a vicious virus, it spreads into our thoughts and attitudes. Instead of having a heart of compassion for people who are trapped in their sin, we start to point an accusing finger of condemnation at them. But by being judgmental toward others, we make ourselves guilty of a far greater sin than the ones we're pointing at.

Jesus told a parable of a Pharisee and a tax collector who both went to the temple to pray. The Pharisee was proud of the fact that he wasn't a worthless "sinner" like the tax collector who had the audacity to approach God. In contrast, the tax collector beat his chest and begged God for His mercy to fall upon him and cover his sinful self. It was the broken sinner who was justified that day, not the judgmental Pharisee (Luke 18:10–14). God was all ears when a heart was breaking, but He didn't even listen to the utterances of judgment.

A strange thing happens as we harbor a judgmental heart. We actually become estranged from the very God we are supposed to be a witness for. Is it any wonder that those who find themselves in such a state are unable to lead others into the kingdom? They've forgotten the fact that apart from God's grace, they too would be set adrift in their sin. Without the sense of their own need for God's grace, they can't properly communicate it to others. It's sort of like selling a product you don't know anything about.

Every once in a while, we need to examine our hearts to see if we've grown judgmental. Are we ridiculing or reconciling? Are we patronizing or praying? Are we criticizing or consoling? I pray we would have a renewed sense of our own need for God's grace and that in so doing, we would be effective in sharing it.

Whom do you tend to be judgmental toward?

Apologize to the people you've been guilty of judging.

WHAT'S AT STAKE?
DAY 357

For the law of the Spirit of life in Christ Jesus has made me free from <u>the law of sin and death</u>.
(Romans 8:2 NKJV)

It has been well said that "a law without consequences is just good advice." In other words, there has to be some sort of penalty attached to a law in order for it actually to be a law. The Bible speaks of *the law of sin and death*, which underscores the fact that there are real consequences attached to sin. Those consequences are eternal and terrible:

For the wages of sin is death . . . . (Romans 6:23 NKJV)

"If your hand causes you to sin, cut it off. It is better for you to enter into life maimed, rather than having two hands, to go to hell, into the fire that shall never be quenched—where 'Their worm does not die And the fire is not quenched.'" (Mark 9:43–44 NKJV)

I need to make this heavy for a moment because God does. His Word teaches us that there's a literal place of torment and torture called hell. Originally created for Satan and his demons (Matthew 25:41), it also serves as a place of punishment for the sins of mankind. People can be sentenced there once their earthly life ends (Hebrews 9:27), at which point they will experience an unquenchable eternal fire. Anyone who has suffered burns of *any* degree can begin to imagine what it must be like to be in this everlasting condition! The only way for people to avoid hell is to have their sins covered by the blood of Jesus, which occurs as they place their faith in His saving work on the cross (John 3:16).

Most of us know these truths, but how many of us grasp the true horror of hell and are moved to action by it? Has hell just become theoretical for us, or are we convinced of its reality, believing that many (if not most) of the people we know are just a heartbeat away from being there? When we appreciate what's at stake for those who don't know Him, we'll want to make the most of our opportunities to lead others to Christ, embracing our responsibility as Christ's witnesses.

How real is hell to you?

What will you do with this knowledge?

<u>For the love of Christ compels us</u>, because we judge thus: that if One died for all, then all died; and He died for all, that those who live should live no longer for themselves, but for Him who died for them and rose again. (2 Corinthians 5:14–15 NKJV)

We've taken the time to examine what it truly means to be a witness for Jesus Christ. We've looked at a lot of the do's and don'ts when it comes to sharing the Gospel and at some of the reasons why people reject it. We've looked at what it means to serve as salt and light in this world and have even been challenged by the consequences that exist for those who don't know Jesus. But before we close out this subject, we need to be reminded of the one thing that puts all of this together and makes the Gospel message real in our lives—love.

As gifted and skilled as the apostle Paul was, he attributed his effectiveness as an apostle, missionary, and witness to the love of Christ. He didn't act out of a sense of guilt, frustration, or self-promotion. Love—and love alone—compelled him to impact his world for Jesus.

That's the way it needs to be in our lives. When we base our evangelistic efforts on anything other than the love God pours into our hearts, we'll miss His mark for us in this area. Love stirs the sense of urgency we need in preaching the Gospel, it produces persistence and perseverance when we feel rejected, it teaches us the perfect balance between tact and truthfulness, and it forces every fear in our heart to flee (1 John 4:18).

I was grieved by the recent statistic that **95 percent of all Christians never lead another person to Christ.** If Christians would allow God's love to invade their lives more, they would be compelled to share the Good News, just like Paul did. It's my earnest prayer that we will be so immersed in God's love that we can't help but be worthy witnesses to Him and His Gospel.

What part does God's love play in being a witness?

When was the last time God's love compelled you to do something?

FOOLISH FELLOWSHIP

Do not be unequally yoked together with unbelievers. For what fellowship has righteousness with lawlessness? And what communion has light with darkness? And what accord has Christ with Belial? Or what part has a believer with an unbeliever? (2 Corinthians 6:14–15 NKJV)

Fellowship is an incredibly powerful force, and for that reason, God issues us a warning in the preceding passage: *Do not be unequally yoked together with unbelievers.* A lot of people don't know what this illustration means, but it made perfect sense when Paul wrote this to believers who were living in an agrarian culture. When a farmer plowed his field, he usually had a pair of oxen to pull the plow. But the two oxen had to move together in tandem in order to be productive. A yoke made of wood was placed over the necks of the oxen, linking and aligning them together as they moved forward to plow.

Now carry this over into the spiritual realm. We are all walking through life, and hopefully, we're focused on following the course God has called us to. This can be difficult enough by ourselves, but what happens when we yoke ourselves to people who aren't believers? We'll want to go one way, and they'll want to pull us in the opposite direction. In the process, we'll leave the path the Lord has laid out for us. You can see the danger in being yoked to the wrong type of person.

The key to preventing this is to be wise when it comes to our fellowship. When we're in fellowship with people who care about the things of God, there's always a common authority for our conduct. But if we're spending time with those who don't know (much less respect) God, then there's bound to be compromise in some area of our lives sooner or later. Let's avoid foolish fellowship by limiting the influence the unsaved have on us and by being around those who are on the same spiritual page.

What does *"Do not be unequally yoked together with unbelievers"* mean?

Give some examples of how this has happened in your life. What were the results?

We love Him because He first loved us. (1 John 4:19 NKJV)

We hear a lot about worship these days. Just take a look at some of the hottest-selling CDs in the Christian market and you'll see many that are worship-oriented. We all want to worship, but I've found that our perspective of worship needs to be right in order for it to be what God intended.

It's possible to place a lot of emphasis on how we worship. We can make it all about the proper angle to raise our arms or just the right positioning of our hands. Or maybe we have become preoccupied with tapping our feet to the beat of the song being played.

We can also get caught up with where we worship. I know a few folks who feel that in order to truly connect with God, they need to be in the midst of His creation. Because their worship depends on the conditions of their environment, they hang out at the beach or get lost somewhere in the woods in an effort to worship.

It's even possible to be overly focused on when we worship. There are four different worship services to choose from at our church on any given weekend. I'm sure there are some who feel that Saturday night is the real time to worship and also those who feel the same way about the Sunday service they regularly attend.

Another common misconception is that it's all about what type of music our worship is set to. Some people have a hard time singing fast songs while others don't like to sing slow songs. Some prefer hymns while others want a more contemporary style of music.

We need to understand that our worship isn't a matter of how, where, when, or what. It's a matter of why. Until we understand why we worship God, we'll miss out on true worship. Our adoration for God needs to come from our knowledge that He loves us so much that He was willing to die for us (1 John 4:19). When we see how much He loves us, it will move us toward a true worship of Him.

Where does our worship of God begin?

What do you focus on when it comes to your worship?

GOD'S LAW
DAY 361

For the wages of sin is death, but the gift of God is eternal life in Christ Jesus our Lord.
(Romans 6:23 NKJV)

Imagine life without laws. No criminal laws to protect your personal property and privileges. No moral laws to prevent people from disrespecting your dignity. No traffic laws to keep one car from colliding with another. No physical laws, such as gravity, to keep people from flying off into outer space. It doesn't take too much imagination to see that life would be crazy, chaotic, and confusing without laws. Laws are good because they provide us with structure, and within that structure, we find safety.

There are also certain spiritual laws that God has put into place that also provide structure and safety. The Bible declares, *the wages of sin is death*, which is another way of saying that God's law demands for sin to be punished and judged. God's perfect holiness demands that every unholy thing receive the perfect measure of His wrath. God will never break this law because He knows that without it, chaos and calamity would follow.

This is bad news for us because we are born sinners (Romans 3:23). And yet, there's a ray of hope that shines through at the end of this law—*but the gift of God is eternal life in Christ Jesus our Lord*. Jesus Christ, who deserved no punishment Himself, received the wrath that mankind's sin had incurred. Because Jesus' slate was clean, God was able to write out our death sentence on Him. By doing so, the law that demands perfect punishment was perfectly satisfied by His sacrifice.

Through God's law we find a sense of structure, and through Jesus' sacrifice, we find a sense of safety. We simply need to believe and receive it:

"For God so loved the world that He gave His only begotten Son, that whoever believes in Him should not perish but have everlasting life. For God did not send His Son into the world to condemn the world, but that the world through Him might be saved." (John 3:16–17 NKJV)

What spiritual law is being declared in Romans 6:23?

What makes your salvation secure?

. . . God tested Abraham, and said to him, "Abraham!" And he said, "Here I am." Then He said, "Take now your son, your only son Isaac, whom you love, and go to the land of Moriah, and offer him there as a burnt offering on one of the mountains of which I shall tell you." So Abraham rose early in the morning and saddled his donkey, and took two of his young men with him, and Isaac his son . . . . And Abraham said to his young men, "Stay here with the donkey; the lad and I will go yonder and worship, and we will come back to you." (Genesis 22:1–5 NKJV)

The first time that the word *worship* shows up in Scripture is here in Genesis 22:5. What I find amazing is that it comes in the context of God asking Abraham to sacrifice his son, Isaac. Understand that for decades Abraham had cried out and pleaded to God for a son. It was when Abraham was 100 years old that Isaac was finally born to him! If there was anything near and dear to Abraham's heart, it was his long-awaited and much-beloved son. And yet, God calls Abraham to offer him up as a sacrifice, which is what he sets out to do.

Notice how the Bible describes Abraham's attitude at this point; it says that he went forward with an attitude of worship. This is amazing because at this point, Abraham doesn't know how the story ends. He doesn't know that the angel of the Lord will come at the last minute and tell him to put down his knife. In this moment of the unknown, Abraham makes the decision to worship his God.

This shows us something very powerful about worship—it can happen (and even thrive) during unknown and scary moments in our lives. We can still worship even when we don't know how the story ends. And it's in these times of worship that we hear God's divine direction and guidance.

But the Angel of the LORD called to him from heaven and said, "Abraham, Abraham!" So he said, "Here I am." And He said, "Do not lay your hand on the lad, or do anything to him; for now I know that you fear God, since you have not withheld your son, your only son, from Me." (Genesis 22:11–12 NKJV)

What do we learn from Abraham's decision to worship?

What scary situation are you facing right now, and what are you going to do in the midst of this trial?

HE WANTS TO TALK
DAY 363

Hear, O LORD, when I cry with my voice! Have mercy also upon me, and answer me. When You said, "Seek My face," My heart said to You, "Your face, LORD, I will seek." (Psalm 27:7–8 NKJV)

Prayer is so well represented in God's Word that we could examine it from an infinite number of angles. But we see a particularly powerful principle of prayer when we look at it through the window of David's relationship with the Lord. Notice how he describes both his heart and God's heart at the point of prayer. God said to David, *"Seek My face,"* and David cried out, *"LORD, I will seek."* See how they match? That's because David's desire to pray to God was actually an echo of God's desire to talk to him.

Here's how it works in our lives. Have you ever had a longing deep inside of you to cry out to God? In those moments, it's the Lord who's motivating and drawing you heavenward toward His throne. He wants to talk to you, so He says, by His Spirit, *"Seek My face,"* and you should respond, *Lord, I will seek your face.*

This is a powerful point because often we believe God's too busy or preoccupied to be bothered with us. We think, He has the cosmos to take care of. Why would He want to bother with my puny problems? This is so wrong. Our urge to pray is not a matter of our inherent goodness. Apart from God, all of us have turned away from Him (Romans 3:10–12). When we desire to seek God's face, it's a matter of His Spirit tugging on our hearts because He is the one who wants to talk to us in the first place.

The next time you sense the stirring to pray, remember that it's the Lord's way of telling you that He wants to talk.

What motivates you to pray? Knowing this, how should you respond when you sense the stirring to pray?

What hinders your prayer time? Are you willing to cut these distractions from your daily routine?

But know that the LORD has set apart for Himself him who is godly; The LORD will hear when I call to Him. (Psalm 4:3 NKJV)

I love David's declaration. In the midst of a mighty trial, he cries out without any inhibition or hesitation, The LORD will hear when I call to Him. You can't help but admire his confidence when it comes to his connection to the Lord through prayer. But the reason we admire David's confidence so much is because often we lack confidence when it comes to our own prayer lives.

If you've been a believer for any amount of time, you know what I'm talking about. From time to time, you will hit those "spiritual dry spells," where things just don't seem the same. Prayer suddenly starts to become a chore, and you just don't sense a powerful connection to God like you did when you first fell in love with Him. His heart can seem so distant, and before you know it, you may find yourself questioning if God is even listening to you. *Maybe He's too busy to hear me. Perhaps He's spending time with someone who He really likes. Or maybe He just turns the channel when He starts to hear my voice.* Rather than succumb to these false feelings, rise up in faith and declare as David did, *The LORD will hear when I call to Him.*

If you don't pray with confidence, then your prayers will be rendered ineffective because they aren't being offered in faith. But God's Word says you can be confident that God hears your prayers when you ask according to His will.

Now this is the confidence that we have in Him, that if we ask anything according to His will, He hears us. (1 John 5:14 NKJV)

Why is confidence so critical to prayer?

Have you ever thought that God wasn't listening to you? How do feel about it after reading 1 John 5:14?

YOU'RE HIS WORKMANSHIP
DAY 365

For we are His workmanship, created in Christ Jesus for good works, which God prepared beforehand that we should walk in them. (Ephesians 2:10 NKJV)

Salvation is not the end of the Christian life; it's just the beginning. Once we're saved, we discover that God has charted out an adventurous course for us to follow. That course involves a succession of exciting experiences where we model our Master by ministering to others. It has been well said, "We've been saved to serve."

As we start to walk in these good works, the Bible describes us as God's workmanship. In the original Greek the word used here for *workmanship* is *poiema*, which is where we get our word *poem*. The idea is that we are so special to God that He looks at our lives as a poet or artist would look at his or her life's labor.

Recently, I found myself at an upscale art gallery. I'm the type of person who's fascinated by colors, hues, and brush strokes, and I took my time to pore over every detail of the paintings on display. I even asked the gallery manager to turn off the overhead lights so I could see the paintings from another perspective. I was amazed by how different the images and lines looked in different types of light. I could have spent hours engrossed in the details that the artists had embedded into their works.

That's the way God looks at us as we continue to walk in the good works that He has prepared for us. It fills His heart with joy to watch us as we're slowly shaped into men and women that resemble Him by the way we love and serve others.

Are you walking in good works by serving others? List some examples.

Pray that God will make you more sensitive to the good works that He has planned for you.

DIGGING IN THE ACTIVE WORD JOURNAL

Digging in the Active Word is a devotional journal that will challenge and encourage you in your daily walk. You'll start off each new month with a look at one of the twelve apostles. See yourself in the lives of these twelve men who turned the world upside down in the name of Jesus Christ. Digging in the Active Word is spiral bound, so it's great for journaling!

MY GOD STORY

Meet a very real, personal God in this collection of extraordinary stories of people just like you who found peace, forgiveness, joy, and love in some surprising places. Includes a helpful Scripture reference guide for every topic covered in the book!

DEVOTIONARY

Discover what God's Word has to say about real-life topics from A to Z in *Devotionary* by Pastor Bob Coy. This resource is designed to help you grow in your understanding of seventy-seven different spiritual issues, including adversity, evangelism, joy, prayer, wisdom, and zeal. Whether you are seeking personal guidance or equipping yourself to share with others, this devotional is an invaluable tool for applying the practical and timeless principles of God's Word.

ONE SURRENDERED LIFE

In *One Surrendered Life*, Pastor Bob Coy shares the incredible journey from his fast-paced existence as an executive at Capitol Records to his supernatural walk with Christ where he has become the pastor of one of the fastest-growing churches in the country. Pastor Bob lovingly reveals that God has a plan for you and shares how you can discover your remarkable story through the grace of God. His story highlights God's ability to transform any life from heathen to holy. He is a true example of what God can do through even one surrendered life.

DREAMALITY

Somewhere between childhood and adulthood, many of us let go of our dreams. We stop trusting that anything will be different. We stop hoping that anything could get better. We stop expecting life to be full of excitement, anticipation, joy, fun, and hope. Often optimism is replaced by anger, frustration, and bitterness. But it doesn't have to be that way. Bob Coy, senior pastor of the seventeen thousand-member Calvary Chapel Fort Lauderdale, believes that hope can be revived and we can rekindle in our hearts the expectation of something more. Using the biblical story of Joseph as a recurring analogy, Coy looks to God as our dream-deliverer as well as the source of our dreams. He asserts that, as we come to understand God's heart toward us and the bigger picture of our lives, we can reclaim and live out our dreams.

The Active Word
Calvary Chapel Fort Lauderdale
2401 West Cypress Creek Road Fort Lauderdale, Florida 33309
866.977.9673   FAX 954.977.9774
www.calvaryftl.org/bookstore